INTELLIGENT IOT
ANALYTICS

INTELLIGENT IoT
ANALYTICS

Concepts and
Real-World Applications

Dr. Adhiguna Mahendra
Ekki Rinaldi

MERCURY LEARNING AND INFORMATION
Boston, Massachusetts

MERCURY LEARNING AND INFORMATION
121 High Street, 3rd Floor
Boston, MA 02110
info@merclearning.com

A. Mahendra. *Intelligent IoT Analytics: Concepts and Real-World Applications.*
ISBN: 978-1-5015-2341-0

The publisher recognizes and respects all marks used by companies, manufacturers, and developers as a means to distinguish their products. All brand names and product names mentioned in this book are trademarks or service marks of their respective companies. Any omission or misuse (of any kind) of service marks or trademarks, etc. is not an attempt to infringe on the property of others.

Library of Congress Control Number: 2025949306
242526321   This book is printed on acid-free paper in the United States of America.

Our titles are available for adoption, license, or bulk purchase by institutions, corporations, etc.

All of our titles are available in digital format at various digital vendors.

To my beloved wife Anissa, whose unwavering support, patience, and strength
have carried me through every challenge.

And to my three sons — Farrel, Rafale, and Xavier —
Your curiosity, imagination, and boundless energy are the true
inspiration behind this work.

You remind me every day why we build intelligent systems: to make the world a
safer, smarter, and more compassionate place for the future you will shape.

With all my love and gratitude.

—Dr. Adhiguna Mahendra

CONTENTS

PREFACE

In an era of unprecedented urbanization and technological advancement, the convergence of the Internet of Things (IoT) and Big Data analytics has emerged as a transformative force in shaping the cities of tomorrow. This book, *Intelligent IoT Analytics: Concept and Real-World Applications*, serves as a comprehensive guide to understanding, implementing, and leveraging these cutting-edge technologies to create more efficient, sustainable, and livable urban environments.

The concept of smart cities has rapidly evolved from a futuristic vision to a present-day reality, with municipalities worldwide embracing digital solutions to address the complex challenges of urban life. At the heart of this transformation lies the Internet of Things - a vast network of interconnected devices that collect, transmit, and analyze data in real-time. When combined with the power of Big Data analytics, IoT creates unprecedented opportunities for urban planners, policymakers, and citizens to make informed decisions and optimize city operations.

This book is designed to bridge the gap between theoretical concepts and practical applications, offering readers a deep dive into the world of intelligent IoT analytics within the context of smart cities. Whether you are a city official, an urban planner, a technology professional, or a student of urban studies, this comprehensive resource will equip you with the knowledge and insights needed to navigate the rapidly evolving landscape of smart urban technologies.

This book was written not only from a conceptual standpoint but also from the author's years of hands-on experience in designing, developing, and operationalizing IoT systems in Smart Cities. The insights within come from working directly with the complexities of real-world deployments: integrating heterogeneous sensors, developing middleware, building data pipelines, and operationalizing analytics frameworks that support mission-critical environments.

Importance of IoT and Big Data in Urban Development and Smart Cities

The potential of IoT and Big Data to revolutionize urban development cannot be overstated. These technologies offer a myriad of solutions to longstanding urban challenges, from traffic congestion and energy consumption to public safety and environmental sustainability.

Transformative Potential

IoT and Big Data analytics are reshaping the urban landscape in profound ways:

1. Real-time Monitoring and Response: IoT sensors deployed throughout the city provide a continuous stream of data on everything from air quality to traffic flow, enabling rapid response to emerging issues. This real-time capability allows city managers to address problems proactively, often before they escalate into more significant challenges.

2. Predictive Maintenance: By analyzing patterns in sensor data, cities can anticipate infrastructure failures before they occur, reducing downtime and maintenance costs. This approach not only saves money but also enhances the reliability of critical urban systems, from transportation networks to utility grids.

3. Resource Optimization: Smart metering and analytics help cities manage resources like water and energy more efficiently, reducing waste and environmental impact. By providing detailed insights into consumption patterns, these technologies enable more precise resource allocation and encourage conservation efforts.

4. Enhanced Public Services: From intelligent transportation systems to smart waste management, IoT and Big Data improve the quality and efficiency of public services. These technologies enable cities to tailor services to the specific needs of their residents, improving overall quality of life.

5. Data-Driven Decision Making: Access to comprehensive, real-time data empowers city leaders to make more informed decisions about urban planning and resource allocation. This data-centric approach leads to more effective policies and better long-term outcomes for urban communities.

The integration of IoT and Big Data analytics into urban infrastructure is not just about technological advancement; it represents a fundamental shift in how cities are managed and experienced. By creating a digital nervous system for urban environments, these technologies enable a level of responsiveness and adaptability that was previously unimaginable.

Key Challenges Addressed

The adoption of IoT and Big Data analytics offers solutions to several critical urban challenges:

1. Traffic Congestion: Intelligent traffic management systems can reduce congestion, improve mobility, and decrease emissions. By analyzing real-time traffic data from sensors, cameras, and connected vehicles, cities can optimize traffic light timing, suggest alternative routes, and even predict and prevent traffic jams before they occur.

2. Energy Efficiency: Smart grids and building management systems optimize energy consumption, reducing costs and environmental impact. These systems can balance energy supply and demand in real-time, integrate renewable energy sources more effectively, and enable dynamic pricing to encourage off-peak consumption.

3. Public Safety: IoT-enabled surveillance and emergency response systems enhance public safety and reduce crime rates. From smart streetlights that brighten when they detect movement to predictive policing algorithms that help allocate law enforcement resources more effectively, these technologies are making cities safer for residents and visitors alike.

4. Environmental Sustainability: Real-time monitoring of air and water quality allows for more effective environmental protection measures. IoT sensors can detect pollution levels, identify sources of contamination, and trigger automated responses to mitigate environmental risks.

5. Urban Planning: Data-driven insights inform better urban design decisions, creating more livable and sustainable cities. By analyzing patterns of movement, resource usage, and social interactions, urban planners can design spaces that better serve the needs of residents and promote community well-being.

6. Healthcare Access: IoT and Big Data analytics can improve the delivery of healthcare services in urban areas. From telemedicine platforms that connect patients with healthcare providers remotely to predictive models that anticipate disease outbreaks, these technologies have the potential to make healthcare more accessible, efficient, and proactive.

7. Waste Management: Smart waste management systems use IoT sensors to optimize collection routes, reduce operational costs, and minimize environmental impact. These systems can detect when bins are full, plan the most efficient collection routes, and even sort waste for better recycling outcomes.

The ability of IoT and Big Data to address these challenges simultaneously and in an integrated manner is what makes them so powerful in the context of smart cities. By creating a holistic, data-driven approach to urban management, these technologies enable cities to tackle complex, interconnected problems more effectively than ever before.

Potential Benefits

The adoption of IoT and Big Data in smart cities offers significant benefits to various stakeholders:

1. For Citizens:
   • Improved quality of life through better public services
   • Enhanced safety and security in urban environments
   • More efficient and convenient transportation options
   • Greater transparency and engagement with city governance
   • Personalized services tailored to individual needs and preferences
   • Healthier living environments with reduced pollution and improved sustainability

2. For Governments:
   • More efficient resource allocation and significant cost savings
   • Improved decision-making capabilities based on real-time data
   • Enhanced ability to respond to citizen needs and emergencies
   • Better long-term planning and sustainability initiatives
   • Increased citizen satisfaction and trust in government services
   • Ability to attract businesses and talent with advanced urban infrastructure

3. For Businesses:
   • New opportunities for innovation and service provision in urban markets
   • Access to valuable urban data for product development and market research

- Improved infrastructure supporting business operations and logistics
- Potential for public-private partnerships in urban development projects
- Enhanced ability to tailor products and services to local urban needs
- Opportunities to contribute to and benefit from the circular economy

4. For the Environment:
   - Reduced carbon emissions through optimized energy use and transportation
   - More effective conservation of natural resources
   - Improved air and water quality through real-time monitoring and management
   - Enhanced ability to respond to environmental emergencies and natural disasters
   - Promotion of sustainable urban development practices

5. For Urban Planners and Researchers:
   - Access to unprecedented amounts of data for urban studies and research
   - Ability to test and validate urban planning theories in real-time
   - Enhanced tools for modeling and simulating urban environments
   - Opportunities for interdisciplinary collaboration in urban development

The realization of these benefits requires careful planning, implementation, and ongoing management of IoT and Big Data systems. It also necessitates a collaborative approach involving government agencies, private sector entities, academic institutions, and citizens. By working together, these stakeholders can harness the full potential of intelligent IoT analytics to create truly smart, sustainable, and livable cities.

How This Book is Structured

To provide a comprehensive understanding of intelligent IoT analytics in smart cities, this book is organized into four main parts, each focusing on a crucial aspect of the subject:

Part I: Foundations of IoT and Big Data for Smart Cities

This section lays the groundwork for understanding the fundamental concepts and technologies underlying smart city initiatives. It covers:

- Chapter 1: Introduction to IoT for Smart Cities
- Chapter 2: Real-time Big Data for IoT
- Chapter 3: Digital Twin Cities

Chapter 1: "Introduction to IoT for Smart Cities" provides a historical context for the development of IoT technologies and their application in urban environments. It explores the evolution of smart city concepts, from early experiments in urban technology to the comprehensive, data-driven approaches of today. The chapter also examines key milestones in IoT adoption for urban applications and analyzes pioneering smart city projects worldwide, such as those in Barcelona, Singapore, and Amsterdam.

A highlight of this chapter is a detailed case study on the role of IoT in enhancing urban life in Nusantara, Indonesia's planned smart capital city. This case study offers insights into the ambitious Integrated Command and Control Center (ICCC) concept and provides a comprehensive overview of the proposed IoT implementations in Nusantara. By examining this large-scale project, readers will gain an understanding of both the potential benefits and the challenges involved in implementing IoT at a city-wide scale.

Chapter 2: "Real-time Big Data for IoT" delves into the critical role of Big Data in smart city operations. It begins with a detailed explanation of the four V's of Big Data - Volume, Velocity, Variety, and Veracity - and their specific relevance to IoT data in urban contexts. The chapter then explores the importance of real-time data streaming and low-latency processing in urban environments, using examples from traffic management and emergency response systems to illustrate the value of real-time analytics.

This chapter also addresses the challenges of implementing real-time systems at the city scale, including issues of data integration, processing power, and network infrastructure. It provides strategies for overcoming these challenges and maximizing the value of real-time Big Data in smart city applications.

Chapter 3: "Digital Twin Cities" introduces the concept of Digital Twins and their transformative potential in urban planning and management. The chapter traces the evolution of Digital Twins from their origins in industrial applications to their current use in complex urban systems. It outlines the key components of a city-scale Digital Twin and explores the benefits of this technology for urban planning, simulation, and optimization.

A significant portion of this chapter is dedicated to case studies of successful Digital Twin implementations in world-class smart cities. By examining projects such as Virtual Singapore and Helsinki's Digital Twin, readers will gain insights into the technologies used, challenges overcome, and outcomes achieved. The chapter concludes with a discussion of lessons learned and best practices for implementing Digital Twins in smart cities of various scales.

Part II: Design and Architecture of IoT Big Data Analytics Platforms

This part delves into the practical aspects of designing and implementing IoT and Big Data systems for smart cities. It includes:

- Chapter 4: Choosing the Right Technology Stack
- Chapter 5: Integrating the Human Dimension into Smart Cities

Chapter 4: "Choosing the Right Technology Stack" provides a comprehensive overview of the various technology options available for smart city implementations. It begins with a detailed comparison of proprietary vendors such as Vantiq, Azure IoT, and AWS IoT, analyzing their features, strengths, and specific use cases in smart city contexts. The chapter then explores open-source solutions like ThingsBoard, OpenRemote, and Node-RED, discussing their architecture, customization options, and community support.

A key focus of this chapter is on evaluating the best fit for technology stacks based on different city scales and needs. It considers factors such as city size, existing infrastructure, budget constraints, and available technical expertise. The chapter also addresses critical considerations such as scalability requirements for growing urban environments and the importance of interoperability and standards compliance. Case studies of technology stack selection in various city sizes provide practical insights into the decision-making process.

Chapter 5: "Integrating the Human Dimension into Smart Cities" emphasizes the critical importance of user-centric design in IoT implementations. It begins by outlining the principles of user-centered design in IoT contexts and discusses accessibility considerations for diverse urban populations. The chapter explores the delicate balance between automation and human control and addresses the ethical and privacy concerns that arise in user-centric IoT design.

A significant portion of this chapter is dedicated to strategies for public engagement and feedback on IoT systems. It covers the design of intuitive applications and dashboards for IoT systems, including best practices for data visualization, responsive design for multi-device access, and personalization options. The chapter also explores innovative approaches to citizen participation, including the use of gamification strategies to encourage public engagement. A detailed case study of a successful citizen engagement project in a smart city IoT implementation provides practical insights into effective public involvement strategies.

Part III: Technical Aspects of IoT and Big Data Analytics

This section provides a deep dive into the technical underpinnings of IoT and Big Data systems, covering:

- Chapter 6: Core Principles of IoT
- Chapter 7: IoT Protocols and Computing
- Chapter 8: Realtime IoT Data Analytics
- Chapter 9: Designing Effective Data Lakes for IoT Systems
- Chapter 10: Machine Learning for IoT
- Chapter 11: Securing the IoT Ecosystem

Chapter 6: "Core Principles of IoT" lays the foundation for understanding the technical aspects of IoT systems. It begins with an in-depth exploration of sensors, endpoints, and power systems commonly used in smart city applications. The chapter discusses various types of sensors, their characteristics, and selection criteria for different urban use cases. It also addresses critical considerations in power management, including battery life optimization and innovative energy harvesting solutions.

The chapter then delves into communication and network systems for IoT, providing an overview of IoT communication protocols such as MQTT, CoAP, and HTTP. It explores wireless technologies crucial for IoT deployments in urban environments, including LoRaWAN, NB-IoT, and 5G. The chapter also addresses the challenges of implementing IoT networks in urban settings, such as interference, coverage issues, and scalability requirements.

Chapter 7: "IoT Protocols and Computing" builds on the previous chapter by providing a detailed comparison of edge and cloud computing paradigms in IoT contexts. It explores the benefits and challenges of edge computing, including latency reduction, bandwidth savings, and enhanced privacy. The chapter also discusses the principles of computation in IoT, covering data processing models, distributed computing concepts, and resource management strategies.

A significant portion of this chapter is dedicated to edge computing, exploring its benefits and challenges in detail. It examines the potential of edge AI and machine learning, discussing both the opportunities and limitations of these technologies in resource-constrained environments. The chapter includes a case study of a successful implementation of edge computing in a smart city project, providing practical insights into the real-world application of these concepts.

Chapter 8: "Realtime IoT Data Analytics" focuses on the critical aspect of processing and analyzing IoT data in real-time. It begins by outlining the principles and applications of real-time data processing, exploring streaming analytics frameworks and technologies. The chapter then delves into the design and optimization of data flow, covering topics such as data ingestion patterns, streaming protocols, and strategies for optimizing data flow in low-latency and high-throughput scenarios.

The chapter also addresses the challenges of processing and consuming data on the cloud, exploring cloud-based stream processing architectures and serverless computing options for IoT data processing. It provides strategies for scaling cloud-based IoT analytics and optimizing data storage and retrieval for real-time access. The chapter concludes with a detailed case study on building IoT data analytics in the edge and cloud using AWS, offering a practical walkthrough of an end-to-end IoT analytics solution.

Chapter 9: "Designing Effective Data Lakes for IoT Systems" explores the principles and practices of Data Lakes in the context of IoT and smart cities. It begins by defining Data Lakes and comparing them with traditional data warehouses. The chapter then delves into the architecture components of Data Lakes, including storage solutions, metadata management, and data cataloging. It also addresses critical aspects such as data ingestion strategies for IoT data streams and data governance in Data Lake environments.

A highlight of this chapter is a comprehensive case study on implementing an IoT Data Lake in a smart city context. This case study examines the architecture and technology stack used, the challenges faced during implementation, and the solutions developed. It also analyzes the benefits realized from the Data Lake implementation and discusses future scalability and expansion plans.

Chapter 10: "Machine Learning for IoT" focuses on the application of artificial intelligence and machine learning techniques to IoT data in smart city contexts. The chapter begins by exploring the development of AI models for data prediction and analysis, covering topics such as feature engineering for IoT sensor data, model training strategies, and techniques for handling the unique challenges of IoT data streams, such as imbalanced data and concept drift.

The chapter then delves into the implementation of machine learning in smart city solutions, exploring use cases such as predictive maintenance, traffic forecasting, and energy optimization. It addresses the challenges of deploying ML models in resource-constrained IoT environments and discusses model compression and optimization techniques. The chapter also explores the ethical considerations involved in AI-driven decision-making for urban management.

A significant portion of this chapter is dedicated to a detailed case study of a machine learning implementation in a smart city IoT project. This case study examines the entire process from data pipeline development to model deployment and monitoring in production environments. It concludes with a quantitative and qualitative assessment of the impact of the ML implementation on urban operations.

Chapter 11: "Securing the IoT Ecosystem" addresses the critical aspect of security in IoT implementations for smart cities. The chapter begins by exploring the unique security challenges in IoT environments, including device constraints, scale, and heterogeneity. It introduces threat modeling techniques specific to IoT systems in smart cities and discusses relevant security standards and frameworks, such as the NIST Cybersecurity Framework for IoT.

The chapter then delves into best practices for safeguarding data and privacy in IoT systems. It covers data protection strategies, including encryption methods suitable for resource-constrained devices, anonymization techniques, and access control mechanisms. The chapter also explores privacy-preserving techniques such as differential privacy and federated learning, which are particularly relevant in the context of smart city data.

A significant portion of this chapter is dedicated to a case study on securing IoT systems for a smart city. This case study provides an in-depth analysis of a comprehensive IoT security implementation, detailing the technical and organizational measures put in place. It also examines incident response and recovery procedures and discusses strategies for continuous improvement and adaptation to evolving threats.

Part IV: Application Domains in Smart Cities

The final part of the book explores real-world applications of IoT and Big Data analytics across various urban domains:

Chapter 12: "Smart Public Services" focuses on how IoT and Big Data analytics are enhancing public safety and comfort in urban environments. The chapter begins by exploring IoT applications in fire systems, pollution monitoring, and disaster prevention. It examines the use of IoT-enabled early warning systems for natural disasters, air quality monitoring and management using distributed sensors, and smart fire detection and response systems.

A highlight of this chapter is a detailed case study on improving safety and security with IoT in a specific city. This case study examines the technologies used, their integration with existing systems, and the measurable improvements achieved in response times and incident prevention. It also explores public perception and engagement with these new systems, providing insights into the social aspects of implementing smart public services.

Chapter 13: "Smart Water and Energy Management" delves into the application of IoT in resource management for cities. The chapter begins by exploring smart metering technologies for water and energy consumption, discussing how these systems provide real-time data to both utilities and consumers. It then examines IoT applications in leak detection and prevention for water distribution networks, highlighting how these technologies can significantly reduce water loss and associated costs.

The chapter also explores demand response systems for energy grid optimization, discussing how IoT enables more efficient balancing of energy supply and demand. It concludes with an examination of how IoT facilitates the integration of renewable energy sources into urban power grids. A comprehensive case study on optimizing energy resources with IoT in a specific city provides practical insights into the implementation and impact of these technologies.

Chapter 14: "Smart Mobility and ATMS" focuses on advancements in transportation and mobility solutions, with a particular emphasis on Advanced Traffic Management Systems (ATMS). The chapter begins by exploring real-time traffic monitoring and adaptive traffic signal control systems, discussing how these technologies can significantly reduce congestion and improve traffic flow.

The chapter then examines smart parking systems and parking space optimization, exploring how IoT can help cities better manage their parking resources. It also discusses the integration of multimodal transportation using IoT, exploring how these technologies can create more seamless and efficient urban transportation networks.

A significant portion of this chapter is dedicated to a case study on implementing an Advanced Public Transportation System (APTS) in a smart city. This case study examines the IoT technologies used for real-time tracking and passenger information, their integration with other city systems, and the impact on public transit efficiency and ridership.

Chapter 15: "Smart Buildings" explores the application of IoT in building management and automation. The chapter begins by examining energy management and HVAC optimization in smart buildings, discussing how IoT sensors and analytics can significantly reduce energy consumption. It then explores occupancy detection and space utilization technologies, which can help building managers optimize the use of space and resources.

The chapter also covers predictive maintenance for building systems, exploring how IoT can help prevent equipment failures and reduce maintenance costs. It concludes with a discussion of indoor air quality monitoring and control systems, which are becoming increasingly important in the wake of global health concerns.

A detailed case study on implementing IoT for smart buildings in an urban setting provides practical insights into the deployment of these technologies at scale. This case study examines the IoT devices and systems deployed throughout a large building or complex, their integration with city-wide systems, and the quantifiable improvements achieved in energy efficiency, occupant comfort, and operational costs.

These concluding chapters highlight the future direction of Intelligent IoT Analytics in the context of smart cities. Chapter 16 explores how AI Agents are transforming command center operations through a three-layer architecture that unifies data, AI, and user interfaces. Chapter 17 looks ahead to the emerging technologies, challenges, and opportunities shaping the next generation of IoT ecosystems. These chapters offer a clear, forward-looking view of how IoT, AI, and agentic systems will redefine smart city management.

Summary

The book concludes with a comprehensive recap of the key concepts and methodologies covered throughout the text. It reflects on the interdependencies between different smart city domains and discusses critical success factors for implementing IoT solutions in urban environments.

The conclusion also looks to the future of IoT and Big Data in urban development, exploring emerging technologies such as 6G networks and quantum computing, and their potential impact on smart cities. It offers predictions for the evolution of smart cities over the next decade and discusses potential paradigm shifts in urban planning and management.

Finally, the book offers key takeaways and encouragement for innovators in the field of smart cities. It emphasizes the importance of continued innovation and experimentation in this rapidly evolving domain and concludes with a call to action for sustainable and inclusive smart city development.

By offering this blend of theoretical foundations, technical insights, and practical applications, *Intelligent IoT Analytics: Concept and Real-World Applications* aims to serve as a comprehensive resource for anyone interested in the transformative potential of IoT and Big Data analytics in shaping the cities of the future. As readers embark on this journey through the pages that follow, they will explore cutting-edge technologies and innovative approaches that are redefining urban life in the 21st century.

The challenges facing our cities are complex and multifaceted, but the potential of IoT and Big Data to address these challenges is immense. By harnessing these technologies thoughtfully and responsibly, we have the opportunity to create urban environments that are not only more efficient and sustainable but also more equitable and livable for all citizens. It is our hope that this book will inspire and guide the next generation of urban innovators, policymakers, and technologists in their efforts to build the smart cities of tomorrow.

Dr. Adhiguna Mahendra
Ekki Rinaldi

CHAPTER 1

INTRODUCTION TO IOT FOR SMART CITIES

U rban areas globally confront escalating challenges from rapid demographic expansion, constrained resource availability, and intensifying environmental pressures that compromise service delivery and sustainability objectives. These mounting pressures demand innovative approaches to urban management and governance. The integration of Internet of Things technologies offers a comprehensive framework for real-time monitoring, analysis, and optimization across municipal operations. Interconnected networks of sensors, devices, and analytics platforms enable continuous situational awareness and adaptive control mechanisms, supporting applications ranging from dynamic traffic coordination in Barcelona to utility management systems that enhance operational efficiency and resident quality of life. Documented implementations, including congestion management and parking systems in European pilot programs, and advanced water and environmental monitoring networks, demonstrate how IoT capabilities are fundamentally reshaping municipal workflows and public services with quantifiable results[1].

This comprehensive book explores fundamental concepts and practical applications of intelligent IoT analytics within smart city environments, connecting architectural principles with domain-specific implementations across mobility, energy, water, public safety, environmental monitoring, and health sectors. Subsequent chapters analyze how urban centers deploy sensor networks for air quality monitoring, demand-side energy optimization, multimodal transportation coordination, and emergency response systems, emphasizing analytics pipelines that transform raw telemetry data into actionable operational decisions. Case studies incorporate international experiences, including European open-data dashboards and integrated command platforms such as Amsterdam's circular economy initiatives and Nusantara's Integrated Command and Control Center, illustrating how centralized analytics coordinate cross-departmental actions and support evidence-based governance at municipal scale.

Large-scale implementation, however, presents significant challenges requiring systematic consideration: protecting citizen privacy, securing cybersecurity for critical infrastructure systems, addressing the digital divide, and integrating legacy infrastructure with modern platforms and standards. IoT programs must establish comprehensive data protection protocols, authentication systems, and lifecycle security measures, while ensuring equitable access and building the interoperability

---

1 Whaiduzzaman, M., Barros, A., Chanda, M., Barman, S., Sultana, T., Rahman, M. S., Roy, S., & Fidge, C. (2022). A review of emerging technologies for IoT-based smart cities. *Sensors*, 22(23), 9271.

necessary to prevent fragmented systems and pilot-stage stagnation that inhibit scalable deployment. Within this context, the primary objective provides urban planners, technology professionals, and policymakers with practical guidance to evaluate, design, and deploy secure, interoperable, and human-centered IoT analytics that advance urban livability and resilience. Through detailed analysis of successful implementations and examination of project failures, this book establishes a practical roadmap for developing sustainable, citizen-focused smart cities that effectively address contemporary urban challenges while preparing for future technological developments.

HISTORICAL BACKGROUND OF IOT DEVELOPMENT

The history of the Internet of Things spans successive industrial eras, beginning with mechanization and electrification and culminating in the digital foundations that enable connected sensing and control at scale. Early milestones include World War II radar and IFF systems and Harry Stockman's 1948 paper on communication by reflected power, which laid conceptual roots for RFID, a cornerstone technology for IoT identification and data capture. A seminal demonstration of connected devices emerged in the early 1980s when Carnegie Mellon researchers linked a Coca-Cola vending machine to ARPANET to report stock and temperature, predating the coining of the term "Internet of Things" by Kevin Ashton in 1999 to describe RFID-driven, machine-readable supply chains[2].

During the Digital Revolution, advances in artificial intelligence, machine learning, and first-generation sensor networks provided the substrate for distributed sensing and actuation, while architectural work matured connectivity and interoperability for heterogeneous "things" on the Internet. The ecosystem coalesced in the 2000s with the emergence of cyber-physical systems as a unifying lens for computation tightly coupled with physical processes, alongside the rise of cloud computing and big data analytics that enabled scalable storage and processing of telemetry streams for urban applications. By the early 2010s, these trajectories converged in the Industrial Internet, signaling a shift from isolated gadgets to end-to-end IoT platforms capable of operating intelligent infrastructure across city services.

TABLE 1.1 A timeline showing the evolution of the IoT in an urban context.

Industrial Revolution	1760s	Mechanization
Electrical Revolution	1850s	Mass Production
Digital Revolution	1940s	RFID
	1950s	AI & Digitization
	1960s	Machine Learning
	1970s	1st Gen Sensor Network
	1980s	3D Printing
	1991	Internet of Things (IoT)
	2005	CPS
	2006	Cloud Computing
	2008	Big Data
	2011	Industry
Industrial Internet	2012	Industrial Internet

---

2 Paolone, G., Iachetti, D., Paesani, R., Pilotti, F., Marinelli, M., & Di Felice, P. (2022). A holistic overview of the Internet of Things ecosystem. Internet of Things, 3(4), 398–434.

TECHNOLOGICAL ADVANCEMENTS ENABLING IOT

Advances across components, networks, and computing have rapidly expanded the feasibility and impact of the Internet of Things in cities, directly building on the historical trajectory outlined in the preceding timeline from embedded systems and networked sensing to large-scale, data-driven operations. Miniaturized sensors and processors, driven by MEMS fabrication and low-power microcontrollers, now embed intelligence in compact devices, while improved batteries and on-device power management reduce maintenance cycles in dense urban deployments. Complementary energy harvesting options, including vibration and ambient sources, further extend node lifetimes by supplementing small batteries, particularly in hard-to-service locations typical of utility, transport, and building systems.

Low-power wide-area networks have become core enablers of city-scale connectivity, offering long range and multi-year battery operation for sparse telemetry workloads across streets, buildings, and underground assets. LoRaWAN, NB-IoT, LTE-M, and related protocols trade throughput for energy efficiency and coverage, with comparative studies guiding selection by latency tolerance, mobility, and reliability requirements in applications such as metering, waste, and environmental sensing. Deployed correctly, LPWANs support massive device counts with low operating cost; ongoing research addresses performance optimization, mobility, and security hardening to sustain reliability at urban scale. Practical evaluations in smart environments show LPWAN suitability for critical alerts and inclusive services, such as emergency assistance for vulnerable users in buildings and campuses, with high delivery reliability under realistic conditions[3].

Cloud and edge computing jointly provide the processing backbone that transforms raw telemetry into operational decisions, with edge nodes reducing latency, bandwidth usage, and privacy exposure by filtering and acting on data near sources, and the cloud aggregating, learning, and coordinating across domains. Real-time edge analytics frameworks demonstrated in traffic, energy, and environmental use cases show faster control loops and lower network load, while maintaining model quality and security at the periphery of the network. This edge-to-cloud continuum underpins resilient urban services, allowing local autonomy during backhaul disruptions and centralized optimization when connectivity is available.

Artificial intelligence and machine learning elevate IoT from sensing to intelligence, enabling forecasting, anomaly detection, and adaptive control that drive measurable improvements in service quality and resource efficiency across mobility, energy, and environment. MLassisted resource allocation on constrained networks further improves energy use and capacity, illustrating how analytics codesign with communications can extend device life and service reliability in dense urban deployments[4].

3 R. Marini, K. Mikhaylov, G. Pasolini and C. Buratti, "Low-Power Wide-Area Networks: Comparison of LoRaWAN and NB-IoT Performance," in *IEEE Internet of Things Journal*, vol. 9, no. 21, pp. 21051–21063, 1 Nov. 1, 2022, doi: 10.1109/JIOT.2022.3176394.

4 Q. M. Qadir, "Low Power Wide Area Networks; Promising Technologies for IOT Applications," *2023 9th International Engineering Conference on Sustainable Technology and Development (IEC)*, Erbil, Iraq, 2023, pp. 1–1, doi: 10.1109/IEC57380.2023.10438828.

IOT IN URBAN CONTEXTS

The application of IoT in urban environments has led to the emergence of smart cities, where interconnected devices and data analytics are used to enhance various aspects of urban living. IoT technology optimizes transportation and mobility in a smart city, making systems more efficient and reducing congestion. Energy management is also improved through smarter grids and consumption monitoring, while water and waste management benefits from automated systems that ensure better resource allocation. Real-time surveillance and emergency response systems strengthen public safety and security, while environmental monitoring helps track pollution and other ecological factors. Additionally, health care and social services are enhanced through IoT-driven innovations that improve accessibility and efficiency. Finally, urban planning and governance are streamlined through data-driven decision-making, enabling more responsive and sustainable city management.

KEY COMPONENTS OF IOT IN SMART CITIES

The IoT ecosystem in smart cities encompasses diverse application domains, each serving essential urban functions through interconnected technologies and data-driven systems. These components work collaboratively to enhance operational efficiency, sustainability, and quality of life across multiple sectors. The comprehensive nature of IoT deployment in urban environments includes twelve critical domains:

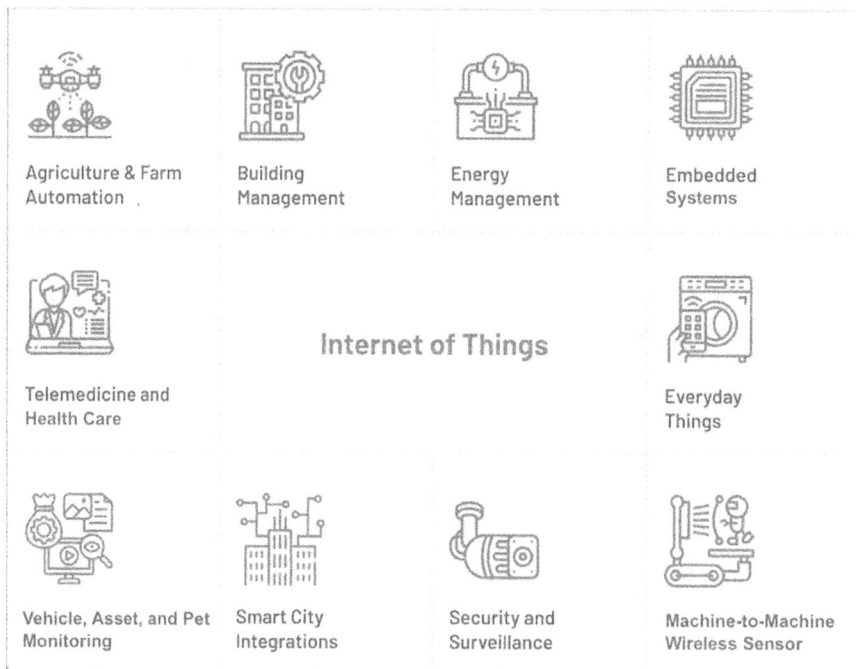

Agriculture & Farm Automation	Building Management	Energy Management	Embedded Systems
Telemedicine and Health Care		Internet of Things	Everyday Things
Vehicle, Asset, and Pet Monitoring	Smart City Integrations	Security and Surveillance	Machine-to-Machine Wireless Sensor

FIGURE 1.1 Critical components of IoT in smart cities.

Agriculture and Farm Automation integrates precision farming, vertical cultivation, and controlled environment agriculture within urban boundaries. IoT-enabled systems monitor soil conditions, automate irrigation based on moisture and weather data, and optimize resource usage in vertical farms through sensors that track temperature, humidity, and nutrient levels. Urban agricultural initiatives reduce food miles, enhance food security, and support circular economy principles by utilizing smart irrigation controllers and automated harvesting systems.

Building Management use IoT technologies to optimize energy consumption, enhance occupant comfort, and improve operational efficiency across residential, commercial, and industrial structures. Smart building systems integrate HVAC controls, lighting automation, occupancy sensors, and environmental monitoring to reduce energy waste and maintain optimal indoor conditions.

Energy Management utilize smart grid technologies, renewable energy integration, and demand-side management to create resilient and sustainable power systems. IoT devices monitor energy generation from solar panels, wind turbines, and other renewable sources while optimizing distribution based on real-time demand patterns. Smart meters provide granular consumption data, enabling dynamic pricing, load balancing, and grid stability management across urban energy networks.

Embedded Systems form the technological foundation supporting all IoT applications through microcontrollers, sensors, and communication modules that collect, process, and transmit data. These systems enable edge computing capabilities, reducing latency and improving response times for critical urban services while supporting diverse communication protocols from LoRaWAN to 5G networks.

Telemedicine and Healthcare extend medical services through remote monitoring, wearable devices, and digital health platforms that improve accessibility and reduce healthcare costs. IoT-enabled health systems support chronic disease management, emergency response coordination, and population health monitoring through continuous data collection and analysis.

Everyday Things is consumer IoT devices including smart appliances, wearables, and connected vehicles that enhance daily life while contributing to broader smart city data ecosystems. These devices support personalized services, energy efficiency, and improved convenience for urban residents.

Vehicle, Asset, and Pet Monitoring provides real-time tracking and management capabilities for transportation systems, infrastructure assets, and public safety applications. Connected vehicle technologies support traffic optimization, fleet management, and autonomous transportation systems that reduce congestion and emissions.

Smart City Integrations coordinate cross-domain systems through unified platforms that enable data sharing, interoperability, and holistic urban management. These integration platforms support evidence-based decision-making, resource optimization, and coordinated responses to urban challenges.

Security and Surveillance enhance public safety through intelligent monitoring systems, predictive policing, and emergency response coordination. IoT-enabled security networks provide real-time threat detection, automated alerts, and coordinated emergency responses across urban environments.

Machine-to-Machine Wireless Sensor networks enable autonomous communication between devices, supporting industrial automation, infrastructure monitoring, and environmental sensing without human intervention. These networks form the backbone of smart city operations, enabling responsive and adaptive urban systems.

These interconnected components create a comprehensive IoT ecosystem that supports efficient resource management, improved public services, enhanced sustainability, and better quality of life for urban residents.

SMART CITY PROJECTS BENCHMARK

Several leading cities now provide concrete templates for domain-specific IoT deployments and integrated operations, building on the preceding components and architecture to demonstrate measurable public value across mobility, utilities, environment, and governance. Barcelona's portfolio combines smart lighting, irrigation, parking, and open platforms; outcomes reported include multimillion-dollar annual savings on water, increased parking revenue, and energy reductions through LED and sensorized streetlights orchestrated via city platforms such as Sentilo and City OS[5]. Singapore operationalizes a whole-of-government model through the Smart Nation Sensor Platform and the Smart Nation Operations Centre, using lamppost sensors, video analytics, and integrated dashboards to deliver 360-degree situational awareness for incident response and municipal maintenance at scale. Amsterdam advances a collaborative, citizen-centric approach via the Amsterdam Smart City platform and IoT Living Lab, using open data, LPWAN pilots, and living-lab methods to co-create solutions in mobility, circular economy, and public-space interactivity that other municipalities can replicate.

Together, these exemplars show how cities convert sensor networks and connectivity into operational improvements: optimized lighting and water use, dynamic parking and congestion management, and unified monitoring that speeds response and improves service reliability across departments. Cross-city efforts in semantic interoperability for mobility services further illustrate how shared data models and APIs enable parking guidance and travel suggestions that span deployments in Barcelona, Santander, and multiple Korean cities, reducing vendor lock-in and supporting scalable ecosystems. At the network layer, many of these programs rely on LPWAN coverage for cost-effective telemetry of metering, environmental sensing, and waste operations, highlighting both the advantages of long-range, low-energy links and the need to plan for performance and security as deployments grow.

These benchmarks will anchor the chapter's deeper analyses: Barcelona for integrated urban services and economic impact, Singapore for centralized situational awareness and governance, and Amsterdam for open, participatory innovation—each mapping architectural choices to outcomes in energy, mobility, environment, and data-driven operations that inform pragmatic adoption paths for other cities.

Barcelona, Spain

Barcelona has emerged as a leader in smart city initiatives, deploying numerous IoT solutions to enhance urban living. One notable innovation is the city's smart street lighting system, where energy-efficient LED lights adjust their brightness based on pedestrian activity, conserving

---

5 Adler, L. (2016, February 18). How Smart City Barcelona brought the Internet of Things to life. Data-Smart City Solutions, Harvard Kennedy School. *https://datasmart.hks.harvard.edu/news/article/how-smart-city-barcelona-brought-the-internet-of-things-to-life-789*

energy and minimizing light pollution. Another important development is smart waste management, with sensors embedded in waste containers that help optimize collection routes and schedules, reducing operational costs and environmental impact.

In addition, Barcelona introduced IoT-enabled irrigation systems in public parks, which adjust water usage based on real-time data, significantly reducing water consumption. The city's smart parking system uses sensors to direct drivers to available parking spaces, helping to alleviate traffic congestion. Central to these efforts is the City OS, a unified platform that integrates data from various urban systems, enabling more informed and efficient decision-making across the city's services.

Barcelona's initiatives have resulted in significant cost savings, improved resource management, and enhanced quality of life for its citizens.

Singapore

Singapore's Smart Nation initiative exemplifies comprehensive urban digitalization through coordinated implementation of integrated IoT platforms and data-driven governance systems. The foundation of this transformation rests on the Smart Nation Sensor Platform (SNSP)[6], a nationwide infrastructure that connects diverse sensor networks across government agencies to collect, share, and analyze urban data for evidence-based decision-making. This integrated platform eliminates data silos between agencies such as the National Environmental Agency and Land Transport Authority, enabling seamless information exchange through secure protocols and shared analytics capabilities.

Central to Singapore's digital urban management is Virtual Singapore, a comprehensive 3D digital twin that integrates real-time sensor data, satellite imagery, and geographic information systems to create a dynamic virtual representation of the entire city-state. This $73 million digital infrastructure enables urban planners to simulate infrastructure projects, analyze traffic optimization strategies, test disaster response scenarios, and monitor environmental conditions with unprecedented detail and accuracy. The platform supports predictive analytics for urban planning, allowing officials to model the impact of proposed developments and policy changes before implementation.

Smart mobility initiatives demonstrate Singapore's methodical approach to autonomous vehicle integration, prioritizing safety and regulatory frameworks over rapid deployment. The Land Transport Authority conducts controlled autonomous bus trials with safety operators onboard, establishing operational protocols and public confidence before scaling deployment. Current trials focus on data collection for mapping and navigation systems within real traffic conditions, representing a cautious but thorough approach to transforming public transportation.

Amsterdam, Netherlands

Amsterdam exemplifies sustainable smart city development through a collaborative governance model that places citizens at the center of innovation processes. The city's approach to smart energy integrates renewable sources, energy-efficient building systems, and smart grid technologies that balance supply and demand while reducing consumption. In smart mobility,

---

6 Government Technology Agency. (2022, October). GOVTECH: Championing Singapore's digital government journey (Fact sheet). *https://www.developer.tech.gov.sg/our-digital-journey/singapore-digital-government-journey/files/govtech-singapore-digital-government-journey-factsheet.pdf*

Amsterdam has developed comprehensive electric vehicle charging infrastructure and intelligent traffic management systems that reduce congestion and emissions through data-driven optimization. These initiatives demonstrate how IoT technologies can support environmental sustainability while enhancing urban mobility and energy security.

Central to Amsterdam's strategy is the advancement of circular economy principles through sophisticated IoT-enabled waste management systems that optimize sorting, recycling, and resource recovery. Smart waste bins equipped with sensors monitor fill levels, automatically optimizing collection routes and reducing fuel consumption while improving operational efficiency. Machine learning algorithms enhance waste categorization precision, enabling higher recycling rates and supporting circular economy objectives through better material recovery and reuse. The city's waste-to-energy systems use IoT monitoring to optimize biogas production from organic waste, exemplifying how technology can convert waste streams into valuable resources.

Amsterdam's open data platform and participatory governance model foster transparency and citizen engagement through the Amsterdam Smart City (ASC) initiative, which serves as a collaborative forum for public, private, and civic organizations. The ASC platform enables residents to propose projects, participate in decision-making, and contribute to smart city development through bottom-up innovation processes. Living labs established across various neighborhoods provide testing environments for new smart city technologies with active citizen participation, ensuring solutions address real community needs. This collaborative approach demonstrates how successful smart city implementation requires partnership between government, businesses, and residents, creating inclusive digital transformation that prioritizes human-centered design and democratic participation in urban innovation[7].

AN ANALYSIS OF IOT IMPACT ON URBAN PLANNING AND MANAGEMENT

The integration of IoT in urban environments has had a profound impact on urban planning and management practices, such as:

Data-Driven Decision-Making

IoT devices generate enormous amounts of real-time data on different aspects of city life, allowing city officials to make more informed decisions and respond swiftly to dynamic conditions. For instance, traffic management systems can use real-time traffic flow data to adjust signal timings, reducing congestion and improving traffic efficiency. Similarly, energy grids can optimize the balance between supply and demand by leveraging data from smart meters, ensuring more efficient energy distribution.

In addition, emergency services can be deployed more strategically with the help of data collected from sensors and cameras, enabling quicker and more precise responses to incidents. This ability to act on real-time data enhances urban efficiency and safety, making cities more resilient and responsive to the needs of their inhabitants.

---

7 Fraaije, A., van der Meij, M., Vermeeren, A., Kupper, F. & Broerse, J., (2023) "Creating room for citizen perspectives in 'smart city' Amsterdam through interactive theatre", *Research for All* 7(1). doi: *https://doi.org/10.14324/RFA.07.1.05*

Predictive Maintenance

IoT sensors play a crucial role in monitoring the condition of urban infrastructure, supporting predictive maintenance strategies that help reduce costs and enhance service reliability. These sensors can track various aspects of infrastructure, providing early warnings of potential issues. For example, they can monitor the structural integrity of bridges and buildings, allowing officials to address weaknesses before they escalate into costly repairs or safety hazards.

In water distribution systems, IoT sensors can detect leaks at an early stage, preventing significant water loss and avoiding costly disruptions. Similarly, sensors can identify potential failures in electrical grids before they result in outages, ensuring a more stable and efficient power supply. IoT sensors contribute to more sustainable and resilient urban environments by enabling proactive maintenance.

Resource Optimization

IoT solutions enable cities to optimize resource usage, delivering both cost savings and environmental benefits. One example is smart lighting systems that automatically adjust their brightness based on natural light levels and pedestrian activity, conserving energy and reducing light pollution. Similarly, intelligent waste management systems use sensors to optimize collection routes, reducing fuel consumption and operational costs while minimizing environmental impact.

In parks and green spaces, smart irrigation systems equipped with IoT technology can monitor weather and soil conditions to reduce water consumption, ensuring efficient water use without compromising the health of vegetation. These resource-efficient IoT solutions cut costs and support more sustainable urban living.

Improved Public Services

IoT enables city services to run faster, with better targeting, and fewer manual steps. Smart parking sensors detect open spaces and direct drivers via apps or roadside signs, cutting search time and easing congestion. Connected buses and trains publish live arrival times and vehicle load levels to stops and phones, helping commuters plan routes, reduce waiting, and balance demand across the network.

Digital government services, often called e-government, use online portals and mobile apps to deliver public services and information. When linked with IoT data, these services let residents apply for permits, pay utility bills, book public facilities, and report issues with automatic location and photo evidence. Workflows route cases to the right department, provide status updates, and trigger field crews with optimized schedules. The result is faster resolution, lower operating cost, and a clearer, more convenient experience for residents.

Enhanced Urban Planning

IoT data offers urban planners valuable insights into the functioning of cities, facilitating more effective long-term planning. By analyzing pedestrian and vehicle movement patterns, planners can make informed decisions regarding infrastructure development, ensuring that roadways, public transport, and pedestrian pathways meet the needs of the community. This data-driven approach helps create a more efficient urban layout that enhances mobility and accessibility.

Additionally, monitoring air quality and noise levels using IoT sensors provides crucial information for guiding environmental policies, enabling cities to implement strategies that protect public health and improve overall quality of life. Furthermore, studying energy consumption patterns allows planners to anticipate future energy needs, helping to develop sustainable energy solutions that can accommodate population growth and technological advancements. By utilizing IoT data, urban planners can create smarter, more resilient cities that respond to the evolving needs of their inhabitants.

CITIZEN ENGAGEMENT

IoT solutions enable direct communication channels between residents and city governments through digital platforms that streamline service requests and feedback mechanisms. Mobile applications equipped with GPS technology allow citizens to report infrastructure problems such as potholes, broken streetlights, or overflowing waste containers with precise location data and photographic evidence. These systems route reports automatically to the appropriate municipal departments and provide status updates throughout the resolution process. The integration of IoT sensors with reporting platforms enhances accuracy by cross-referencing citizen reports with real-time sensor data, enabling city officials to prioritize responses based on severity and impact. This automated workflow reduces response times, improves service delivery efficiency, and creates a documented record of municipal performance that residents can track and evaluate.

Open data initiatives supported by IoT infrastructure provide citizens with unprecedented access to real-time information about city operations and resource allocation. Sensor networks collect continuous data on air quality, traffic flow, energy consumption, water usage, and waste collection patterns, which is then made available through public portals and application programming interfaces. Citizens, researchers, and community organizations use this data to analyze neighborhood conditions, identify service gaps, and propose evidence-based solutions to local challenges. The availability of granular, location-specific data enables residents to participate in informed discussions about urban planning decisions and hold elected officials accountable for resource management. Academic institutions and civic technology groups often develop visualization tools and analytical platforms that make complex datasets accessible to non-technical users, further democratizing access to municipal information.

Digital governance platforms integrate IoT data streams with participatory budgeting processes, allowing residents to make informed decisions about public investment priorities. These systems present budget proposals alongside relevant performance metrics from sensor networks, enabling citizens to evaluate the potential impact of different spending options. For example, proposals for traffic safety improvements can be supported by data from speed sensors and accident reporting systems, while environmental initiatives can reference air quality and noise monitoring data. The combination of real-time IoT data with structured public input processes creates more transparent and accountable governance mechanisms. Citizens can track the implementation of approved projects through continued sensor monitoring and performance dashboards, creating feedback loops that improve future decision-making processes and strengthen community trust in local government operations.

CHALLENGES AND CONSIDERATIONS

IoT brings clear benefits to urban management, but sustained value depends on confronting a set of cross-cutting risks in governance, engineering, and social equity; the most consequential challenges—and practical mitigations—span privacy and security, interoperability, the digital divide, operational resilience, safety, ethics, and compliance, all of which must be addressed by design in smart-city roadmaps and procurement policies.

Privacy and Security

Smart-city IoT expands the attack surface across heterogeneous devices, networks, and platforms, raising risks to data confidentiality, integrity, and availability, especially where low-cost sensors lack secure boot, credential hygiene, or encrypted storage and transport by default. Effective mitigations include end-to-end encryption, strong authentication, secure software development life cycles, intrusion detection, network segmentation, Zero Trust access, and incident response playbooks tailored to critical urban services. Privacy engineering must cover data at rest and in motion with minimization, pseudonymization, and access control grounded in legal bases and consent where applicable, since weak protections enable linkage attacks and secondary use beyond original purpose.

Interoperability and Open Standards

Lack of interoperability across vendors and domains impedes data sharing and coordinated response, making standards adoption a prerequisite for scale, maintainability, and security baselines across devices, networks, and platforms. International standards bodies provide protocol suites, information models, and conformity frameworks that reduce integration costs and improve assurance, enabling secure interwork among utilities, mobility, buildings, and public safety systems. Cities should mandate standards compliance in RFPs, require open APIs and data schemas, and plan for lifecycle governance so new systems can integrate without custom point-to-point adapters that become technical debt.

Digital Divide and Inclusion

Without inclusive design, smart-city services risk amplifying inequities by privileging connected, digitally literate residents and excluding low-income, elderly, or disabled populations from essential services and civic participation. Programmatic responses pair universal design and multi-channel access (web, phone, kiosk, assisted service) with subsidized connectivity, device access, and digital literacy, while auditing datasets and algorithms for disparate impact on marginalized groups. Governance should establish equity KPIs, community advisory mechanisms, and grievance redress tied to service levels, ensuring benefits of IoT reach all residents rather than a narrow user base.

Over-Reliance on Technology

Dependence on tightly coupled, networked systems increases the blast radius of failures and cyber incidents, threatening continuity of critical services such as power, water, transport, and emergency response. Resilience requires defense-in-depth, segmented architectures, graceful degradation modes, manual fallbacks, and routine exercising of failover, along with cyber-physical tabletop drills covering cascading impacts across domains. Continuous monitoring and anomaly detection using ML can speed detection and containment but must be paired with operational runbooks and trained responders to avoid automation surprises during crises.

Governance and Data Protection by Design

Data protection by design operationalizes privacy and security through consent management, purpose limitation, role-based access, and audit trails, aligning identity and authorization flows with regulatory obligations and citizen expectations. A citywide policy framework should define data categories, retention schedules, sharing rules, and DPIA triggers, while aligning vendor contracts with breach notification, vulnerability disclosure, and patch SLAs to sustain compliance at scale. Integrating privacy-preserving identity, consent orchestration, and contextual access control reduces uncontrolled data propagation and improves accountability across agencies and partners.

Advanced Threat Landscape

As adversaries target IoT gateways and edge nodes, smart-city defenders benefit from layered controls, including encrypted telemetry, signed firmware, secure element key storage, and behavioral baselines for anomaly detection across OT and IT. Emerging approaches combine edge analytics and federated learning to keep raw data local while training models collaboratively, reducing exposure and latency while improving collective detection performance against advanced threats. Research also explores blockchain for tamper-evident logging and trusted data exchange, and Zero Trust frameworks to decouple identity from network location across multi-tenant city platforms.

Standards-Driven Lifecycle Security

Security must align with device constraints and lifecycle events: onboarding, operation, update, and decommissioning, with explicit guidance for secure storage, key rotation, and vulnerability remediation over multi-year deployments. A structured framework maps common IoT attack patterns to violated security goals and mitigation guidelines, tying controls to software lifecycle practices and communications hygiene, while addressing legacy system integration risks during modernization. Cities should require SBOMs, over-the-air update capability, and verifiable attestation to ensure fleet-wide posture can be measured and improved continuously.

Surveillance, Ethics, and Legitimacy

Expansive sensing for safety and optimization can drift into mass surveillance if guardrails are weak, eroding trust and chilling civic life; legitimacy rests on clearly scoped purposes, proportionality, independent oversight, and public transparency. Ethical deployment demands bias testing in analytics, community consultation, opt-out or privacy-enhancing modes where feasible, and periodic review of data value versus societal risk as technologies and norms evolve. Clear accountability lines and accessible appeals reinforce due process when automated decisions affect access to services or enforcement actions.

Connectivity and 5G Security

5G expands bandwidth and device density for city IoT but introduces new radio, core, and slicing threats; securing end-to-end communications requires robust authentication, isolation, and monitoring across heterogeneous wireless stacks and edge sites. A risk-informed 5G strategy inventories dependencies across WSNs, SDR/CR, and RFID layers, addresses known vulnerabilities, and sets requirements for vendor diversity, patch cadence, and supply-chain assurance in radio and edge infrastructure. Operational telemetry across slices and MEC nodes supports rapid containment of lateral movement, preserving availability for life-safety workloads under attack.

AI/ML Security and Accountability

IoT-enabled analytics increasingly rely on ML for detection and decision support, but models face risks of data poisoning, drift, and unfair outcomes, requiring robust MLOps with data provenance, validation, and continuous evaluation. Defense-in-depth combines signature and behavior-based IDS with ML classifiers, yet human-in-the-loop review and red-team testing remain essential to avoid overconfidence in automated judgments that may miss novel attack paths. Documented model cards, audit logs, and calibrated thresholds improve transparency and enable post-incident analysis across safety, mobility, and public-service applications.

Practical Implementation Checklist

- Policy: Citywide cybersecurity and privacy policies with data governance, DPIAs, incident response, and third-party risk management aligned to critical services.
- Architecture: Segmented networks, Zero Trust access, secure OTA updates, SBOMs, and encryption for data at rest/in transit across device–edge–cloud.
- Standards: Procurement mandates for open standards, interoperable APIs, and conformity testing to reduce integration friction and security gaps.
- Equity: Inclusive service design, assisted channels, affordability programs, and bias audits with equity KPIs and public reporting.
- Resilience: Fail-safe modes, manual overrides, backup comms, routine exercises, and cross-domain incident drills simulating cyber-physical cascades.

Addressing these challenges early—through standards-aligned design, rigorous governance, equity commitments, and resilient operations—turns IoT from a fragmented risk surface into a dependable public infrastructure asset for cities.

CASE STUDY: ROLE OF IOT IN ENHANCING URBAN LIFE – NUSANTARA CAPITAL CITY

Nusantara, Indonesia's planned new capital city, provides an excellent case study for examining the role of IoT in enhancing urban life. As a purpose-built smart city, Nusantara offers a unique opportunity to implement IoT solutions from the ground up, potentially setting new standards for smart city development worldwide.

Background on the Nusantara Project

In 2019, the Indonesian government announced plans to relocate the country's capital from Jakarta to East Kalimantan on the island of Borneo. The new capital, Nusantara, is envisioned as a smart, sustainable city that will address many of the challenges Jakarta faces, including overcrowding, traffic congestion, and environmental issues. The project represents one of the most ambitious smart city initiatives globally, with comprehensive planning that integrates IoT technologies from the initial design phase.

Important features of the Nusantara project include the following:

1. a planned area of 256,000 hectares
2. expected population of 1.5 million people by 2045
3. focus on sustainability and green technology
4. integration of smart city technologies from the initial planning stages

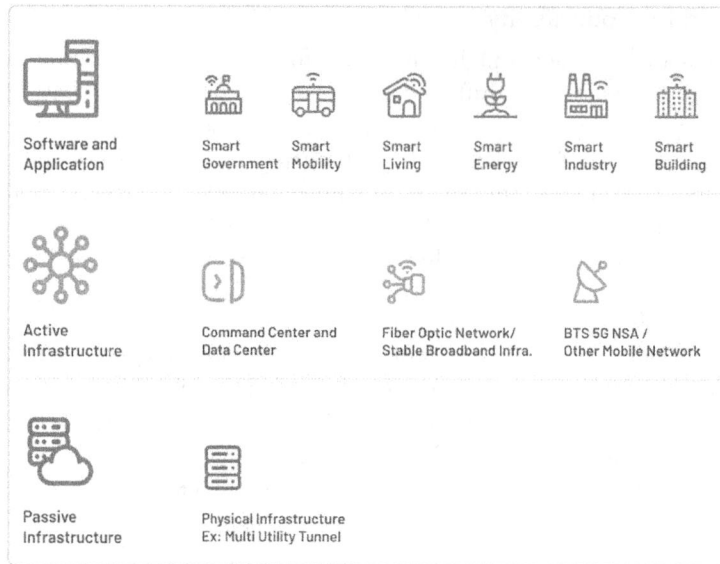

FIGURE 1.2 Nusantara's smart design plan from Nusantara's Blueprint.

The Integrated Command and Control Center (ICCC)

The Nusantara's smart city plan incorporates the Integrated Command and Control Center (ICCC), which will serve as the central system for the city's IoT infrastructure. The ICCC functions as a city's central nervous system, combining real-time monitoring of urban infrastructure with advanced data analytics. Through its centralized platform, the ICCC enables swift decision-making and efficient resource allocation across city departments. The system coordinates emergency responses and integrates diverse smart city applications—from traffic management to on environmental monitoring, creating a unified approach to urban operations management.

The ICCC will enable city officials to manage Nusantara's operations efficiently and respond quickly to any issues that arise.

IoT Implementations in Nusantara

Nusantara's planners have proposed a wide range of IoT implementations to enhance urban life:

1. Smart Transportation: Nusantara will deploy several connected solutions to make travel easier and greener. Traffic signals will link to AI-driven controls that monitor road conditions and adjust signal timing to ease congestion. Sensors in parking areas will send live updates on available spaces to drivers' smartphones or roadside signs, cutting search time. Electric vehicle charging stations will use smart meters to set prices based on demand and grid load, encouraging off-peak charging. Pilot lanes for self-driving shuttle services will test autonomous vehicles under real-world conditions. Finally, all public transit—buses, light rail, and ferries—will share a single platform for live vehicle locations and cashless fare payments. These systems work together to reduce delays, lower emissions, and make daily commutes more predictable.

2. Smart Energy Management: A city-wide intelligent grid will use sensors and automated controls to balance supply and demand, cutting transmission losses and preventing outages. Renewable sources, solar panels, wind turbines, and biomass generators, link to the network so output can be monitored and adjusted in real time. Streetlights with motion detectors and ambient-light sensors will dim when no one is nearby and brighten when pedestrians or vehicles approach, saving power and boosting safety. In public and commercial buildings, energy-management platforms gather data on HVAC, lighting, and equipment use, suggesting adjustments to cut peak loads and lower costs. In homes, smart meters and in-house dashboards give residents instant feedback on electricity use and allow timed control of appliances. These systems create an adaptive energy environment that reduces waste and supports a low-carbon future.

3. Smart Water Management: End-to-end monitoring of water flow and quality will keep supply systems efficient and safe. Sensors at treatment plants and along pipelines measure chemical levels, turbidity, and pressure, alerting operators to anomalies before they affect consumers. Digital meters in homes and businesses report usage every hour, helping detect leaks early and guiding conservation campaigns. In parks and green corridors, automated irrigation controllers draw on weather forecasts and soil-moisture data to water only when needed. Pumps and valves in drainage networks use predictive analytics to anticipate heavy rainfall and open or close gates to prevent flooding. This integrated approach reduces water loss, safeguards public health, and strengthens resilience against droughts and storms.

4. Smart Waste Management: Waste collection and processing will follow data-driven routes rather than fixed schedules. Bins fitted with level sensors signal when they need emptying, allowing trucks to visit only full containers. At sorting centers, robotic arms guided by computer vision separate recyclables with high accuracy. Organic waste moves to on-site digesters, where conditions are monitored for optimal biogas production. Residual material goes to advanced waste-to-energy plants, where sensors control temperature and emissions to meet environmental standards. A mobile app lets residents report overflowing bins or request bulk-pickup services. Real-time tracking of each collection vehicle and processing facility ensures the system adapts to changing demands, cuts costs, and maximizes resource recovery.

5. Environmental Monitoring: Nusantara will deploy a city-wide sensor network to keep constant watch on both natural and built environments. Fixed air-quality stations across neighborhoods will feed data on pollutants and weather to a central platform, enabling swift action when levels exceed safety thresholds. Acoustic monitors along major roads and in public squares will log noise in real time, guiding zoning rules and quieter pavement designs. Neighborhood microclimate units will track temperature, humidity, and rainfall, allowing park irrigation and flood-prevention systems to adapt instantly. In forested corridors around the city, soil probes will report moisture and nutrient status, while camera traps and acoustic sensors will monitor wildlife movements and habitat health. Together, these systems ensure planners and residents have a clear, up-to-date view of Nusantara's environmental wellbeing.

6. Public Safety and Security: Nusantara's safety network ties together smart cameras, emergency systems, and citizen alerts into a single command center. Cameras with built-in analytics will flag loitering, crowd surges, or traffic accidents and relay live feeds to response

teams. A citywide network of panic buttons and connected call stations will pinpoint incidents down to the street corner, cutting dispatch times. River-level and rainfall sensors in vulnerable zones will push flood warnings via sirens, street panels, and mobile apps well before water levels crest. Smart streetlights will brighten when motion is sensed and can flash alerts to draw attention during emergencies. A dedicated safety app will stream real-time alerts to residents, allow instant reporting of hazards or crimes, and track response crews, forging a partnership between citizens and authorities in keeping Nusantara secure.

7. Smart Health Care: Nusantara's health system will link clinics, hospitals, and homes through a single digital backbone. Telemedicine hubs in community centers and the mobile app will let residents consult doctors by video, cutting travel for routine check-ups. Wearable and bedside monitors will feed vital signs such as heart rate, oxygen levels, glucose into hospital dashboards, alerting staff the moment readings stray from safe ranges. Smart ambulances will stream patient data and live camera views en route, giving emergency departments time to ready the right specialists and equipment. All records will sync to a unified health platform, ensuring test results and treatment plans travel securely between providers. Environmental health sensors for air and water quality will feed outbreak models, helping public-health teams contain threats before they spread.

8. Smart Education: Smart education initiatives utilize IoT and digital technologies to enhance the learning environment and streamline campus operations. IoT-enabled smart classrooms are equipped with interactive learning tools, such as smart boards and connected devices, allowing teachers and students to engage in dynamic, technology-driven educational experiences. These tools foster a more collaborative and engaging learning atmosphere. Digital learning platforms offer personalized content delivery, adapting to the needs and learning styles of individual students. These platforms support remote learning, resource sharing, and real-time feedback, creating a flexible and tailored educational experience. Campus safety and security systems, integrated with IoT technology, monitor access points and provide real-time alerts, ensuring a safe environment for students and staff.

9. Smart Governance: Smart governance integrates IoT technologies with digital platforms to enhance public service delivery. IoT-enabled sensors and systems feed real-time data into e-government services, enabling citizens to interact with live urban systems through mobile apps and web portals. These platforms combine IoT-gathered infrastructure data with blockchain-based security for transparent operations, from voting systems to public service monitoring. AI-powered chatbots utilize this IoT network to provide context-aware responses to citizen inquiries, creating a data-rich, responsive government infrastructure that adapts to real-time urban needs.

10. Smart Buildings: Smart buildings integrate IoT technologies to enhance operational efficiency, safety, and comfort. Building management systems optimize energy use by monitoring and controlling lighting, heating, and cooling, reducing waste and operational costs. Occupancy sensors improve space utilization by adjusting resources based on real-time usage, while indoor air quality monitoring systems ensure a healthy environment by detecting pollutants and adjusting ventilation. Predictive maintenance systems, enabled by IoT sensors, identify potential issues in building infrastructure before they cause disruptions, reducing downtime and repair costs. Smart access control and security systems provide enhanced safety by automating entry management and monitoring building security in real-time.

FUTURE TRENDS AND DEVELOPMENTS IN IOT FOR SMART CITIES

As IoT technologies continue to evolve, several trends are likely to shape the future of smart cities:

1. 5G and Beyond: The implementation of 5G networks will enable faster, more reliable connections for IoT devices, supporting applications that require high bandwidth and low latency. This will facilitate the deployment of more sophisticated IoT solutions in urban environments, such as autonomous vehicles and augmented reality applications. As 6G technology develops, even more advanced IoT applications may become possible.

2. Edge Computing: The increasing use of edge computing will allow for more processing to be done closer to the source of data generation. This will reduce latency, improve privacy, and enable real-time decision-making for critical applications. In smart cities, edge computing could be particularly useful for applications like traffic management and emergency response systems.

3. Artificial Intelligence and Machine Learning: Artificial intelligence and machine learning will play an increasingly important role in analyzing the vast amounts of data generated by IoT devices in smart cities. These technologies will enable more sophisticated predictive analytics, autonomous decision-making, and personalized services for citizens.

4. Digital Twins: The development of more comprehensive and accurate digital twins of cities will enable better planning, simulation, and optimization of urban systems. These virtual replicas will integrate real-time data from IoT sensors to provide a dynamic representation of the city's operations.

5. Blockchain and Distributed Ledger Technologies: Blockchain technology could be used to enhance security, transparency, and trust in smart city systems. Applications could include secure voting systems, transparent supply chain management, and decentralized energy trading platforms.

6. Internet of Everything (IoE): The IoE extends the IoT beyond connected devices to include people, processes, and data. In smart cities, this could lead to more holistic and integrated approaches to urban management, where all elements of the urban ecosystem are interconnected and optimized.

7. Autonomous Systems: As AI and IoT technologies advance, we can expect to see more autonomous systems in smart cities. This could include self-driving vehicles, autonomous drones for delivery and surveillance, and self-managing energy grids.

8. Quantum Computing: While still in its early stages, quantum computing could potentially revolutionize data processing and encryption in smart cities. This could enable more complex simulations and optimization problems to be solved, enhancing urban planning and management.

9. Advanced Sensors and Actuators: The development of more sophisticated and miniaturized sensors will enable more detailed and comprehensive data collection in urban environments. New types of actuators could allow for more precise control of city systems.

10. Sustainable and Environmentally-friendly (Green) IoT: There will be an increasing focus on developing IoT solutions that are energy-efficient and environmentally friendly. This

could include the use of biodegradable sensors, energy harvesting technologies, and circular economy principles in IoT device design.

11. **Human-Centric Design:** Future IoT implementations in smart cities are likely to place greater emphasis on human-centric design, ensuring that technology enhances rather than replaces human interactions and experiences in urban environments.

12. **Augmented and Virtual Reality:** AR and VR technologies, combined with IoT, could transform how citizens interact with their urban environment, offering new ways to visualize data, navigate cities, and participate in urban planning processes.

ETHICAL CONSIDERATIONS IN IOT IMPLEMENTATION FOR SMART CITIES

As IoT becomes more pervasive in urban environments, it is crucial to address the ethical implications of these technologies.

1. **Privacy:** The widespread deployment of sensors and cameras in smart cities raises significant privacy concerns. There is a need to balance the benefits of data collection with citizens' right to privacy.

2. **Data Ownership and Control:** Clear policies need to be established regarding who owns the data collected by IoT devices in public spaces and how this data can be used.

3. **Surveillance and Freedom:** The potential for IoT systems to enable pervasive surveillance could infringe on citizens' freedom and autonomy. Safeguards need to be put in place to prevent misuse of these technologies.

4. **Digital Divide:** As smart city services become more integral to urban life, there is a risk of exacerbating existing inequalities if access to these services is not equitable.

5. **Algorithmic Bias:** Artificial intelligence and machine learning algorithms used in smart city applications need to be carefully designed and monitored to avoid perpetuating or amplifying existing biases.

6. **Transparency and Accountability:** There should be transparency in how IoT systems are implemented and used in smart cities, with clear mechanisms for accountability.

7. **Environmental Impact:** The production, deployment, and disposal of IoT devices need to be considered from an environmental perspective to ensure that smart city initiatives contribute to overall sustainability goals.

8. **Human-Centric Design:** Smart city technologies should be designed to enhance human experiences and well-being, rather than prioritizing efficiency at the expense of human factors.

9. **Cybersecurity and Resilience:** As cities become more dependent on IoT systems, ensuring the security and resilience of these systems becomes a critical ethical consideration.

10. **Informed Consent:** Citizens should be informed about the data being collected about them and have the ability to opt-out of certain data collection practices where possible.

Addressing these ethical considerations will be crucial for building trust and ensuring the long-term success of IoT implementations in smart cities.

CONCLUSION

The Internet of Things has come a long way since researchers first connected a Coca-Cola vending machine to the internet in the 1980s. What started as a simple way to check soda inventory has grown into a network of billions of connected devices that can make cities smarter, safer, and more efficient. The timeline from basic RFID tags in the 1940s to today's advanced AI-powered systems shows how technology builds on itself to create new possibilities.

Smart cities represent the most practical use of IoT technology today. When sensors, data networks, and analytics work together, they can solve real urban problems. Traffic flows better when signals adjust to actual conditions. Energy systems waste less power when buildings and grids communicate. Emergency services respond faster when they get instant alerts from across the city. Water systems detect leaks before they become major problems.

The case of Nusantara shows how a city can be designed from the ground up with smart technology. The Integrated Command and Control Center will connect all city services, from transportation to environmental monitoring. Citizens will access government services through a single app, making daily tasks simpler. The city plans to use renewable energy, manage waste efficiently, and provide quality healthcare and education through digital platforms.

However, building smart cities is not just about adding more technology. Cities must protect citizen privacy and data security. They need to ensure that digital services work for everyone, including older residents and those with disabilities. The technology should make life easier, not create new barriers or exclude people who cannot access digital tools.

As cities around the world face growing populations and limited resources, IoT offers practical solutions. The key is implementing these technologies in ways that truly serve residents while building systems that are secure, reliable, and fair for all citizens.

CHAPTER 2

REAL-TIME BIG DATA FOR IoT

R eal-time big data analytics is essential for modern smart cities as they manage increasingly complex urban systems through Internet of Things (IoT) deployments. The continuous generation of massive data streams from sensors, devices, and infrastructure requires sophisticated processing capabilities that can deliver actionable insights within seconds or minutes rather than hours or days. This chapter examines the fundamental concepts underlying real-time big data processing for IoT applications, exploring how cities can effectively capture, process, and analyze the enormous volumes of information generated by their connected infrastructure.

The convergence of IoT technologies with advanced analytics platforms creates unprecedented opportunities for urban optimization, from traffic flow management to energy distribution and public safety monitoring. However, this convergence also presents significant technical challenges related to data volume, processing speed, system reliability, and analytical accuracy. Understanding these challenges and the solutions available to address them forms the foundation for successful smart city implementations that can scale from pilot projects to city-wide deployments.

UNDERSTANDING BIG DATA IN SMART CITY CONTEXTS

Big data in smart city environments utilizes datasets that exceed the processing capabilities of traditional database systems and analytical tools. The exponential growth in IoT device deployments across urban infrastructure generates data streams that require specialized architectures and processing frameworks to extract meaningful insights. These datasets exhibit characteristics that distinguish them from conventional data processing scenarios, necessitating new approaches to storage, analysis, and real-time decision-making.

The complexity of urban data stems not only from its scale but also from the diverse sources and formats involved in smart city operations. Traffic management systems generate structured numerical data, while surveillance networks produce unstructured video streams, and environmental sensors create time-series measurements with varying temporal resolutions. This heterogeneity requires flexible data processing architectures that can accommodate multiple data types while maintaining the performance characteristics necessary for real-time urban management. Figure 2.1 explains the popular 4Vs in big data in a smart city context.

VOLUME
Scale of Data

181 zettabytes of total global data generation projected for 2025

73 zettabytes specifically from IoT devices contributing to this total

402.74 million terabytes created daily worldwide

VARIETY
Different Forms of Data

8+ major categories including energy, smart governance, healthcare, buildings, mobility, infrastructure, technology, and citizens

29+ billion IoT devices projected worldwide by 2030

5+ core application areas for smart city implementations

VELOCITY
Analysis of Streaming Data

Under 5 milliseconds latency achieved through edge computing

100x faster anticipated speeds with 6G trials by 2030

400x faster AI analysis compared to previous methods

VERACITY
Uncertainty of Data

90% of all data created in 2025 will require security measures

50% of data will actually be protected with adequate security

26.92% of data will need cognitive AI processing for quality assurance

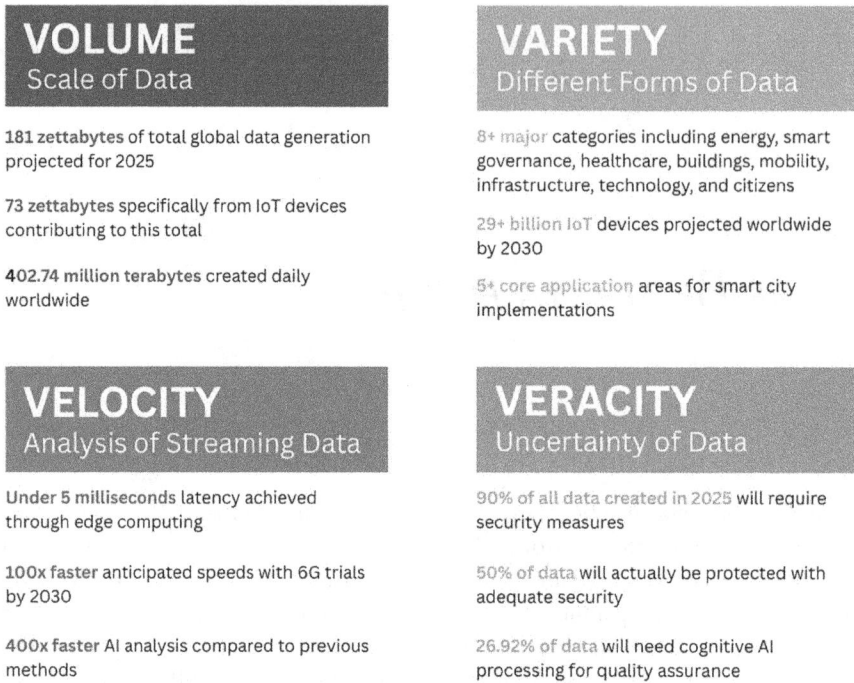

FIGURE 2.1 An infographic illustrating the 4 Vs of big data (volume, velocity, variety, and veracity) in the context of smart cities.

Volume: Scale of Data Generated by IoT Devices

The large *volume* of data generated by IoT devices in smart cities challenges traditional data processing approaches. Modern urban environments deploy thousands of sensors and connected devices that continuously generate measurements, creating data streams measured in terabytes and petabytes annually. Traffic monitoring systems exemplify this challenge, where a single intersection equipped with comprehensive sensor arrays can produce several gigabytes of data daily through vehicle detection, speed measurement, and flow analysis.

Smart energy infrastructure contributes significantly to urban data volumes through the widespread deployment of intelligent metering systems. A metropolitan area serving one million households with smart meters collecting readings every fifteen minutes generates over 35 billion individual data points each year. This continuous data collection enables detailed analysis of energy consumption patterns but requires robust storage and processing infrastructure to handle the sustained data ingestion rates.

Environmental monitoring networks add to the urban data volume through distributed sensor deployments that measure air quality, noise levels, temperature, humidity, and other atmospheric conditions. These networks can generate terabytes of environmental data over time, particularly when deployed at the high spatial and temporal resolutions necessary for accurate pollution tracking and climate monitoring. The cumulative effect of multiple environmental parameters measured across hundreds or thousands of locations creates substantial data management challenges.

Video surveillance systems represent one of the most data-intensive components of smart city infrastructure. High-definition security cameras can generate up to 180 gigabytes of video data daily, and cities typically deploy thousands of cameras across their territories. The resulting data volumes can reach petabyte scales annually, requiring specialized storage solutions and processing capabilities for both real-time monitoring and historical analysis.

The challenge of storage for these large amounts of data extends to the computational resources required for processing these massive datasets. Traditional database systems often cannot manage the sustained write rates and query loads generated by high-volume IoT deployments, necessitating distributed computing architectures and specialized database technologies designed for big data applications. Cities must invest in scalable infrastructure that can grow with their IoT deployments while maintaining acceptable performance for real-time applications.

Velocity: Speed of Data Generation and Processing Requirements

The *velocity* of big data in smart cities refers to the speed at which data is generated and the corresponding requirements for rapid processing and analysis. Urban systems often require real-time or near-real-time responses to changing conditions, making data processing velocity as critical as volume management. Traffic control systems exemplify these requirements, where signal timing adjustments must occur within seconds of detecting changing traffic patterns to maintain optimal flow conditions.

Energy grid management represents another domain where data velocity is crucial for system stability and efficiency. Smart grid systems must process data from thousands of sensors and meters instantaneously to detect supply-demand imbalances, equipment failures, or grid instabilities. The ability to respond within milliseconds or seconds can prevent cascading failures and maintain reliable power delivery across urban areas. This requires stream processing technologies capable of handling millions of events per second while maintaining low latency for critical control decisions.

Public safety applications demonstrate the life-critical importance of high-velocity data processing in urban environments. Emergency response systems must analyze incoming data from multiple sources including emergency calls, sensor networks, and surveillance systems to coordinate rapid response efforts. Real-time analysis of video feeds and sensor data enables immediate detection of incidents and automated alerting of appropriate response teams, potentially saving lives through faster emergency response times.

Public transportation systems rely on high-velocity data processing to provide accurate service information and optimize operations. Real-time tracking of buses, trains, and other transit vehicles requires continuous processing of GPS data, passenger counting information, and schedule adherence metrics. This data must be processed immediately to provide accurate arrival predictions, identify service disruptions, and implement dynamic route adjustments that maintain service reliability.

The technical implementation of high-velocity data processing requires specialized streaming technologies that can handle continuous data flows without the delays associated with traditional batch processing approaches. Stream processing frameworks like Apache Kafka and Apache Flink enable cities to process millions of events per second while maintaining the low latencies required for real-time urban management applications.

Variety: Different Types of Data from Diverse Sources

The *variety* of big data in smart cities refers the diverse types and formats of data generated by heterogeneous IoT deployments across urban infrastructure. This diversity presents significant integration challenges as cities must combine structured numerical data from sensors with unstructured content from video systems, semi-structured data from web services, and spatial information from location-based systems. The ability to effectively integrate and analyze these diverse data types determines the success of comprehensive smart city analytics initiatives.

Structured data forms the foundation of many smart city applications through standardized sensor measurements and device telemetry. Temperature sensors, energy meters, traffic counters, and similar devices generate numerical data with consistent formats and well-defined schemas. This structured data enables straightforward statistical analysis and time-series modeling but represents only a portion of the total information available in smart city environments.

Semi-structured data includes information formatted using standards like JSON or XML that provide organizational properties without the rigid constraints of relational database schemas. Many IoT devices communicate using these formats to transmit complex information including device status, configuration parameters, and multi-dimensional measurements. While more flexible than structured data, semi-structured formats require specialized processing techniques to extract and analyze the embedded information effectively.

Unstructured data presents the greatest integration challenges but often contains the most valuable insights for urban management. Video surveillance systems generate continuous streams of visual information that require computer vision techniques for automated analysis. Audio data from noise monitoring systems and social media content provide additional unstructured information sources that can enhance understanding of urban conditions and citizen experiences.

Spatial data adds geographic context to urban analytics through GPS coordinates, mapping information, and location-based measurements. Vehicle tracking systems, mobile device location data, and geographic sensor networks generate spatial datasets that require specialized geographic information system (GIS) capabilities for effective analysis. The integration of spatial data with other data types enables location-aware analytics that can identify geographic patterns and optimize location-specific services.

Time-series data represents a special category that spans multiple data types but shares common temporal characteristics. Most IoT sensors produce time-stamped measurements that create long sequences of observations over time. Effective analysis of time-series data requires specialized techniques for trend detection, seasonality analysis, and temporal correlation identification across multiple data streams.

Veracity: Ensuring Data Quality and Reliability

Data *veracity* in smart city environments refers to the accuracy, consistency, and trustworthiness of information collected from distributed IoT systems. The reliability of urban analytics and decision-making depends fundamentally on data quality, making veracity a critical consideration for successful smart city implementations. Poor data quality can lead to incorrect conclusions, ineffective policies, and reduced public trust in smart city initiatives.

Sensor accuracy represents a primary concern for data veracity in IoT deployments. Environmental factors, device aging, calibration drift, and manufacturing variations can all contribute to measurement errors that compromise data quality. Temperature sensors may drift over time due to component aging, air quality monitors can be affected by local interference sources, and traffic sensors may produce inaccurate counts due to environmental conditions or physical obstructions.

Data transmission errors introduce additional quality concerns as information travels from IoT devices through network infrastructure to central processing systems. Network congestion, electromagnetic interference, hardware failures, and software bugs can all result in data corruption, packet loss, or transmission delays that affect data integrity. Wireless communication systems are particularly susceptible to environmental interference that can degrade signal quality and introduce transmission errors.

Security threats pose significant risks to data veracity through potential manipulation of IoT devices or data streams by malicious actors. Cybersecurity attacks targeting smart city infrastructure can introduce false data, disrupt communications, or compromise device functionality. The distributed nature of IoT deployments creates multiple potential attack vectors that must be secured to maintain data integrity.

Data consistency challenges arise when integrating information from multiple sources with different update frequencies, measurement units, timestamp formats, and data schemas. Ensuring temporal synchronization across systems operating on different schedules requires careful coordination and standardization efforts. Inconsistent data formats can lead to integration errors that compromise analytical accuracy.

Implementing robust data quality assurance requires comprehensive validation processes that operate at multiple levels of the data processing pipeline. Real-time validation techniques can identify obvious errors or anomalies as data is received, while statistical analysis methods can detect more subtle quality issues through pattern recognition and outlier detection. Redundant sensor deployments provide cross-validation capabilities for critical measurements, enabling automatic detection of sensor failures or calibration problems.

Importance of Each Aspect in the Context of Smart Cities

The four dimensions of big data each play distinct but interconnected roles in enabling effective smart city operations. Understanding the specific importance of volume, velocity, variety, and veracity helps cities prioritize their investments and design systems that address the most critical requirements for their specific applications and objectives

The ability to handle massive data volumes enables cities to conduct comprehensive analysis of urban operations that would be impossible with smaller datasets. Large-scale data collection provides the statistical power necessary for accurate trend identification, pattern recognition, and predictive modeling across complex urban systems. Traffic optimization algorithms require extensive historical data to identify recurring patterns and develop effective control strategies, while energy demand forecasting depends on long-term consumption data from thousands of meters to achieve acceptable accuracy.

Comprehensive data coverage also enables cities to identify correlations and relationships between different urban systems that might not be apparent from limited datasets. The interaction between traffic patterns and air quality, the relationship between weather conditions and energy consumption, and the correlation between public events and transportation demand all require large-scale data analysis to quantify and understand. These insights enable more effective urban planning and policy development.

High-velocity data processing capabilities enable cities to respond rapidly to changing conditions and implement dynamic management strategies that optimize urban operations in real-time. Traffic management systems that can adjust signal timing within seconds of detecting congestion can significantly reduce travel times and emissions compared to static timing plans. Emergency response systems that process and analyze incoming data streams immediately can coordinate faster and more effective responses to incidents.

Real-time processing also enables predictive capabilities that allow cities to anticipate problems before they occur. Energy grid management systems that can detect developing instabilities within milliseconds can implement corrective actions that prevent widespread blackouts. Public transportation systems that process real-time data can identify potential service disruptions early and implement alternative routing or additional capacity to maintain service reliability.

The ability to integrate diverse data types provides cities with comprehensive understanding of urban operations that enables more effective decision-making and policy development. Combining structured sensor data with unstructured video content and social media information creates a more complete picture of urban conditions than any single data source could provide. This holistic view enables cities to identify complex relationships and develop more nuanced responses to urban challenges.

Data variety also enables cities to validate findings across multiple information sources and reduce the risk of making decisions based on incomplete or biased data. Cross-validation between different data types increases confidence in analytical results and helps identify potential data quality issues that might not be apparent from single-source analysis.

Ensuring data quality and reliability is essential for maintaining public trust in smart city initiatives and ensuring that urban management decisions are based on accurate information. Poor data quality can lead to ineffective policies, wasted resources, and reduced citizen confidence in government technology initiatives. High-quality data enables more accurate analysis, better decision-making, and more effective urban services.

Data veracity also supports regulatory compliance and accountability requirements that are increasingly important for public sector technology deployments. Accurate data collection and processing enable cities to demonstrate the effectiveness of their programs, comply with reporting requirements, and maintain transparency with citizens and oversight bodies.

The exploration of real-time big data analytics for IoT in smart city environments reveals a complex ecosystem where the four fundamental dimensions—volume, velocity, variety, and veracity—operate as interconnected pillars supporting effective urban management. The massive scale of data generation from distributed IoT infrastructure creates unprecedented opportunities for comprehensive urban analysis, enabling city officials to understand patterns and relationships that were previously invisible. However, this volume must be coupled with high-velocity processing capabilities to deliver the real-time insights necessary for dynamic urban operations, from traffic signal optimization to emergency response coordination.

The integration of diverse data types across urban systems provides the holistic understanding required for effective decision-making, while robust data quality assurance mechanisms ensure that these decisions are based on reliable information. The case studies and technical implementations discussed demonstrate that successful smart city deployments require balanced attention to all four dimensions, as deficiencies in any single area can compromise the entire system's effectiveness. Cities that prioritize volume without addressing velocity limitations find themselves unable to respond to time-critical situations, while those that focus on speed without ensuring data quality risk making decisions based on inaccurate information.

The technical challenges of implementing city-scale real-time analytics systems extend beyond pure computational considerations to encompass organizational, economic, and ethical dimensions. The infrastructure requirements for processing petabyte-scale data streams while maintaining sub-second response times demand significant capital investments and sophisticated technical expertise. However, the successful integration of edge computing architectures with cloud-based analytics platforms demonstrates viable pathways for achieving the performance characteristics necessary for effective urban management while maintaining cost-effectiveness and scalability.

Looking forward, the continued evolution of IoT technologies and analytics capabilities will further enhance cities' abilities to optimize their operations and improve citizen services. The convergence of artificial intelligence, 5G networks, and advanced sensor technologies promises even greater opportunities for real-time urban optimization. Cities that successfully navigate these complexities will be positioned to deliver more efficient, sustainable, and responsive urban services that enhance quality of life for their residents while establishing foundations for continued technological advancement and urban innovation.

REAL-TIME STREAMING BIG DATA FOR URBAN DECISION-MAKING

Real-time streaming big data analytics represents a fundamental paradigm shift in how cities approach urban management and governance. Unlike traditional data processing methods that rely on batch operations and historical analysis, real-time streaming enables continuous data capture, processing, and analysis as information flows from thousands of IoT sensors, devices, and systems throughout the urban environment. This capability allows city officials to move beyond reactive responses to proactive, data-driven decision-making that can address urban challenges as they emerge.

Real-Time Data Streaming Concepts

Real-time data streaming involves the continuous generation, capture, processing, and analysis of data without significant delay. In smart city contexts, this technology processes data as it flows through urban systems, analyzing information within seconds or minutes rather than hours or days. The core principle centers on handling "data in motion" rather than "data at rest," enabling immediate insights that support time-critical urban operations.

The fundamental architecture of real-time streaming systems comprises several important components that work together to enable continuous data processing. Data ingestion layers capture information from diverse sources including traffic sensors, environmental monitors, energy meters, and surveillance systems. Stream processing engines then analyze this data in real-time, applying filtering, transformation, aggregation, and analytical algorithms to extract meaningful insights. Finally, output layers deliver processed information to dashboards, automated control systems, and decision-making platforms that enable immediate action.

Event time versus processing time represents a critical distinction in streaming systems. *Event time* refers to when data events actually occurred in the physical world, while *processing time* indicates when the system analyzes the data. Managing the relationship between these temporal dimensions becomes essential for accurate real-time analytics, particularly in urban environments where network delays and system latencies can impact decision-making accuracy.

Windowing techniques enable meaningful analysis of continuous data streams by grouping events within specific temporal boundaries. Tumbling windows create fixed-size, non-overlapping time intervals that allow for consistent periodic analysis. Sliding windows provide overlapping intervals that enable continuous monitoring of evolving conditions. Session windows adapt dynamically based on data characteristics, particularly useful for analyzing user behavior patterns or event sequences.

Importance of Low-Latency Data Processing in Urban Environments

Low-latency data processing is an important part of effective real-time urban management, enabling cities to respond to changing conditions within seconds rather than minutes or hours. In emergency response scenarios, processing delays can mean the difference between preventing incidents and responding after they occur. Traffic management systems require sub-second response times to adjust signal timing based on current congestion patterns, while energy grid management needs millisecond response capabilities to prevent cascading failures during demand fluctuations.

Public safety applications demonstrate the life-critical importance of low-latency processing in urban environments. Real-time analysis of surveillance video feeds, emergency communications, and sensor networks enables immediate detection of security threats, natural disasters, or public health emergencies. Automated alerting systems can dispatch emergency responders within seconds of incident detection, potentially saving lives through faster response times. Similarly, crowd management systems can identify dangerous overcrowding situations and implement protective measures before injuries occur.

Environmental monitoring represents another domain where processing speed directly impacts public welfare. Air quality sensors must detect pollution spikes immediately to trigger protective measures such as traffic restrictions or public health warnings. Water quality monitoring systems require instant analysis capabilities to identify contamination events and prevent public exposure. Real-time weather monitoring enables rapid responses to severe weather conditions that could threaten public safety or infrastructure.

The technical implementation of low-latency processing requires sophisticated streaming architectures that minimize delays at every stage of the data pipeline. Edge computing deployments bring processing capabilities closer to data sources, reducing transmission delays and enabling local decision-making for time-critical applications. Stream processing frameworks like Apache Kafka and Apache Flink provide the computational infrastructure necessary for handling millions of events per second while maintaining consistent low latencies.

Use Cases Demonstrating the Value of Real-time Analytics

Traffic management systems exemplify the transformative impact of real-time analytics on urban operations. Los Angeles' ATSAC/ATCS evaluations reported reductions in travel times, delays, stops, air emissions, and fuel use, with performance varying by corridor and period; benefits are not uniform across all contexts. These systems can reduce travel times and significantly decrease traffic-related emissions by minimizing congestion and idle time. The continuous analysis of traffic patterns enables predictive adjustments that prevent congestion before it occurs, rather than simply responding after bottlenecks form.

Energy management represents another critical application area where real-time analytics delivers substantial benefits. Smart grid systems use streaming data from thousands of meters and sensors to balance supply and demand instantaneously, while real-time pricing mechanisms allow both consumers and automated systems to adjust energy usage in response to grid conditions. Such flexibility helps reduce peak loads and stabilize the grid, thereby preventing blackouts and enhancing overall system efficiency. Predictive analytics further contribute by identifying potential equipment failures before they occur, enabling proactive maintenance that mitigates service disruptions. However, the implementation of real-time pricing models is not without challenges. For households with limited flexibility in energy consumption such as working-class individuals constrained by fixed work schedules,higher costs during peak hours may create an inequitable burden. This raises ethical and socio-economic considerations in smart city energy management, underscoring the need for balancing efficiency gains with fairness, affordability, and inclusivity in automated decision-making systems.

Public transportation optimization demonstrates how real-time analytics can improve both operational efficiency and citizen experience. Transit agencies use GPS tracking, passenger counting systems, and mobile app data to provide accurate arrival predictions and identify service disruptions immediately. Dynamic route adjustments based on real-time conditions help maintain schedule reliability, while predictive analytics enable proactive capacity management during special events or peak travel periods. These systems have shown measurable improvements in on-time performance and passenger satisfaction.

Environmental monitoring applications can support the public health benefits of real-time urban analytics. Beijing implemented comprehensive air quality monitoring networks that provide real-time pollution data to support immediate decision-making. When air quality deteriorates rapidly, automated systems can implement traffic restrictions, industrial controls, or public health advisories within minutes. This rapid response capability helps protect public health and demonstrates the potential for data-driven environmental management.

Water management systems illustrate the infrastructure protection benefits of real-time analytics. Smart water networks monitor pressure, flow rates, and quality parameters continuously to detect leaks, contamination, or system failures immediately. Real-time analysis enables automated responses such as valve adjustments or pump controls that can prevent water loss, maintain service quality, and protect public health. Predictive analytics help optimize maintenance schedules and prevent costly infrastructure failures.

Waste management optimization represents an emerging application area where real-time analytics can improve both efficiency and environmental outcomes. Smart waste bins equipped with sensors provide real-time fill level data that enables dynamic collection routing. This optimization can reduce collection costs by 30–50% while improving service reliability. Real-time monitoring also enables rapid response to overflow situations or maintenance needs, preventing environmental and public health issues.

Public safety applications demonstrate the security benefits of real-time urban analytics. Video analytics systems can identify suspicious activities, crowd dynamics, or emergency situations automatically, enabling faster response times than human monitoring alone. Integration with other city systems allows for coordinated responses that can include traffic management, emergency services deployment, and public communication systems. Moscow's implementation of AI-enhanced surveillance helped solve over 3,000 crimes in 2018-2019 using a video surveillance system with facial recognition, according to the Ministry of Internal Affairs press service[1].

These use cases collectively demonstrate that real-time streaming big data analytics enables a fundamental shift from reactive to proactive urban management. Rather than simply responding to problems after they occur, cities can anticipate challenges, prevent issues, and optimize operations continuously based on current conditions and predictive insights. This capability represents a critical foundation for creating more efficient, sustainable, and livable urban environments that can adapt dynamically to changing needs and conditions.

The success of these implementations relies on the integration of multiple technologies including IoT sensors, edge computing, cloud platforms, and advanced analytics. As these technologies continue to evolve and costs decrease, the potential for real-time urban analytics will expand, enabling even more sophisticated applications that can address the complex challenges facing modern cities.

CHALLENGES IN IMPLEMENTING REAL-TIME SYSTEMS AT THE CITY SCALE

The deployment of real-time big data analytics systems within urban environments presents multifaceted challenges that span technical, organizational, and socio-economic dimensions. These challenges become particularly acute when scaling from pilot projects to city-wide implementations, where the complexity increases exponentially with the size and diversity of the urban ecosystem. Understanding and addressing these challenges is essential for successful smart city initiatives that can deliver sustained benefits to urban communities.

Infrastructure and Technical Constraints

The foundational challenge lies in establishing robust computational and network infrastructure capable of supporting real-time data processing at metropolitan scale. Urban environments require distributed computing architectures that can handle petabyte-scale data volumes while maintaining sub-second response times for critical applications such as emergency response systems and traffic management. The heterogeneous nature of existing urban infrastructure often necessitates significant capital investments in fiber-optic networks, edge computing nodes, and high-performance computing clusters.

Modern smart city projects typically integrate 10 to 12 advanced technologies including IoT sensors, AI surveillance systems, smart lighting, traffic management platforms, and real-time analytics engines. Achieving interoperability between these diverse systems represents one of the most significant technical hurdles, as each system must communicate efficiently with others to deliver real-time functionality and insights. The lack of standardized protocols and data formats across different vendors and technologies creates substantial integration complexity that can delay deployment and increase costs.

Network latency and bandwidth limitations present additional technical barriers, particularly in dense urban areas where electromagnetic interference and physical obstacles can degrade signal quality. The deployment of 5G networks, while promising enhanced connectivity, requires

1 Gubko, V., Novogonskaya, M., Stepanov, P., & Yundina, M. (2023). AI and administration of justice in Russia. International Penal and Penitentiary Foundation (A-07-23).

substantial coordination between telecommunications providers and municipal authorities, often involving lengthy regulatory approval processes and significant financial commitments. Legacy infrastructure constraints further complicate deployment efforts, as aging electrical and telecommunications systems may lack the capacity to support modern IoT and analytics requirements.

Edge computing architectures, while essential for achieving low-latency processing, introduce their own technical challenges. Deploying and maintaining thousands of edge computing nodes across an urban area requires sophisticated management systems that can handle remote monitoring, software updates, and hardware maintenance. The distributed nature of these systems creates multiple points of potential failure that must be addressed through comprehensive redundancy and fault tolerance mechanisms.

Data Integration and Interoperability

The heterogeneous nature of urban data sources creates substantial integration challenges that extend beyond simple technical compatibility. Municipal systems typically involve legacy infrastructure with disparate data formats, communication protocols, and temporal synchronization requirements. Achieving semantic interoperability across systems developed by different vendors and deployed over decades requires sophisticated middleware solutions and extensive data harmonization efforts.

Urban data streams exhibit significant diversity in format, granularity, and quality characteristics. Traffic sensors might generate structured numerical data every second, while environmental monitoring systems may report semi-structured measurements hourly, and social media feeds provide unstructured text data continuously. Integrating these diverse data types for coherent real-time analysis requires advanced Extract, Transform, Load (ETL) processes that can handle multiple data formats while maintaining processing speed.

The temporal dimension of data integration presents particular complexity, as different systems may operate on varying time scales and update frequencies. Synchronizing these diverse data streams for coherent real-time analysis requires advanced stream processing capabilities and careful consideration of temporal alignment algorithms. Event ordering and timestamp management become critical issues when combining data from systems with different clock synchronization mechanisms.

Data quality and consistency challenges are amplified in real-time environments where traditional batch processing validation techniques are not feasible. Ensuring data accuracy across multiple sources while maintaining processing speed requires automated quality assessment mechanisms that can identify and correct errors in real-time. The lack of standardized data quality metrics across different urban systems complicates the development of comprehensive quality assurance frameworks.

Scalability and Performance Engineering

Scaling real-time analytics systems to accommodate millions of IoT devices across a metropolitan area introduces significant engineering challenges. The system architecture must support horizontal scaling while maintaining data consistency and processing accuracy. This requires sophisticated distributed computing frameworks capable of dynamic load balancing and resource allocation based on fluctuating data volumes and processing demands.

Performance optimization becomes increasingly complex as system scale increases. Query optimization strategies that work effectively for thousands of data points may become computationally prohibitive when applied to millions of concurrent data streams. The challenge extends beyond raw computational capacity to include memory management, storage optimization, and network resource allocation across distributed computing nodes.

Real-time processing requirements create additional scalability constraints, as systems must maintain consistent performance characteristics even as data volumes grow. Traditional scaling approaches that simply add more computing resources may not be sufficient if they introduce latencies that compromise real-time processing capabilities. This necessitates careful architectural design that can scale capacity without degrading response times.

Storage and retrieval optimization for real-time access represents another significant scalability challenge. As data volumes grow exponentially, traditional database systems often cannot maintain the read and write performance necessary for real-time applications. This requires specialized storage solutions optimized for time-series data and high-throughput operations, along with sophisticated caching and indexing strategies.

Data Quality and Reliability Assurance

Ensuring data quality and reliability across thousands of heterogeneous sensors and devices presents substantial operational challenges. Sensor drift, calibration errors, and environmental interference can compromise data accuracy, while network disruptions and device failures can result in data loss or corruption. Implementing comprehensive data validation and quality assurance mechanisms at city scale requires automated anomaly detection systems, redundant sensor deployments, and sophisticated error correction algorithms.

The challenge is compounded by the need to maintain data quality standards while processing data in real-time. Traditional batch processing approaches that allow for extensive data cleaning and validation must be adapted for streaming environments where decisions must be made based on potentially incomplete or noisy data. This requires advanced statistical techniques and machine learning algorithms that can identify and compensate for data quality issues in real-time.

Environmental factors unique to urban deployments create additional data quality challenges. IoT sensors deployed in city environments must contend with extreme temperatures, electromagnetic interference, physical vandalism, and air pollution that can affect measurement accuracy. Developing sensors robust enough to maintain accuracy in these challenging conditions while remaining cost-effective for large-scale deployment requires significant engineering investment.

Data provenance and lineage tracking become critical for maintaining system reliability but introduce additional computational overhead. Understanding the source and processing history of each data point is essential for debugging issues and ensuring analytical accuracy, but tracking this information across millions of data streams requires sophisticated metadata management systems that can operate at city scale.

Privacy, Security, and Regulatory Compliance

The pervasive nature of city-scale IoT deployments raises significant privacy and security concerns that must be addressed through comprehensive governance frameworks. Real-time systems must implement end-to-end encryption, secure authentication mechanisms, and privacy-preserving analytics techniques while maintaining the performance characteristics required for time-critical applications. The distributed nature of urban IoT systems creates multiple potential attack vectors that must be secured against increasingly sophisticated cyber threats.

Regulatory compliance adds additional complexity, as municipal systems must adhere to evolving data protection regulations such as GDPR while enabling the data sharing necessary for effective urban analytics. The challenge lies in implementing privacy-by-design principles that protect individual privacy without compromising the analytical capabilities required for effective urban management. This requires sophisticated anonymization techniques and access control mechanisms that can operate in real-time environments.

Data sovereignty issues become particularly complex in smart city implementations that may involve multiple jurisdictions, private sector partners, and international technology vendors. Ensuring that data processing and storage comply with local regulations while enabling cross-jurisdictional cooperation for regional challenges requires careful legal and technical coordination.

Organizational and Governance Challenges

The implementation of city-scale real-time systems requires unprecedented coordination across multiple municipal departments, external contractors, and technology vendors. Traditional organizational structures may be inadequate for managing the interdisciplinary collaboration required for successful deployment. This necessitates new governance models that can effectively coordinate technical implementation with policy development and public engagement.

Change management presents additional challenges, as real-time systems often require modifications to established workflows and decision-making processes. Training municipal staff to effectively utilize new analytical capabilities while maintaining operational continuity requires comprehensive professional development programs and careful transition planning. Resistance to change within established bureaucratic structures can significantly delay implementation and reduce system effectiveness.

The rapid pace of technological evolution creates additional organizational challenges, as municipal staff must continuously update their skills to keep pace with advancing technologies. Building internal technical capabilities while managing external vendor relationships requires sophisticated project management and strategic planning that may exceed the experience of many municipal organizations.

Economic and Financial Considerations

The total cost of ownership for city-scale real-time systems extends far beyond initial capital investments to include ongoing operational expenses, maintenance costs, and system upgrade requirements. The rapid pace of technological evolution in IoT and analytics platforms creates additional financial risks, as systems may require significant upgrades or replacements within shorter timeframes than traditional municipal infrastructure.

Budget allocation across multiple fiscal years and departments creates additional complexity, particularly when benefits may be realized across different organizational units than those bearing implementation costs. Developing sustainable financing models that can support long-term system evolution while demonstrating clear return on investment remains a significant challenge for municipal authorities.

Cost control becomes increasingly difficult as system complexity grows, with integration efforts often requiring significantly more resources than initially anticipated. The need for specialized technical expertise that may not be available within municipal organizations can result in substantial consulting costs and dependency on external vendors.

Technical Debt and System Evolution

The pressure to deploy functional systems quickly can result in technical debt that becomes increasingly difficult to address as systems scale. Architectural decisions made during pilot phases may prove inadequate for city-wide deployment, requiring substantial refactoring or complete system redesigns. Managing this technical debt while maintaining operational systems requires careful planning and significant technical expertise.

The challenge is compounded by the need to continuously evolve systems to incorporate new technologies and address changing urban requirements. Maintaining system flexibility while ensuring stability and reliability requires sophisticated software engineering practices and comprehensive testing frameworks that may exceed the technical capabilities of many municipal organizations.

Legacy system integration presents ongoing challenges as cities must continue operating existing infrastructure while implementing new capabilities. The need to maintain backward compatibility while enabling new functionality creates architectural constraints that can limit system performance and increase complexity.

These challenges underscore the complexity of implementing real-time big data analytics at urban scale and highlight the need for comprehensive planning, substantial technical expertise, and sustained organizational commitment to achieve successful deployment and operation of city-scale real-time systems. Success requires addressing not only technical challenges but also organizational, financial, and social considerations that affect system adoption and long-term sustainability.

DESIGN AND OPTIMIZATION OF DATA FLOW: INGESTING AND STREAMING DATA FROM THE EDGE

The design and optimization of data flow architectures represent fundamental challenges in modern smart city implementations, where vast amounts of data generated at the network edge must be efficiently collected, processed, and transmitted to analytical platforms. The proliferation of IoT devices across urban infrastructure creates unprecedented demands on data ingestion systems that must handle heterogeneous data types, varying transmission rates, and diverse quality-of-service requirements while maintaining real-time processing capabilities.

Effective data flow design encompasses the entire pathway from sensor data generation to actionable insights, requiring careful consideration of edge processing capabilities, network bandwidth limitations, and cloud infrastructure scalability. Smart cities typically deploy thousands of interconnected devices that generate continuous data streams, necessitating architectures that can accommodate both real-time streaming requirements and batch processing needs. The challenge lies in creating systems that optimize resource utilization across the entire data pipeline while ensuring data quality, security, and accessibility for multiple stakeholders.

Edge-to-Cloud Data Architecture Framework

The foundational architecture for IoT data flow in smart cities operates through a hierarchical processing model that distributes computational tasks across edge devices, fog nodes, and cloud infrastructure. This three-tier approach enables efficient data processing by placing computational resources closer to data sources while maintaining centralized coordination and long-term storage capabilities. Edge devices perform initial data collection and basic filtering operations, reducing the volume of data that must be transmitted over network connections.

Fog computing nodes serve as intermediate processing layers that aggregate data from multiple edge sources, perform local analytics, and implement intelligent data routing decisions. These intermediate nodes provide crucial buffering capabilities that accommodate network connectivity fluctuations while ensuring continuous data availability for time-critical applications. The fog layer enables sophisticated preprocessing operations including data validation, format standardization, and preliminary anomaly detection before transmitting refined datasets to cloud infrastructure.

Cloud infrastructure provides the computational scale necessary for complex analytics, machine learning model training, and long-term data warehousing. The hierarchical architecture ensures that each processing tier operates at optimal efficiency while maintaining overall system resilience through redundant data paths and distributed processing capabilities. This approach particularly benefits smart city applications where data processing requirements vary significantly across different operational domains and temporal patterns.

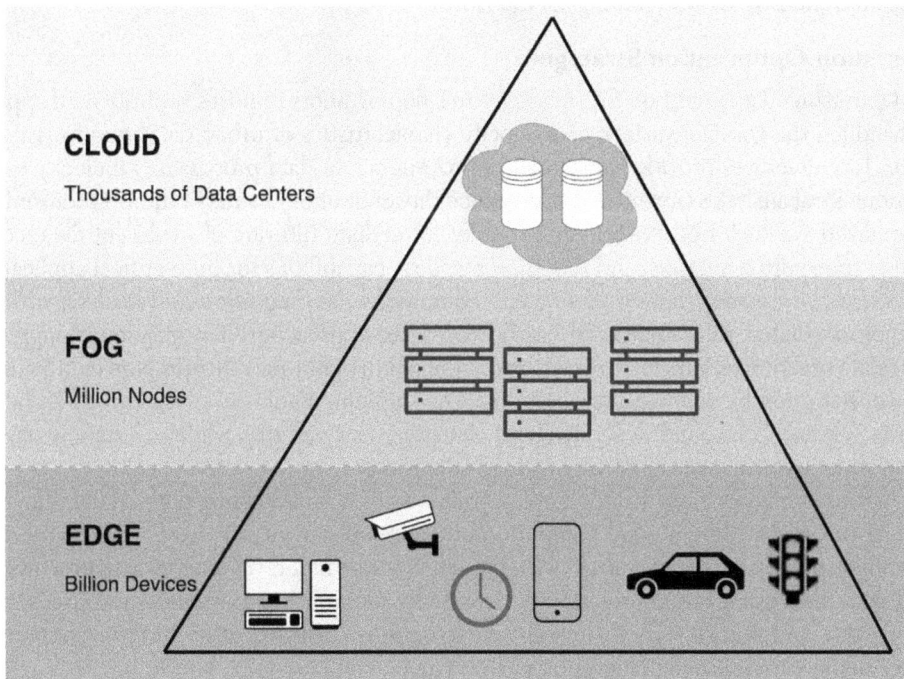

FIGURE 2.2 Hierarchical edge-to-cloud data flow architecture.

Streaming Protocols and Communication Frameworks

The selection and optimization of communication protocols significantly impact the efficiency and reliability of IoT data streaming in urban environments. Message Queuing Telemetry Transport (MQTT) has emerged as the dominant protocol for IoT communications due to its lightweight overhead, publish-subscribe architecture, and built-in quality-of-service mechanisms. MQTT's minimal 2-byte header and TCP-based reliability make it particularly suitable for scenarios requiring guaranteed message delivery and persistent connections across variable network conditions.

Constrained Application Protocol (CoAP) provides an alternative approach optimized for resource-constrained devices operating in low-power environments. CoAP's UDP-based transport reduces network overhead and enables multicast communications, making it effective for applications where battery life and bandwidth conservation are priorities. The protocol's RESTful design facilitates integration with web services while supporting both confirmable and non-confirmable message types to balance reliability with efficiency requirements.

Advanced streaming architectures increasingly integrate MQTT with Apache Kafka to create robust data pipelines that combine IoT device connectivity with enterprise-scale data processing capabilities. This integration enables bidirectional data flow where MQTT handles device-to-cloud communications while Kafka provides the scalable message queuing and stream processing infrastructure necessary for real-time analytics. The combination allows organizations to leverage MQTT's IoT-optimized features alongside Kafka's distributed computing capabilities for comprehensive data streaming solutions.

Data Ingestion Optimization Strategies

Optimizing data ingestion for smart city IoT deployments requires sophisticated approaches to handling the volume, variety, and velocity characteristics of urban data streams. Edge computing architectures provide substantial improvements in data processing efficiency by implementing local analytics capabilities that reduce the amount of raw data requiring transmission to centralized systems. Local processing enables immediate filtering of irrelevant data, compression of transmitted datasets, and real-time response capabilities for time-critical applications.

Stream processing frameworks enable continuous data ingestion and analysis without the latency associated with traditional batch processing approaches. These systems support real-time data transformation, enrichment, and aggregation operations that prepare data for immediate consumption by analytical applications. The implementation of event-driven architectures allows systems to respond dynamically to changing data patterns while maintaining consistent processing performance across varying load conditions.

Resource management strategies play crucial roles in maintaining optimal data flow performance across distributed edge computing environments. Dynamic load balancing algorithms distribute processing tasks among available edge nodes based on current resource availability and data processing requirements. These systems monitor computational resources, network bandwidth, and storage capacity in real-time to optimize task allocation and prevent bottlenecks that could compromise data ingestion performance.

Quality of Service and Fault Tolerance Mechanisms

Maintaining consistent data quality and system reliability represents critical requirements for smart city data architectures where service disruptions can impact public safety and urban operations. Quality of Service (QoS) frameworks establish performance guarantees for different types of data streams based on their criticality and time sensitivity. Emergency response systems require ultra-low latency processing with guaranteed delivery, while environmental monitoring applications may tolerate higher latency in exchange for improved energy efficiency.

Fault tolerance mechanisms including redundant data paths, error correction codes, and checkpoint-based recovery systems ensure system resilience in the face of hardware failures or network disruptions. These systems must be designed to minimize performance impact while providing comprehensive protection against data corruption or loss. Distributed architectures implement automatic failover capabilities that redirect data streams to alternative processing nodes when primary systems become unavailable, maintaining service continuity without manual intervention.

Data integrity validation processes verify the accuracy and completeness of transmitted information throughout the entire data pipeline. Checksums, digital signatures, and temporal consistency checks identify potential data corruption or transmission errors before they propagate to analytical systems. These validation mechanisms operate continuously in the background to maintain data quality while minimizing computational overhead that could impact real-time processing performance.

Performance Monitoring and Optimization

Continuous monitoring of data flow performance provides essential insights for maintaining optimal system operation and identifying potential bottlenecks before they impact service delivery. Real-time metrics collection systems track key performance indicators including data throughput rates, processing latencies, error frequencies, and resource utilization across all components of the data architecture. These monitoring systems enable proactive optimization strategies that adjust system parameters based on observed performance patterns and predicted future demands.

Adaptive optimization algorithms automatically adjust data flow parameters to maintain optimal performance under changing operational conditions. These systems monitor network bandwidth utilization, processing queue lengths, and response times to dynamically modify data compression ratios, transmission frequencies, and processing priorities. Machine learning algorithms analyze historical performance data to predict optimal configuration settings for different operational scenarios and automatically implement appropriate adjustments.

Performance optimization extends to energy consumption management, particularly important for battery-powered edge devices deployed throughout urban infrastructure. Power-aware computing strategies balance processing performance with energy efficiency requirements through dynamic frequency scaling, selective sensor activation, and intelligent sleep scheduling. These approaches ensure sustainable operation of distributed IoT networks while maintaining adequate data collection and processing capabilities for smart city applications.

PROCESSING AND CONSUMING DATA ON THE CLOUD

Cloud computing platforms provide the essential infrastructure and services necessary for processing and consuming massive volumes of IoT data at scale. As IoT deployments generate data streams that exceed the capacity of edge processing alone, cloud-based systems offer the computational power, storage capacity, and analytical capabilities required to extract meaningful insights from distributed sensor networks. The transition from edge to cloud processing represents a critical component in comprehensive IoT analytics architectures, enabling sophisticated analysis, long-term data retention, and integration with enterprise systems.

The fundamental architecture of cloud data processing for IoT applications relies on distributed computing principles that enable horizontal scaling across multiple computational nodes. This distributed approach ensures that data processing capabilities can expand dynamically to accommodate varying workloads while maintaining consistent performance characteristics. Modern cloud platforms leverage containerization technologies, microservices architectures, and serverless computing models to provide flexible, resilient, and cost-effective solutions for IoT data analytics.

Distributed Computing Architectures for IoT Data Processing

Distributed computing frameworks form the backbone of cloud-based IoT data processing systems, enabling organizations to handle massive data volumes through parallel processing across multiple computing nodes. These architectures decompose complex data processing tasks into smaller, independent units that can be executed simultaneously across different machines, significantly reducing overall processing time while improving system reliability through redundancy and fault tolerance mechanisms.

The implementation of distributed computing for IoT applications requires careful consideration of data partitioning strategies, load balancing algorithms, and coordination mechanisms that ensure efficient resource utilization. Data partitioning techniques divide large datasets based on temporal boundaries, geographic regions, or device categories, allowing processing nodes to work on specific data subsets without interference. This approach enables linear scalability where additional computing resources directly translate to proportional improvements in processing throughput.

Fault tolerance represents a critical design consideration in distributed IoT data processing systems where individual node failures must not compromise overall system functionality. Advanced distributed architectures implement automatic failure detection, data replication strategies, and dynamic task redistribution mechanisms that maintain continuous operation even when significant portions of the computing infrastructure become unavailable. These resilience features ensure that smart city operations can continue uninterrupted despite hardware failures or network disruptions.

Resource management frameworks coordinate the allocation of computational resources across distributed systems based on real-time demand patterns and priority requirements. Dynamic scaling algorithms monitor system performance metrics and automatically provision additional computing resources during peak load periods while releasing unnecessary resources during low activity times. This elastic resource management enables cost-effective operations by ensuring organizations only pay for computing capacity they actually utilize.

Monolithic   Microservices

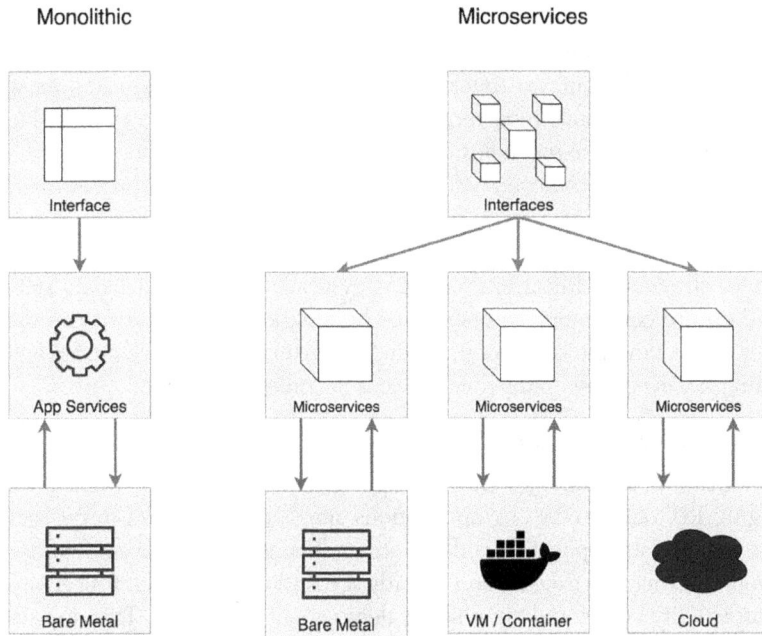

FIGURE 2.3 Comparison of monolithic and microservices architecture.

Microservices Architecture for Scalable IoT Platforms

Microservices architecture represents a fundamental shift from monolithic application designs toward modular, independently deployable service components that can scale individually based on demand patterns. This architectural approach particularly benefits IoT data processing systems where different analytical tasks require varying computational resources and have distinct scaling requirements. By decomposing complex data processing workflows into discrete microservices, organizations can optimize resource allocation and improve system maintainability.

The implementation of microservices for IoT data processing enables specialized optimization of individual service components based on their specific computational requirements. Data ingestion services can be optimized for high-throughput operations with minimal latency, while machine learning services can be configured with GPU acceleration for model training and inference tasks. This granular optimization approach results in significant improvements in overall system efficiency compared to monolithic architectures where all components must share the same resource configuration.

Communication patterns between microservices require careful design to ensure efficient data flow while maintaining loose coupling between service components. Event-driven communication models enable asynchronous data processing where services publish events to message queues and other services consume these events based on their processing capabilities. This approach prevents performance bottlenecks that could occur when slower services delay faster components, enabling optimal utilization of available computational resources.

Service discovery and load balancing mechanisms ensure that microservices can locate and communicate with each other efficiently in dynamic cloud environments. Automated service registration systems maintain real-time directories of available service instances, while intelligent load balancers distribute incoming requests across multiple service replicas based on current performance metrics. These mechanisms enable seamless scaling operations where new service instances can be added or removed without disrupting ongoing data processing operations.

Data consistency management across distributed microservices presents unique challenges that require sophisticated coordination mechanisms. Event sourcing patterns maintain complete audit trails of all data modifications, enabling systems to reconstruct data states at any point in time and ensure consistency across service boundaries. Saga patterns coordinate multi-step transactions across multiple services, providing mechanisms to handle partial failures and maintain data integrity even when individual services become unavailable.

Containerization and Orchestration Technologies

Containerization technologies provide lightweight, portable environments for deploying and managing IoT data processing applications across diverse cloud infrastructure platforms. Containers encapsulate application code, runtime dependencies, and configuration settings into standardized units that can execute consistently across different computing environments, eliminating compatibility issues and simplifying deployment processes. This approach particularly benefits IoT applications where data processing components must operate reliably across heterogeneous infrastructure configurations.

Container orchestration platforms automate the deployment, scaling, and management of containerized applications across clusters of computing nodes. These platforms provide sophisticated scheduling algorithms that optimize resource allocation based on application requirements, node capabilities, and current system load conditions. Intelligent placement decisions ensure that containers with complementary resource requirements are co-located on the same nodes while distributing CPU-intensive and memory-intensive workloads across different machines.

Dynamic scaling capabilities enable container orchestration systems to automatically adjust the number of running container instances based on real-time demand patterns. Horizontal pod autoscaling monitors application performance metrics and provisions additional container replicas when processing queues exceed predefined thresholds. This automatic scaling ensures that IoT data processing systems can handle sudden spikes in data volume without manual intervention while minimizing resource costs during low activity periods.

Network management within containerized environments requires sophisticated coordination to ensure efficient communication between distributed application components. Software-defined networking solutions provide overlay networks that enable secure communication between containers regardless of their physical location within the cluster. These networking abstractions simplify application development by providing consistent connectivity models while implementing advanced security policies and traffic management capabilities.

Storage orchestration capabilities ensure that containerized applications can access persistent data storage resources reliably across node failures and scaling operations. Dynamic volume provisioning automatically creates storage resources as applications require them, while storage class definitions specify performance characteristics and backup policies for different data types. These storage management features enable stateful IoT applications to maintain data persistence even as containers are created, destroyed, and migrated across computing nodes.

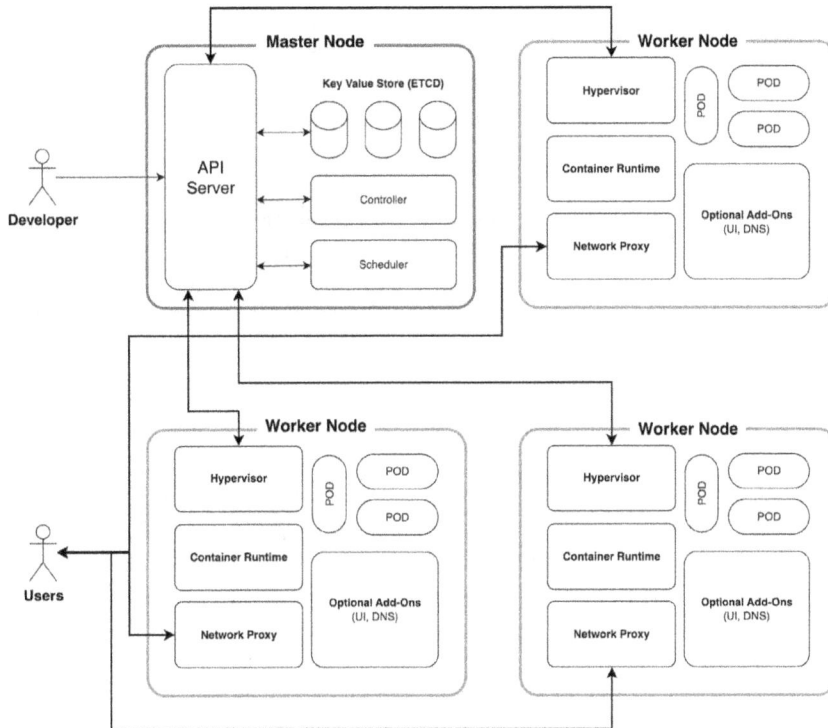

FIGURE 2.4 Kubernetes cluster architecture showing master and worker nodes, components, and workflow for container orchestration in the cloud.

Stream Processing Frameworks and Real-Time Analytics

Stream processing frameworks enable continuous analysis of data as it flows through IoT systems, providing immediate insights and enabling rapid response to changing conditions. These frameworks process data incrementally as individual events arrive rather than waiting for complete datasets to accumulate, significantly reducing latency between data generation and actionable insights. This real-time processing capability proves essential for smart city applications where immediate responses can prevent incidents or optimize resource utilization.

The implementation of stream processing requires sophisticated windowing mechanisms that define how continuous data streams are segmented for analysis. Tumbling windows process non-overlapping time intervals, while sliding windows enable analysis of overlapping time periods to detect trends and patterns that span multiple measurement intervals. Session windows group related events based on activity patterns rather than fixed time boundaries, enabling analysis of user interactions or device usage patterns that vary in duration.

State management within stream processing systems enables complex analytical operations that require maintaining context across multiple data events. Stateful operations such as aggregations, joins, and pattern detection require persistent storage of intermediate results that can survive application restarts and node failures. Advanced state management solutions provide automatic backup and recovery mechanisms that ensure analytical continuity even during infrastructure disruptions.

Exactly-once processing semantics ensure that stream processing applications produce consistent results even when processing failures occur. These guarantees prevent duplicate processing of data events while ensuring that no events are lost during system failures. Implementing exactly-once semantics requires coordination between data sources, processing frameworks, and output destinations to maintain consistent state across all system components.

Integration capabilities enable stream processing frameworks to consume data from multiple sources while producing results to various analytical and operational systems. Source connectors provide standardized interfaces for ingesting data from message queues, databases, and file systems, while sink connectors deliver processing results to visualization tools, alerting systems, and data warehouses. This integration flexibility enables organizations to incorporate stream processing into existing analytical workflows without requiring significant infrastructure modifications.

Serverless Computing Models for Event-Driven Processing

Serverless computing architectures enable event-driven data processing where computational resources are automatically provisioned in response to specific triggers or data events. This approach eliminates the need for pre-allocated server capacity by dynamically creating execution environments only when processing tasks are required. For IoT applications with irregular data patterns or sporadic processing requirements, serverless models provide cost-effective solutions that scale from zero to handle massive workloads automatically.

Function-as-a-Service platforms provide execution environments for small, focused code units that perform specific data processing tasks. These functions can be triggered by various events including HTTP requests, message queue deliveries, file uploads, or scheduled intervals. The stateless nature of serverless functions enables unlimited parallel execution, allowing systems to process thousands of concurrent data events without complex coordination mechanisms.

Cold start optimization techniques minimize the latency associated with provisioning new execution environments for serverless functions. Advanced platforms implement container reuse strategies that maintain warm execution environments for frequently invoked functions while implementing efficient bootstrapping processes for new function instances. These optimizations ensure that time-sensitive IoT applications can achieve sub-second response times even when scaling from zero active instances.

Cost optimization in serverless architectures results from precise billing models that charge only for actual execution time rather than allocated capacity. This pricing approach particularly benefits IoT applications with unpredictable workload patterns where traditional server-based architectures would require overprovisioning to handle peak demands. Serverless models enable organizations to pay proportionally for actual usage while maintaining the ability to handle sudden spikes in data volume.

Integration patterns enable serverless functions to coordinate complex data processing workflows through event-driven communication mechanisms. Function composition allows simple processing units to be combined into sophisticated analytical pipelines where the output of one function triggers the execution of subsequent functions. This approach enables organizations to build complex data processing systems from simple, reusable components that can be developed and maintained independently.

Data Lake Architectures and Storage Optimization

Data lake architectures provide scalable storage solutions for massive volumes of structured and unstructured IoT data while supporting diverse analytical workloads. Unlike traditional data warehouses that require predefined schemas and data transformation processes, data lakes enable organizations to store raw data in its native format and apply schema-on-read approaches when specific analytical requirements are identified. This flexibility proves essential for IoT applications where data formats and analytical requirements evolve continuously.

Tiered storage strategies optimize cost and performance by automatically moving data between different storage classes based on access patterns and retention requirements. Hot storage tiers provide high-performance access for frequently analyzed data, while warm and cold storage tiers offer cost-effective solutions for historical data that requires occasional access. Automated lifecycle management policies ensure that data transitions between storage tiers based on predefined rules without manual intervention.

Data partitioning and indexing strategies enable efficient query performance across massive datasets stored in data lake environments. Temporal partitioning organizes data by time periods to support efficient time-range queries, while geographic partitioning enables location-based analysis. Advanced indexing techniques create metadata structures that enable query engines to locate relevant data quickly without scanning entire datasets.

Schema evolution capabilities ensure that data lake architectures can accommodate changing data formats and structures without requiring migration of existing data. Schema registries maintain versioned metadata descriptions that enable analytical tools to interpret data correctly regardless of when it was originally stored. This evolutionary approach enables organizations to adapt to new IoT device types and data formats without disrupting existing analytical workflows.

Query optimization engines provide high-performance analytical capabilities across data lake storage systems through distributed processing and intelligent caching mechanisms. Columnar storage formats optimize data compression and query performance for analytical workloads, while predicate pushdown techniques minimize data transfer by filtering irrelevant data at the storage level. These optimizations enable complex analytical queries to execute efficiently even across petabyte-scale datasets.

Time Series Database Integration and Performance Optimization

Time series databases provide specialized storage and query capabilities optimized for temporal data patterns commonly generated by IoT sensor networks. These databases implement compression algorithms specifically designed for time-stamped data, achieving storage densities significantly higher than general-purpose databases while maintaining query performance for time-based analytical operations. The optimization extends to indexing strategies that enable efficient retrieval of data based on time ranges, device identifiers, and measurement types.

High-frequency data ingestion capabilities enable time series databases to handle millions of data points per second from distributed IoT sensor networks. Batch ingestion mechanisms buffer incoming data points to optimize write performance, while real-time ingestion capabilities ensure that critical measurements are immediately available for analysis. Advanced ingestion systems implement backpressure mechanisms that prevent memory overflow during peak data volumes while maintaining data durability guarantees.

Downsampling and aggregation strategies enable efficient storage and analysis of long-term historical data by automatically reducing data resolution over time. Recent data maintains full resolution for detailed analysis, while older data is progressively aggregated into hourly, daily, or weekly summaries. These retention policies ensure that databases maintain historical context while controlling storage costs and query performance for long-term trend analysis.

Distributed architecture implementations enable time series databases to scale horizontally across multiple nodes while maintaining consistent query performance. Sharding strategies distribute data across nodes based on time ranges or device identifiers, enabling parallel query processing that scales linearly with cluster size. Replication mechanisms ensure data durability and availability even when individual nodes fail, while automatic rebalancing capabilities redistribute data as cluster composition changes.

Integration capabilities connect time series databases with analytical tools, visualization platforms, and machine learning frameworks through standardized query interfaces and data export mechanisms. SQL-compatible query languages enable data scientists to leverage existing analytical tools, while streaming interfaces provide real-time data feeds for continuous monitoring and alerting applications. These integration features ensure that time series data can be incorporated into comprehensive analytical workflows alongside other data sources.

Machine Learning Pipeline Integration and Model Deployment

Machine learning pipeline architectures enable automated training, validation, and deployment of analytical models using IoT data streams processed within cloud environments. These pipelines implement continuous integration and deployment practices that ensure models remain accurate and relevant as data patterns evolve over time. Automated data preprocessing, feature engineering, and model training workflows reduce the manual effort required to maintain effective analytical capabilities.

Model versioning and experiment tracking systems maintain comprehensive records of model training processes, enabling data scientists to reproduce results and compare different approaches systematically. Version control mechanisms track changes to training data, model parameters, and code implementations, while automated testing frameworks validate model performance across different datasets and deployment scenarios. These practices ensure that machine learning models maintain consistent quality standards throughout their lifecycle.

Real-time model serving architectures provide low-latency inference capabilities that enable immediate application of machine learning insights to incoming IoT data streams. Containerized model serving environments ensure consistent execution characteristics across different deployment platforms while enabling automatic scaling based on inference demand. Advanced serving systems implement A/B testing capabilities that enable gradual rollout of new models while monitoring their performance compared to existing implementations.

Feature store architectures centralize the management of processed data features used for machine learning model training and inference. These systems ensure that feature engineering pipelines produce consistent results across training and production environments while providing versioning capabilities that enable reproducible model development. Automated feature validation ensures that data quality issues are detected before they impact model performance.

AutoML capabilities reduce the expertise required to develop effective machine learning models by automating algorithm selection, hyperparameter tuning, and model architecture optimization. These systems can automatically evaluate multiple modeling approaches and select optimal configurations based on performance metrics and computational constraints. This automation enables organizations to leverage machine learning capabilities without requiring extensive data science expertise while ensuring that models achieve optimal performance for specific IoT analytical requirements.

Data Quality Management and Monitoring Systems

Data quality management frameworks ensure that IoT data processed within cloud environments maintains accuracy, completeness, and consistency standards necessary for reliable analytical insights. These systems implement automated validation rules that detect anomalies, missing values, and inconsistencies in real-time data streams before they propagate to analytical systems. Quality monitoring dashboards provide immediate visibility into data health metrics, enabling rapid identification and resolution of issues that could compromise analytical accuracy.

Anomaly detection algorithms identify unusual patterns in IoT data streams that may indicate sensor malfunctions, network issues, or security threats. Statistical approaches establish baseline patterns for normal data behavior and flag deviations that exceed predefined thresholds, while machine learning algorithms adapt to evolving data patterns and detect subtle anomalies that static rules might miss. These detection systems enable proactive maintenance and security responses that prevent minor issues from developing into significant operational problems.

Data lineage tracking systems maintain comprehensive records of data transformations and processing steps throughout the entire analytical pipeline. These records enable organizations to trace the origin of analytical results back to original data sources and understand how processing decisions impact final insights. When data quality issues are identified, lineage information enables rapid identification of affected analytical results and facilitates corrective actions.

Automated data validation frameworks implement business rules and constraints that ensure data consistency across different systems and time periods. These validation systems can detect schema violations, referential integrity issues, and business logic violations in real-time, preventing corrupted data from affecting analytical processes. Validation results are integrated with monitoring systems to provide immediate alerts when data quality standards are not met.

Performance monitoring systems track the efficiency and resource utilization of data processing pipelines to ensure optimal system operation. These systems monitor metrics including processing latency, throughput rates, error frequencies, and resource consumption across all components of the data processing infrastructure. Automated alerting capabilities notify operators when performance metrics exceed acceptable thresholds, enabling proactive intervention before issues impact user experiences.

Security and Compliance Frameworks for Cloud Data Processing

Security frameworks for cloud-based IoT data processing implement comprehensive protection mechanisms that address threats throughout the entire data lifecycle. These frameworks encompass data encryption during transmission and storage, access control mechanisms that enforce least-privilege principles, and network security measures that prevent unauthorized access to processing infrastructure. Multi-layered security approaches ensure that compromise of individual security controls does not expose entire systems to attack.

Identity and access management systems provide centralized authentication and authorization capabilities that control access to data processing resources based on user roles and operational requirements. These systems implement fine-grained permissions that enable users to access only the specific data and processing capabilities required for their responsibilities. Advanced authorization frameworks support dynamic access policies that adjust permissions based on context such as time of day, geographic location, or current security threat levels.

Data privacy protection mechanisms ensure that IoT data processing complies with regulatory requirements while enabling necessary analytical operations. Anonymization and pseudonymization techniques remove or obscure personally identifiable information while preserving data utility for analytical purposes. Differential privacy algorithms add controlled noise to analytical results to prevent individual data subjects from being identified while maintaining statistical accuracy of aggregate insights.

Audit logging systems maintain comprehensive records of all data access and processing activities to support compliance requirements and security investigations. These logs capture detailed information about user activities, data transformations, and system events with tamper-evident storage mechanisms that ensure log integrity. Automated analysis of audit logs can detect suspicious activities and policy violations in real-time, enabling rapid response to potential security incidents.

Compliance automation frameworks ensure that data processing operations adhere to regulatory requirements through automated policy enforcement and compliance monitoring. These frameworks implement data retention policies that automatically delete or archive data according to regulatory requirements, while data residency controls ensure that sensitive data remains within specified geographic boundaries. Continuous compliance monitoring provides real-time assessment of regulatory adherence and identifies potential violations before they result in penalties.

As smart city IoT deployments continue expanding, the sophistication and scale of cloud-based data processing systems will require continuous evolution to address emerging challenges and opportunities. The integration of artificial intelligence capabilities with distributed processing frameworks will enable more intelligent resource allocation and automated optimization of data processing workflows. Edge-cloud hybrid architectures will provide seamless data processing capabilities that span from device-level analytics to large-scale cloud computations, enabling comprehensive urban intelligence systems that can respond to conditions at multiple temporal and spatial scales.

DATA STORAGE AND RETRIEVAL OPTIMIZATION FOR REAL-TIME ACCESS

Optimizing data storage and retrieval for real-time access represents a critical challenge in cloud-based IoT analytics systems, where response times must remain consistently low despite massive data volumes and complex query patterns. Effective optimization requires specialized storage technologies, intelligent indexing strategies, and carefully designed data architectures that balance performance, cost, and scalability requirements.

Time Series Database Optimization

Time series databases provide specialized storage and query optimization for IoT data characterized by timestamp-based organization and high ingestion rates. These databases implement column-oriented storage architectures that group related temporal measurements together, enabling efficient compression and rapid retrieval of time-bounded data ranges. Specialized compression algorithms exploit the temporal patterns inherent in IoT sensor data, often achieving compression ratios significantly higher than general-purpose databases while maintaining query performance.

The design principles underlying time series optimization focus on write-heavy workloads typical of IoT deployments where thousands of sensors continuously generate measurements. Time-based indexing structures organize data chronologically to support efficient range queries and temporal aggregations without requiring full table scans. These optimizations prove particularly effective for smart city applications where analytical queries frequently involve time-based filtering, temporal aggregations, and trend analysis across extended historical periods.

Modern time series database implementations demonstrate substantial performance improvements over traditional relational databases for IoT workloads, with some systems achieving ingestion rates exceeding millions of data points per second while maintaining sub-second query response times for complex analytical operations. These performance characteristics enable real-time dashboard updates, immediate anomaly detection, and interactive exploration of historical trends across massive IoT datasets spanning multiple years of continuous sensor measurements.

Data Partitioning Strategies

Effective data partitioning is fundamental to achieving scalable performance in large-scale IoT systems. Time-based partitioning aligns naturally with IoT data patterns, enabling efficient query pruning and automated data lifecycle management. Range-based partitioning works effectively for time-series data where queries typically focus on specific temporal ranges, while hash-based partitioning provides even distribution for unpredictable access patterns.

IoTDB implements sophisticated partitioning algorithms specifically designed for time-series data, combining series partitioning for schema management with time partitioning for data organization. This dual-layer approach enables efficient handling of both device-specific queries and time-range analytics while maintaining manageable partition sizes. The system distinguishes between hot and cold partitions based on access patterns, optimizing storage and retrieval strategies accordingly.

Caching Layer Implementation

Multi-tier caching strategies significantly improve query performance by storing frequently accessed data in high-speed memory systems. Redis and Memcached provide distributed caching solutions that can maintain query results, aggregated data, and frequently accessed time series in memory for sub-millisecond access times. Effective caching strategies implement cache-aside patterns for read-heavy workloads and write-through patterns for applications requiring immediate consistency.

Advanced caching implementations for IoT analytics include edge caching for geographically distributed data access, adaptive caching that adjusts strategies based on access patterns, and hierarchical caching that balances memory usage with access frequency. The challenge lies in maintaining cache consistency while minimizing invalidation overhead, particularly for applications that require real-time data freshness.

In-memory Database Integration

In-memory databases provide exceptional performance for applications requiring sub-millisecond response times by eliminating disk I/O bottlenecks entirely. These systems leverage volatile RAM for persistent data storage, achieving dramatic improvements in query processing times compared to traditional disk-based systems. In-memory databases prove particularly valuable for real-time fraud detection, high-frequency algorithmic trading, and personalized recommendation engines that require immediate insights.

The integration of in-memory databases with IoT analytics requires careful consideration of data volatility and persistence requirements. Hybrid approaches that combine in-memory processing with persistent storage systems provide optimal performance while ensuring data durability. Technologies like Apache Ignite and SAP HANA offer distributed in-memory capabilities that can scale horizontally while maintaining consistency across multiple nodes.

Query Optimization Techniques

Advanced query optimization techniques significantly improve performance for complex IoT analytics workloads. Time-range indexing enables rapid identification of relevant data within specific temporal boundaries, while tag-based indexing facilitates efficient filtering based on device metadata. Materialized views pre-compute frequently accessed aggregations, eliminating the need for expensive real-time calculations.

Query execution plan optimization analyzes query patterns to determine the most efficient processing strategies, often implementing parallel execution across multiple nodes to reduce response times. Approximate query processing techniques provide near-instantaneous results for exploratory analytics where perfect accuracy is less critical than response speed. These optimization approaches enable real-time analytics capabilities even for complex queries involving millions of data points.

The implementation of comprehensive optimization strategies requires continuous monitoring and adjustment based on actual usage patterns and performance metrics. Successful IoT analytics systems combine multiple optimization techniques tailored to specific workload characteristics, achieving the low-latency performance required for real-time decision-making while maintaining cost efficiency and scalability.

ETHICAL CONSIDERATIONS IN REAL-TIME BIG DATA ANALYTICS FOR IOT

As we implement real-time big data analytics for IoT in smart city contexts, it is crucial to consider the ethical implications of these technologies. The pervasive nature of IoT devices and the vast amount of data they collect raise significant concerns about privacy, security, and the potential for misuse of information. This section explores key ethical considerations and proposes guidelines for responsible implementation of IoT analytics.

Privacy Concerns

One of the major challenges in smart cities is data collection, as IoT devices often passively gather information without explicit user consent. This necessitates the implementation of clear consent mechanisms, along with options for opting out where possible. To address privacy concerns, a privacy by design approach should be adopted, limiting data collection to only what is essential for the intended purpose.

The privacy by design framework was originally developed by Dr. Ann Cavoukian during her tenure as Information and Privacy Commissioner of Ontario, Canada, in the 1990s. Recognizing the inadequacy of reactive privacy measures, Dr. Cavoukian proposed seven foundational principles that embed privacy protection into the very architecture of systems and technologies from the beginning rather than treating privacy as an afterthought. This proactive approach gained international recognition when the International Assembly of Privacy Commissioners and Data

Protection Authorities unanimously adopted the framework in 2010, and it was subsequently incorporated into the European Union's General Data Protection Regulation (GDPR) under Article 25.

The seven foundational principles of privacy by design include: proactive prevention rather than reactive remediation, privacy as the default setting, full functionality through positive-sum solutions, end-to-end security, visibility and transparency, respect for user privacy, and embedding privacy throughout the system lifecycle. These principles prove particularly relevant for smart cities where Dr. Cavoukian recommends immediate de-identification of personal data collected from vehicles, pedestrians, or buildings to preserve anonymity while maintaining analytical utility.

Data anonymization also presents challenges, as even anonymized datasets can be re-identified when combined with other data sources. Advanced techniques like differential privacy must be utilized, and anonymization processes regularly audited to mitigate re-identification risks. Differential privacy provides mathematical guarantees for individual privacy protection by adding carefully calibrated noise to data query results, ensuring that analytical insights remain useful while preventing individual identification. This technique has proven particularly effective in smart healthcare systems and traffic management applications where sensitive personal information requires absolute protection while enabling aggregate pattern analysis.

Location privacy represents another significant concern, as many IoT devices track users' locations, potentially revealing sensitive personal information about daily routines, work locations, and social connections. Strict controls on location data collection and aggregation practices are vital to protect individual privacy, requiring implementation of spatial anonymization techniques, temporal data separation, and granular location data controls that prevent inference attacks while maintaining urban planning capabilities.

Security Concerns

Security is a critical concern for IoT devices in smart cities, as they are vulnerable to hacking and unauthorized access. To address this, robust security measures must be implemented at all levels, including encryption, strong authentication, and regular updates to systems. Additionally, IoT devices often have limited computational resources, making traditional security measures difficult to implement. Therefore, security protocols specifically designed for resource-constrained devices, such as secure boot processes and trusted platform modules, are essential. The distributed nature of IoT networks creates multiple points of vulnerability, requiring network segmentation, monitoring, and the use of dedicated networks like VPNs for IoT devices. Clarity around data ownership is also important in public spaces, where IoT devices collect significant amounts of data. Cities need to establish clear policies on data ownership and involve stakeholders in developing these policies, ensuring transparency and fairness in data usage.

Data Ownership and Control

Another challenge in smart cities is the uncertainty surrounding data ownership, particularly when IoT devices collect data in public spaces. To address this, cities must establish clear policies that define data ownership and usage rights, ensuring transparency in how data is managed. It is essential to involve a broad range of stakeholders, including citizens, in the development of these policies to ensure trust and collaboration. Additionally, ensuring individuals have access to their own data and the ability to transfer it between services is crucial for empowering users. Implementing systems that facilitate data portability, such as developing APIs that allow individuals to access and export their personal data in standard formats, is a critical step towards data transparency and control in smart cities.

Algorithmic Bias and Fairness

One of the major challenges in IoT data and algorithms is the risk of reflecting and amplifying existing societal biases. To mitigate this, cities and organizations must regularly audit their data and algorithms for bias, ensuring that the systems remain fair and equitable. One strategy is using diverse datasets to train algorithms and incorporating fairness metrics in their evaluation to minimize biased outcomes. Additionally, the complexity of big data analytics often leads to opacity in decision-making processes, which can erode public trust. To address this, it is crucial to develop explainable AI and transparent analytics practices, where algorithmic decisions are communicated in understandable terms. Providing mechanisms for individuals to appeal automated decisions further supports accountability and fairness in smart city initiatives.

Governance and Accountability

The rapidly evolving rules and regulations for data protection and privacy, such as GDPR and CCPA, present a significant challenge for IoT initiatives. To ensure compliance, it is essential to implement a robust compliance management system and regularly audit data practices against these regulatory requirements. Beyond compliance, ethical oversight is equally important to ensure that IoT and big data projects respect ethical standards. Establishing ethics committees or review boards to evaluate IoT initiatives can help create an ethical framework tailored to the specific needs of IoT and data analytics. Additionally, gaining public understanding and acceptance of IoT systems is crucial. Transparent communication strategies, including public consultations and accessible information about data collection and usage, can foster trust and encourage public engagement in smart city projects.

Proposed Ethical Guidelines for IoT Analytics Implementation

To ensure the ethical deployment of IoT in smart city environments, several guidelines should be created. First, transparency is crucial. Citizens must be informed about what data is collected, how it is used, and who has access to it. Coupled with this is the need for consent and control, where individuals should have the option to provide informed consent for data collection and maintain control over their personal information. Another important principle is data minimization: only essential data should be collected, and it should be anonymized or deleted once no longer necessary. Security must be embedded at all levels, with security by design protecting data across devices and cloud storage, while privacy by design ensures privacy is considered at every stage of system development.

Furthermore, fairness and non-discrimination require regular audits of data and algorithms to prevent biases and ensure equity, while accountability establishes clear lines of responsibility for data management and protection. Environmental sustainability is also important, as environmental responsibility ensures IoT systems are designed with energy efficiency and e-waste minimization in mind. Finally, accessibility and inclusivity focus on making IoT and data analytics available to all members of society, ensuring that the benefits are shared equitably. An ethical review process should be in place for all IoT projects, ensuring their broader societal impacts are considered and aligned with ethical standards. By following these guidelines, smart city projects can advance while safeguarding individual rights and promoting a fair, sustainable, and inclusive future.

CONCLUSION

Real-time big data analytics for IoT represents a powerful tool for creating smarter, more efficient, and more livable cities. The combination of IoT devices generating vast amounts of data and the ability to process and analyze this data in real-time creates opportunities for urban management and improvement.

We discussed how the four Vs of big data (volume, velocity, variety, and veracity) operate within the context of smart cities, creating both challenges and opportunities. The large amount of data generated by IoT devices in urban environments necessitates new approaches to data storage, processing, and analysis.

The importance of low-latency, real-time data processing was emphasized throughout this chapter. In many smart city applications, from traffic management to emergency response, the ability to quickly analyze data and take action can make a crucial difference. We discussed various architectures and technologies for achieving this, including edge computing, stream processing, and cloud-based analytics platforms.

The future of smart cities lies not just in the technology itself, but in how we choose to apply it. By leveraging real-time big data analytics for IoT thoughtfully and ethically, we have the opportunity to create urban environments that are not only more efficient and sustainable, but also more responsive to the needs and aspirations of their inhabitants.

As this field continues to evolve rapidly, ongoing research, experimentation, and public dialogue will be crucial. The potential benefits are enormous, but so too are the responsibilities. By staying informed about technological developments, remaining mindful of ethical considerations, and always keeping the needs of citizens at the forefront, we can work towards realizing the full potential of real-time big data analytics for IoT in creating the smart cities of tomorrow.

CHAPTER 3

DIGITAL TWIN CITIES

D igital twin technology has emerged as a powerful tool for modeling, simulating, and optimizing complex systems in urban environments. This transformative approach to urban planning and management represents a significant advancement in how cities can understand, monitor, and optimize their operations. By creating comprehensive virtual representations of urban environments, digital twins enable unprecedented capabilities for simulation, analysis, and decision-making that fundamentally change how cities are planned, managed, and operated.

THE IMPORTANCE OF DIGITAL TWINS IN URBAN PLANNING

A *digital twin* is a virtual representation of a physical object or system that serves as a dynamic, real-time model capable of simulating its behavior and performance. In the context of cities, a digital twin constitutes a comprehensive virtual model of the urban environment that encompasses buildings, infrastructure, transportation systems, and human activities. These sophisticated models integrate data from various sources including geographic information systems, sensors, and demographic databases to create comprehensive and dynamic representations of a city's physical environment. Figure 3.1 shows the main components of city-scale digital twin.

Digital twins give cities a live, connected view of how the urban system works. The diagram shows two linked layers: a physical city on the right and a virtual model on the left. Between them flows data and actions. Sensors in the streets, buildings, and vehicles stream data into the twin. Analytics turn that data into insight. Decisions then go back to the city as actions.

- Always-on view: With a twin, planners watch key indicators in real time: traffic flow, transit delays, energy use, water pressure, air quality, and service requests. When a value drifts, alerts fire and teams act fast.
- From data to decisions: The loop in the image—data → analyze → insight → decision → action—captures the daily rhythm of city work. It replaces sporadic reports with a steady cycle that improves services and cuts waste.

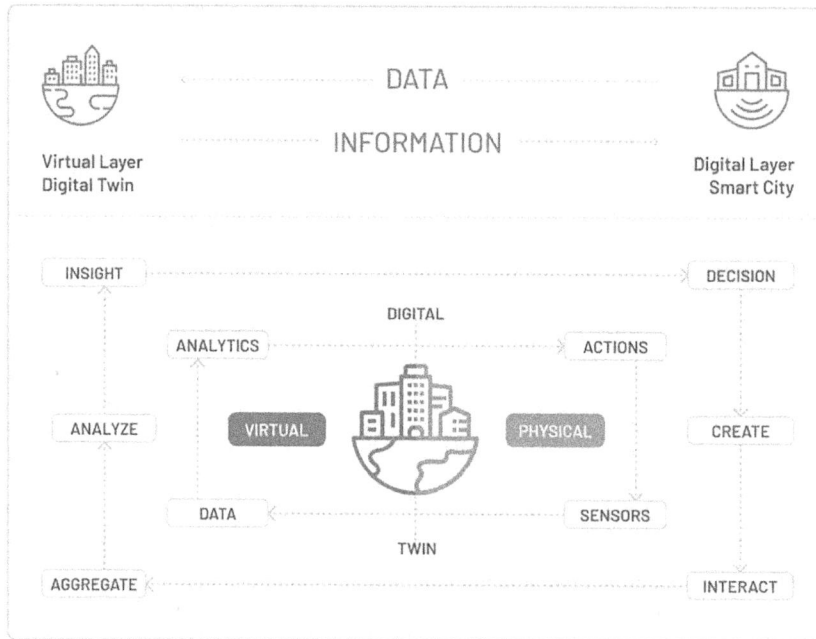

FIGURE 3.1 Main Components of a city-scale digital twin.

- Test before building: The virtual side lets teams run "what-if" scenarios. They can try new bus lanes, signal timing, storm routes, or zoning rules inside the twin first, see impacts, and only then deploy in the street.
- Break down silos: The shared model becomes a common map for transport, utilities, planning, and emergency services. Teams see the same facts, use the same context, and coordinate responses.
- Engage the public: Clear visuals help residents understand plans. People can view proposed changes in a realistic 3D scene, give feedback, and track progress.
- Improve resilience: During heat waves, floods, or outages, the twin brings together live sensor feeds and forecasts. It helps route resources, warn neighborhoods, and recover faster.
- Continuous learning: Each action taken in the city feeds back into the model. Over time, predictions get better, maintenance becomes proactive, and costs fall.

Unlike traditional urban planning tools that rely on static data and models, digital twins are dynamic, continuously updated virtual representations that incorporate live data from various sources including IoT sensors, social media platforms, and other urban data systems. This real-time connectivity transforms the virtual model from a simple visualization tool into an intelligent platform capable of responding to changes and providing insights based on current conditions.

Digital twins support data-driven decision-making for urban management by providing evidence-based insights that help city officials make informed decisions. Rather than relying on intuition or limited data sets, urban planners can access comprehensive, real-time information about city operations and use advanced analytics to identify patterns, predict trends, and optimize resource allocation.

The technology also enhances collaboration between different stakeholders in urban development by providing a shared platform where government agencies, private sector partners, and citizens can visualize and discuss urban plans and policies. This collaborative approach leads to more transparent decision-making processes and helps build trust between city authorities and residents.

Evolution of Digital Twins from Industrial Applications to Urban Contexts

Digital twins began in industrial engineering and have steadily expanded into the urban domain. This section traces the key ideas, technologies, and practices that enabled the shift from product-centric twins to city-scale, data-driven twins for planning and operations.

Early roots in engineering and space programs

- 1960s–1980s: Manufacturers used computational models to test designs before physical prototyping. These early practices established the core principle of mirroring a physical asset with a digital representation for analysis and optimization.
- 1970: Space programs demonstrated the value of "mirrored" systems to diagnose issues and guide operations when direct access to the physical asset was impossible. The approach validated the idea that a faithful replica—digital or physical—can support real-time decision-making for complex, high-risk systems.
- 1991: Conceptual foundations matured with the vision of software that represents and monitors real-world systems at scale, anticipating the rise of always-on digital counterparts.

Industrial maturation and enabling technologies

- Asset lifecycle focus: In manufacturing, twins tracked performance from design through maintenance, reducing downtime and improving quality. Standardized telemetry, supervisory control systems, and condition-based maintenance practices made digital monitoring routine.
- Compute and cloud: Affordable high-performance computing and elastic cloud services allowed continuous ingestion and analysis of high-volume telemetry. This shift lowered entry barriers and made large, persistent twins feasible beyond plant floors.
- 3D modeling and game engines: Advances in 3D GIS, photogrammetry, LiDAR, and real-time rendering (e.g., physics-based and game-engine pipelines) enabled immersive, interactive models. Teams could navigate complex assets and environments, annotate them, and run simulations with realistic behavior.

Transition from assets to systems and networks

- From single machines to fleets: Twins expanded from individual equipment to connected fleets (e.g., vehicles, turbines), introducing challenges in data federation, identity, versioning, and synchronization across many instances.
- Standards and semantics: Open data schemas and ontologies improved interoperability. Shared semantics made it possible to link telemetry, maintenance records, and spatial context across suppliers and agencies.

- Real-time analytics: Stream processing, feature stores for time-series, and low-latency inference turned twins from static dashboards into operational decision tools. Predictive maintenance and anomaly detection became common at scale.

Expansion into the urban context

- Data abundance: Cities deployed IoT sensors for traffic, transit, utilities, environment, and safety. Open data programs and mobile devices added event streams and context, while building information models (BIM) and cadastral data supplied structural detail.
- City-scale visualization: Municipalities combined semantic city models (e.g., CityGML-style structures) with reality meshes derived from aerial imagery and street-level scans. The result was a unified spatial canvas that could host both analytics and public engagement.
- Simulation as a core engine: Urban twins embraced multi-physics and multi-agent simulations: traffic flow, crowd movement, stormwater routing, heat distribution, energy demand, and air quality. Planners could test "what-if" scenarios safely, compare interventions, and anticipate spillover effects across systems.

Operating model and governance shifts

- Cross-agency coordination: Twins provided a shared view for transport, utilities, planning, emergency management, and public works. This reduced siloed decisions and improved response alignment during events and planned works.
- Lifecycle integration: City projects linked planning, permitting, construction, operations, and maintenance in one environment. As-built updates flowed back into the model, keeping the twin accurate over time.
- Public participation: Visual and accessible models helped residents understand proposals and impacts. Feedback loops improved plan legitimacy and refined design choices earlier in the process.

Capabilities that define city digital twins today

- Live data loop: Continuous streams from sensors and systems update the model in near real time, enabling monitoring, alerting, and automated actions.
- Predictive and prescriptive analytics: Forecasts, risk scoring, and optimization guide resource allocation and service levels across traffic, energy, waste, water, and safety.
- Interoperable fabric: APIs, shared schemas, and data contracts allow agencies and vendors to plug into a common platform without rigid lock-in.
- Privacy and security by design: Access controls, data minimization, and differential views protect sensitive information while keeping the twin useful for operations and public transparency.

Main Components of a City-scale Digital Twin

A comprehensive digital twin of a city integrates multiple technological components that work together to create a dynamic, interactive model of the urban environment. These components form the technological foundation that enables the creation and operation of city-scale digital twins.

The 3D city model serves as the visual and spatial foundation of the digital twin, providing a detailed three-dimensional representation of the city's physical environment. This model encompasses buildings, infrastructure, natural features, and terrain, created using advanced technologies including LiDAR scanning, photogrammetry, and building information modeling. The model provides accurate spatial context for all data integration and analysis activities.

The IoT sensor network constitutes the "nervous system" of the digital twin, consisting of sensors deployed throughout the city to collect real-time data on various urban processes. These sensors monitor traffic flow, air quality, energy consumption, water usage, noise levels, and numerous other parameters that characterize urban life. Environmental sensors measure air quality, temperature, humidity, and noise levels, while traffic sensors monitor vehicle flow, pedestrian movement, and parking availability. Smart meters track energy and water consumption in buildings, and cameras equipped with computer vision capabilities provide visual monitoring of urban spaces.

The data integration platform serves as the central hub for collecting, processing, and integrating data from the diverse sources that feed the digital twin. This platform handles the complex task of managing and synthesizing data streams from IoT sensors, city databases, social media, weather services, and other relevant sources. The platform includes extract, transform, and load processes to standardize data from different sources and ensure compatibility across the system.

The simulation engine provides the computational capabilities necessary for modeling and simulating various urban processes and scenarios based on integrated data and 3D models. This engine can run complex simulations including agent-based modeling of human behavior, computational fluid dynamics for air flow analysis, and physics-based simulations for infrastructure performance. The simulation capabilities enable predictive modeling and scenario testing that are central to the value proposition of digital twins.

Visualization interface components provide tools for presenting the digital twin and its associated data in intuitive and interactive formats. These interfaces support both 2D and 3D representations and can incorporate virtual reality, augmented reality, and mixed reality technologies to provide immersive experiences. Web-based visualization tools enable broad access to digital twin capabilities across different devices and platforms.

Analytics and AI components provide advanced analytical capabilities for deriving insights, making predictions, and optimizing urban processes. Machine learning algorithms can identify patterns in urban data, predict future trends, and support automated decision-making. These components enable real-time analytics platforms that can process streaming data from IoT sensors and provide dynamic updates to digital twin models.

APIs and integration interfaces provide mechanisms for connecting the digital twin with other urban management systems and enabling third-party applications to access and utilize the digital twin's data and capabilities. These interfaces support interoperability and enable the digital twin to serve as a platform for urban innovation.

Security and privacy framework components ensure the security of the digital twin and protect the privacy of citizens' data. This framework includes encryption systems, access controls, data anonymization techniques, and privacy protection protocols that are essential for maintaining public trust and regulatory compliance.

The integration and orchestration of these diverse technological components creates a powerful platform for urban modeling, analysis, and decision-making that can transform how cities are planned, managed, and operated.

BENEFITS OF DIGITAL TWINS FOR URBAN PLANNING, SIMULATION, AND OPTIMIZATION

Digital twins offer benefits for urban planning, simulation, and optimization by enabling cities to address complex challenges with innovative, data-driven solutions. These benefits span multiple domains of urban management and create value for city administrators, planners, businesses, and citizens.

Enhanced Urban Planning Capabilities

Digital twins revolutionize urban planning by providing dynamic visualization and analysis capabilities that far exceed traditional planning tools. Urban planners can visualize and analyze proposed developments within the context of the existing urban environment, enabling more informed decision-making about land use, infrastructure development, and urban growth patterns. The technology supports scenario testing where planners can simulate various development options and assess their potential impacts before making final decisions.

The collaborative nature of digital twins fosters improved stakeholder engagement in planning processes. Government agencies, private sector partners, and community members can interact with shared visual models that make complex planning concepts more accessible and understandable. This enhanced collaboration leads to more transparent decision-making processes and helps build consensus around development plans.

Digital twins enable comprehensive impact assessment for proposed developments, allowing planners to evaluate how new projects might affect traffic patterns, environmental conditions, economic activity, and quality of life. This holistic approach to impact assessment helps prevent unintended consequences and ensures that development decisions consider all relevant factors.

Real-time Monitoring and Management

The real-time data integration capabilities of digital twins provide continuous oversight of urban systems and infrastructure, enabling early detection of issues and rapid responses to emergencies or anomalies. City managers can monitor the performance of transportation networks, utility systems, public facilities, and environmental conditions from integrated dashboards that provide comprehensive situational awareness.

This monitoring capability extends to predictive maintenance applications where digital twins can analyze infrastructure performance data to predict when maintenance will be needed, reducing costs and preventing service disruptions. The technology enables proactive management approaches that address problems before they become critical.

Emergency response capabilities are significantly enhanced through digital twins that can provide real-time information about city conditions during crises. First responders can access current information about traffic conditions, infrastructure status, and population distribution to optimize their response strategies. The systems can also simulate emergency scenarios to improve preparedness and response planning.

Advanced Simulation and Scenario Testing

Digital twins enable sophisticated simulation capabilities that allow cities to test potential policies, infrastructure changes, and development scenarios in virtual environments before implementation. This "what-if" analysis capability is invaluable for understanding the potential consequences of different choices and optimizing urban operations.

Cities can simulate the impacts of new transportation policies, evaluate the effectiveness of different infrastructure designs, and assess the potential effects of climate change on urban systems. Traffic management systems can be tested virtually to optimize signal timing, routing, and congestion management strategies.

The simulation capabilities extend to long-term planning applications where cities can model different growth scenarios and assess their sustainability implications. This forward-looking analysis helps cities prepare for future challenges and opportunities while ensuring that current decisions support long-term urban goals.

Citizen Engagement and Transparency

Digital twins significantly enhance citizen engagement by providing intuitive visualizations of urban data and plans that make complex information more accessible to the public. Citizens can interact with 3D models of their neighborhoods to understand proposed developments, explore traffic management plans, and visualize the potential impacts of various urban policies.

Interactive platforms created through digital twins allow citizens to provide feedback on urban plans and participate more meaningfully in planning processes. This participatory approach leads to better-informed public decisions and stronger community support for urban initiatives.

Transparency in decision-making is improved through digital twins that can demonstrate how data and analysis inform urban policies. Citizens can access the same information that city officials use to make decisions, building trust and accountability in urban governance.

Resource Optimization and Efficiency

Digital twins identify inefficiencies in energy, water, and infrastructure management systems, enabling cities to optimize resource allocation and reduce waste. Energy consumption patterns can be analyzed to identify opportunities for efficiency improvements, while water management systems can be optimized to reduce losses and improve distribution.

Infrastructure maintenance schedules can be optimized based on actual performance data rather than predetermined timelines, reducing costs while improving system reliability. The technology enables data-driven resource allocation that ensures city resources are deployed where they can have the greatest impact.

Operational efficiency improvements result from the comprehensive view of city operations that digital twins provide. City departments can coordinate more effectively when they have shared access to real-time information about urban conditions and performance metrics.

Environmental Management and Sustainability

Digital twins play a critical role in environmental management by providing continuous monitoring of air quality, noise pollution, water quality, and other environmental factors. This monitoring capability enables cities to identify pollution sources, track environmental trends, and evaluate the effectiveness of environmental policies.

Cities can simulate the environmental impacts of proposed developments and assess their effects on sustainability goals. Urban heat island effects can be modeled to inform green infrastructure planning, while carbon emission patterns can be analyzed to support climate action planning.

The technology supports the development of strategies for sustainability and resilience by enabling cities to model different approaches to reducing environmental impacts and improving resource efficiency. Renewable energy integration can be optimized through simulations that account for local conditions and demand patterns.

Economic Benefits and Development

Digital twins help reduce costs in urban planning and management by improving the efficiency of decision-making processes and reducing the risk of costly mistakes. Infrastructure projects can be optimized through virtual testing before construction begins, reducing change orders and construction delays.

The technology attracts investment by providing sophisticated tools for analyzing market conditions, assessing development opportunities, and demonstrating the potential returns on urban investments. Cities with advanced digital twin capabilities can position themselves as innovation leaders, attracting businesses and talent.

New business opportunities are created within the digital twin ecosystem as companies develop applications, services, and solutions that leverage digital twin data and capabilities. This innovation ecosystem can become a source of economic growth and job creation.

Improved Urban Mobility

Urban mobility benefits significantly from digital twin applications that optimize traffic flow, reduce congestion, and improve transportation system performance. Real-time traffic management systems can adjust signal timing and routing recommendations based on current conditions, while long-term transportation planning can be informed by comprehensive analysis of mobility patterns.

Virtual testing of mobility solutions enables cities to evaluate new transportation options, such as bike-sharing systems, autonomous vehicles, or new transit lines, before making investments. This testing capability reduces the risk associated with transportation investments and helps ensure that new mobility options meet community needs.

Public transportation systems can be optimized through digital twins that analyze ridership patterns, route efficiency, and service reliability. This optimization leads to improved service quality and higher ridership levels.

Enhanced Disaster Preparedness and Response

Digital twins enable cities to simulate disaster scenarios, including floods, earthquakes, fires, and other emergencies, to improve preparation and response capabilities. Evacuation routes can be optimized based on population distribution and infrastructure conditions, while emergency resource allocation can be planned more effectively.

The technology supports real-time emergency management by providing current information about city conditions during crises. Emergency responders can access updated information about infrastructure damage, population distribution, and resource availability to coordinate their response efforts.

Recovery planning is enhanced through digital twins that can model the impacts of disasters and evaluate different recovery strategies. This capability helps cities rebuild more effectively and incorporate resilience improvements into recovery efforts.

Facilitation of Smart City Initiatives

Digital twins serve as integration platforms that bring together various smart city technologies and data streams, enabling a holistic approach to urban management. Rather than managing separate smart city applications in isolation, cities can use digital twins to coordinate these systems and maximize their combined value.

The technology fosters innovation by providing a platform for developing and testing new urban solutions. Researchers, entrepreneurs, and technology companies can use digital twin data and capabilities to create innovative applications that address urban challenges.

Comprehensive urban management is enabled through digital twins that provide city officials with the tools and information needed to manage complex urban systems effectively. This capability is essential for addressing the growing complexity of modern cities and ensuring that urban development supports community goals and values.

These comprehensive benefits demonstrate the transformative potential of digital twins to enhance urban planning, management, and citizen quality of life. As cities continue to grow and face increasingly complex challenges, digital twins provide essential tools for creating more efficient, sustainable, and livable urban environments. The technology represents a fundamental shift toward data-driven, evidence-based urban management that can help cities address current challenges while preparing for future opportunities and risks.

CASE STUDIES: SUCCESSFUL IMPLEMENTATIONS OF DIGITAL TWINS IN SMART CITIES

The practical applications and potential of digital twins in urban contexts are best illustrated through a comprehensive examination of successful implementations across diverse global cities. These case studies demonstrate how different urban environments have utilized digital twin technology to address unique challenges and achieve specific objectives in their smart city initiatives.

Virtual Singapore

Virtual Singapore represents the world's most comprehensive and ambitious digital twin project, establishing Singapore as the pioneer in country-scale digital twin implementation. Initiated in 2014 through a collaborative partnership between the Singapore government, the National Research Foundation, Singapore Land Authority, and various technology partners, the project emerged from Singapore's Smart Nation initiative and addressed critical urban challenges in one of the world's most densely populated city-states.

The project's foundation is a modern geospatial stack that builds a dynamic, high-resolution 3D model of the entire island nation. This virtual model covers buildings, infrastructure, transport networks, and natural features with survey-grade precision. Positional accuracy is within about 10 cm, meaning any mapped point in the model is expected to be no more than 0.1 m from its true location on the ground. The city acquired this detail using airborne LiDAR and vehicle-mounted sensors to capture terrain and surface geometry across the full 721 km² area, producing more than 50 TB of geospatial data from 160,000 high-resolution aerial images collected over 41 days.

The technological framework integrates real-time data streams from multiple sources, including IoT sensors, government databases, environmental monitoring systems, and population tracking mechanisms. This integration creates a living digital ecosystem that continuously updates to reflect current conditions across Singapore. The platform using Dassault Systèmes' 3DEXPERIENCE City technology to maintain and operate the comprehensive digital model, providing advanced simulation capabilities for urban planning, disaster management, and environmental monitoring.

Virtual Singapore's applications span multiple critical domains of urban management. Urban planners utilize the platform to visualize proposed developments within existing urban contexts, enabling comprehensive impact assessment before implementation. The system supports sophisticated scenario testing where planners can simulate various development options and evaluate their effects on traffic patterns, environmental conditions, and infrastructure capacity. This capability has proven particularly valuable in Singapore's constrained land environment where development decisions carry significant long-term implications[1].

Environmental management represents another major application domain where Virtual Singapore demonstrates substantial value. The platform integrates real-time climate and topographical data to assess urban heat island effects, optimize green space planning, and evaluate environmental impacts of proposed developments. Solar panel placement optimization represents a notable success story where the digital twin analyzed city-wide sunlight exposure patterns to identify optimal locations for renewable energy installations, contributing to Singapore's sustainability objectives.

Disaster management capabilities within Virtual Singapore enable comprehensive scenario simulations for emergency preparedness and response planning. The platform can model various disaster scenarios including flooding, earthquakes, and other emergencies to optimize evacuation routes, resource allocation, and emergency response strategies. This predictive capability enhances Singapore's resilience against natural disasters and supports evidence-based emergency planning.

Important outcomes from the Virtual Singapore project include enhanced urban planning efficiency through data-driven decision-making processes. Development proposals can now be evaluated within comprehensive urban contexts, reducing planning uncertainties and improving development outcomes. Environmental monitoring capabilities have improved through continuous data collection and analysis, enabling proactive environmental management strategies. The platform has also supported Singapore's position as a global leader in smart city innovation, attracting international attention and investment in urban technology development.

Virtual Singapore's implementation faced several significant challenges that provide valuable lessons for other cities. Data integration complexity required sophisticated systems to manage diverse data formats and sources while maintaining quality and consistency. The project team addressed this through development of comprehensive data standards and integration

---

1 United Nations Development Programme. (2021). Handbook on smart urban innovations. UNDP Global Centre for Technology, Innovation, and Sustainable Development. *https://undp.org*

protocols that ensure compatibility across different data streams. Privacy and security concerns surrounding comprehensive urban data collection required implementation of robust protection measures including data anonymization, access controls, and encryption systems.

Computational demands for maintaining and operating a country-scale digital twin necessitated scalable cloud infrastructure capable of processing massive data volumes in real-time. The project addressed this through partnership with cloud computing providers and implementation of distributed processing architectures. Ongoing maintenance and updates require continuous investment in data collection, system updates, and technology advancement to ensure the digital twin remains current and useful.

The collaborative approach adopted by Virtual Singapore (a representation is shown in Figure 3.2) demonstrates the importance of multi-stakeholder engagement in digital twin development. The project brought together government agencies, academic institutions, and private sector partners to create a comprehensive platform that serves diverse needs. This collaboration model has proven essential for creating digital twins that address complex urban challenges requiring interdisciplinary expertise and diverse perspectives.

FIGURE 3.2 Virtual Singapore 3D representation, taken from GovTech Singapore.

Helsinki's Digital Twin

Helsinki's digital twin initiative represents a comprehensive approach to urban digitalization that has positioned Finland's capital as a global leader in open data and citizen-centric smart city development. The project emerged from Helsinki's broader digitalization strategy aimed at becoming the world's most functional city through technology integration across all aspects of city planning, construction, and maintenance.

The Helsinki digital twin project, officially known as Helsinki 3D+, launched as a one-million-euro initiative (approximately $1.1 million USD)[2] designed to create practical and versatile digital city models and to deliver value through citywide digital twin implementation. The project brought together three collaborating organizations: the Helsinki City Environment Division, responsible for strategic planning, traffic management, and urban development; Helsinki 3D+, responsible for creating and maintaining the 3D models and digital twins; and Forum Virium Helsinki, the city-owned innovation company that facilitates smart city development and citizen engagement. Figure 3.3 shows the 3D model of Helsinki.

---

2 Bentley Systems. (n.d.). Improving the environment with a city-scale digital twin: City of Helsinki (Helsinki 3D+). *https://www.bentley.com/company/esg-user-project-city-of-helsinki/*

FIGURE 3.3 A 3D model of the digital twin of Helsinki City, taken from *engineering.com*.

The technological foundation of Helsinki's digital twin encompasses two complementary 3D city models that work together to provide comprehensive urban representation. The first component consists of a smart, semantic city information model based on the open CityGML standard, designed for advanced city analytics with unlimited data enrichment capabilities. This model supports complex urban analyses including energy efficiency planning, greenhouse gas emission assessments, and environmental impact evaluations. The second component features a visually high-quality reality mesh model created from aerial photographs using computerized calculations, providing realistic visualization capabilities for online services and public engagement.

Helsinki achieved a significant milestone by becoming the first Nordic city to create a semantic CityGML 3D model covering its entire urban area. The semantic model incorporates detailed building information including materials, age, energy characteristics, and usage patterns, enabling sophisticated analysis capabilities. The *reality mesh model* offers photorealistic visualization with dimensional accuracy within 20 centimeters of actual conditions, making it suitable for both professional planning applications and public engagement initiatives.

The digital twin integration extends beyond basic 3D modeling to incorporate comprehensive urban data from multiple city departments and systems. The platform connects with existing Geographic Information Systems, urban management platforms, and IoT sensor networks to create a unified data environment. This integration enables real-time updates and dynamic modeling capabilities that reflect current urban conditions and support responsive city management.

Open data represents a fundamental principle underlying Helsinki's digital twin strategy. The city makes both the semantic CityGML model and reality mesh model available as open data, enabling access for researchers, businesses, citizens, and other stakeholders. This open approach has fostered innovation and collaboration while promoting transparency in urban planning and decision-making processes. The availability of high-quality 3D city data has attracted international research interest and supported development of various applications and services by third-party developers.

Helsinki's digital twin applications span multiple urban management domains with demonstrable impacts on city operations. Urban planning processes have been enhanced through 3D visualization capabilities that enable planners, developers, and citizens to better understand proposed developments and their impacts. The digital twin supports shadow analysis, view corridor assessments, and environmental impact evaluations that inform planning decisions. Building permit processes have become more efficient through automated checks and 3D visualizations that reduce administrative burden and improve approval timelines.

Construction project management represents another significant application area where Helsinki's digital twin provides substantial value. The platform enables visualization of construction impacts on surrounding areas, helping planners anticipate disruptions and optimize project scheduling. Construction firms can coordinate more effectively using shared 3D models that provide common reference points for project planning and execution. The digital twin also supports public communication about construction projects by providing clear, accessible visualizations that reduce community concerns and complaints.

Energy efficiency planning has benefited from Helsinki's semantic city model capabilities. The detailed building information enables analysis of energy consumption patterns, identification of efficiency improvement opportunities, and planning of district-level energy systems. Solar energy potential analysis represents a specific application where the digital twin evaluates building surfaces for solar panel installations, supporting renewable energy development initiatives.

Citizen engagement has been significantly enhanced through Helsinki's digital twin implementation. Citizens can access user-friendly interfaces that allow exploration of 3D city models, review of proposed developments, and participation in planning processes. The platform provides transparent access to planning information and enables meaningful public input on urban development projects. Mobile-friendly interfaces ensure broad accessibility across different demographic groups and technical skill levels.

The Kalasatama digital twin project within Helsinki demonstrates neighborhood-scale digital twin implementation. This 0.27-square-mile area served as a pilot project for advanced digital twin applications including smart city solution testing and citizen participation facilitation. The Kalasatama digital twin used OpenCities Planner to present smart city solutions and enable community engagement in urban development planning. This pilot project established methodologies and best practices that have been scaled across the broader Helsinki digital twin initiative.

Helsinki's digital twin has achieved several significant outcomes that demonstrate its value for urban management and development. Planning processes have become more efficient through improved visualization and analysis capabilities. Development review timelines have been reduced through automated compliance checking and enhanced stakeholder communication. Public participation in planning has increased through accessible digital interfaces that make complex planning concepts understandable to non-technical audiences.

International recognition of Helsinki's digital twin reflects its success and innovation. The project has received attention from urban planning and smart city communities worldwide, with Helsinki's approaches being studied and adapted by other cities. The combination of technical excellence, open data principles, and citizen engagement has created a model that balances innovation with public interest and democratic participation.

Data management challenges associated with large-scale 3D models necessitated robust storage and processing systems. Helsinki addressed this through cloud-based infrastructure and distributed computing approaches that ensure reliable performance. Integration with existing city systems required careful planning and phased implementation to minimize disruptions to ongoing operations.

Boston's Digital Twin

Boston's digital twin initiative represents a sophisticated approach to urban planning and climate resilience that has established the city as a leader in evidence-based urban management. The project emerged from Boston's long-standing commitment to data-driven planning and the recognition that complex urban challenges require comprehensive analytical tools for effective decision-making.

Boston's digital twin effort took shape after early discussions in the mid-2000s about using the city's growing data assets to support 3D planning and public engagement. By 2005, planners and GIS teams were cataloging core datasets: water and sewer networks, transportation assets, tax parcels, building footprints, and zoning layers and exploring how a unified 3D environment could improve review of major projects and neighborhood plans. The Boston Planning & Development Agency (BPDA) and the city's GIS group began standardizing data, defining update cycles, and testing 3D scenes for shadow, view, and massing studies. These steps laid the groundwork for a citywide model that could serve both expert users and the public.

In 2015, the city formalized this vision by building an operational 3D city model and associated workflows. The team integrated current building stock, transportation infrastructure, vegetation, daylight and shadow analysis, and points of interest. Proposed and under-construction developments were added with effective dates, creating a time-aware view that tracks Boston's growth. A public version of the model was released in 2018, giving residents and developers a common reference for project review and community meetings. Figure 3.4 shows a GIS city-model-guided development scenario near Boston Common.

Technically, Boston's digital twin is anchored in advanced 3D GIS. It combines authoritative base layers (parcels, utilities where permissible, roads, transit, and open space) with detailed building geometry and attributes. The platform supports:

- Massing, daylight, and shadow tests across seasons and times of day.
- Visibility and view-corridor checks for historic and sensitive areas.
- Evaluation of proposed projects against zoning envelopes and design guidelines.
- Scenario comparisons that show cumulative effects of multiple developments.

This combination of curated data, regular updates, and time-enabled 3D views turned the model into a practical planning tool. It speeds internal review, provides consistent visuals for public dialogue, and reduces rework by letting teams detect conflicts early[3].

Boston's digital twin integrates data from multiple city departments and external sources to create a comprehensive urban information system. The platform incorporates data from the city's Assessing Department, the Boston Planning and Development Agency's Article 80 development review process, and Climate Ready Boston resilience planning initiatives. This integration enables cross-departmental coordination and supports holistic approaches to urban management that consider interactions between different city systems.

FIGURE 3.4 A GIS city-model-guided development near Boston Common, taken from Esri.

The platform utilizes Esri's ArcGIS Urban technology to provide Web-based access to 3D city models and analytical capabilities. This cloud-based approach ensures broad accessibility across different devices and user groups while supporting collaborative planning processes. The system provides both quantitative analysis tools for detailed measurements and qualitative visualization capabilities for stakeholder communication and public engagement.

Boston's digital twin applications focus particularly on development review and urban planning processes where the platform provides substantial value for city officials, developers, and citizens. The most prominent application involves shadow analysis for proposed developments, particularly in relation to Boston Common and the Public Garden. Massachusetts state law, specifically the Boston Common Shadow Law, restricts new building shadows on these historic public spaces, creating specific analytical requirements for development review.

The digital twin enables comprehensive shadow analysis that evaluates proposed developments' impacts on public spaces throughout different seasons and times of day. Quantitative assessments provide detailed measurements of shadow duration and coverage, while qualitative visualizations enable stakeholders to understand shadow impacts intuitively. This analytical

---

3 Cote, P. B., & Bennett, C. (2023). A city-wide 3D model for Boston, MA, USA. In L. Wan et al. (Eds.), Digital twins for smart cities: Conceptualisation, challenges and practices (Chapter 5.2). Emerald Publishing Limited.

capability supports compliance with shadow protection laws while enabling informed decision-making about development proposals.

Urban heat island analysis represents another significant application where Boston's digital twin supports climate resilience planning. The platform can integrate temperature data with building information, surface materials, and vegetation coverage to identify areas experiencing elevated temperatures. This analysis informs strategies for green infrastructure development, building design requirements, and urban cooling initiatives that improve community resilience to climate change.

Climate change adaptation planning utilizes Boston's digital twin to evaluate sea level rise impacts and flood risks throughout the city. The platform integrates climate projections with detailed topographical and infrastructure data to model potential flooding scenarios. This capability supports development of flood protection measures, infrastructure upgrades, and land use planning strategies that account for changing climate conditions.

Development impact assessment benefits from the digital twin's ability to visualize proposed projects within existing urban contexts. Planners can evaluate how new developments affect neighborhood character, infrastructure capacity, transportation patterns, and public space access. This comprehensive impact analysis supports more informed development decisions and improves coordination between development projects and city infrastructure planning.

Public engagement has been enhanced through Boston's digital twin by providing accessible visualizations that help citizens understand complex planning concepts. The platform enables virtual exploration of proposed developments and their impacts, supporting meaningful public participation in planning processes. This engagement capability builds community trust and ensures that development decisions reflect community priorities and concerns.

The Boston digital twin has achieved several significant outcomes that demonstrate its value for urban planning and management. Development review processes have become more efficient through automated analysis capabilities and improved stakeholder communication. The platform enables rapid assessment of development proposals against various criteria including shadow impacts, zoning compliance, and infrastructure compatibility, reducing review timelines while maintaining thorough analysis.

Enhanced collaboration between city departments has resulted from shared access to comprehensive urban data and analysis tools. The digital twin provides a common platform where different departments can coordinate their activities and understand the implications of their decisions for other city systems. This coordination improves overall city management effectiveness and reduces conflicts between different municipal initiatives.

Evidence-based policy development has been supported through the digital twin's analytical capabilities that provide data-driven insights for policy decisions. Climate resilience planning, zoning regulations, and development policies can be informed by comprehensive analysis of their potential impacts and effectiveness. This analytical foundation improves policy quality and supports more confident decision-making by city officials.

International recognition of Boston's digital twin reflects its success and innovation in urban planning technology. The project received the Special Achievement in GIS Award at the 2018 Esri User Conference and has been presented at national planning conferences as a model for other cities. This recognition has positioned Boston as a leader in digital twin technology and attracted interest from other municipalities seeking to implement similar capabilities.

Boston's digital twin implementation has encountered several challenges that provide valuable lessons for other cities. Maintaining accuracy and currency of 3D models requires ongoing investment in data collection and processing capabilities. The city has addressed this through partnerships with technology providers and development of automated data update processes that ensure the digital twin reflects current conditions.

Ensuring user accessibility across different technical skill levels has required careful interface design and training programs. The city has developed multiple access points for the digital twin, including professional-grade analytical tools for planners and user-friendly visualization interfaces for public engagement. This multi-tiered approach ensures that the digital twin serves diverse user needs effectively.

Integration with existing city systems and processes required careful planning to minimize disruptions while maximizing benefits. Boston has pursued gradual integration approaches that build on existing data systems and workflows rather than requiring complete replacement of established processes. This incremental strategy has reduced implementation risks while ensuring that the digital twin adds value to existing city operations.

TECHNOLOGIES USED IN DIGITAL TWIN CITIES

Digital twin cities represent a convergence of multiple advanced technologies that work together to create comprehensive virtual replicas of urban environments. The successful implementation of digital twin cities relies on sophisticated technological infrastructure that enables data capture, processing, visualization, and interaction. These technologies form the foundation of smart city initiatives and provide the foundation for data-driven urban management and planning. Figure 3.5 illustrates the key building blocks that enable a city digital twin—from sensing and compute to visualization and operational response.

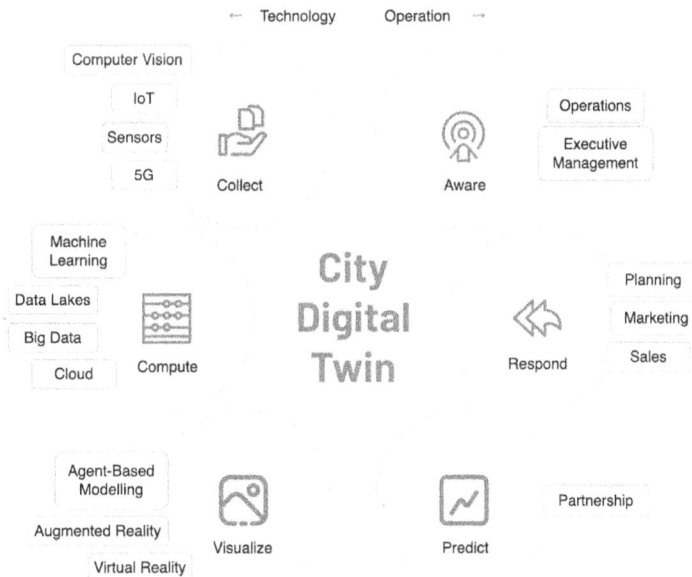

FIGURE 3.5 Technologies used in digital twin cities.

Before diving into each technology in detail, it helps to see how they connect as one continuous loop. On the left side of Figure 3.5 are the core enablers: IoT, cloud, 5G, AI, and big data platforms that collect and compute large volumes of city information. At the center is the city digital twin, which turns raw streams into structured knowledge through models, semantics, and context. On the right are operational functions: awareness, response, planning, and executive decision-making that use insights to guide day-to-day services and long-term investments.

The diagram also highlights two cross-cutting capabilities. First, visualization tools, including AR/VR and 3D mapping, allow experts and the public to explore scenarios, understand trade-offs, and validate plans. Second, partnerships cross agencies, utilities, academia, and industry keep the ecosystem open and interoperable so that new data sources and applications can plug in without rebuilding the platform.

Read the image as a workflow rather than a parts list:

- Collect: Sensors, connected assets, and operational systems stream events and measurements into the platform.
- Compute: Cloud and edge resources process data in real time, apply AI models, and maintain trustworthy histories.
- Visualize: 3D city models and immersive tools provide a shared view for analysis and engagement.
- Predict: Analytics and simulations forecast demand, risk, and performance across domains.
- Aware and Respond: Operations centers use alerts and playbooks to act, while planners and executives use evidence to set policy and allocate budgets.

The following subchapters unpack each area: data collection, communications, compute and storage, analytics and AI, visualization and interaction, and integration and governance showing how they come together to deliver a reliable, scalable city digital twin.

3D Modeling and Visualization Technologies

3D modeling and visualization technologies form the visual and spatial foundation of digital twin cities, providing detailed representations of urban environments that serve as the basis for all subsequent analysis and simulation activities. These technologies enable the creation of accurate, immersive, and interactive models that capture the complex geometry and spatial relationships within urban systems.

LiDAR Technology

Light Detection and Ranging (LiDAR) is a high-precision method for building detailed 3D views of a city. A LiDAR unit emits laser pulses and records how long each pulse takes to return after striking a surface. By combining the travel time with the speed of light and the exact position and orientation of the sensor, the system computes a distance for every pulse. Millions of these measurements form a "point cloud" that captures the shape of buildings, roads, trees, utilities, and ground surfaces.

Airborne LiDAR typically reaches horizontal and vertical accuracy on the order of 10 cm when flown at appropriate altitude with proper calibration and ground control. In practical terms, this means that the position of a measured point in the resulting dataset is expected to be within about 0.1 m of its true location. Such precision is sufficient for city-scale digital twins that need reliable roof forms, façade planes, curb lines, and terrain models for simulations and permitting.

A refined LiDAR workflow includes:

- Sensor calibration and boresight alignment to remove systematic bias.
- Integration with GNSS and inertial measurement units (IMU) to track sensor position and attitude during flight or drive.
- Use of ground control points and quality checks to validate accuracy.
- Classification of points (ground, building, vegetation, water, utilities) and derivation of products such as digital terrain models (DTM), digital surface models (DSM), and building footprints.
- Fusion with imagery and BIM/GIS layers to add semantics and textures, improving both analysis and visualization.

For urban twins, LiDAR's advantages are clear: consistent coverage, high fidelity in height and form, and the ability to penetrate gaps in vegetation to recover true ground. Regular re-flights keep the model current as construction and street changes occur, preventing geometry drift over time.

FIGURE 3.6 LiDAR based aerial imaging to track construction progress.

Integration of LiDAR data with other data sources enhances the overall quality and completeness of digital twin models. When combined with photogrammetric imagery, LiDAR provides both accurate geometric information and realistic visual textures, creating comprehensive digital representations that support both analytical and visualization applications. The technology enables automated feature extraction processes that can identify and classify urban elements such as buildings, roads, trees, and other infrastructure components.

Photogrammetry

Photogrammetry technology enables the creation of detailed 3D models from overlapping photographs, providing an efficient and cost-effective method for generating realistic digital representations of urban environments. Modern photogrammetric techniques utilize sophisticated algorithms to extract three-dimensional information from multiple perspective views, creating dense point clouds and textured 3D models that capture both geometric and visual characteristics of urban features.

Aerial photogrammetry, conducted using aircraft or unmanned aerial vehicles, provides comprehensive coverage of urban areas while maintaining high resolution and detail. The technology can capture fine-scale features and textures that complement the geometric precision provided by LiDAR systems. When combined with advanced image processing algorithms, photogrammetry generates photorealistic 3D models that enable intuitive visualization and public engagement applications.

The integration of photogrammetry with machine learning techniques enhances automated feature extraction and classification capabilities. Modern systems can automatically identify and categorize urban elements such as buildings, roads, vegetation, and water bodies from photogrammetric imagery. This automated processing capability significantly reduces the time and cost associated with creating and updating comprehensive 3D city models.

Building Information Modeling

Building Information Modeling (BIM) technology provides detailed digital representations of individual buildings that include comprehensive geometric, material, and operational information. BIM models contain rich semantic data about building components, systems, and properties, enabling sophisticated analysis of energy performance, structural integrity, and maintenance requirements. When integrated into city-scale digital twins, BIM data provides building-level detail that supports precise simulation and optimization of urban systems.

The semantic richness of BIM data enables advanced analytics that consider building characteristics, usage patterns, and performance metrics. Energy efficiency analysis, structural assessment, and maintenance planning applications benefit from the detailed information contained within BIM models. Modern BIM systems support lifecycle management of building assets, tracking changes and updates throughout the operational life of structures.

Integration challenges arise when connecting BIM data with city-scale models due to differences in data formats, coordinate systems, and levels of detail. However, successful integration provides powerful capabilities for multi-scale analysis that spans from individual building components to city-wide systems. Standardized data exchange formats and interoperability protocols facilitate the incorporation of BIM data into broader digital twin platforms.

Geographic Information Systems

Geographic Information Systems (GIS) provide the spatial framework for organizing and analyzing diverse urban data within digital twin platforms. GIS technology manages geospatial data layers that include administrative boundaries, land use classifications, transportation networks, utility systems, and environmental features. The spatial analysis capabilities of GIS enable complex queries and modeling operations that consider geographic relationships and spatial patterns within urban environments.

Modern GIS platforms support three-dimensional data management and visualization capabilities that complement traditional two-dimensional mapping functions. Advanced spatial analysis tools enable sophisticated modeling of urban processes such as traffic flow, pollutant dispersion, and infrastructure capacity analysis. The integration of GIS with real-time data streams creates dynamic mapping capabilities that support operational monitoring and management of urban systems.

Web-based GIS platforms enable broad accessibility and collaborative use of spatial data within digital twin systems. Cloud-based GIS services provide scalable infrastructure for managing large urban datasets while supporting diverse user communities including city officials, planners, researchers, and citizens. APIs and web services facilitate integration with other urban management systems and third-party applications.

Game Engines and Real-time Rendering

Game engine technologies such as Unity and Unreal Engine provide advanced real-time 3D visualization capabilities that enable immersive interaction with digital twin models. These platforms offer sophisticated rendering engines capable of displaying complex urban scenes with realistic lighting, shadows, materials, and atmospheric effects. The real-time capabilities enable interactive exploration and manipulation of 3D city models, supporting planning and design applications.

Advanced rendering techniques, including ray tracing, global illumination, and physically-based materials, create photorealistic visualizations that enhance understanding and communication of urban designs. These visual capabilities support public engagement activities where citizens can explore proposed developments and provide feedback based on realistic representations of future urban conditions.

Game engines provide robust frameworks for implementing interactive applications that combine 3D visualization with data integration and analysis capabilities. Virtual reality and augmented reality applications built using game engines enable immersive experiences that place users within digital twin environments. These platforms support the development of collaborative tools that enable multiple users to explore and modify urban designs simultaneously.

Web-based 3D Visualization

Web-based 3D visualization technologies enable broad accessibility to digital twin models through standard Web browsers, eliminating the need for specialized software installations. Technologies such as WebGL, CesiumJS, and Three.js provide powerful 3D rendering capabilities that operate within Web browser environments. These platforms support the display of complex urban geometries, satellite imagery, and real-time data overlays within accessible web applications.

Cloud-based rendering services enhance the performance and accessibility of Web-based 3D visualization by offloading computational requirements to remote servers. This approach enables high-quality visualization experiences on diverse devices including smartphones, tablets, and desktop computers. Progressive loading techniques ensure responsive performance even when accessing large-scale urban models over network connections.

Integration with Web-based data services enables the dynamic visualization of real-time urban data within 3D city models. APIs and Web services provide mechanisms for incorporating sensor data, traffic information, environmental conditions, and other dynamic urban information into interactive visualizations. This integration creates living digital twins that reflect current urban conditions and enable real-time monitoring and analysis.

IoT and Sensor Technologies

Internet of Things and sensor technologies provide the real-time data streams that create digital twin cities, enabling dynamic modeling and responsive management of urban systems. These technologies create comprehensive sensing networks that monitor diverse aspects of urban life, from environmental conditions to infrastructure performance and human activities.

Environmental Sensors

Environmental sensing systems monitor air quality, temperature, humidity, noise levels, and other environmental parameters that affect urban livability and public health. Advanced sensor networks deploy monitoring stations throughout urban areas to capture spatial and temporal variations in environmental conditions. These systems provide continuous data streams that enable real-time assessment of environmental quality and support evidence-based policy making.

Air quality monitoring represents a critical application of IoT sensors, which track pollutants including particulate matter, nitrogen dioxide, ozone, and carbon monoxide. Modern sensor technologies provide cost-effective alternatives to traditional monitoring stations while maintaining acceptable accuracy levels for urban management applications. Dense networks of air quality sensors enable fine-scale mapping of pollution patterns and identification of emission sources.

Noise pollution monitoring utilizes acoustic sensors to measure sound levels and identify sources of urban noise. These systems support enforcement of noise regulations and provide data for urban planning decisions that consider acoustic comfort. Advanced acoustic monitoring systems can automatically classify sound sources and distinguish between traffic noise, construction activities, and other urban sound sources.

Traffic and Mobility Sensors

Traffic monitoring systems utilize diverse sensor technologies to capture vehicle movement, pedestrian flow, and transportation system performance throughout urban areas. These systems provide real-time data about traffic conditions, congestion patterns, and modal usage that support dynamic traffic management and transportation planning applications.

LiDAR and computer vision technologies enable accurate vehicle counting and classification while providing detailed information about traffic flow characteristics. Advanced traffic sensors can distinguish between different vehicle types, measure speeds and spacing, and detect traffic incidents automatically. This information supports adaptive traffic signal control and dynamic route guidance systems that optimize traffic flow in real-time.

Parking sensors monitor occupancy levels in parking facilities and on-street parking spaces, providing real-time information to drivers while supporting parking management strategies. Smart parking systems reduce the time spent searching for parking spaces, thereby decreasing traffic congestion and vehicle emissions. Mobile applications provide drivers with real-time parking availability information and enable reservation and payment services.

Smart Meters and Utility Monitoring

Smart metering systems provide detailed monitoring of energy and water consumption at building and district levels, enabling precise tracking of resource utilization patterns. These systems support demand response programs, leak detection, and energy efficiency initiatives that optimize urban resource management. Advanced analytics applied to smart meter data can identify consumption anomalies, predict demand patterns, and optimize utility system operations.

Smart water meters enable detection of leaks and water waste while providing consumers with detailed usage information that promotes conservation. Real-time monitoring capabilities support rapid response to system failures and enable proactive maintenance strategies that reduce service disruptions. Integration with weather data and irrigation systems enables optimized water management that considers local conditions and demand patterns.

Energy monitoring extends beyond electricity to include gas, heating, and cooling systems that provide comprehensive views of building energy performance. Smart grid integration enables bidirectional energy flows that support distributed renewable energy generation and energy storage systems. These capabilities facilitate the transition to sustainable energy systems while maintaining grid stability and reliability.

Computer Vision and Video Analytics

Computer vision technologies enable automated analysis of video streams from security cameras and traffic monitoring systems throughout urban areas. Advanced image processing algorithms can automatically detect incidents, count pedestrians and vehicles, monitor crowd densities, and assess infrastructure conditions. These capabilities provide cost-effective alternatives to human monitoring while enabling comprehensive coverage of urban areas.

Crowd monitoring applications utilize computer vision to assess pedestrian densities and flow patterns in public spaces, supporting event management and public safety operations. These systems can detect unusual crowd behaviors and potential safety hazards while providing data for optimizing public space designs and managing large events.

Infrastructure monitoring applications use computer vision to assess the condition of roads, bridges, and buildings from imagery captured by vehicles, drones, or fixed cameras. Automated defect detection algorithms can identify potholes, cracks, and other maintenance issues while enabling systematic tracking of infrastructure conditions over time. This information supports proactive maintenance strategies that extend asset lifecycles and reduce costs.

Wireless Communication Technologies

Advanced wireless communication systems including 5G, LoRaWAN, and other low-power wide-area networks enable efficient data transmission from distributed sensor networks. These technologies support massive deployment of IoT devices while providing reliable connectivity for mission-critical urban applications. Low-power communication protocols extend battery life for wireless sensors while enabling cost-effective deployment across large urban areas.

5G networks provide high-bandwidth, low-latency connectivity that supports real-time applications including autonomous vehicles, augmented reality, and remote control of urban systems. Edge computing capabilities integrated with 5G networks enable local processing of sensor data, reducing latency and bandwidth requirements while supporting responsive urban applications.

Mesh networking technologies enable resilient communication systems that maintain connectivity even when individual network components fail. These systems support emergency communications and ensure continuity of critical urban services during disasters or system failures. Self-healing network capabilities automatically route communications around failed components while maintaining system performance.

Data Integration and Management Technologies

Effective data integration and management are crucial for handling the large volumes of diverse data in digital twin cities. They create the foundation for digital twin cities, handling the massive volumes of diverse data generated by urban sensors, systems, and activities. These technologies ensure that data from multiple sources can be effectively combined, processed, and utilized to support urban decision-making and optimization.

Big Data Platforms

Big data platforms provide the foundational infrastructure for managing the massive volumes of heterogeneous data generated by urban systems. Modern cities generate data from thousands of sensors, millions of citizens, and numerous municipal systems, creating data management challenges that require scalable, distributed computing architectures. Apache Hadoop and Apache Spark are two big data platforms that enable distributed storage and processing of large-scale urban datasets.

These platforms support diverse data types including structured data from databases, semi-structured data from sensors, and unstructured data from social media and multimedia sources. Advanced data processing frameworks enable complex analytics operations including pattern recognition, predictive modeling, and optimization algorithms that operate across massive datasets. Stream processing capabilities handle real-time data ingestion and processing requirements for responsive urban applications.

The integration of big data platforms with cloud computing services provides scalable infrastructure that can grow with urban data requirements. Elastic computing resources enable cities to handle peak data loads during emergencies or special events while maintaining cost-effective operations during normal conditions. Distributed storage systems provide fault tolerance and high availability that ensure critical urban data remains accessible.

Cloud Computing Platforms

Cloud platforms are the backbone of city-scale digital twins. They supply elastic compute, durable storage, high-throughput networking, managed analytics, and secure application hosting without the need for large capital expenditure. Major providers offer building blocks for ingesting sensor streams, storing petabytes of geospatial and time-series data, training AI models, and serving interactive 3D experiences for planners and residents. This elasticity is essential because city workloads are bursty—traffic events, storms, and large public gatherings can multiply data volume and processing needs within minutes.

- Infrastructure as a Service (IaaS). Virtual machines, containers, GPUs, and high-performance disks can be scaled up or down on demand. This is useful for LiDAR processing, large simulation runs and backfills of historical telemetry. Policy-driven autoscaling keeps costs aligned with actual use while meeting service-level objectives.

- Platform as a Service (PaaS). Managed services for streaming, time-series databases, geo-spatial processing, and machine learning reduce operational burden. Pre-built pipelines accelerate common tasks such as ingesting IoT data, running ETL on geospatial layers, training demand-forecasting models, and exposing APIs for agency systems.
- Software as a Service (SaaS). Ready-to-use applications—asset management, work-order systems, traffic analytics dashboards, or permitting portals—can plug into the twin via APIs. SaaS shortens time-to-value for departments that need outcomes rather than bespoke engineering.
- Multi-cloud and hybrid patterns. Cities often combine more than one cloud with on-premises sites. Reasons include proximity to legacy systems, data-sovereignty rules, and the need for deterministic latency for operational control. A hybrid approach lets sensitive datasets remain on city infrastructure while less sensitive workloads (e.g., public 3D visualization) run in the public cloud.
- Edge integration. Compute placed at intersections, stations, depots, plants, and district hubs filters, aggregates, and analyzes data close to the source. This reduces backhaul traffic and supports low-latency actions such as adaptive signals, sub-second grid controls, and safety alerts. Cloud services coordinate model training, policy distribution, and fleet-wide monitoring, while the edge executes real-time inference.

Managing vendor lock-in and service retirement
Cloud benefits come with risks that must be managed explicitly:

- Lock-in risks. Proprietary data formats, closed APIs, and provider-specific services can make migration costly. Mitigations:
  - Use open standards and portable formats for core assets: CityGML/IFC for 3D/built environment, OGC APIs for geospatial, MQTT/AMQP/HTTP for device messaging, and Apache Parquet/ORC for analytical storage.
  - Build to cloud-agnostic abstractions. Favor containers and Kubernetes over provider-specific runtimes; use infrastructure-as-code (e.g., Terraform) with modules that target multiple providers.
  - Separate data from compute. Keep authoritative datasets in storage systems that support standard interfaces and lifecycle policies independent of specific analytics engines.
  - Contractual safeguards. Include exit clauses, data-egress support, and migration assistance in master agreements.
- Service and sensor retirement. Providers may deprecate managed services or devices over time, and hardware vendors may discontinue sensors or gateways.
  - Adopt a tiered dependency policy. Core capabilities (identity, messaging, storage) should rely on widely supported services with long roadmaps; experimental features stay at the edge of the architecture.
  - Design for substitution. Encapsulate vendor services behind internal APIs so replacements can be swapped with minimal downstream change. Maintain compatibility test suites.
  - Lifecycle planning. Track end-of-support dates for cloud services and field hardware. Budget for rolling upgrades and phased sensor replacements; prefer vendors that commit to long-term firmware and security updates.

- Digital twin continuity. Keep model schemas, metadata catalogs, and event contracts under city control so upstream or downstream changes do not break the operational twin.

Cost, performance, and governance considerations

- FinOps discipline. Monitor consumption by domain (traffic, water, energy), set budgets and alerts, and right-size resources. Use reserved or savings plans for steady workloads and on-demand for bursts.
- Data governance. Enforce classification, retention, and residency policies across clouds. Apply role-based access control, attribute-based policies, and differential views for public portals.
- Reliability and resilience. Distribute critical components across regions and zones; practice disaster recovery with automated backups and periodic restore drills. For 24/7 operations centers, choose architectures that fail over without manual intervention.
- Observability. End-to-end logging, metrics, and traces across edge, network, and cloud layers are mandatory for troubleshooting and compliance audits.

Taken together, cloud, hybrid, and edge resources provide the scale and reliability required for a living city model. A deliberate strategy for portability, lifecycle management, and governance ensures that the digital twin remains sustainable even as vendors, services, and devices change.

Data Lakes and Storage Systems

Data lake architectures provide flexible storage systems that can accommodate diverse urban data types without requiring predefined schemas or structures. Unlike traditional databases that require structured data formats, data lakes can store raw sensor data, images, videos, text documents, and other unstructured information in their native formats. This flexibility enables cities to collect and store data first and determine analysis requirements later.

Modern data lake implementations provide governance and security capabilities that ensure data quality and protect sensitive urban information. Data cataloging systems enable users to discover and understand available datasets while maintaining metadata that describes data sources, quality, and usage restrictions. Version control and lineage tracking capabilities support reproducible analysis and ensure data integrity throughout processing pipelines.

Integration with analytics platforms enables direct analysis of data stored in data lakes without requiring extensive data transformation processes. Machine learning frameworks can access diverse datasets directly from data lakes, enabling advanced analytics that consider multiple data sources simultaneously. This capability supports sophisticated urban modeling that incorporates sensor data, social media information, economic indicators, and other diverse data sources.

ETL and Data Integration Tools

Extract, transform, and load (ETL) processes provide a disciplined way to bring data from many city systems into one platform where it can be analyzed together. ETL connects to source systems, standardizes formats and units, harmonizes schemas, and loads the results into trusted stores used by the digital twin. This is the backbone that lets information from utilities, transportation, permitting, environment, public safety, and finance work as one model.

Beyond batch jobs, today's integration stacks also support streaming and near–real-time pipelines. Event ingestion services, stream processors, and change data capture (CDC) track inserts, updates, and deletes in source databases and publish only the deltas. The twin is then refreshed continuously while preserving a history of versions for audits, trend analysis, and scenario testing. This combination, incremental updates plus controlled historical snapshots—keeps the twin both current and traceable.

Quality is enforced throughout the pipeline. Data quality rules check completeness, valid ranges, coordinate systems, timestamps, and referential integrity. Profiling highlights anomalies such as duplicate asset IDs or out-of-order sensor readings. Cleansing steps fix common issues (unit conversion, trimming text, deduplication), while enrichment adds context such as spatial joins to parcels, networks, and districts. Failed records are quarantined to a review queue with clear diagnostics, so stewards can correct sources rather than masking problems downstream.

A robust integration layer for city digital twins typically includes:

- Connectors to relational databases, time-series stores, message buses, files, and APIs from city and partner systems.
- Schema management and metadata catalogs that define authoritative sources, ownership, and refresh schedules.
- Idempotent, versioned pipelines that support reprocessing without creating duplicates.
- Master data and entity resolution to reconcile the same asset across departments (e.g., a road segment, pipe, or building).
- Security controls: row/column masking, role-based access, and lineage so every metric can be traced to its origin.

With these practices, ETL and streaming integration keep the digital twin reliable, timely, and ready for operational use, whether for live dashboards, predictive models, or regulatory reporting.

Application Programming Interface Management and Integration Platforms

Application programming interface (API) management platforms provide standardized mechanisms for accessing and sharing urban data across different systems and applications. APIs enable digital twin platforms to integrate with existing municipal systems, third-party applications, and external data sources while maintaining security and access control. Well-designed API architectures support ecosystem development where multiple organizations can build applications that utilize urban data.

API gateways provide security, authentication, and rate limiting capabilities that protect urban data while enabling authorized access. These systems log API usage and monitor performance while providing analytics about data utilization patterns. API versioning capabilities ensure backward compatibility while enabling continuous improvement of data services.

Microservices architectures built around APIs enable modular development of digital twin capabilities that can be independently updated and scaled. This approach supports incremental implementation of digital twin features while enabling integration with diverse urban systems. Container-based deployment platforms facilitate the management and scaling of microservices across distributed computing infrastructure.

Blockchain and Distributed Ledger Technologies

Blockchain technologies provide secure and transparent mechanisms for managing urban data sharing and transactions. Distributed ledger systems enable trusted data exchange between different municipal departments and external organizations without requiring centralized control authorities. Smart contracts automate data sharing agreements and ensure compliance with privacy and security requirements.

Blockchain-based identity management systems provide secure authentication for urban data access while protecting citizen privacy. These systems enable fine-grained access control that ensures individuals and organizations can only access data they are authorized to use. Audit trails maintained on blockchain systems provide transparency about data usage while supporting regulatory compliance requirements.

Token-based incentive systems built on blockchain platforms can encourage citizen participation in urban data collection and validation activities. These systems reward individuals for contributing sensor data, reporting infrastructure issues, or participating in urban planning processes. Decentralized governance mechanisms enable stakeholder participation in decisions about urban data management and usage policies.

Simulation and Analytics Technologies

Advanced simulation and analytics technologies enable digital twin cities to model complex urban processes, predict future conditions, and optimize system performance. These technologies transform raw urban data into actionable insights that support evidence-based decision-making and proactive urban management.

Agent-Based Modeling

Agent-based modeling represents a powerful simulation approach that models urban systems by simulating the behavior and interactions of individual entities such as people, vehicles, and businesses. These models capture the complex dynamics that emerge from numerous individual decisions and interactions, providing insights into urban phenomena that cannot be understood through traditional aggregate modeling approaches.

Urban mobility applications utilize agent-based models to simulate individual travel decisions and their cumulative effects on transportation system performance. These models consider factors such as departure times, route choices, mode preferences, and destination selection while accounting for interactions between travelers through congestion and competition for resources. Advanced agent-based transportation models can evaluate the impacts of new infrastructure, policy changes, and emerging technologies such as autonomous vehicles.

Social and economic applications of agent-based modeling examine how individual decisions about housing, employment, and consumption create neighborhood-level patterns and city-wide trends. These models consider factors such as income, preferences, social networks, and market dynamics while tracking how individual choices aggregate to create urban development patterns. Such models support evaluation of housing policies, economic development strategies, and social equity initiatives.

Energy system applications employ agent-based models to simulate the behavior of energy consumers, producers, and grid operators in urban energy systems. These models consider individual decisions about energy consumption, renewable energy adoption, and demand response participation while modeling their combined effects on grid performance and energy costs. The models support evaluation of energy policies, grid modernization strategies, and renewable energy integration scenarios.

Machine Learning and Artificial Intelligence

Machine learning technologies enable digital twin cities to automatically discover patterns in urban data, make predictions about future conditions, and optimize system performance. These technologies process massive datasets generated by urban sensors and systems to extract insights that would be impossible to identify through traditional analytical methods.

Predictive analytics applications utilize machine learning algorithms to forecast urban conditions such as traffic congestion, energy demand, air quality, and infrastructure failures. These models learn from historical data patterns while incorporating real-time information to provide accurate short-term and long-term predictions. Predictive capabilities enable proactive management strategies that address problems before they become critical.

Pattern recognition systems identify anomalies and trends in urban data that indicate potential issues or opportunities for improvement. Machine learning algorithms can detect unusual patterns in energy consumption that indicate equipment failures, identify traffic flow anomalies that suggest incidents, and recognize environmental conditions that pose health risks. Automated anomaly detection enables rapid response to urban problems while reducing the burden on human operators.

Optimization applications utilize machine learning to find optimal solutions for complex urban management problems. These systems can optimize traffic signal timing, resource allocation, service scheduling, and infrastructure planning while considering multiple objectives and constraints. Reinforcement learning algorithms enable systems to continuously improve their performance through interaction with urban environments.

Classification and clustering algorithms organize urban data into meaningful categories that support planning and management decisions. These techniques can classify neighborhoods based on development patterns, categorize infrastructure based on condition assessments, and cluster citizens based on service needs. Machine learning-enabled classification supports targeted interventions and resource allocation strategies.

Computational Fluid Dynamics

Computational fluid dynamics provides sophisticated simulation capabilities for modeling air flow, pollutant dispersion, and thermal conditions within urban environments. CFD simulations support urban planning decisions by predicting how building designs, street layouts, and infrastructure modifications will affect local climate conditions and air quality.

Urban wind modeling applications utilize CFD to assess how buildings and infrastructure affect wind patterns within cities. These simulations guide building design decisions that optimize natural ventilation while avoiding wind-related comfort problems in public spaces. Wind modeling supports evaluation of renewable energy potential for urban wind generation systems and helps identify optimal locations for wind-sensitive infrastructure.

Air quality modeling integrates CFD with emission inventories and meteorological data to simulate pollutant concentrations throughout urban areas. These models predict how traffic patterns, industrial activities, and weather conditions combine to create air quality conditions in different neighborhoods. CFD-based air quality models support policy evaluation and emission reduction strategies while identifying areas where additional monitoring or interventions may be needed.

Urban heat island analysis utilizes CFD to model thermal conditions and identify strategies for reducing urban temperatures. These simulations evaluate how different surface materials, vegetation patterns, and building designs affect local temperature conditions. Heat modeling supports climate adaptation planning and guides urban design decisions that improve thermal comfort while reducing energy consumption for cooling.

Digital Physics Engines

Digital physics engines provide realistic simulation of physical processes within urban environments, enabling accurate modeling of water flow, structural dynamics, and mechanical systems. These simulation capabilities support infrastructure planning, emergency preparedness, and operational optimization by providing detailed understanding of physical system behavior.

Flood modeling applications utilize physics engines to simulate water flow through urban drainage systems and across urban surfaces during storm events. These simulations predict flood risks and evaluate the effectiveness of different stormwater management strategies. Physics-based flood models support infrastructure design decisions and emergency response planning while identifying areas that require improved drainage capacity.

FIGURE 3.7 Digital Twin for Flood simulation and modeling in Jakarta.

Structural analysis applications employ physics engines to simulate the performance of buildings and infrastructure under various loading conditions. These simulations assess structural integrity, identify potential failure modes, and optimize maintenance schedules. Physics-based structural models support safety assessments and guide decisions about infrastructure upgrades and replacements.

Traffic flow simulation utilizes physics engines to model vehicle dynamics and traffic flow phenomena with high fidelity. These models consider factors such as acceleration, braking, lane changing, and collision avoidance while simulating realistic traffic behavior. Physics-based traffic models support evaluation of traffic management strategies and infrastructure designs while providing accurate inputs for air quality and noise modeling.

Real-time Analytics Platforms

Real-time analytics platforms process streaming data from urban sensors and systems to provide immediate insights that support operational decision-making. These systems handle high-velocity data streams while maintaining low latency requirements for time-critical applications such as emergency response and traffic management.

Stream processing frameworks including Apache Kafka, Apache Storm, and Apache Flink enable real-time analysis of sensor data as it arrives from urban monitoring systems. These platforms support complex event processing that can detect patterns and correlations across multiple data streams simultaneously. Real-time analytics enable immediate response to urban conditions while providing continuous monitoring of system performance.

Dashboard and visualization systems present real-time analytics results in formats that support rapid decision-making by urban operators. Interactive dashboards provide customizable views of urban conditions while alerting systems notify operators about critical situations that require immediate attention. Mobile-accessible dashboards enable field personnel to access real-time information while responding to urban incidents.

Edge computing integration brings analytics capabilities closer to data sources, enabling low-latency processing of time-critical urban data. Edge analytics platforms can process sensor data locally while sending only summarized information to central systems. This approach reduces network bandwidth requirements while enabling real-time response to local conditions.

Visualization and User Interface Technologies

Advanced visualization and user interface technologies make digital twin cities accessible and useful to diverse stakeholders including city officials, planners, researchers, businesses, and citizens. These technologies translate complex urban data and models into intuitive, interactive experiences that support understanding, collaboration, and decision-making.

Virtual Reality Technologies

Virtual reality (VR) technologies create immersive experiences that enable users to explore and interact with digital twin cities in three-dimensional environments. VR applications show users virtual representations of urban spaces where they can "walk" through streets, "enter" buildings, and observe urban systems from perspectives that would be impossible in the physical world.

Urban planning applications utilize VR to enable stakeholders to experience proposed developments before construction begins. Planners can create virtual walkthroughs of new neighborhoods, transportation systems, and public spaces that allow citizens to provide informed feedback about design proposals. VR experiences help non-technical stakeholders understand complex planning concepts while enabling more meaningful participation in planning processes.

Training and education applications employ VR to provide realistic simulations of urban environments for emergency responders, maintenance workers, and planning professionals. Virtual reality training enables personnel to practice emergency procedures, learn about infrastructure systems, and develop skills in safe, controlled environments. Educational applications enable students and the public to explore urban systems and understand complex relationships between different city components.

Collaborative design platforms built with VR technology enable multiple stakeholders to work together within shared virtual environments. These platforms support remote collaboration where participants from different locations can meet within virtual urban spaces to discuss projects and make design decisions. Collaborative VR environments enable more inclusive planning processes that engage diverse stakeholders regardless of their physical location.

Research and analysis applications utilize VR to enable immersive exploration of urban data and simulation results. Researchers can visualize complex datasets within three-dimensional urban contexts while manipulating variables and observing their effects in real-time. VR-based analysis tools enable intuitive understanding of urban phenomena while supporting hypothesis generation and testing.

Augmented Reality Technologies

Augmented reality (AR) technologies overlay digital information onto real-world views, enabling users to access urban data and digital twin information while navigating physical urban environments. AR applications enhance understanding of urban systems by providing contextual information that would not be visible to the naked eye.

Infrastructure management applications utilize AR to provide maintenance workers with real-time information about buried utilities, building systems, and equipment specifications. Workers equipped with AR devices can see virtual overlays showing pipe locations, electrical circuits, and maintenance histories while working on physical infrastructure. This capability reduces errors and improves efficiency while enhancing worker safety.

Urban planning applications employ AR to enable visualization of proposed developments within existing urban contexts. Citizens and stakeholders can use AR devices to see how new buildings or infrastructure would appear within their actual neighborhoods. This capability enables more informed public participation in planning processes while reducing misunderstandings about development proposals.

Navigation and wayfinding applications integrate AR with digital twin data to provide enhanced guidance within urban environments. AR applications can display real-time information about public transportation, parking availability, and points of interest while providing context-aware directions. These applications improve urban accessibility while helping visitors and residents navigate complex urban environments more effectively.

Educational and tourism applications utilize AR to provide interactive experiences that enhance understanding of urban history, culture, and systems. AR applications can overlay historical information onto current urban scenes, provide explanations of urban infrastructure, and offer interactive tours of urban attractions. These applications increase public engagement with urban environments while promoting civic education and cultural awareness.

Mixed Reality Platforms

Mixed reality (MR) platforms combine elements of virtual and augmented reality to create hybrid experiences that blend physical and digital urban environments. MR applications enable users to interact with digital twin information while maintaining awareness of their physical surroundings, creating versatile tools for urban planning, management, and education.

Collaborative planning applications utilize mixed reality to enable stakeholders to work together on urban design projects within shared physical and virtual spaces. MR platforms support co-location scenarios where multiple participants can manipulate virtual urban models while discussing projects face-to-face. These applications enhance collaboration while enabling more natural interaction with digital twin information.

Data visualization applications employ mixed reality to present urban data within spatial contexts that enhance understanding and analysis. Users can visualize sensor data, simulation results, and analytical outputs as three-dimensional overlays within physical urban environments. MR visualization enables intuitive understanding of spatial patterns and relationships within urban data while supporting field-based analysis and decision-making.

Training and simulation applications utilize mixed reality to create realistic learning environments that combine physical and virtual urban elements. Emergency responders can practice procedures within physical spaces enhanced with virtual hazards and scenarios. Infrastructure workers can train on virtual equipment overlaid within real maintenance environments, providing safe and cost-effective training opportunities.

Web-based Visualization Platforms

Web-based visualization platforms provide broad accessibility to digital twin information through standard Web browsers, eliminating barriers to access while supporting diverse user communities. These platforms utilize modern Web technologies to deliver sophisticated visualization capabilities without requiring specialized software installations.

Interactive mapping applications built with technologies such as Leaflet, Mapbox, and OpenLayers provide Web-based access to urban data and digital twin models. These platforms support real-time data visualization, layer management, and interactive analysis tools that enable users to explore urban information effectively. Web-based mapping supports broad public access to urban data while enabling collaborative analysis and decision-making.

Dashboard and monitoring applications utilize Web technologies to provide real-time views of urban system performance. These platforms present sensor data, system status, and analytical results in formats that support operational decision-making. Web-based dashboards enable access from diverse devices while supporting role-based customization for different user types.

Citizen engagement platforms employ Web-based visualization to enable public participation in urban planning and governance processes. These platforms provide accessible interfaces for exploring urban data, reviewing planning proposals, and providing feedback on municipal services. Web-based engagement tools reduce barriers to participation while enabling more inclusive urban governance.

Natural Language and Voice Interfaces

Natural language interfaces enable users to interact with digital twin systems using conversational queries and commands, making complex urban data more accessible to non-technical users. These interfaces utilize natural language processing and voice recognition technologies to translate user requests into appropriate system actions and data retrievals.

Voice-activated query systems allow users to request information about urban conditions, system performance, and planning scenarios using spoken commands. These systems can answer questions about traffic conditions, air quality, service availability, and infrastructure status while providing context-appropriate responses. Voice interfaces enable hands-free interaction that supports field operations and accessibility requirements.

Conversational analytics platforms utilize natural language interfaces to enable sophisticated analysis of urban data through natural language queries. Users can request complex analytical operations using everyday language while receiving results in understandable formats. These interfaces make advanced analytics capabilities accessible to broader user communities while reducing the technical expertise required for urban data analysis.

Automated reporting systems employ natural language generation to create readable summaries of urban conditions and system performance. These systems can automatically generate daily reports, emergency notifications, and planning documents that communicate complex information in accessible language. Natural language reporting enables efficient communication of urban information while reducing the burden on human analysts.

Interactive assistance systems provide conversational interfaces that guide users through complex urban data exploration and analysis tasks. These systems can provide step-by-step guidance for using digital twin capabilities while offering contextual help and suggestions. Conversational assistance reduces learning curves for new users while supporting more effective utilization of digital twin capabilities across diverse user communities.

The integration of these diverse visualization and interface technologies creates comprehensive platforms that serve the varied needs of different stakeholders within urban ecosystems. By providing multiple ways to access and interact with digital twin information, these technologies ensure that urban data and insights can be effectively utilized by everyone from technical specialists to everyday citizens, promoting more inclusive and effective urban governance and planning processes.

THE CHALLENGES OF IMPLEMENTING DIGITAL TWINS IN SMART CITIES

The implementation of digital twins in smart cities presents numerous challenges that need to be addressed for successful deployment. Here are some of the primary challenges and strategies to overcome them.

Data Integration and Standardization

A significant challenge in implementing IoT for smart cities is the issue of data being siloed in different departments and systems, often with diverse formats and standards, which hinders successful integration and collaboration.

To overcome this, cities can develop citywide data standards and protocols that enable efficient data sharing across various departments. Implementing data integration platforms capable of handling diverse data formats is essential, along with utilizing ETL processes to standardize data from different sources. Adopting open data standards further enhances interoperability, ensuring that various systems can communicate effectively.

For example, Helsinki's digital twin project successfully introduced a citywide 3D data model standard, which ensured consistency across departments and facilitated smooth data integration, demonstrating the importance of unified standards in smart city initiatives.

Data Quality and Accuracy

Ensuring the accuracy and reliability of data from various sources, including IoT sensors and legacy systems, is a critical challenge in smart city development.

To address this, cities can implement robust data validation and cleaning processes to ensure that data is consistent and trustworthy. Machine learning algorithms can be employed for anomaly detection and continuous improvement of data quality, helping to identify and correct errors in real time.

Establishing data governance frameworks is also essential for maintaining high standards of data quality across the city's systems.

Additionally, regular calibration and maintenance programs for IoT sensors can ensure their ongoing accuracy and performance.

For instance, Singapore's digital twin integrates automated data quality checks and machine learning algorithms to detect and rectify anomalies, demonstrating the effectiveness of these strategies in maintaining reliable data for smart city applications.

Privacy and Security Concerns

Protecting sensitive urban data and ensuring citizen privacy while maintaining the utility of a digital twin is a challenge in smart city projects.

Cities can implement strong encryption and access control measures to safeguard data from unauthorized access. Anonymization and aggregation techniques can be applied to sensitive data to protect individual privacy while still allowing for meaningful analysis.

Additionally, developing clear data usage policies and obtaining the necessary consents from citizens helps ensure transparency and trust.

Regular security audits and penetration testing further enhance data protection by identifying vulnerabilities. For example, Boston's digital twin project implemented a comprehensive data privacy framework that includes data anonymization and strict access controls, demonstrating how privacy can be maintained in smart city initiatives.

Scalability and Performance

Managing the computational demands of processing and analyzing large volumes of urban data in real-time is a significant challenge for smart city projects. To address this, cities can utilize cloud computing and distributed processing technologies, allowing for scalable and flexible data handling. Implementing edge computing enables local processing of IoT data, reducing latency and easing the load on central systems. Data compression and efficient storage technologies help in managing large datasets, while optimizing 3D models and simulations improves performance. An example of this approach is Virtual Singapore, which uses a scalable cloud infrastructure to meet the computational demands of its citywide digital twin.

User Adoption and Training

Ensuring that city officials and other stakeholders can effectively use and benefit from the digital twin presents a challenge in smart city projects. To address this, cities can develop intuitive user interfaces tailored to the specific needs of different user groups, ensuring accessibility and ease of use. Comprehensive training programs for city staff, alongside user guides and documentation for digital twin applications, help enhance understanding and engagement. Implementing a phased rollout approach allows for gradual adoption, enabling stakeholders to familiarize themselves with the technology over time.

For example, Helsinki's digital twin project included extensive user training programs and the development of user-friendly interfaces designed for different stakeholder groups, ensuring a smooth transition and effective utilization.

Cost and Resource Constraints

Managing the significant costs associated with developing and maintaining a city-scale digital twin is driven by the complexity of integrating diverse data sources, advanced simulations, and the infrastructure required for real-time updates. To address this, cities can implement a phased approach to spread costs over time and make the investment more manageable. Public-private partnerships offer a way to share financial burdens and technical expertise, while open-source technologies can further reduce development expenses. Additionally, pilot projects and case studies help demonstrate return on investment (ROI), making the project more attractive to stakeholders. For example, Amaravati's digital twin project successfully utilized public-private partnerships to share costs and leverage expertise from the private sector.

Real-time Data Processing

Processing and analyzing large volumes of real-time data from IoT sensors and other sources is a significant challenge due to the need for quick decision-making and efficient data management. To address this, cities can implement stream processing technologies that enable real-time data analysis, ensuring that insights are delivered without delay. Edge computing further supports this by processing data closer to the source, reducing latency and network bandwidth requirements. Optimizing data pipelines ensures efficient, low-latency processing, while implementing advanced data storage and retrieval mechanisms enables the swift handling of large datasets. For example, Singapore's digital twin utilizes cutting-edge stream processing technologies to manage real-time data from thousands of IoT sensors across the city.

Model Accuracy and Validation

Ensuring that digital twin models accurately represent real-world urban systems and processes poses a significant challenge, as discrepancies can lead to ineffective decision-making and planning. To address this issue, it is crucial to implement rigorous validation processes that compare model outputs with real-world data, ensuring that the digital twin reflects actual conditions.

Utilizing three domains for further exploration (uncertainty and sensitivity analysis, model validation for systems of systems, and the integration of expert knowledge with empirical data) helps to reveal the limitations of the models and their responses to varying. Furthermore, engaging domain experts in the development and validation process ensures that the models are grounded in real-world knowledge and expertise. For instance, Boston's climate resilience digital twin regularly undergoes validation against observed climate data and expert reviews, ensuring its accuracy and reliability in planning and response efforts.

Interoperability and Integration

Ensuring that a digital twin can seamlessly integrate with existing city systems and third-party applications is a critical challenge that requires a multifaceted approach.

One effective solution is to adopt open standards and APIs for data exchange, which promote interoperability between diverse systems. Implementing service-oriented architectures can further facilitate this integration by enabling modular and scalable components that communicate effectively with one another.

Comprehensive documentation detailing the integration processes is essential for guiding developers and stakeholders through the implementation phases.

Additionally, creating development sandboxes allows third-party developers to experiment with integrations without impacting live systems, encouraging innovation and collaboration. A noteworthy example of this approach in action is Helsinki's digital twin project, which successfully implemented open APIs and standards, enabling smooth integration with both existing city systems and external applications.

LESSONS LEARNED AND BEST PRACTICES FOR IMPLEMENTING DIGITAL TWINS IN SMART CITIES

The implementation of digital twins in various smart cities around the world has yielded valuable lessons and best practices. These insights can guide other cities in their digital twin initiatives.

Start with Clear Objectives and Use Cases

Successful digital twin projects are rooted in well-defined objectives and specific use cases, ensuring that the digital twin effectively addresses urban challenges. To achieve this, it is crucial to identify key urban issues that the digital twin can tackle, which helps in aligning its capabilities with real-world needs. Engaging stakeholders throughout the process allows for a deeper understanding of their needs and priorities, fostering collaboration and buy-in. Developing a comprehensive roadmap with clear milestones and deliverables provides a structured approach to implementation, guiding the project from inception to completion. Starting with pilot projects enables teams to demonstrate value and gather insights before scaling up, ensuring that lessons learned inform broader applications. A noteworthy example is Helsinki's digital twin project, which commenced with specific use cases in urban planning and building permit processes, enabling focused development and a clear demonstration of the digital twin's value to stakeholders.

Adopt a Collaborative and Inclusive Approach

Digital twin projects significantly benefit from collaboration across various city departments, academia, industry, and citizens, creating a holistic approach to urban management. Establishing cross-departmental working groups facilitates coordinated efforts, guiding the development of the digital twin to meet diverse city needs. Engaging academic institutions for research and innovation support enhances the project with cutting-edge knowledge and methodologies. Partnerships with technology companies provide essential expertise and resources, ensuring that the digital twin is built on a solid technological foundation. Involving citizens through participatory design processes and open data initiatives fosters transparency and ensures that the digital twin aligns with community needs and expectations. A prime example of this collaborative approach is Virtual Singapore, which involved multiple government agencies, universities, and technology companies, fostering innovation while ensuring the digital twin's broad applicability across various urban applications.

Prioritize Data Governance and Standards

Robust data governance frameworks and standards are crucial for the successful implementation of digital twins, ensuring that data is managed effectively and ethically throughout the project lifecycle. Developing citywide data standards and protocols allows for consistency and interoperability, enabling seamless data exchange among various systems. Establishing clear data ownership and sharing agreements clarifies responsibilities and fosters collaboration between stakeholders, which is essential for effective data management. Implementing comprehensive data privacy and security policies safeguards sensitive information, protecting citizens' rights and building trust in the digital twin initiative. Additionally, creating data quality assurance processes ensures that the data utilized by the digital twin is accurate and reliable, ultimately enhancing the model's effectiveness. An exemplary case is Boston's digital twin project, which implemented a comprehensive data governance framework that ensured data quality, privacy, and interoperability across city systems, laying a strong foundation for the project's success.

Design for Scalability and Flexibility

Digital twins must be designed with scalability and adaptability in mind to effectively respond to evolving urban needs and technologies. Utilizing cloud-based and distributed computing architectures ensures that the digital twin can handle increased data loads and user demands without compromising performance. Implementing modular design principles allows for easy updates and expansions, enabling the system to evolve alongside changing requirements. Adopting open standards and APIs facilitates integration and interoperability with existing systems and third-party applications, fostering collaboration and innovation. Moreover, planning for the incorporation of emerging technologies, such as 5G and AI, enhances the digital twin's capabilities and ensures its relevance in a rapidly changing technological landscape. A notable example is Singapore's digital twin, which was designed with a scalable cloud infrastructure and modular architecture, enabling continuous expansion and seamless integration of new technologies.

Focus on User Experience and Adoption

The success of digital twins depends on user adoption and effective utilization by various stakeholders. To facilitate this, it is crucial to develop intuitive and user-friendly interfaces tailored to different user groups, ensuring that all stakeholders can navigate the system with ease. Comprehensive training and support programs are essential to empower users with the necessary skills and knowledge to maximize the digital twin's potential. Additionally, creating use case demonstrations and best practice guides can help illustrate practical applications and inspire confidence in using the technology.

Implementing feedback mechanisms for continuous improvement fosters an environment of collaboration, allowing users to voice their experiences and suggest enhancements.

An example of these principles can be seen in Helsinki's digital twin project, which included extensive user training programs and the development of tailored interfaces for urban planners, citizens, and other stakeholders, promoting widespread engagement and successful adoption.

Implement Robust Security Measures

Security is paramount in digital twin projects due to the sensitive nature of urban data involved. To safeguard this data, it is essential to implement end-to-end encryption for both data transmission and storage, ensuring that information remains secure throughout its lifecycle. Utilizing strong authentication and access control mechanisms can further protect against unauthorized access and breaches. Conducting regular security audits and penetration testing helps identify vulnerabilities and reinforces the overall security posture of the digital twin. Additionally, developing incident response plans prepares organizations to swiftly address potential security breaches, minimizing their impact. An exemplary case is Singapore's digital twin, which incorporates advanced security measures, including encryption, access controls, and regular security audits, effectively protecting sensitive urban data from potential threats.

Utilize Existing Infrastructure and Data

Building on existing city infrastructure and data resources can significantly accelerate the development of digital twins. By integrating with current Geographic Information Systems (GIS) and urban management systems, cities can leverage established frameworks and data to enhance the functionality of their digital twins. Utilizing existing Internet of Things (IoT) sensor networks and data collection processes allows for the seamless incorporation of real-time information, enriching the digital twin's capabilities. Moreover, tapping into available open data resources and historical datasets can provide a robust foundation for modeling and analysis. Strategically identifying and addressing data gaps ensures that the digital twin remains comprehensive and relevant. An example of this approach is Boston's climate resilience digital twin, which effectively built upon existing GIS data and climate monitoring systems, thereby accelerating its development and ensuring alignment with the city's existing processes.

Plan for Long-term Sustainability

Digital twin projects necessitate a long-term commitment and strategic planning for their ongoing development and maintenance. To ensure sustainability, cities should develop funding models such as public-private partnerships that can support continuous investment over time. Establishing robust governance structures facilitates effective management and ongoing development, ensuring that the digital twin remains aligned with evolving urban needs. Additionally, implementing processes for regular updates and technology refreshes is vital to keep the digital twin relevant in the face of rapid technological advancements. Fostering a digital twin ecosystem that encourages collaboration among stakeholders can drive long-term innovation and adaptability. A notable example of this approach is Amaravati's digital twin project, which integrated long-term sustainability planning from the beginning, forming partnerships with technology companies and academic institutions to support ongoing development and enhancement.

Emphasize Interoperability and Open Standards

Interoperability and the adoption of open standards are essential for maximizing the value and longevity of digital twin projects. To achieve this, cities should prioritize the use of open data standards and formats that facilitate seamless data exchange between various systems. Implementing open APIs is crucial for ensuring easy access to data and integration with existing urban management platforms. Additionally, active participation in industry standardization efforts can help shape best practices and promote consistency across digital twin implementations. Encouraging the development of third-party applications and services fosters a diverse ecosystem that enhances the digital twin's functionality. An example of this is Helsinki's digital twin project, which successfully adopted open standards and APIs, allowing for smooth integration with existing city systems and creating a vibrant ecosystem of third-party applications that extend its capabilities.

Measure and Communicate Impact

Demonstrating and effectively communicating the impact of digital twin initiatives is vital for securing ongoing support and fostering widespread adoption. To achieve this, cities should develop key performance indicators (KPIs) that quantitatively measure the outcomes and benefits of their digital twin projects. Regular evaluations should be conducted, with results published to maintain transparency and accountability. Sharing success stories and case studies with stakeholders and the public can help illustrate the tangible benefits of digital twins, thereby building trust and enthusiasm. Additionally, utilizing the digital twin itself as a tool to visualize and communicate urban improvements can enhance understanding and engagement among citizens and decision-makers. For instance, Virtual Singapore regularly publishes case studies and impact assessments that highlight the value of its digital twin in various urban planning and management scenarios. By implementing these lessons learned and best practices, cities embarking on digital twin initiatives can avoid common pitfalls and maximize the benefits of this transformative technology.

FUTURE TRENDS AND DEVELOPMENTS IN DIGITAL TWIN CITIES

As technology continues to evolve and cities gain more experience with digital twins, several trends and developments are shaping the future of this field.

AI and Machine Learning Integration

The integration of AI and machine learning capabilities into digital twins is an emerging trend that significantly enhances advanced analytics and supports autonomous decision-making in smart cities. This integration makes it possible for potential developments such as self-optimizing urban systems capable of real-time adjustments based on AI predictions, along with advanced pattern recognition techniques for early detection of urban issues. Additionally, AI-driven scenario planning and policy recommendation systems can empower city planners to make informed decisions grounded in predictive analytics. For instance, Singapore is actively exploring the application of AI within its digital twin to optimize traffic flow and predict maintenance needs for urban infrastructure, exemplifying how AI can transform urban management and operational efficiency.

Internet of Things and 5G Integration

The expansion of IoT sensor networks, coupled with the integration of 5G technology, may revolutionize real-time data collection and processing in smart cities. This trend enables ultra-low latency updates to digital twins, allowing for immediate responsiveness to urban dynamics. Additionally, the implementation of Massive Machine Type Communications (mMTC) facilitates the establishment of dense networks of IoT devices, significantly increasing the volume and variety of data that can be captured. Furthermore, this technological advancement supports enhanced mobile augmented reality applications that leverage digital twin data, enriching user interactions and decision-making. For example, Helsinki is planning to incorporate 5G technology into its digital twin infrastructure, aiming to unlock sophisticated real-time applications that will elevate urban management and improve citizen engagement.

Digital Twin Federation

The development of federated digital twin ecosystems is emerging as a significant trend, enabling interaction and data sharing across city and regional boundaries. This evolution facilitates cross-border urban planning and management capabilities, allowing cities to collaboratively address shared challenges and optimize resource allocation. Standardized protocols for digital twin interoperability will be essential in creating seamless connections among various systems, enhancing data exchange and cooperation. Moreover, these federated systems can pave the way for global marketplaces that offer digital twin applications and services, fostering innovation and collaboration among stakeholders. For instance, the European Union is actively exploring the concept of a federated European digital twin, which aims to support continent-wide urban and environmental management, promoting a unified approach to tackling pressing issues across Europe.

Quantum Computing Applications

The exploration of quantum computing capabilities is becoming a pivotal trend in addressing complex urban optimization problems. With its ability to perform ultra-fast simulations of intricate urban systems, quantum computing has the potential to revolutionize the way cities analyze and manage resources. This technology could enable real-time optimization of city-scale resource allocation, allowing for more efficient and responsive urban planning and management. Additionally, quantum computing promises enhanced cryptography techniques to secure sensitive data within digital twins, further safeguarding urban infrastructure.

Citizen-Centric Digital Twins

The trend toward increased citizen engagement and participatory design in digital twin development is reshaping how urban environments are managed and planned. This shift emphasizes the creation of personalized urban services tailored to individual citizen data, enhancing the relevance and responsiveness of city initiatives. Crowdsourced data collection and validation processes are becoming integral to the development of digital twins, enabling residents to actively contribute to the accuracy and comprehensiveness of urban models. Furthermore, citizen-driven urban planning and policy-making platforms are emerging, allowing community members to visualize and provide input on urban development projects. An exemplary case is Amsterdam, where citizen-centric digital twin applications are being developed to engage residents in meaningful dialogue about urban growth and transformation, fostering a more inclusive and democratic approach to urban governance.

Digital Twin as a Service (DTaaS)

The emergence of cloud-based digital twin platforms offered as a service (DTaaS) is transforming how cities and urban planners can utilize digital twin technology. This trend enables scalable and cost-effective digital twin solutions that cater to smaller cities, allowing them to access advanced modeling and analytics without the need for extensive infrastructure investments. Additionally, the development of marketplaces for digital twin applications and datasets fosters a collaborative environment where cities can share resources and innovations. Standardized tools and APIs are being introduced to streamline the digital twin development process, making it easier for various stakeholders to integrate and utilize these technologies.

Enhanced Visualization and Immersive Experiences

The development of more sophisticated visualization technologies is enhancing the interaction between users and digital twins, creating immersive experiences that foster better understanding and engagement. Potential advancements in this area include photorealistic real-time rendering of entire cities, enabling users to navigate and explore urban environments with incredible detail and accuracy. Additionally, haptic interfaces may allow users to "feel" digital twin data, providing tactile feedback that enhances the interpretation of complex information. Further innovation could involve brain-computer interfaces, which would enable direct interaction with digital twins through neural signals, opening up new avenues for user engagement and data manipulation. An example of this trend can be seen in Boston, where the city is exploring the integration of advanced virtual reality and augmented reality technologies to enhance public engagement with its climate resilience digital twin, facilitating greater community involvement in urban planning and decision-making processes.

Integration with Autonomous Systems

The increasing integration of digital twins with autonomous urban systems, such as self-driving vehicles and drones, can change urban management and transportation. Potential developments in this domain include real-time path planning and traffic management for autonomous vehicles, allowing them to navigate complex urban environments more efficiently while minimizing congestion. Additionally, drones could be employed for automated updating of digital twin 3D models, ensuring that the virtual representation of the city remains accurate and up-to-date. Furthermore, autonomous urban service robots can utilize digital twin data to optimize their operations, enhancing service delivery in public spaces. A notable example of this trend can be found in Singapore's approach, where the city is integrating its digital twin with autonomous vehicle testbeds to optimize routing and traffic management, ultimately improving urban mobility and operational efficiency.

Blockchain and Distributed Ledger Technologies

The exploration of blockchain and distributed ledger technologies is enabling more secure and transparent urban data management in smart cities. This trend includes potential developments such as decentralized governance models for digital twins, which can enhance transparency and accountability in urban planning and management. Additionally, smart contracts could automate urban service delivery, streamlining processes and reducing administrative overhead. Tokenization of urban assets and services may also emerge, allowing for more efficient transactions and ownership models within the city. A prominent example of this trend can be found in Dubai, which is actively exploring the use of blockchain technology in its digital twin initiative. This integration aims to enhance data security while enabling new urban services, thereby encouraging innovation and improving urban resilience.

ETHICAL CONSIDERATIONS IN DIGITAL TWIN CITIES

As digital twins become increasingly prevalent in urban planning and management, addressing the ethical implications of these technologies is essential. Important ethical considerations include privacy and data protection, as digital twins collect vast amounts of data, including sensitive information about citizens and their behaviors. To mitigate privacy concerns, cities must ensure informed consent for data collection and use, implement robust data anonymization techniques, and establish clear policies on data retention and deletion.

Balancing the benefits of data-driven insights with individual privacy rights is critical. The European Union's General Data Protection Regulation (GDPR) exemplifies this approach by requiring explicit consent for data collection and processing in digital twin implementations.

Security and cybersecurity risks also pose significant ethical challenges, as digital twins are attractive targets for cyberattacks. Cities must implement robust security measures to protect against unauthorized access and develop incident response plans to address potential threats.

In addition, ensuring algorithmic bias and fairness is crucial, as AI and machine learning algorithms used in digital twins can perpetuate or exacerbate existing biases in urban planning and decision-making. To combat this issue, cities should ensure diversity in data sources and development teams, conduct regular audits for algorithmic bias, and provide transparency in decision-making processes. Boston's climate resilience digital twin project, which includes regular audits of predictive models, demonstrates a proactive approach to identifying and mitigating potential biases in urban planning.

Moreover, addressing the "digital divide" and ensuring equitable access to digital twin resources is essential for fostering inclusivity in smart cities. This involves providing alternative means of engagement for those without digital access and considering the needs of diverse user groups in interface design. Transparency and accountability in urban decision-making processes are also paramount, necessitating clear explanations of how digital twin data informs decisions and mechanisms for public oversight. Cities like Amsterdam have adopted public dashboards to help citizens understand the decision-making processes driven by digital twin data. Ultimately, a comprehensive framework addressing these ethical considerations is vital for the successful and equitable deployment of digital twin technologies in urban environments, ensuring that they benefit all community members while safeguarding individual rights and societal values.

CONCLUSION

Digital twin cities represent a powerful convergence of technologies that have the potential to transform urban planning, management, and governance. By creating comprehensive virtual replicas of urban environments, digital twins enable unprecedented capabilities for simulation, analysis, and optimization of city systems.

Throughout this chapter, we explored the concept and importance of digital twins in urban contexts, examining their main components and the benefits they offer for urban planning, simulation, and optimization. We discussed how digital twins can enhance decision-making processes, improve resource allocation, and facilitate more effective responses to urban challenges.

The case studies of successful digital twin implementations in cities like Singapore, Helsinki, Amaravati, and Boston provided valuable insights into the practical applications and benefits of this technology. These examples demonstrate how digital twins can be applied to a wide range of urban issues, from traffic management and environmental monitoring to climate resilience planning and citizen engagement.

We also examined the technologies that enable digital twin cities, including advanced 3D modeling and visualization tools, IoT and sensor networks, big data analytics platforms, and AI and machine learning systems. The integration of these technologies creates powerful platforms for urban modeling and analysis.

However, the implementation of digital twins in urban contexts is not without challenges. We discussed issues such as data integration and standardization, privacy and security concerns, scalability, and user adoption. The lessons learned and best practices derived from pioneering digital twin projects provide valuable guidance for addressing these challenges.

We explored emerging trends and developments in digital twin technology, including the integration of AI and 5G, the development of federated digital twin ecosystems, and the potential applications of quantum computing. These advancements promise to further enhance the capabilities and impact of digital twins in urban environments.

Finally, we considered the ethical implications of digital twin technologies, highlighting the need for careful consideration of issues such as privacy, algorithmic bias, digital divide, and the long-term societal impacts of these systems.

As we move forward, the key to realizing the full potential of digital twin cities lies in balancing technological innovation with ethical considerations and human-centric design. By doing so, we can harness the power of digital twins to create more efficient, sustainable, and livable urban environments that benefit all citizens.

The future of urban planning and management is increasingly digital, and digital twins will play a crucial role in shaping the smart cities of tomorrow. As this technology continues to evolve, ongoing research, experimentation, and collaboration between cities, technology providers, academia, and citizens will be essential to unlock its full potential and address the complex challenges of 21st-century urbanization.

CHAPTER 4

Choosing the Right Technology Stack

The technology stack is a foundational element for effective IoT deployment in smart cities. It represents a structured collection of technologies, platforms, protocols, and tools that collectively enable the collection, transmission, storage, and analysis of data across interconnected urban systems. The suitability of the chosen stack strongly influences whether an IoT initiative creates long-term value or results in complexity and inefficiency.

An IoT stack is typically organized into multiple layers, each fulfilling a distinct function within the broader ecosystem. The foundational layer consists of devices, sensors, and actuators that directly interact with the physical environment. The communication layer supports connectivity by providing reliable data transfer through diverse protocols and network infrastructures. The data management layer ensures that information is processed, stored, and analyzed at scale, while the application layer delivers interfaces and business logic that translate raw data into actionable services. A security layer spans across all components, ensuring confidentiality, integrity, and resilience of the system.

The layered stack approach provides a flexible yet comprehensive architecture for cities, where heterogeneous systems must interoperate. For example, traffic flow optimization or air quality monitoring requires seamless linking of sensor nodes, data processing platforms, management dashboards, and decision-making tools. This integration depends on harmonizing hardware, communication protocols, cloud and edge systems, as well as analytical frameworks.

Smart city environments are especially complex because they combine diverse data sources, support multiple communication standards, and need scalability to serve growing urban populations. Cities must therefore balance advanced technical capabilities with practical constraints, including financial resources, long-term maintainability, and compatibility with existing infrastructure. Poor alignment of components in the technology stack may result in integration problems, dependency on specific vendors, or escalating operational costs that undermine the expected benefits.

In selecting technologies, decision-makers also navigate between open-source and proprietary approaches. Each option presents trade-offs in flexibility, support, sustainability, and security. The decision should be guided not by brand recognition alone but by the specific requirements of the project, the skill sets available, and the future scalability of the entire ecosystem.

OPEN SOURCE VS. PROPRIETARY SOLUTIONS

The decision to use either open source or proprietary solutions influences every aspect of an IoT deployment. This choice influences not only initial costs but also long-term flexibility, security posture, and the ability to innovate and adapt to changing requirements.

Open source solutions provide access to source code, enabling organizations to examine, modify, and redistribute software according to their specific needs. This transparency fosters collaboration among developers worldwide, often resulting in rapid innovation cycles and community-driven improvements. Examples include platforms like Eclipse IoT, ThingsBoard, and Node-RED, which have gained widespread adoption for their flexibility and extensive feature sets. Figure 4.1 shows the comparison between open-source and proprietary solutions.

Proprietary solutions, in contrast, offer controlled development environments with dedicated vendor support and often more polished user interfaces. Companies like Microsoft with Azure IoT, Amazon with AWS IoT Core, and Google with Cloud IoT provide comprehensive platforms backed by substantial engineering resources and enterprise-grade support services. These solutions typically feature integrated security frameworks, streamlined deployment processes, and extensive documentation.

Technology Stack	Open Source Software	Proprietary Software
Entirety of software code base meets OSS requirements	YES	NO
Unrestricted distribution of software and license	YES	NO
Inclusion of source code	YES	NO
Allows derived works	YES	NO
License is technology-neutral/not dependent on other proprietary technology	YES	NO (Usually)

FIGURE 4.1 Comparison between open-source and proprietary solutions.

The ecosystem surrounding each approach differs significantly. Open source communities often comprise volunteers and organizations contributing to shared goals, creating diverse perspectives and rapid problem-solving capabilities. However, this distributed development model can sometimes result in inconsistent quality or delayed feature implementations. Proprietary vendors maintain focused development teams with clear roadmaps and accountability structures, but their priorities may not always align with specific customer requirements.

Interoperability considerations also vary between approaches. Open source solutions typically embrace open standards and protocols, facilitating integration with diverse systems and avoiding vendor-specific dependencies. Proprietary platforms may offer excellent integration within their own ecosystems but can create challenges when connecting with external systems or migrating to alternative platforms.

Proprietary Solutions

Proprietary solutions represent commercial offerings developed and maintained by technology vendors who retain exclusive control over the source code, feature development, and licensing terms. These solutions typically provide comprehensive, integrated platforms designed to address specific market needs with professional support structures and guaranteed service levels.

Leading proprietary platforms in the IoT analytics space include Microsoft Azure IoT Suite, Amazon Web Services IoT Core, Google Cloud IoT Core, IBM Watson IoT Platform, and specialized smart city platforms from companies like Cisco, Oracle, and SAP. These platforms offer end-to-end solutions encompassing device management, data ingestion, real-time processing, machine learning capabilities, and visualization tools within unified ecosystems.

The proprietary approach emphasizes reliability, security, and enterprise-grade features. Vendors invest heavily in research and development, security auditing, and compliance certifications to meet stringent requirements of government and enterprise customers. These solutions often include advanced features such as automated scaling, built-in security protocols, disaster recovery mechanisms, and integration with existing enterprise systems.

Proprietary platforms typically provide comprehensive documentation, training programs, and professional services to accelerate implementation. The vendor relationship includes ongoing technical support, regular updates, and access to new features as they become available. This support structure proves particularly valuable for organizations with limited internal technical expertise or those requiring rapid deployment timelines.

Open Source Solutions

Open source solutions provide access to source code, enabling organizations to modify, customize, and redistribute software according to their specific needs. The open source ecosystem for IoT analytics includes robust platforms such as Apache Kafka for data streaming, Apache Spark for large-scale data processing, InfluxDB for time-series data storage, Grafana for visualization, and TensorFlow or PyTorch for machine learning applications.

The open source approach offers unprecedented flexibility and customization capabilities. Organizations can adapt solutions to unique requirements, integrate disparate systems, and avoid vendor lock-in scenarios. The collaborative nature of open source development often results in rapid innovation, with global communities contributing improvements, bug fixes, and new features at accelerated pace compared to traditional proprietary development cycles.

Many successful smart city implementations utilize open source components to build tailored solutions. Cities like Barcelona, Amsterdam, and Helsinki have developed sophisticated IoT analytics platforms using combinations of open source tools, creating systems that precisely match their operational requirements and budget constraints. These implementations demonstrate the viability of open source approaches for large-scale, mission-critical urban applications.

The open source ecosystem provides extensive community support through forums, documentation wikis, and collaborative development platforms. While this support differs from commercial vendor relationships, the collective knowledge and experience of global developer communities often provides solutions to complex technical challenges more rapidly than traditional support channels.

The Advantages and Disadvantages of Each Approach

Proprietary Solution Advantages

Proprietary solutions excel in providing comprehensive, integrated platforms with guaranteed support levels and professional accountability. The vendor relationship ensures access to expert technical support, regular security updates, and feature enhancements aligned with market demands. These solutions typically offer superior documentation, training resources, and implementation services that accelerate deployment timelines.

The integrated nature of proprietary platforms reduces complexity in system architecture and integration challenges. Vendors design their solutions to work seamlessly together, minimizing compatibility issues and reducing the technical expertise required for implementation and maintenance. This integration extends to security features, with vendors implementing comprehensive security frameworks and maintaining compliance with industry standards and government regulations.

Proprietary solutions provide predictable licensing models and clear accountability structures. When issues arise, organizations have direct recourse to vendor support teams with defined service level agreements and escalation procedures. This accountability proves crucial for mission-critical smart city applications where system downtime directly impacts citizen services and urban operations.

Proprietary Solution Disadvantages

The primary limitation of proprietary solutions lies in vendor lock-in scenarios that restrict future flexibility and increase long-term costs. Organizations become dependent on vendor roadmaps, pricing decisions, and strategic directions that may not align with evolving city requirements. Migration away from proprietary platforms often requires significant investment in system redesign and data migration efforts.

Licensing costs for proprietary solutions can escalate significantly as deployments scale, particularly for usage-based pricing models common in cloud platforms. These costs may become prohibitive for large-scale smart city implementations that process massive data volumes or support extensive sensor networks. Additionally, customization capabilities remain limited to vendor-provided configuration options and APIs.

Open Source Solution Advantages

Open source solutions provide unparalleled flexibility and customization capabilities, enabling organizations to create precisely tailored systems that address unique requirements. The absence of licensing fees for core software components can result in substantial cost savings, particularly for large-scale deployments. Organizations retain complete control over their technology stack, avoiding vendor lock-in and maintaining freedom to modify or replace components as needs evolve.

The collaborative nature of open source development often produces more secure and robust software through extensive peer review and testing by global developer communities. Security vulnerabilities are typically identified and addressed more rapidly than in proprietary systems, with fixes available immediately rather than waiting for vendor release cycles.

Open source solutions enable organizations to build internal technical expertise and maintain complete understanding of their systems. This knowledge transfer proves valuable for long-term maintenance, troubleshooting, and system evolution. Additionally, the transparency of open source code facilitates security auditing and compliance verification processes required for government applications.

Open Source Solution Disadvantages

Open source implementations require significant internal technical expertise for selection, integration, configuration, and ongoing maintenance of multiple software components. Organizations must invest in skilled development teams capable of managing complex, distributed systems and resolving integration challenges between different open source projects.

The distributed nature of open source support can complicate troubleshooting and issue resolution. While community support provides valuable resources, organizations cannot rely on guaranteed response times or professional accountability when critical issues arise. This limitation may prove problematic for mission-critical smart city applications requiring high availability and rapid issue resolution.

Integration complexity increases significantly when combining multiple open source components, each with different configuration requirements, update cycles, and compatibility considerations. Organizations must manage these complexities internally, requiring ongoing investment in system administration and development resources.

TOTAL COST OF OWNERSHIP CONSIDERATIONS

Total cost of ownership analysis extends far beyond initial licensing or development costs to encompass the complete lifecycle expenses of IoT analytics platforms. This comprehensive evaluation includes direct costs such as software licensing, hardware infrastructure, and implementation services, as well as indirect costs including internal resource allocation, training, maintenance, and opportunity costs associated with different technological approaches.

Initial Implementation Costs

Proprietary solutions typically require substantial upfront investments in licensing fees, professional services, and specialized training. These costs provide immediate access to comprehensive platforms and expert implementation support but represent significant capital expenditure. Cloud-based proprietary solutions may reduce initial costs through subscription models but create ongoing operational expenses that scale with usage.

Open source implementations require different initial investments focused on internal development resources, system integration efforts, and infrastructure setup. While software licensing costs remain minimal, organizations must invest in skilled personnel capable of designing, implementing, and configuring complex distributed systems. These implementation costs vary significantly based on system complexity and internal technical capabilities.

Operational and Maintenance Expenses

Ongoing operational costs differ substantially between proprietary and open source approaches. Proprietary solutions include predictable licensing fees, support contracts, and vendor-managed updates within defined cost structures. However, these costs often escalate with system growth, user adoption, and feature utilization, potentially creating budget pressures for expanding smart city initiatives.

Open source solutions require ongoing investment in internal technical teams responsible for system maintenance, security updates, and performance optimization. While direct licensing costs remain low, personnel expenses for specialized technical roles can exceed proprietary licensing fees, particularly for complex, large-scale deployments requiring 24/7 operational support.

Scalability and Growth Costs

Proprietary platforms often implement usage-based pricing models that increase costs proportionally with data volumes, device connections, or user access. These scaling costs can become prohibitive for successful smart city initiatives that experience rapid growth in sensor deployments and data processing requirements. Additionally, vendor pricing changes or strategic shifts can impact long-term budget planning and system sustainability.

Open source solutions provide more predictable scaling costs primarily related to infrastructure resources and personnel requirements. Organizations can optimize costs through efficient system design and resource utilization without vendor-imposed limitations or pricing escalations. However, scaling complexity may require additional technical expertise and system architecture investments.

Risk and Opportunity Costs

Vendor dependency in proprietary solutions creates risks related to business continuity, pricing changes, and strategic alignment. Organizations may face significant migration costs if vendor relationships deteriorate or strategic directions diverge. These risks must be quantified and included in total cost calculations.

Open source approaches involve different risk profiles related to technical complexity, community support sustainability, and internal capability requirements. Organizations must evaluate their capacity to manage these risks against potential cost savings and flexibility benefits. The opportunity cost of internal resource allocation to system management versus other strategic initiatives represents another critical consideration in total cost evaluation.

The total cost of ownership analysis, other than strictly financial considerations, include strategic value, operational flexibility, and long-term sustainability factors that impact overall smart city initiative success. This comprehensive evaluation enables informed decision-making that aligns technology choices with organizational capabilities, budget constraints, and strategic objectives for urban intelligence and citizen service delivery.

EVALUATING THE BEST FIT FOR THE TECHNOLOGY STACK FOR DIFFERENT CITY SCALES AND NEEDS

The selection of an appropriate technology stack for smart city initiatives requires comprehensive evaluation of factors that vary significantly based on city size, resources, and specific urban challenges. This evaluation process must account for scalability requirements, interoperability considerations, and implementation complexities that differ across municipal scales and contexts.

Scalability Requirements for Growing Urban Environments

Urban environments face distinct scalability challenges that technology stacks must address effectively. The scalability demands vary dramatically between small municipalities with hundreds of IoT devices and major metropolitan areas managing millions of connected endpoints.

Device and Infrastructure Scaling

Smart city platforms must be designed to support significant growth in the number of connected devices and sensors. Research indicates that such platforms must be capable of handling not only millions of devices that form the IoT infrastructure but also large numbers of users and software components accessing platform services. In addition, the system must effectively store and process vast volumes of city-related data generated continuously by these sources. Scalability needs may vary depending on the operating context, but they should always be considered a fundamental requirement during the early stages of any smart city initiative.

The underlying architecture plays a decisive role in determining scalability. Traditional monolithic architectures are structured as single, unified systems in which all components such as data management, communication, and application logic are tightly interconnected and deployed together. While this design can simplify early development, it has limitations when applied to large-scale IoT environments. Scaling a monolithic system typically requires replicating the entire application, which is inefficient when only certain functions experience increased demand. Furthermore, changes in one part of the system often require redeployment of the whole application, resulting in reduced agility.

By contrast, microservice-based architectures separate the system into small, independent services that perform specific functions. Each microservice can be scaled individually based on demand, making it possible to allocate resources more efficiently. For instance, a service that processes high-frequency sensor data can be scaled vertically or horizontally without affecting the rest of the system. Empirical evaluations, such as those conducted on the InterSCity platform, highlight how loosely coupled microservices improve elasticity and resilience. They allow different scaling strategies to be applied to individual services according to their workload characteristics, enhancing the platform's ability to manage rapid growth and fluctuating demands.

Adopting a microservice approach therefore strengthens scalability, fault isolation, and maintainability, critical attributes for urban IoT infrastructures that must remain functional and responsive under continuous technological and demographic pressures.

Data Volume and Processing Scaling

Growing urban environments generate exponentially increasing data volumes that require sophisticated processing capabilities. Smart cities use IoT equipment and communication technology to closely connect with citizens, collecting and analyzing a variety of data in the city to optimize the efficiency of urban operations and social services. This challenge involves not only storing massive amounts of data but processing them in real-time for immediate decision-making.

Modern smart city implementations utilize distributed computing architectures to manage this complexity. Platforms like Haikou Smart City Management Platform use Hadoop cluster construction technology, Hdfs distributed file storage technology, Zookeeper cluster technology, Kafka cluster technology, and Hbase storage technology to integrate, process, and integrate large numbers of real-time data streams. These technologies perform large amounts of calculations and analyses on data and make real-time predictions.

Performance and Response Time Scaling

Scalability involves maintaining acceptable performance levels as the system load increases. Real-time IoT analytics pipelines demonstrate impressive performance metrics, with a throughput of 5,000 events per second alongside a very low latency of 50 milliseconds, indicating how urban information flow is processed efficiently. This performance level enables cities to process massive data streams while maintaining responsive services for citizens and administrators.

Edge computing architectures provide additional scaling benefits by distributing processing closer to data sources. Edge-based systems improve availability, scalability, and interoperability while providing data analysis and alerting functionalities. This distributed approach reduces bandwidth requirements and improves response times for time-critical applications.

Network and Communication Scaling

The communication infrastructure must be capable of scaling in response to the rapid increase of connected devices and the resulting data transmission demands. In smart city contexts, diverse device populations generate both high-volume and low-volume data streams that must be transmitted efficiently and reliably. Low-power wide-area networks (LPWAN) have emerged as an important solution for large-scale deployments due to their ability to provide extensive coverage at low energy consumption and cost. Among the different LPWAN technologies, LoRaWAN is frequently adopted in urban environments, as it offers cost-effective connectivity for large numbers of battery-powered sensors. Research highlights its effectiveness in addressing challenges of scalability, energy efficiency, and high deployment expenditures, making it well-suited for massive sensor networks that characterize smart city infrastructures.

In addition to network protocol selection, architectural approaches critically shape the scalability of communication systems. Container-based architectures provide significant advantages in this regard. Studies indicate that containerized LoRaWAN deployments allow system designers to run identical network software across diverse and distributed hosts. Containers simplify configuration and management, streamline the emulation of large-scale deployments, and lower resource overhead compared to virtual-machine-based alternatives. By encapsulating LoRaWAN network elements in containers, scalability testing and service orchestration can be achieved while maintaining high reproducibility and reducing operational complexity.

Interoperability and Standards Compliance

Interoperability represents a fundamental requirement for successful smart city technology implementations. The absence of standardized interfaces creates fragmented systems that cannot communicate effectively, limiting the potential benefits of smart city investments.

Standards Framework and Implementation

Multiple international standards organizations have developed frameworks to address smart city interoperability challenges. The oneM2M standards initiative has emerged as a foundational framework for IoT interoperability. Analysis of oneM2M-based systems reveals that optimal framework choice depends on specific quality constraints, with some platforms excelling in performance while others offer advantages in ease of setup for smaller-scale implementations.

The United Nations approved the Y-MIM Standard (Minimal Interoperability Mechanisms) to enhance interoperability across smart city solutions and digital public infrastructures worldwide. This standard aims to enable better integration and communication between different systems by standardizing minimal requirements for interoperability and facilitating seamless exchange of data, services, and applications across different platforms and jurisdictions.

Multi-Level Interoperability Requirements

Smart city interoperability encompasses multiple technical layers that must function cohesively. Research identifies five types of interoperability requirements: syntactic, semantic, network, middleware, and security interoperability. Each type has different requirements and must be addressed systematically to achieve comprehensive system integration.

Syntactic interoperability addresses data format compatibility between systems. *Semantic interoperability* ensures that data meaning remains consistent across different platforms and applications. *Network interoperability* enables communication across diverse network technologies and protocols. *Middleware interoperability* facilitates integration between different software platforms and services. *Security interoperability* ensures consistent security policies and mechanisms across all system components.

Data Integration and Exchange Standards

Effective data integration requires standardized data models and exchange protocols. The Open Geospatial Consortium has developed standards including CityGML, IndoorGML, and SensorThings API that enable integration of IoT resources and city models. These standards support multiple views of urban entities including building-level, room-level, opening-level, and device-level perspectives.

Modern platforms implement microservice architectures to facilitate data exchange. Each function of the system is constructed as a single microservice, with different data services and governance solutions configured according to application scenarios. Services can be deployed independently with resources between microservices isolated, improving system flexibility and scalability.

Cross-Domain Integration Challenges

Smart cities consist of multiple application domains such as transportation, energy, healthcare, and public safety that must integrate and interoperate seamlessly. Achieving this integration requires systematic approaches that enable distinct domains to share data, processes, and services. Standards-based frameworks play a critical role by providing common models and reference structures for representing complex urban systems, thereby facilitating coordination among diverse stakeholders.

One approach to enable interoperability is the use of domain-specific languages (DSLs) that are built upon established *smart city reference architectures*. These reference architectures, developed in international initiatives such as ISO/IEC, ITU-T, and organizations like ETSI, provide methodological guidelines for structuring smart city platforms, data models, and services. By tailoring DSLs to these reference architectures, cities can achieve interoperability across heterogeneous domains while aligning with the requirements and priorities of urban stakeholders. This ensures that solutions developed for one sector—such as mobility—can interact effectively with those from another, such as environmental monitoring or public health.

A key challenge lies in bridging the gaps between different IoT standards and technologies adopted by various cities or domains within the same city. To address this, three primary interworking models are typically applied:

1. Standardized interface approaches: use common, globally recognized APIs or standards (e.g., NGSI-LD, oneM2M) to allow systems in different domains to communicate directly.

2. Interworking proxy solutions: employ intermediary gateways or middleware that translate between protocols or data models used in different domains or cities.

3. Semantic integration methods: use ontologies and semantic web technologies to align meaning across diverse datasets and systems, enabling interoperability even in cases of heterogeneous data representations.

Selection of an interworking model depends on factors such as the existing maturity level of city infrastructures, the degree of heterogeneity across systems, and the long-term roadmap for cross-city or cross-domain service continuity.

CASE STUDIES OF TECHNOLOGY STACK SELECTION

Real-world implementations provide valuable insights into how different city sizes approach technology stack selection based on their unique requirements, resources, and constraints.

Small City Implementation: Saint-Sulpice-la-Forêt, France

The smallest documented smart city implementation demonstrates that scale does not preclude smart city benefits. Saint-Sulpice-la-Forêt, with only 1,500 inhabitants, deployed just 27 sensors on water, gas, and electricity meters and in public buildings. The IoT installation cost approximately 24,000 dollars, with money saved on energy consumption reduction expected to exceed costs within five years.

This implementation focused on essential utility monitoring rather than comprehensive smart city services. The simple technology stack enabled early leak detection and precise real-time consumption monitoring across all parts of the town. The mayor could identify where to focus renovation investments based on data-driven insights rather than guesswork.

The success factors included focused scope, manageable technology complexity, and clear return on investment metrics. The implementation demonstrates that smart city benefits are achievable at very small scales when technology selection aligns with specific municipal needs and capabilities.

Medium City Implementation: Karanganyar Regency, Indonesia

Medium-sized cities face different challenges in smart city implementation, as demonstrated by Karanganyar Regency's experience. The smart city journey was documented in the Regional Medium-Term Development Plan (RPJMD) 2018–2023, which included digital governance, e-public services, traffic and transportation monitoring, and information systems to support economic and social development. However, the implementation encountered significant infrastructure, structural, and institutional challenges that limited the scope of deployment.

The technology implementation required addressing three categories of problems: technology infrastructure limitations, particularly an uneven distribution of reliable internet connectivity and limited data centers; human resources and budget constraints, where skilled personnel for IoT analytics, cybersecurity, and system integration were scarce and financial allocations remained modest; and institutional and policy gaps, including the absence of standardized frameworks to connect existing e-government systems with IoT-based smart city services. These issues illustrate the complexity of technology stack selection for medium cities that must balance ambitious objectives with resource constraints.

The approach emphasized improvisation and incremental adaptation aligned with local government capacities, rather than adopting comprehensive technology stacks designed for larger metropolitan areas. For example, instead of deploying city-wide IoT networks simultaneously, Karanganyar prioritized sectoral applications such as digital administration for public services and limited-scale smart environmental monitoring. This pragmatic strategy reflects the reality that medium-sized cities must customize smart city pathways based on local priorities and readiness, while gradually building capacity to integrate more advanced technologies.

This case highlights the importance of aligning smart city technology choices with regional development plans, fiscal capacity, and human resource readiness. It also reveals how medium-sized cities benefit from scalable, modular technology stacks that allow gradual expansion. By pursuing stepwise deployment rather than full-scale implementation, Karanganyar provides a useful model for other medium-sized municipalities seeking to operationalize smart city goals under constrained conditions.

Large City Implementation: Surabaya, Indonesia

Surabaya's smart city project demonstrates how large cities can leverage comprehensive technology stacks to address urban sustainability challenges. The implementation focuses on digitalization of city infrastructure for improved sustainability, with quantitative analysis of impact on sustainability indicators.

The technology stack encompasses multiple domains including waste management, transportation, energy systems, and citizen services. Research shows statistically significant improvements in sustainability indicators, with waste reduction behavior and community satisfaction being particularly important outcomes. The comprehensive approach required sophisticated technology integration across multiple municipal departments and services.

Demographic factors including age, income, and digital literacy significantly influence sustainability outcomes, requiring technology stacks that accommodate diverse citizen capabilities and preferences. This complexity necessitates more sophisticated user interface design and citizen engagement strategies compared to smaller implementations.

Metropolitan Implementation: Singapore Smart Nation

Singapore's Smart Nation initiative represents one of the most comprehensive smart city technology deployments globally. The implementation began by deploying a comprehensive network of 110,000 lampposts equipped with sensors, creating foundational IoT infrastructure for multiple applications.

The technology stack utilizes 5G wireless networks, extensive fiber optic infrastructure, and sophisticated IoT sensor networks covering environmental monitoring, traffic management, and urban planning applications. The scale requires advanced data analytics platforms capable of processing massive data streams from hundreds of thousands of connected devices.

The Singapore approach emphasizes integrated platform development that connects multiple urban systems and services. This integration enables cross-domain optimization and coordinated responses to urban challenges that span multiple municipal functions and services.

Technology Architecture Comparison Across Scales

Small cities typically implement focused, single-purpose technology stacks that address specific problems like utility monitoring or basic environmental sensing. The technology architecture remains simple with direct device-to-cloud connectivity and basic analytics capabilities.

Medium cities require more sophisticated architectures that can integrate multiple systems while remaining manageable with limited technical resources. Edge computing architectures provide benefits by reducing bandwidth requirements and enabling local processing capabilities.

Large cities implement comprehensive platforms with microservices architectures, distributed computing capabilities, and advanced analytics frameworks. The technology stack must support real-time processing of massive data volumes while maintaining high availability and performance.

Metropolitan areas require enterprise-grade platforms with extensive redundancy, multi-cloud deployments, and sophisticated integration capabilities. The architecture must support coordination across multiple municipal agencies and integration with regional and national systems.

BEST PRACTICES FOR TECHNOLOGY STACK SELECTION

Successful technology stack selection requires systematic evaluation of technical, economic, and organizational factors that influence long-term implementation success. These best practices emerge from analysis of successful and unsuccessful smart city implementations across diverse urban contexts.

Requirements Assessment and Prioritization

Effective selection of a technology stack begins with a comprehensive assessment of current capabilities, future requirements, and strategic objectives. A city-wide evaluation should consider the condition of existing infrastructure and identify areas where smart technologies may be integrated or optimized. This assessment must cover not only technical capabilities, but also organizational readiness (governance capacity, workforce skills) and budget constraints, as these factors directly influence the feasibility and sustainability of technology choices.

A priority-based implementation approach is widely regarded as an effective strategy for managing complexity and ensuring successful outcomes. Projects should be prioritized according to potential impact, technical and financial feasibility, and alignment with long-term urban development goals. Implementation is commonly structured as a phased process, starting with pilot projects that allow cities to test and validate technologies before undertaking full-scale deployment. This phased trial-and-error approach reduces risk and builds institutional learning capacity.

The innovation sandbox concept further supports effective prioritization by providing a structured environment in which proposed projects are evaluated against transparent criteria. An innovation sandbox defines which types of initiatives are "in scope" and which are not, based on considerations such as: alignment with municipal development objectives, clearly defined problems addressed, expected costs, available resources, and the respective institutional jurisdiction. This framework prevents resource fragmentation and ensures concentrated investment in projects that produce measurable benefits.

Technical Architecture Considerations

Modern smart city platforms increasingly rely on distributed, service-oriented architectures that enhance scalability, performance, and adaptability. Microservice-based architectures are particularly beneficial, as they allow independent scaling and management of discrete system components while also supporting the integration of technologies and vendors from multiple sources (Dragoni et al., 2017). This modular structure enables cities to adapt more rapidly to evolving technical requirements.

Integration of edge computing provides additional advantages by reducing bandwidth demand, lowering latency, and improving service reliability. Through localized data processing, edge-based systems enhance scalability and interoperability across heterogeneous infrastructures. This is especially valuable for time-sensitive applications such as intelligent traffic control, public safety monitoring, or energy grid management, where real-time responsiveness is critical.

Container-based deployment strategies offer practical benefits in managing distributed and complex smart city systems. Containerization ensures that identical software environments can be deployed consistently across diverse infrastructure nodes, simplifying configuration and orchestration processes. It also lowers operational costs by enabling resource-efficient emulation of large-scale deployments, thereby allowing iterative testing before city-wide rollouts.

Interoperability and Standards Integration

Technology stack selection must prioritize interoperability from the initial design phase. Cities should develop interoperability standards to ensure that new technologies can be integrated with existing systems. This includes adopting recognized industry standards and ensuring compatibility with regional and national systems.

The adoption of open standards provides long-term benefits for technology evolution and vendor independence. Standards-based approaches facilitate integration between different application domains and enable cities to avoid vendor lock-in scenarios that limit future flexibility.

Data governance frameworks should be established early to ensure consistent data management across different system components. Cities should invest in data management systems that can integrate data from different sources, enabling unified views of city operations.

Procurement and Partnership Strategies

Smart city technology procurement requires specialized approaches that differ from traditional municipal purchasing processes. Cities should create procurement policies and processes specifically designed for innovation projects. These policies must accommodate pilot projects, performance-based contracting, and iterative development approaches.

Public-private partnerships offer valuable mechanisms for accessing private sector expertise and reducing financial burdens. PPPs can bring specialized knowledge and skills that may not be available within government agencies while sharing costs of smart city initiatives. However, these partnerships require careful structuring to ensure public interests remain protected.

Vendor evaluation should emphasize long-term partnership potential rather than focusing solely on initial costs. Cities should evaluate vendors based on their ability to provide ongoing support, technology evolution, and integration capabilities with existing and planned systems.

Implementation and Evolution Planning

Successful technology stack implementations require comprehensive planning for ongoing adaptation and evolution. Cities should establish systems for ongoing adaptation and feedback collection, ensuring technology roadmaps remain flexible and responsive to changing circumstances. This includes provisions for technology updates, capability expansion, and integration of emerging technologies.

Community engagement strategies must be integrated into technology selection and implementation processes. Cities should develop strategies for involving citizens in project planning and establishing feedback channels for continuous improvement. This engagement ensures that technology deployments address actual citizen needs and gain community support.

Long-term maintenance planning ensures sustainability and continued innovation of smart city technologies. Cities should develop comprehensive maintenance plans that keep systems at the forefront of technological advancements while ensuring reliable operation. This includes provisions for staff training, technology refresh cycles, and capability enhancement programs.

Performance Measurement and Optimization

Evaluating a technology stack requires the establishment of comprehensive performance measurement frameworks. Cities should implement holistic key performance indicators (KPIs) that go beyond narrow technical measurements such as latency, throughput, or uptime, and instead incorporate broader dimensions of urban performance. Holistic KPIs are rooted in the concept of multidimensional evaluation, combining technical metrics (system reliability, scalability, interoperability), infrastructure service quality (coverage, availability, and cost-efficiency), and societal outcomes (citizen satisfaction, environmental benefits, economic value creation, and governance transparency). This inclusive approach has been widely applied in urban innovation assessments, evolving from earlier practices in e-government measurement, where technical efficiency alone was found to be insufficient for capturing community impact. For smart cities, holistic KPIs therefore serve as a framework to ensure that technology investments contribute directly to improving quality of life, service delivery, and municipal performance.

To support continual improvement, continuous monitoring and optimization processes must be embedded into the technology stack. Real-time analytics capabilities are essential, enabling cities to track system health, detect anomalies, evaluate operational efficiency, and measure citizen engagement in real time. This includes monitoring metrics such as application response times, energy consumption, or service availability, alongside social indicators like public service adoption rates, citizen feedback trends, and perceived benefit levels. By linking system performance with user-level outcomes, cities can ensure that deployed technologies remain aligned with strategic objectives and evolving community needs.

Data-driven decision making acts as the backbone of this process. By systematically analyzing collected data, cities can identify performance bottlenecks, optimize resource usage, and forecast areas where future investments yield the greatest impact. This analytical approach improves governance efficiency, reduces waste, and allows for the early adaptation of systems in response to emerging challenges such as population growth, climate pressures, or shifts in mobility patterns.

Successful selection and management of a technology stack depends on tailoring solutions to city-specific factors, including scale, resource availability, institutional capacity, and long-term priorities. The most effective technology stacks balance complexity with operational readiness, ensuring sustainability while offering a clear pathway for gradual innovation. Through systematic evaluation and optimization guided by holistic KPIs, cities can create technology ecosystems that generate measurable improvements in both operational efficiency and community well-being, while establishing a strong foundation for continued digital growth.

CHALLENGES IN TECHNOLOGY STACK SELECTION FOR SMART CITIES

While selecting the right technology stack is crucial for the success of smart city initiatives, several challenges can complicate this process. Understanding and addressing these challenges is essential for making informed decisions and ensuring the long-term viability of smart city projects.

Rapid Technological Evolution

One of the primary challenges faced by cities in the pursuit of smart city solutions is the rapid pace of technological advancement in fields such as the Internet of Things (IoT) and artificial intelligence (AI). This fast evolution can complicate the selection process, making it difficult for urban planners and decision-makers to choose solutions that will remain relevant and effective over the long term.

To mitigate this challenge, cities should adopt flexible, modular architectures that can accommodate new technologies as they emerge. This approach allows for the successful integration of innovative solutions without necessitating a complete overhaul of existing systems. Additionally, prioritizing solutions with strong upgrade paths and backward compatibility ensures that current investments remain viable as technology evolves, thereby protecting the city's infrastructure from obsolescence.

Moreover, engaging in ongoing technology monitoring and assessment is essential for staying informed about emerging trends and advancements. By establishing a framework for continuous evaluation, cities can adapt their strategies and technology stacks proactively, ensuring that they harness the latest innovations while avoiding the pitfalls of outdated or ineffective solutions. This proactive stance enhances the effectiveness of smart city initiatives and ensures long-term sustainability and relevance in an ever-changing technological landscape.

Integration with Legacy Systems

Other challenge many cities face in their transition to smart city technologies is the need to integrate existing legacy systems with new solutions. This integration can be both complex and costly, often requiring extensive planning and resources to ensure seamless functionality across various platforms.

To address this challenge, cities should first conduct a thorough assessment of their existing systems and evaluate their integration capabilities. Understanding the strengths and limitations of legacy systems will help urban planners identify potential hurdles and develop targeted strategies for integration. Additionally, selecting new technologies that offer robust API support and integration tools is essential. These features facilitate smoother communication between systems, making it easier to share data and functionalities.

Furthermore, considering the implementation of middleware solutions can significantly streamline the integration process. Middleware acts as a bridge, enabling different systems to communicate effectively and share data, thereby reducing the complexity associated with direct integration. Finally, cities should plan for phased replacements of legacy systems where necessary, allowing for a gradual transition that minimizes disruption while ensuring that new technologies are fully integrated and operational. By taking these strategic steps, cities can effectively navigate the complexities of integrating legacy systems with new smart city technologies, ultimately enhancing their operational efficiency and service delivery.

Data Silos and Interoperability Issues

Another challenge cities encounter in their smart city initiatives is the existence of operational silos among different departments and systems. These silos hinder effective data sharing and integration, making it difficult to utilize the full potential of smart technologies and achieve coordinated urban management.

To address this challenge, cities should first implement a citywide data strategy and governance framework. Such a framework establishes clear guidelines for data management, sharing, and usage, ensuring that all departments adhere to consistent standards. Additionally, selecting technologies that support open standards and common data formats is essential. This approach enhances compatibility between different systems and encourages collaboration by simplifying the process of data exchange.

Moreover, developing a central data platform or data lake can significantly facilitate data sharing across departments. This centralized repository allows for the aggregation of data from various sources, making it accessible to all stakeholders involved in urban planning and management. Finally, fostering a culture of collaboration and data sharing across city departments is crucial. Encouraging interdepartmental communication and teamwork promotes the use of shared data in decision-making processes, leading to more integrated and effective smart city initiatives. By taking these strategic actions, cities can overcome silos and create a more cohesive, data-driven urban environment.

Security and Privacy Concerns

The implementation of smart city technologies frequently necessitates the collection and processing of vast amounts of data, which raises significant concerns regarding security, privacy, and adherence to data protection regulations. As cities strive to harness the power of data for improved urban management, they must address these critical issues to foster trust and ensure compliance.

To mitigate security and privacy risks, cities should prioritize technologies with strong built-in security features. This includes selecting platforms and devices that offer advanced encryption, secure access controls, and regular security updates. In addition, it is essential to implement comprehensive security policies and practices across the entire smart city ecosystem. These policies should encompass data governance, incident response protocols, and regular security audits to safeguard sensitive information against potential breaches.

Ensuring compliance with data protection laws such as GDPR and CCPA is essential, backed by privacy-by-design, data minimization, strong encryption, access control, and auditability throughout the stack. Cities should institutionalize Privacy Impact Assessments, consent management, and transparent notices, while mapping data flows and enforcing vendor due diligence to maintain trust and accountability.

Breach readiness must be explicit: maintain an incident response plan with rapid detection, containment, forensic analysis, and documented decision paths; notify the supervisory authority within 72 hours under GDPR and inform affected individuals without undue delay where high risk exists, providing actionable guidance and phased updates if details are incomplete. Mitigation measures include encrypting data at rest and in transit, least-privilege and privileged access controls, well-defined data retention and deletion, and continuous monitoring to reduce impact and prevent recurrence. Transparent post-incident communication, credit/identity protection offers when warranted, and corrective actions reporting help repair harm and sustain citizen confidence in smart city services.

As smart city initiatives expand, the underlying technology stack must effectively manage increasing data volumes, a growing number of connected devices, and heightened user demands without sacrificing performance. This challenge necessitates careful planning and the adoption of strategies that prioritize scalability and efficiency.

To ensure scalability, cities should choose technologies with proven scalability in similar contexts. This involves selecting platforms and solutions that have successfully supported other smart city projects, thereby minimizing the risk of performance issues as demand grows. Additionally, cities should design for horizontal scalability from the outset. This approach allows the technology stack to distribute the load across multiple servers or nodes, enabling it to accommodate increased traffic and data processing needs seamlessly.

Implementing performance monitoring and optimization practices is crucial for maintaining system efficiency. By regularly analyzing system performance metrics, cities can identify potential bottlenecks and address them proactively. Furthermore, considering cloud-based solutions can significantly enhance scalability and flexibility. Cloud platforms offer the ability to quickly scale resources up or down based on demand, allowing cities to adapt to changing needs without heavy investments in physical infrastructure. By adopting these strategies, urban areas can ensure their technology stacks remain robust and responsive as smart city initiatives continue to evolve.

Vendor Lock-in

Relying excessively on proprietary technologies can lead to vendor lock-in, constraining future flexibility and potentially escalating costs for smart city projects. This dependency can hinder a city's ability to adapt to emerging technologies or shift to more cost-effective solutions. Therefore, it is important to implement strategies that mitigate these risks and promote a more agile technology environment.

To avoid vendor lock-in, cities should prioritize open standards and interoperable solutions. By opting for technologies that adhere to widely accepted standards, cities can facilitate easier integration with diverse systems and reduce reliance on any single vendor. Additionally, developing a multi-vendor strategy can significantly decrease dependence on one provider. This approach allows cities to utilize various technologies and solutions, fostering a more competitive and flexible ecosystem.

Moreover, ensuring data portability and the capability to migrate to alternative solutions is essential. Cities should focus on solutions that allow for easy extraction and transfer of data, thus safeguarding against potential challenges associated with switching vendors. Finally, city planners must carefully evaluate long-term contracts and licensing agreements to identify any potential pitfalls or restrictive terms. By adopting these strategies, urban planners can cultivate a technology landscape that remains adaptable and responsive to future needs while minimizing the risks associated with vendor lock-in.

Skill Gaps and Resource Constraints

Many cities encounter significant challenges due to shortages of skilled personnel necessary to implement and maintain advanced smart city technologies. The rapid evolution of these technologies often outpaces the availability of trained professionals, hindering effective deployment and ongoing support. To address this pressing issue, urban planners and city officials must adopt proactive strategies that focus on building and nurturing the local talent pool.

One effective strategy is to invest in training and skill development for existing staff. By offering professional development opportunities, cities can enhance their workforce's capabilities and empower employees to adapt to new technologies. Additionally, forging partnerships with local universities and technology companies can facilitate knowledge transfer and provide valuable resources for training programs. Collaborative efforts can create a bridge between academia and industry, ensuring that educational institutions align their curricula with the evolving demands of smart city initiatives.

Another approach to mitigating personnel shortages is to consider managed services or cloud-based solutions that can alleviate the burden on in-house IT staff. By outsourcing certain functions to specialized providers, cities can maintain operational efficiency while focusing their internal resources on critical areas. Furthermore, developing internship and apprenticeship programs can help cultivate local talent, offering students hands-on experience in smart city technologies and fostering a future workforce equipped to tackle urban challenges. Together, these strategies can create a sustainable pipeline of skilled professionals essential for advancing smart city initiatives.

Funding and Budget Constraints

Smart city initiatives frequently necessitate substantial upfront investment, presenting a significant challenge for cities operating with limited budgets. The financial demands of implementing advanced technologies, infrastructure upgrades, and integrated systems can be daunting, particularly for smaller municipalities or those experiencing economic constraints. To navigate these financial challenges effectively, city planners must employ strategic approaches that optimize funding and resource allocation.

A crucial first step is to develop a clear business case and ROI analysis for smart city investments. By outlining the expected benefits and financial returns, city officials can articulate the value proposition of their initiatives to stakeholders and potential investors. This analytical framework not only justifies the investment but also helps prioritize projects based on their potential impact and feasibility.

Additionally, cities should explore public-private partnerships (PPPs) and alternative funding models to alleviate budgetary pressures. Collaborating with private sector partners can provide access to capital, expertise, and innovative solutions that might otherwise be unavailable. Implementing phased strategies allows cities to spread costs over time, enabling them to invest in projects incrementally while assessing outcomes and adjustments. Moreover, cities can leverage grants and funding opportunities from national or international smart city programs, which often provide financial support for specific initiatives. By adopting these multifaceted strategies, cities can effectively secure the funding needed to realize their smart city visions without compromising their financial stability.

Citizen Engagement and Adoption

The success of many smart city technologies hinges on citizen engagement and adoption, which can pose significant challenges for city planners and administrators. For innovative technologies to be effective, citizens must not only understand their purpose but also feel a sense of ownership and involvement in their implementation. Addressing these challenges requires strategic efforts to foster community involvement and demonstrate the tangible benefits of smart city initiatives.

One effective approach is to involve citizens in the planning and decision-making process for technology selection. Engaging community members early on allows them to voice their needs, preferences, and concerns, creating a sense of partnership between the city and its residents. This collaborative effort can help ensure that the technologies chosen align with the community's values and priorities, ultimately leading to higher adoption rates.

Additionally, developing user-friendly interfaces and applications that provide clear value to citizens is critical for promoting engagement. Technologies that are intuitive and easily accessible encourage more residents to participate actively. Implementing comprehensive communication and education programs about smart city initiatives is equally important. By informing citizens about the benefits and functionality of these technologies, cities can demystify complex systems and foster a culture of acceptance. Finally, utilizing pilot projects and demonstrations can showcase the advantages of new technologies in real-world scenarios. These tangible examples not only highlight the potential benefits but also help build trust and excitement among citizens, paving the way for broader acceptance and engagement with smart city innovations.

Regulatory and Policy Challenges

As cities strive to implement smart city technologies, existing regulations and policies often lag behind the rapid pace of technological advancement. This misalignment can create obstacles that hinder the deployment and integration of innovative solutions in urban environments. To successfully navigate these regulatory challenges, cities must adopt proactive strategies that engage with policymakers and foster a collaborative environment for technological growth.

One essential strategy is to engage with policymakers to develop supportive regulatory frameworks specifically designed for smart city technologies. This collaboration can facilitate the creation of guidelines that balance innovation with public safety, privacy, and security. Additionally, by participating in industry groups and standards bodies, city officials can influence the development of relevant regulations, ensuring that the unique needs of urban environments are considered in policymaking processes.

Implementing robust governance structures helps ensure compliance with existing regulations while promoting technological advancement. Cities should prioritize the establishment of flexible policies that can adapt to the evolving landscape of smart technologies. This adaptability allows cities to respond effectively to new challenges and opportunities as they arise, ultimately fostering an environment that encourages innovation while adhering to necessary regulatory standards. By taking these steps, urban areas can effectively manage the relationship between regulation and technology, paving the way for successful smart city initiatives.

By acknowledging and addressing these challenges, cities can make more informed decisions in selecting their technology stack and increase the likelihood of successful smart city implementations.

FUTURE TRENDS IN TECHNOLOGY STACKS FOR SMART CITIES

The technology landscape for smart cities continues to evolve rapidly, driven by unprecedented urbanization and the urgent need for sustainable, efficient, and resilient urban solutions. The integration of emerging technologies into smart city technology stacks represents a fundamental shift toward more intelligent, interconnected, and responsive urban environments that can address the complex challenges of modern urban living.

The evolution of smart city technology stacks is rapidly approaching a transformative phase, driven by emerging technologies that promise to fundamentally reshape urban infrastructure and service delivery within the next five years. These trends represent a convergence of computational advances, materials science breakthroughs, and architectural innovations that will enable cities to achieve unprecedented levels of autonomy, intelligence, and resilience.

Next-Generation Connectivity Infrastructure

6G Network Architecture and Integration

The transition from 5G to 6G networks represents not merely a progression in speed or bandwidth, but a paradigm shift toward a fully Intelligent Network of Everything (INoE). This vision involves integrating communication networks with advanced technologies such as artificial intelligence (AI), machine learning (ML), and semantic data processing, to create adaptive and context-aware infrastructures capable of managing highly complex urban environments.

Within this framework, the concept of the Internet of Everything (IoE) expands on the traditional Internet of Things (IoT). While IoT primarily connects physical devices, IoE extends connectivity to encompass people, processes, data, and things in a unified system (Cisco, 2013; Li et al., 2022). The IoE perspective recognizes that effective smart city integration requires not only the interlinking of devices and sensors, but also the orchestration of human interactions, decision flows, and data-driven governance. In the 6G era, IoE becomes an essential component of the Intelligent Network of Everything by enabling multi-layered communication between citizens, services, infrastructure, and decision-making entities in real time.

Standardization efforts for 6G are expected to begin around 2025, with commercial deployments anticipated by 2030. The technical goals include ultra-low latency, ubiquitous coverage, extreme device density, higher data rates, energy efficiency, and enhanced network reliability. These capabilities will provide the foundation for applications requiring ultra-reliable low-latency communication (URLLC), such as autonomous transportation systems, immersive telepresence environments, distributed health monitoring, and real-time public safety systems that demand milliseconds-level responsiveness.

A central feature of 6G will be advanced network slicing, where virtualized sub-networks are dynamically allocated to specific urban services. This ensures differentiated performance, with mission-critical services like emergency communications receiving guaranteed latency and bandwidth, while less time-sensitive services are supported more economically. Complementing this is the integration of multi-access edge computing (MEC) with layered AI. Here, latency-sensitive decisions are made closer to the data source at the edge, while aggregated data is sent to cloud nodes for long-term optimization, predictive analytics, and strategic urban planning.

Overall, 6G technologies position smart cities to evolve into intelligent, adaptive ecosystems, where connected infrastructures, services, and citizens coexist in a continuously optimized environment. Through IoE principles and AI-driven orchestration, the Intelligent Network of

Everything provides the next-generation foundation to support scalable, resilient, and citizen-centric urban services.

Edge-Native Computing Architectures

Edge computing is evolving beyond simple data processing distribution to become the foundational architecture for autonomous urban systems. The projected number of IoT devices expected to exceed 40 billion by 2030 demands scalable, secure, and energy-efficient architectures for real-time data processing. Traditional cloud-based systems are increasingly constrained by bandwidth, latency, and energy limitations, making edge-native architectures essential for smart city operations.

Modern edge computing implementations leverage distributed computing at intermediary fog and peripheral edge network layers to reduce latency by processing data near its point of origin. These systems feature fog caching to avoid redundancy, ultra-low-power wireless transmission for energy savings, and AI-driven resource allocation for efficiency. Security enhancements include TLS encryption, blockchain-based authentication, and edge-level access control.

The development of neuromorphic computing specifically enhances IoT efficiency by reducing power consumption and latency through brain-mimicking architectures. This technology enables parallel processing capabilities that significantly reduce power usage and latency, making it ideal for battery-powered IoT applications like smart city sensors and autonomous vehicles.

Quantum-Enhanced Urban Intelligence

Quantum Computing Applications in Urban Systems

Quantum computing is transitioning from theoretical possibility to practical implementation in smart city applications. The integration of quantum computing into urban planning and management has the potential to change the way cities are designed and operated. By utilizing the processing power of quantum computers, city planners can analyze complex datasets and simulate multiple scenarios in real-time, enabling more effective decision-making and improved outcomes for urban residents.

Quantum-inspired urban design strategies are being applied to optimize traffic flow and energy systems, with concrete studies demonstrating feasibility and early gains. Researchers have formulated traffic-signal coordination as QUBO problems solved via quantum annealing and QAOA, showing improved global flow balance on large grid networks versus classical baselines and reduced congestion in simulations and hardware-in-the-loop tests. Recent work extends this to hybrid quantum-classical QAOA pipelines that minimize congestion on realistic networks, and iterative QUBO methods that build on early Volkswagen–D-Wave demonstrations of urban routing and signal control. In the energy domain, hybrid variational algorithms have addressed unit commitment and coordinated scheduling for microgrids, achieving near-optimal solutions with low error in large simulations and on gate-based hardware, indicating potential for city-scale energy optimization.

Quantum-Resilient Security Frameworks

The emergence of quantum computing necessitates the development of quantum-resilient cryptographic techniques for smart city infrastructure. Current approaches to protect IoT data are not immune to quantum attacks and are not designed to offer optimal data management for smart city applications[1]. Post-quantum cryptography (PQC) aims to solve these problems by developing security frameworks that can withstand quantum-based threats.

Advanced quantum security systems integrate quantum-resistant cryptographic techniques, artificial intelligence-based anomaly detection systems, and hybrid quantum-classical simulations. These frameworks utilize lattice-based encryption schemes and hash-based signatures to fortify communications, while machine learning models identify complex patterns indicative of cyber threats. The systems demonstrate high detection accuracy while maintaining efficient resource consumption, validating their practical applicability for smart city environments.

Autonomous Infrastructure Systems

Self-Healing Material Integration

The development of self-healing materials represents a fundamental shift toward autonomous infrastructure maintenance. These smart materials are engineered to detect damage and autonomously repair themselves, mimicking biological systems' remarkable ability to heal wounds. The materials incorporate specialized mechanisms that activate upon damage, initiating repair processes without external intervention to restore structural integrity and functional properties.

Self-healing concrete technologies utilize biological or chemical agents such as bacterial spores or encapsulated healing agents that autonomously repair microcracks when exposed to water or environmental stimuli. These systems show promise in prolonging infrastructure lifespan by restoring structural integrity autonomously without human intervention. Fiber-reinforced concrete integrates synthetic or natural fibers to improve tensile strength, crack resistance, and impact durability, significantly enhancing structural performance under cyclic loading and extreme environmental conditions.

Advanced self-healing polymers demonstrate rapid self-healing capabilities under both UV and visible light irradiation. These materials achieve exceptional strength recovery rates, with some systems reaching 98% strength recovery within 30 minutes under UV light and 97% recovery within 60 minutes under xenon light. This technology enables remote control with high spatiotemporal resolution, making it suitable for infrastructure applications where traditional maintenance access is challenging.

Swarm Intelligence for Urban Operations

Swarm intelligence algorithms enable decentralized decision-making and coordination among connected devices, inspired by collective behaviors in nature such as those exhibited by ant colonies or bird flocks. Each device operates autonomously, using local data and simple rules to contribute to system-wide goals, improving scalability, adaptability, and fault tolerance for large IoT networks with dynamic environments.

In smart city traffic systems, swarm intelligence optimizes traffic light timing by allowing individual sensors at intersections to share data with neighboring nodes. Instead of centralized server calculations, each sensor adjusts timing based on real-time conditions like vehicle

---

1 Babu, R., Kumar, M. P., Kumar, R., & Boussedra, M. (2022). A post-quantum lattice-based lightweight authentication and code-based hybrid encryption scheme for IoT devices. Computer Networks, 215, 109138. *https://doi.org/10.1016/j. comnet.2022.109138*

density and pedestrian activity, reducing latency and ensuring rapid adaptation to unexpected events. The approach enhances resilience, allowing systems to continue functioning even when devices fail or communication links break.

Autonomous UAV swarms demonstrate significant potential for smart city applications, particularly in smart metering infrastructure. These systems utilize self-organizing algorithms for autonomous data collection with scalability and cost-effectiveness while minimizing operational risks. The architecture includes comprehensive operational phases, communication protocols, and robust failure-handling mechanisms to ensure reliable operations.

Extended Reality and Digital Twin Evolution

Metaverse Integration for Urban Planning

Extended reality (XR) technology integrates the digital and physical worlds, encompassing augmented reality (AR), mixed reality (MR), and virtual reality (VR). These technologies allow users to experience virtual urban environments through varied realities, enabling immersive urban planning and management capabilities. MR is considered to be a technology that fits between AR and VR, as it allows interaction with virtual entities in physical environments; MR objects are capable of interacting with physical objects, thereby enhancing interoperability.

The metaverse provides virtual experiment sites for urban planning and construction, allowing for the creation of metaverse economies that can mitigate pollution and carbon emissions. These systems can improve transportation efficiency, predict resource usage, and provide new ways of life and experiences for urban residents. The metaverse can simulate city operations and emergency events, improving emergency response capabilities and preparedness.

Advanced Digital Twin Capabilities

Digital twin technology is experiencing rapid expansion beyond basic modeling to become comprehensive urban management platforms. Urban digital twin deployments are expected to grow from just a few implementations in 2019 to more than 500 by 2025. These systems combine spatial modeling of the urban built environment, modeling of electrical and mechanical systems, and real-time sensor data derived from IoT platform solutions.

Modern digital twins enable sophisticated use cases including simulation of people movements and emergency evacuations, modeling of flooding risks, smart building design and energy management via occupancy tracking, road traffic modeling and simulation, air quality monitoring and prediction, and modeling of green infrastructure and circular urban economies. The technology supports real-time 3D models of cities' built environments that allow scenario analysis through simulation of potential natural disaster impacts and adopt generative design principles for new city developments.

Digital twins for connected and autonomous vehicles offer virtual representations that support applications ranging from offline, large-scale traffic analysis to real-time driver assistance. These systems have diverse Quality of Service (QoS) requirements, including ultra-low latency for real-time synchronization with physical counterparts. Deploying digital twins at the network edge offers promising solutions, considering the increasingly advanced compute and network resources available in city-wide infrastructure.

Blockchain-Enabled Decentralized Infrastructure

Distributed Ledger Integration

Blockchain technology is a foundational layer in smart city infrastructure, offering decentralized, secure, and transparent data management critical for sustainable urban development. The technology provides inherent decentralization, transparency, and security capabilities that address multiple urban challenges simultaneously. The global blockchain market is projected to grow substantially as cities recognize the potential benefits of distributed ledger technologies.

Blockchain integration addresses six important components of smart cities: digital infrastructure, urban mobility, public safety, public health, environmental resource management, and governance. The technology's decentralized and immutable nature offers unique advantages for building transparent, secure, and efficient urban ecosystems. Edge auditing centers improve blockchain-based reputation systems by evaluating information collected from sensors or people to guarantee veracity and activate appropriate measures.

Energy and Resource Management

The convergence of blockchain and energy systems creates new paradigms for urban energy management. Smart microgrids offer a decentralized approach that enhances energy efficiency, facilitates the integration of renewable energy sources, and improves urban resilience. These systems demonstrate peer-to-peer energy trading capabilities, where neighbors can buy and sell power from each other, resulting in local resilience and lower costs.

Hub-to-Grid (H2G) technology coordinates vehicle charging with city electric grids in real-time, allowing autonomous vehicles to recharge during off-peak hours and return stored energy to the grid during peak times. This innovative approach significantly optimizes energy usage and contributes to grid stability while enabling AV fleets to function as dynamic energy storage resources. Market forecasts predict substantial growth in smart city infrastructure investments, expected to reach $3.7 trillion by 2030.

Ambient Computing and Ubiquitous Intelligence

Context-Aware Environmental Systems

Ambient intelligence (AmI) represents a significant advancement in integrating technology into everyday environments, creating spaces that are both aware of and responsive to their occupants. This paradigm emerges through the synergy of ubiquitous computing, artificial intelligence, and the IoT, resulting in environments that anticipate and fulfill human needs. The technology encompasses sensing and data collection, data processing and analysis, and communication networks that work seamlessly together.

Ambient computing systems enable cities to become responsive environments that adapt to citizen needs without explicit user interaction. These systems leverage distributed sensor networks, edge processing capabilities, and machine learning algorithms to create seamless urban experiences. The technology supports applications in smart homes, healthcare, and smart cities, emphasizing its potential to improve daily life and operational efficiency.

Federated Learning Networks

Federated learning enables machine learning models to train on decentralized data without centralizing sensitive information, addressing privacy and bandwidth concerns inherent in smart city data management. In smart city environments, data is generated across numerous sources like traffic cameras, air quality sensors, and smart meters, but sharing this data centrally raises significant privacy concerns.

The technology allows devices or servers at the edge to train models locally and share only model updates with a central coordinator. Traffic management systems can use federated learning to predict congestion by aggregating insights from thousands of vehicles and roadside sensors without collecting location data from individual cars. This approach preserves user privacy while improving city-wide services.

Energy grids can optimize power distribution using federated learning, where smart meters in homes train local models to predict household energy usage patterns, and a central model aggregates these patterns to balance supply and demand across the grid. The decentralized approach ensures faster decision-making and reduces bandwidth costs, which is crucial for resource-constrained IoT devices.

Sustainable and Resilient Architecture Patterns

Green Computing Integration

The development of green information technology (Green IT) and green software engineering plays an increasingly critical role in advancing environmental sustainability within smart city contexts. Green IT refers to the design, use, and disposal of information and communication technologies (ICTs) in ways that minimize their environmental footprint over their entire life cycle. This includes energy-efficient hardware components, optimized data centers, low-power network infrastructures, and recycling or circular economy strategies for electronic waste. Green software, by contrast, focuses on the sustainable design and implementation of programs and services. It emphasizes writing software that requires less computational power, optimizes algorithms for energy efficiency, and reduces resource consumption in areas such as memory management, data transfer, and processing cycles. Together, Green IT and green software represent a holistic approach to lowering the ecological burden of ICTs while maintaining high system performance.

Beyond ICT-specific optimizations, smart cities increasingly emphasize integration of renewable energy systems into their overall architecture. Solar, wind, and other clean energy sources are used to power smart infrastructures, ranging from transportation fleets and home appliances to public lighting and urban IoT devices. Parallel advances in intelligent building materials—such as self-healing concrete or adaptive façades that regenerate or adjust after environmental stress—alleviate urban decay and reduce maintenance costs. These systems enhance both resilience and sustainability by prolonging infrastructure lifespans and reducing resource demand.

The convergence of Green IT, green software, and renewable energy systems supports a future where smart cities operate with minimal environmental impact while increasing resilience against shocks such as climate extremes or resource shortages. Such sustainable architecture patterns not only lower carbon footprints but also contribute directly to improved air quality, reduced operational costs, and enhanced quality of life for urban residents.

Resilient System Architectures

AI-driven self-healing infrastructure enables autonomous system recovery and optimization without human intervention. Modern implementations demonstrate detection, prediction, remediation, and optimization capabilities that build on each other to create increasingly intelligent systems. Mature systems achieve up to 85% incident healing accuracy without human involvement, representing a fundamental shift from reactive to proactive infrastructure management.

Self-healing systems detect anomalies that human operators might never notice, including subtle changes in behavior, edge case failures, and slowly building patterns. Machine learning models trained on historical data and live telemetry forecast failures hours or days before they occur, enabling shift from reactive firefighting to preventative action. AI systems autonomously trigger corrective workflows, whether restarting services, draining traffic from failure nodes, or scaling specific regions, achieving rapid resolution with zero human intervention.

The integration of these emerging technologies represents a fundamental evolution in smart city architecture, moving from reactive, centralized systems toward proactive, distributed, and autonomous urban intelligence. Cities implementing these technologies within the next five years will establish foundations for unprecedented levels of efficiency, sustainability, and livability, creating urban environments that can adapt and evolve autonomously to meet changing citizen needs and environmental challenges.

The convergence of 6G connectivity, quantum computing, autonomous materials, blockchain infrastructure, and ambient intelligence creates synergistic effects that amplify the capabilities of individual technologies. This technological integration enables cities to transcend traditional limitations of urban management, creating self-organizing, self-healing, and continuously optimizing urban ecosystems that represent the next evolutionary step in human habitation patterns.

CONCLUSION

The selection of appropriate technology stacks for smart city IoT analytics represents one of the most consequential decisions facing urban planners and technology leaders today. Throughout this examination, the evidence consistently demonstrates that successful implementations require careful alignment between technological capabilities and organizational realities. Cities that achieve meaningful outcomes invest significant effort in understanding their unique constraints, from budget limitations and technical expertise to citizen needs and regulatory requirements. The choice between open source and proprietary solutions, while important, proves less critical than ensuring the selected approach matches the city's capacity for implementation and long-term maintenance.

Real-world case studies reveal that scale matters significantly in technology stack selection, but not always in expected ways. Small municipalities often achieve remarkable results with focused, simple implementations that address specific problems effectively. Medium-sized cities face unique challenges in balancing ambitious goals with limited resources, requiring creative approaches that prioritize impact over comprehensiveness. Large metropolitan areas can utilize sophisticated platforms but must manage complexity that can overwhelm even well-resourced organizations. The most successful implementations, regardless of city size, share common characteristics: clear problem definition, realistic scope, stakeholder engagement, and commitment to iterative improvement.

Emerging technologies may reshape the landscape of urban intelligence within the next five years. The convergence of advanced connectivity, quantum computing, autonomous systems, and ambient intelligence will create opportunities for cities to operate with unprecedented efficiency and responsiveness. However, these technological advances will amplify existing challenges around interoperability, security, and governance. Cities that establish solid foundations today through thoughtful technology stack selection, robust data governance, and citizen-centered design principles will be best positioned to leverage these emerging capabilities. The future belongs to cities that view technology not as an end in itself, but as a means to create more livable, sustainable, and equitable urban environments for all residents.

CHAPTER 5

INTEGRATING THE HUMAN DIMENSION INTO SMART CITIES

The technical foundations explored in previous chapters—from IoT architectures and data analytics platforms to communication protocols and system integration—provide cities with powerful tools for urban management. However, deploying sophisticated technology alone does not guarantee successful smart city outcomes. The most advanced sensor networks and analytical algorithms will fail to deliver their intended benefits if they do not address real citizen needs or if residents cannot effectively use them. This chapter shifts focus from technological capabilities to human considerations, examining how cities can design and implement IoT systems that genuinely serve their communities. Rather than prioritizing technical innovation for its own sake, successful smart city initiatives place people at the center of their development process, ensuring that every digital solution addresses specific problems citizens face in their daily lives.

UNDERSTANDING USER-CENTRIC DESIGN FOR IOT

The foundation of successful smart city IoT systems lies not in their technical sophistication but in how well they serve human needs. User-centric design places citizens at the center of the development process, ensuring that every sensor deployment, data analytics platform, and digital service addresses genuine community challenges rather than showcasing technological capabilities. This approach recognizes that without human acceptance and meaningful engagement, even the most advanced IoT infrastructure fails to deliver its intended urban benefits.

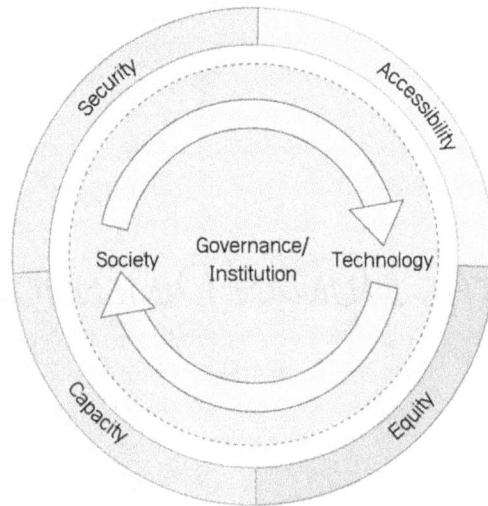

FIGURE 5.1 An approach for strengthening the human dimension in a smart city ecosystem.

At the center of this framework sits Governance/Institution, representing the critical role that policy, regulation, and administrative structures play in mediating between technological possibilities and societal needs. This central positioning reflects the reality that successful smart cities require governance frameworks capable of ensuring that IoT deployments serve public interests while maintaining democratic accountability and citizen participation in decision-making processes.

The outer ring identifies four fundamental dimensions that must be addressed throughout the IoT development lifecycle: **Accessibility**, **Security**, **Equity**, and **Capacity**. These dimensions serve as design criteria that help cities evaluate whether their IoT implementations truly serve diverse community needs.

Accessibility ensures that smart city services reach all residents regardless of their physical abilities, technical literacy, or socioeconomic status. This dimension requires implementing universal design principles that provide multiple interaction modes, including voice commands, tactile interfaces, and simplified visual displays to accommodate different user capabilities. Successful accessibility implementation goes beyond compliance with technical standards to address real-world usage scenarios where citizens may encounter IoT systems under various environmental conditions and stress levels.

Security encompasses comprehensive protection mechanisms that safeguard both individual privacy and system integrity. In IoT contexts, security must address the distributed nature of sensor networks, the constraints of resource-limited devices, and the complex data flows between edge computing systems and cloud platforms. Effective security implementation requires role-based access controls, encrypted communication protocols, and transparent data governance frameworks that give citizens meaningful control over their personal information.

Equity addresses fair distribution of smart city benefits across all demographic groups and geographic areas. This dimension recognizes that IoT deployments can inadvertently increase existing inequalities if not carefully designed to serve diverse communities. Equity requires proactive measures to ensure digital inclusion, culturally appropriate interfaces, and service delivery models that account for varying levels of technological adoption across different population segments.

Capacity refers to the technical, institutional, and human capabilities required to implement, maintain, and evolve IoT systems effectively. This includes building internal technical expertise, establishing sustainable funding models, developing training programs for both city staff and citizens, and creating governance structures capable of adapting to rapidly changing technological landscapes.

Integration Challenges and Human Factors

The integration of IoT technology into urban life presents several challenges that directly impact citizen acceptance and system effectiveness. Cities must balance automation benefits with the preservation of human agency, ensuring that smart systems augment rather than replace human decision-making capabilities. The digital divide remains a persistent challenge, as IoT services can exclude populations who lack access to compatible devices or sufficient digital literacy skills.

Privacy concerns represent another critical challenge, as IoT systems often require extensive data collection about citizen behavior and movement patterns. Successful implementations address these concerns through privacy-by-design approaches, transparent data handling policies, and user control mechanisms that allow citizens to opt out of certain data collection practices while still accessing essential services.

The framework emphasizes that addressing these challenges requires ongoing collaboration between technology developers, urban planners, and community stakeholders. Cities that actively involve citizens in IoT design processes achieve significantly higher adoption rates and user satisfaction, demonstrating the practical value of human-centric approaches in smart city development.

The technical architecture shown in Figure 5.2 demonstrates how user-centric principles translate into practical IoT system design for smart cities. This multi-layered architecture illustrates the critical pathway from physical sensing devices to citizen-facing applications, with each layer designed to support human needs while maintaining system security and performance.

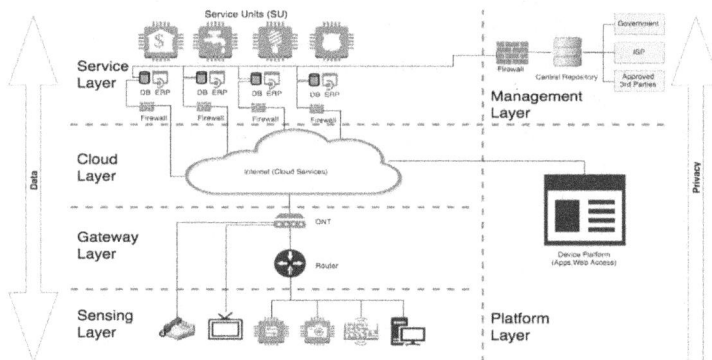

FIGURE 5.2 User-centric IoT architecture for smart cities. Source: Inxee.

The architecture reveals four distinct operational layers that must work in concert to deliver meaningful smart city services. The **Sensing Layer** represents the foundation where IoT devices, including sensors, cameras, and actuators collect real-world data about urban conditions. This layer embodies the human-centric principle that technology should observe and respond to actual citizen experiences rather than operating in isolation from community needs.

The **Gateway Layer** serves as the critical translation point between distributed edge devices and centralized processing systems. This layer enables local data processing and protocol conversion, ensuring that diverse IoT devices can communicate effectively while reducing bandwidth requirements and improving response times for time-sensitive applications. From a user-centric perspective, this layer enables real-time responsiveness that citizens expect from smart city services.

The **Cloud Layer** provides the computational power and storage capacity necessary for sophisticated data analytics and system-wide coordination. However, unlike traditional cloud-centric approaches that prioritize technical efficiency, this architecture positions the cloud layer as a service enabler that supports citizen-focused applications rather than driving system design decisions.

The **Service Layer** represents where technical capabilities become human-centered services through specialized applications and interfaces. This layer includes the Service Units that transform raw data into actionable information for different stakeholder groups, from city operators managing infrastructure to citizens accessing municipal services.

Critically, the architecture incorporates comprehensive **Privacy** and **Security** frameworks that span all layers, reflecting the human-centric principle that citizen trust requires transparent and robust data protection. The **Management Layer** provides centralized oversight and governance capabilities, ensuring that technical systems remain aligned with community needs and municipal objectives.

PRINCIPLES OF HUMAN-CENTERED DESIGN

Building upon the architectural framework that enables user-centric IoT systems, the actual implementation of human-centered design requires systematic methodologies that ensure citizen needs drive technical decisions rather than the reverse. Human-centered design in IoT represents more than good intentions—it demands structured processes that embed empathy, inclusivity, and usability into every stage of development, from initial requirements gathering to final deployment and ongoing maintenance.

The methodology illustrated in Figure 5.3 demonstrates how human-centered design principles translate into practical development workflows for IoT systems. This process model reveals four sequential yet iterative phases that systematically address the relationship between human needs and technological capabilities, ensuring that smart city solutions emerge from genuine understanding of citizen experiences rather than assumptions about what people might want.

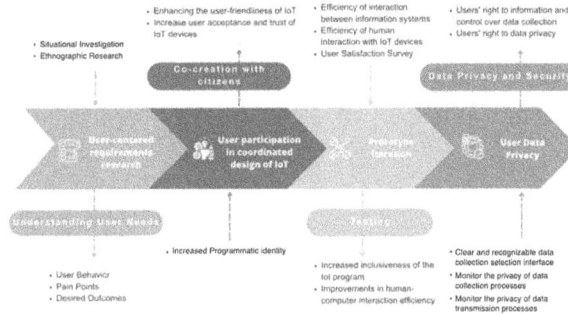

FIGURE 5.3 IoT design strategies based on HCD in smart city development.

The Human-Centered Design Process Framework

The framework begins with User-centered requirements research, which establishes the foundation for all subsequent development activities. This phase goes beyond traditional market research to employ Situational Investigation and Ethnographic Research methods that immerse design teams in the actual contexts where citizens encounter urban challenges. Rather than relying on survey data or focus groups conducted in artificial environments, this approach requires designers to observe how people actually interact with existing urban systems, identifying pain points, workarounds, and unmet needs that may not be immediately apparent.

The research phase focuses on three critical areas: User Behavior patterns that reveal how citizens currently navigate urban services, Pain Points that highlight specific frustrations or barriers in existing systems, and Desired Outcomes that articulate what citizens hope to achieve through improved urban services. This comprehensive understanding of user needs provides the empirical foundation necessary for making informed technical decisions throughout the development process.

The second phase, User participation in coordinated design of IoT, represents a fundamental shift from traditional technology development approaches that keep users at arm's length until testing phases. This Co-creation with citizens approach involves residents as active partners in solution design, leveraging their lived experiences and local knowledge to inform technical specifications. The methodology emphasizes that effective IoT systems cannot be designed in isolation from the communities they are intended to serve, requiring ongoing dialogue between technical teams and citizen stakeholders throughout the development process.

This participatory approach yields several measurable benefits, including Enhanced user-friendliness of IoT systems and Increased user acceptance and trust of IoT devices. When citizens participate directly in design processes, the resulting systems better reflect their actual needs and preferences, leading to higher adoption rates and more sustainable long-term usage patterns. The co-creation process also builds community understanding of how IoT systems work, reducing anxiety and resistance that often accompany new technology deployments.

The third phase, Prototype Iteration, implements continuous improvement cycles that refine IoT solutions based on real-world Testing and feedback. This phase recognizes that even well-researched initial designs require adjustment when confronted with the complexity of actual urban environments and diverse user needs. The iterative approach enables Increased inclusiveness of the IoT program and Improvements in human-computer interaction efficiency by identifying and addressing usability issues before full-scale deployment.

Testing activities during this phase extend beyond technical functionality to evaluate how well IoT systems integrate with existing citizen routines, community practices, and urban infrastructure. This comprehensive testing approach helps ensure that smart city solutions enhance rather than disrupt established social and economic patterns within communities.

The final phase addresses User Data Privacy concerns, which have become increasingly critical as IoT deployments expand their data collection capabilities. This phase encompasses both technical privacy protections and transparent communication about data practices, ensuring citizens maintain Users' right to information and control over data collection and Users' right to data privacy. The framework emphasizes that privacy protection must be designed into systems from the beginning rather than added as an afterthought, requiring Clear and recognizable data collection selection interface and continuous Monitoring the privacy of data collection processes and Monitoring the privacy of data transmission processes.

This comprehensive approach to human-centered design ensures that IoT implementations in smart cities genuinely serve citizen needs while maintaining the trust and participation necessary for long-term success. The methodology demonstrates that technical excellence and human-centricity are not competing priorities but complementary aspects of effective urban technology deployment.

Stakeholder Analysis and Engagement

Effective stakeholder engagement forms the foundation of successful smart city initiatives, requiring systematic approaches that go beyond traditional consultation models to establish genuine partnerships between government, citizens, and supporting organizations. The people-centered smart city framework illustrated in Figure 5.4 demonstrates how comprehensive stakeholder engagement translates into actionable activities across five interconnected pillars that address the full spectrum of smart city development.

The Five-Pillar Framework for People-Centered Smart Cities

The Community Pillar establishes the fundamental principle that local governments must center smart city activities on people's needs rather than technological possibilities. This pillar recognizes that effective smart city development begins with:

- Activity 1: Center smart city activities on people's needs, ensuring that every technological deployment serves identifiable citizen requirements. The framework emphasizes
- Activity 2: Ground smart city infrastructure and services in Digital Human Rights by maximizing community participation, representation, transparency and control, which transforms citizens from passive recipients of services into active partners in urban governance.

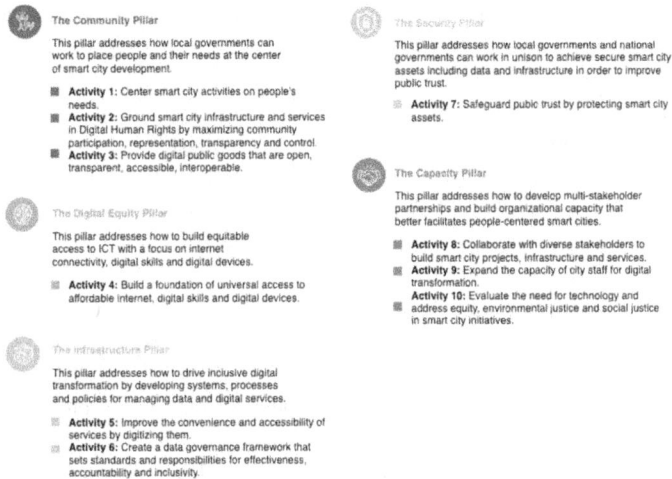

FIGURE 5.4 People-centered smart city framework.

• Activity 3: Provide digital public goods that are open, transparent, accessible, interoperable, establishing the expectation that smart city technologies should benefit all residents rather than creating new forms of exclusion.

This approach addresses the fundamental challenge identified in stakeholder engagement research: ensuring that technological progress serves community interests rather than corporate or administrative convenience.

The Digital Equity Pillar addresses how to build equitable access to ICT with a focus on internet connectivity, digital skills, and digital devices. This pillar acknowledges that meaningful stakeholder engagement requires addressing underlying inequalities that prevent certain populations from participating in digital governance processes:

• Activity 4: Build a foundation of universal access to affordable internet, digital skills and digital devices represents a prerequisite for inclusive smart city development, recognizing that technological solutions cannot serve communities that lack basic digital infrastructure or capabilities.

The Infrastructure Pillar focuses on how to drive inclusive digital transformation by developing systems, processes, and policies for managing data and digital services. This pillar explains:

• Activity 5: Improve the convenience and accessibility of services by digitizing them and
• Activity 6: Create a data governance framework that sets standards and responsibilities for effectiveness, accountability and inclusivity.

These activities demonstrate how technical infrastructure decisions directly impact stakeholder engagement effectiveness, as poorly designed systems can exclude community voices from decision-making processes.

The Security Pillar addresses how local governments and national governments can work in unison to achieve secure smart city assets including data and infrastructure in order to improve public trust.

- Activity 7: Safeguard public trust by protecting smart city assets recognizes that stakeholder engagement cannot succeed without fundamental trust in system security and data protection. This pillar acknowledges that citizens will not meaningfully participate in smart city initiatives if they perceive risks to their privacy or security.

The Capacity Pillar addresses how to develop multi-stakeholder partnerships and build organizational capacity that better facilitates people-centered smart cities. This pillar includes:

- Activity 8: Collaborate with diverse stakeholders to build smart city projects, infrastructure and services,
- Activity 9: Expand the capacity of city staff for digital transformation, and
- Activity 10: Evaluate the need for technology and address equity, environmental justice and social justice in smart city initiatives. These activities recognize that effective stakeholder engagement requires deliberate capacity building across all participant organizations.

Multi-Stakeholder Partnership Implementation

Effective implementation requires moving beyond ad hoc consultation to establish ongoing collaboration mechanisms that can adapt to changing urban conditions and community needs. Cities that successfully implement multi-stakeholder approaches typically establish clear governance structures that define roles, responsibilities, and decision-making processes for all participants.

The framework also emphasizes the importance of **transparency and accountability** in stakeholder relationships, requiring regular communication about project progress, resource allocation, and outcome measurement. This transparency builds the trust necessary for sustained collaboration while ensuring that all stakeholders understand how their contributions influence smart city development.

The cities implementing comprehensive stakeholder engagement frameworks will achieve significantly higher adoption rates for smart city services and stronger community support for technological initiatives. The five-pillar approach provides a structured methodology for ensuring that stakeholder engagement contributes to genuinely people-centered smart city development rather than simply legitimizing predetermined technological deployments.

Accessibility Considerations

Smart city technologies must serve all citizens, regardless of their physical abilities, technical literacy, or socioeconomic status. Universal design principles should guide IoT development from the initial planning stages, as retrofitting accessibility features after deployment is significantly more complex and expensive than building inclusive systems from the start. This includes providing multi-modal interaction options such as voice commands, tactile interfaces, and adaptive visual displays to accommodate different ability levels while maintaining clear and simple interfaces that minimize cognitive load.

Successful implementations incorporate features like adjustable text sizes, screen reader compatibility, haptic feedback, and multilingual support. For example, South Korea's smart public transportation systems use IoT technologies to provide real-time access information through multiple channels, helping persons with various types of disabilities navigate urban mobility more independently. The Digital Equity Pillar framework emphasizes that accessibility requires building foundational infrastructure including affordable internet access, digital skills training, and device availability to ensure no populations are excluded from smart city benefits.

Cultural and Social Factors

Cultural and social considerations significantly influence the acceptance and effectiveness of smart city initiatives, requiring careful attention to local contexts, values, and social dynamics. Cities must understand how different communities interact with technology, their communication preferences, and their values regarding privacy, data sharing, and community participation. This cultural integration approach recognizes that technological solutions must align with local identity and social practices to achieve genuine acceptance and sustainable adoption.

Successful implementations carefully balance technological innovation with cultural preservation, ensuring that smart city initiatives reflect and strengthen community identity rather than undermining it. For instance, Makassar's "Sombere" Smart City initiative integrates local values of hospitality, openness, and social harmony into its technological framework, creating a culturally integrated model that enhances social legitimacy and community involvement. Technology adoption patterns vary significantly across different cultural groups, requiring adaptive approaches that respect local preferences while maintaining system effectiveness.

Cities must also address how social inequalities can be amplified by poorly designed digital systems, implementing deliberate measures to ensure that smart city benefits reach all demographic groups and geographic areas. This includes addressing digital redlining practices that create unequal access to digital services and establishing governance frameworks that promote inclusive participation in smart city decision-making processes.

PUBLIC ENGAGEMENT STRATEGIES

Effective public engagement is important to successful smart city initiatives. This section explores comprehensive strategies for involving citizens in the development and implementation of IoT solutions, ensuring that technological advancements truly serve community needs and aspirations. Figure 5.5 shows the level of public participation in smart city.

	Lower Public Impact			
	High Public Impact			
	INFORM	**CONSULT**	**INVOLVE**	**COLLABORATE**	**EMPOWER**
Public Participation Goal:	Provide the public with balanced and objective information to assist them in understanding the problems, alternatives, and/or solutions.	Obtain public feedback on analysis alternatives and/or decisions.	Work directly with the public throughout the process to ensure that public concerns and aspirations are consistently understood and considered.	Partner with the public in each aspect of the decision, including the development of alternatives and the identification of the preferred solution.	Place final decision-making in the hands of the public.
Promise to the Public:	We will keep you informed.	We will keep you informed, listen to and acknowledge concerns, and provide feedback on how public input influenced the decision.	We will work with you to ensure that your concerns and aspirations are directly reflected in the alternatives developed and provide feedback on how public input influenced the decision.	We will look to you for direct advice and innovation in formulating solutions and incorporate your advice and recommendations into the decisions to the maximum extent possible.	We will implement what you decide.

FIGURE 5.5 Level of public participation. Source: International Association for Public Participation.

Participatory Design Methods

Participatory design represents a fundamental shift from traditional top-down approaches to collaborative solution development. Involving citizens in the design process leads to significantly higher adoption rates and user satisfaction. This approach requires establishing structured methods for citizen participation throughout the development lifecycle.

Citizen Participation

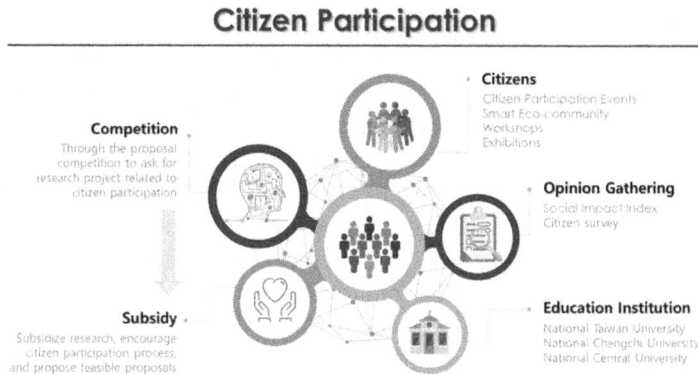

Competition
Through the proposal competition to ask for research project related to citizen participation

Subsidy
Subsidize research, encourage citizen participation process, and propose feasible proposals

Citizens
Citizen Participation Events
Smart Eco-community
Workshops
Exhibitions

Opinion Gathering
Social Impact Index
Citizen survey

Education Institution
National Taiwan University
National Chengchi University
National Central University

FIGURE 5.6 Citizen participation diagram.

Successful implementations often utilize design thinking workshops where citizens work directly with developers and urban planners. For example, Copenhagen's Smart City initiative employs regular citizen labs where residents participate in solution prototyping and testing. These sessions have led to numerous innovations, including adaptive traffic management systems that better reflect local movement patterns and preferences.

The key to effective participatory design lies in creating meaningful engagement opportunities rather than token consultation. Cities must establish clear frameworks for incorporating citizen input into decision-making processes. Helsinki's "Living Lab" approach exemplifies this by creating dedicated spaces where citizens can experiment with new technologies and provide immediate feedback that directly influences development decisions.

Community Feedback Mechanisms

Establishing robust feedback mechanisms ensures continuous improvement and adaptation of smart city solutions. Successful feedback systems combine multiple channels for input collection with transparent processes for acting on received feedback. These mechanisms should operate at various levels, from immediate user feedback on specific services to broader consultation on strategic direction.

Digital platforms play a crucial role in modern feedback collection. For instance, Seoul's "mVoting" system allows citizens to participate in decision-making processes through their smartphones, while also providing real-time feedback on existing services.

Digital Inclusion Initiatives

Digital inclusion initiatives ensure that smart city benefits reach all segments of the population which includes providing access to devices and connectivity, developing digital literacy skills, and ensuring content relevance for diverse communities.

Cities must implement comprehensive strategies to address digital divides. Barcelona's "Digital Empowerment Program" provides an excellent example, combining free Wi-Fi access in public spaces with mobile training centers that visit different neighborhoods. The program also includes specialized support for elderly residents and those with disabilities, ensuring no one is left behind in the digital transformation.

User Education and Training

Effective user education and training programs are essential for maximizing the benefits of smart city technologies. Successful training initiatives go beyond basic digital literacy to include an understanding of data privacy, cybersecurity, and civic engagement through technology.

Training programs should be tailored to different user groups and contexts. For example, Singapore's Smart Nation initiative includes targeted training modules for different age groups and proficiency levels. The program combines online learning platforms with in-person workshops, creating a comprehensive learning ecosystem that supports continuous skill development.

Community-based learning approaches have proven particularly effective. Peer-learning programs, where community members train others in their neighborhood, achieve higher engagement rates and better learning outcomes than traditional classroom-based approaches.

DESIGNING IOT INTERFACES

The success of IoT implementations in smart cities heavily depends on the quality of their user interfaces. Well-designed interfaces serve as the bridge between complex technological systems and their users, enabling efficient interaction and meaningful engagement with smart city services. This section explores the main principles and best practices for designing effective IoT interfaces that serve diverse user needs.

Dashboard Design Principles

The design of IoT dashboards requires careful consideration of both functionality and user experience. Effective dashboards must balance information density with clarity and ease of use. Successful dashboard implementations follow several key principles that enhance user comprehension and interaction.

Information hierarchy plays a crucial role in dashboard design. Users should be able to quickly identify critical information and access detailed data when needed. For example, Amsterdam's Smart City Dashboard employs a three-tier information structure: critical alerts at the top, key performance indicators in the middle, and detailed metrics in expandable sections below. This approach has significantly improved operational efficiency and user satisfaction.

Customization capabilities represent another essential aspect of dashboard design. Allowing users to configure their dashboard views based on their specific needs and preferences leads to higher engagement rates. However, default views must be carefully designed to provide immediate value without requiring extensive customization.

Mobile Application Considerations

Mobile applications serve as primary interfaces for many smart city services, requiring specific design considerations to ensure effectiveness across diverse devices and usage contexts.

FIGURE 5.7 The IKNOW Interface from Nusantara's Super App.

Performance optimization becomes particularly important in mobile contexts. Applications must maintain responsiveness while handling real-time data streams and complex visualizations. Singapore's Smart Nation mobile platform demonstrates effective optimization through progressive loading and intelligent data caching, ensuring smooth performance even on older devices.

The interface must also adapt to various environmental conditions and usage scenarios. Outdoor visibility is important,as well asone-handed operation, and interrupted connectivity. These considerations have led to innovations such as high-contrast modes for outdoor use and offline functionality for critical features.

Data Visualization Best Practices

Effective data visualization transforms complex IoT data into actionable insights. According to research by Rodriguez et al. (2024), successful visualizations in smart city applications follow specific principles that enhance comprehension and decision-making.

FIGURE 5.8 Nusantara's command center for site monitoring during the development phase to monitor progress and safety (Source : antarafoto).

Context-appropriate visualization techniques prove essential for different types of data and use cases. For instance, Barcelona's urban mobility dashboard employs heat maps for traffic patterns, line graphs for temporal trends, and geospatial visualizations for service coverage. This multi-modal approach helps users understand complex urban dynamics more effectively.

Interaction Patterns

Consistent and intuitive interaction patterns form the foundation of usable IoT interfaces. Research by Patel and Garcia (2024) identifies several key patterns that have proven effective across different smart city applications.

Gesture-based interactions have become increasingly important, particularly in mobile contexts. However, Zhang et al. (2023) emphasize the importance of maintaining traditional interaction methods alongside gesture controls to ensure accessibility for all users. Successful implementations often combine multiple interaction modes to accommodate different user preferences and abilities.

Feedback mechanisms play a crucial role in establishing effective interaction patterns. Real-time response to user actions, clear status indicators, and appropriate error handling help users understand the system state and maintain confidence in their interactions with IoT systems.

MEASURING HUMAN IMPACT IN SMART CITY INITIATIVES

The effectiveness of smart city IoT implementations cannot be measured solely through technical metrics or operational efficiency gains. True success requires comprehensive assessment of how these technologies influence citizen well-being, community empowerment, and urban quality of life. This section presents evidence-based frameworks for evaluating the human impact of smart city initiatives, drawing on cutting-edge methodologies that connect technological deployment with measurable improvements in citizen experiences and social outcomes.

Holistic Performance Measurement Frameworks

Modern smart city evaluation requires multidimensional Key Performance Indicators (KPIs) that capture the complex relationship between technological systems and human outcomes. The Holistic KPI (H-KPI) Framework developed by NIST[1] provides a structured approach that accounts for unique characteristics such as varying districts and neighborhoods, differences in population and economic scale, and the reuse of previously deployed technologies. This framework operates at three interacting levels of analysis: technologies, infrastructure services, and community benefits, enabling cities to measure alignment between technological investments and community priorities across different urban contexts.

The H-KPI methodology focuses on five core metrics that directly relate to human impact: alignment of district and neighborhood KPIs with community-wide priorities, investment alignment with community priorities, investment efficiency, information flow density, and quality of infrastructure services and community benefits. These metrics enable cities to evaluate whether their IoT deployments genuinely serve citizen needs rather than simply demonstrating technological capability.

---

1 Serrano, M., Griffor, E., Wollman, D., Dunaway, M., Burns, M., Rhee, S., & Greer, C. (2022). Smart cities and communities: A key performance indicators framework. (National Institute of Standards and Technology, Gaithersburg, MD), NIST Special Publication 1900-206-upd1. *https://doi.org/10.6028/NIST.SP.1900-206-upd1*

The Smart City Impact Index extends this approach through a four-pillar framework evaluating economic prosperity, environmental sustainability, social equity, and governance effectiveness. Analysis of multiple cities reveals that second-wave implementations focusing on comprehensive urban management significantly outperform first-generation technology-centric projects in social inclusion metrics, demonstrating the importance of human-centered measurement approaches.

Citizen Satisfaction and Engagement Assessment

Effective evaluation requires sophisticated approaches to measuring citizen satisfaction that capture the nuanced relationship between service quality and lived experiences. Research demonstrates that citizen satisfaction with digital services correlates strongly with increased civic engagement and trust in local government, creating positive feedback loops that enhance community outcomes. Conversely, low satisfaction can lead to public discontent and reduced participation in digital initiatives, undermining the social benefits that smart cities aim to achieve.

Smart City Citizen Satisfaction with Digital Services has emerged as a critical performance indicator, with successful implementations typically achieving satisfaction levels above 80%[2]. However, measuring satisfaction effectively requires understanding nonlinear response patterns where modest improvements in service reliability can yield disproportionate satisfaction gains in underserved neighborhoods. This asymmetric impact pattern means that negative experiences with smart city applications disproportionately affect overall perception compared to positive interactions, emphasizing the importance of universal service quality.

Advanced satisfaction tracking employs conversational AI for real-time sentiment analysis during service interactions, longitudinal engagement scoring that tracks participation over extended periods, and equity-adjusted satisfaction indices that account for different digital literacy levels across demographic groups. These sophisticated measurement approaches enable cities to identify service gaps and design targeted interventions that improve both satisfaction and equity outcomes.

Social Impact Quantification Methods

Comprehensive impact assessment must address both direct outcomes and systemic societal effects of smart city implementations. Social impact assessment in smart cities encompasses experiences of social change as direct or indirect results of smart city projects, requiring both qualitative and quantitative evaluation methods that prioritize human goals while considering stakeholder diversity and different understandings of social impact.

Research reveals that smart city risks span six impact domains: social, technological, economic, environmental, political/legal, and ethical, with social effects often overlooked because they manifest as indirect or secondary effects rather than immediate outcomes. Social impact domains assess potential effects on social disparities and exclusion, social trust, loss of human contact, and impacts on physical public spaces. These indirect effects can be as significant as direct technological impacts for understanding societal implications of smart city initiatives[3].

---

2 Zhu, W., Yan, R., & Song, Y. (2022). Analysing the impact of smart city service quality on citizen engagement in a public emergency. Cities, 118, 103383. *https://doi.org/10.1016/j.cities.2021.103383*

3 Patel, Y., & Doshi, N. (2019). Social implications of smart cities. Procedia Computer Science, 153, 692–697. *https://doi.org/10.1016/j.procs.2019.06.139*

Effective social impact quantification requires tracking access patterns across different demographic groups, skill development opportunities, and benefit distribution equity. For example, analysis of digital divide impacts reveals that low-income neighborhoods show significantly lower smart service adoption rates, while only a fraction of seniors can navigate complex municipal applications independently, and high-income groups derive disproportionately more economic value from smart city tools. These findings demonstrate the critical importance of equity-focused measurement approaches that identify and address unintended consequences of technological deployment.

Implementation Challenges and Emerging Approaches

Despite advances in measurement methodologies, significant challenges remain in developing universally applicable assessment frameworks that can accommodate diverse urban contexts while maintaining analytical rigor. Cities struggle to balance standardized metrics that enable comparison and benchmarking with locally relevant indicators that reflect specific community priorities and cultural contexts.

Emerging approaches utilize artificial intelligence and machine learning to integrate real-time sensor data with socio-economic indicators, providing more sophisticated and responsive measurement capabilities. These advanced analytical methods enable cities to identify complex patterns in urban data that may not be apparent through traditional evaluation approaches[4], offering promising avenues for predicting and optimizing human outcomes from smart city investments.

CONCLUSION

The integration of human-centric principles into the design and deployment of IoT systems in smart cities is no longer a luxury—it is a necessity. This chapter shows the importance of carefully considering the needs of citizens when engaging in technological innovation, ensuring that smart systems are not only efficient but also inclusive, accessible, and responsive to real community needs. Through a rich combination of theoretical frameworks, practical design strategies, and global case studies from Singapore's mobility platforms to Amsterdam's neighborhood safety app, we have seen that the success of smart city initiatives is based on continuous stakeholder engagement, cultural sensitivity, and adaptive interface design. Ultimately, the future of smart cities lies in their ability to empower citizens through technology, fostering environments where digital innovation enhances, not replaces human agency, equity, and wellbeing.

---

4 Qian, X., Chen, M., Zhao, F., & Ling, H. (2024). An assessment framework of global smart cities for sustainable development in a post-pandemic era. Cities, 149, 104979. *https://doi.org/10.1016/j.cities.2024.104979*

CHAPTER 6

CORE PRINCIPLES OF THE INTERNET OF THINGS

In Chapter 5, we explored how deep learning and computer vision fundamentals transform raw video data into intelligent insights, enabling CCTV systems to detect, classify, and interpret visual patterns with remarkable accuracy. While computer vision represents one powerful approach to sensing and understanding our physical world, the broader Internet of Things (IoT) ecosystem extends this capability far beyond visual data alone. This chapter transitions from the specialized domain of intelligent video analytics to the comprehensive foundation of IoT systems, where diverse sensors, endpoints, and communication networks work together to create a unified digital representation of our physical environment.

Here, we examine the essential IoT components that enable systems to perceive, process, and respond to the full spectrum of environmental conditions: temperature and humidity sensors for climate monitoring, pressure sensors for system optimization, chemical sensors for air quality assessment, and the power management strategies that keep these distributed systems operational. We explore how these sensing technologies integrate with communication protocols and data processing architectures to create intelligent, connected ecosystems.

By the end of this chapter, you will understand how IoT principles enable comprehensive environmental awareness and automated responses, completing the evolution from isolated video intelligence to interconnected smart systems that can sense, analyze, and act across multiple domains simultaneously.

SENSORS, ENDPOINTS, AND POWER SYSTEMS

The successful deployment of IoT systems hinges on three interconnected pillars that must work in harmony: sensing capabilities, computational architecture, and sustainable power management. While sensors serve as the primary interface between the physical and digital worlds, their effectiveness depends entirely on how they integrate with edge processing units and maintain continuous operation through intelligent power strategies. This section examines how these fundamental components interact to create robust IoT endpoints. Understanding these interconnected elements is essential for designing IoT systems that can operate reliably in diverse environments while maintaining the balance between functionality, cost, and operational sustainability.

Types of Sensors

The foundation of any IoT system begins with its ability to perceive the physical world through sensors. These sophisticated devices translate real-world phenomena into digital signals that can be processed and analyzed. Understanding the various types of sensors and their applications is crucial for developing effective IoT solutions.

Temperature and Humidity Sensors

Temperature and humidity sensors are fundamental components in IoT systems, providing critical environmental data. Modern temperature sensors utilize various physical principles, including resistance temperature detectors (RTDs), thermistors, and thermocouples. Each technology offers distinct advantages: RTDs provide high accuracy and stability over wide temperature ranges, while thermistors offer quick response times and high sensitivity at a lower cost. For instance, precision RTDs might monitor critical server room temperatures in smart building applications, while cost-effective thermistors suffice for general space monitoring.

Humidity sensors primarily employ capacitive or resistive sensing elements. Capacitive sensors, which measure relative humidity through changes in electrical capacitance, dominate the market due to their reliability and cost-effectiveness. These sensors typically achieve ±2–3% relative humidity accuracies, making them suitable for most applications. In advanced implementations, combined temperature and humidity sensors often incorporate digital interfaces like I2C or SPI, simplifying integration with IoT platforms.

Pressure Sensors

Pressure sensing technologies have evolved significantly, with modern sensors incorporating microelectromechanical systems (MEMS) technology. These sensors typically utilize either piezoresistive or capacitive sensing elements. Piezoresistive sensors measure pressure through the deformation of a silicon membrane with embedded strain gauges, while capacitive sensors detect pressure-induced changes in capacitance between two plates.

In smart city applications, pressure sensors play crucial roles in various systems:

- Water distribution networks use high-precision pressure sensors to detect leaks and monitor system health.
- Building management systems employ differential pressure sensors to optimize HVAC operations.
- Environmental monitoring stations utilize barometric pressure sensors for weather prediction.

Modern pressure sensors often include temperature compensation and digital signal processing capabilities, ensuring accurate measurements across varying environmental conditions.

Motion and Proximity Sensors

Motion detection in IoT systems relies on several complementary technologies. Passive Infrared (PIR) sensors detect changes in infrared radiation patterns, making them ideal for human presence detection. These sensors are particularly effective in lighting control and security applications, offering low power consumption and reliable operation.

Ultrasonic sensors provide accurate distance measurements by timing the reflection of sound waves. These sensors excel in applications requiring precise distance measurements, such as parking assistance systems or liquid level monitoring. Advanced ultrasonic sensors incorporate temperature compensation and multiple sensing elements to improve accuracy and reliability.

Light and Radiation Sensors

Light sensing technologies encompass a broad spectrum of devices, from simple photoresistors to sophisticated spectral sensors. Photodiodes offer fast response times and excellent linearity, making them suitable for precise light measurement applications. Modern light sensors often incorporate filters and multiple sensing elements to measure different spectral components, enabling applications like color sensing and UV exposure monitoring.

Radiation sensors in IoT applications typically focus on specific types of radiation relevant to the application. For example, UV sensors in smart weather stations monitor sun exposure, while gamma radiation sensors might be deployed in industrial safety systems. These specialized sensors require careful calibration and periodic verification to maintain measurement accuracy.

Chemical and Gas Sensors

The field of chemical sensing has advanced significantly with the development of miniaturized gas sensors suitable for IoT applications. Metal oxide semiconductor (MOS) sensors detect various gases through changes in electrical conductivity when target molecules interact with the sensor surface. These sensors are widely used for monitoring air quality parameters such as volatile organic compounds (VOCs), carbon monoxide, and nitrogen dioxide.

Electrochemical sensors provide more selective detection of specific gases by measuring current generated through chemical reactions. These sensors offer better selectivity than MOS sensors but often require periodic replacement due to sensor element degradation. Modern chemical sensors increasingly incorporate smart features like automatic baseline correction and humidity compensation.

Sound and Vibration Sensors

Acoustic sensing in IoT applications encompasses both audible sound and vibration measurement. MEMS microphones offer digital output and small form factors, making them ideal for noise monitoring and voice interface applications. These sensors often incorporate automatic gain control and noise suppression to improve signal quality.

Vibration sensors, typically based on piezoelectric or MEMS accelerometer technology, enable condition monitoring and predictive maintenance applications. Modern vibration sensors can measure across multiple axes and frequency ranges, providing comprehensive data about machine or structural health. Advanced processing techniques, such as fast Fourier transform (FFT) analysis, are often implemented directly in the sensor module to reduce data transmission requirements.

Power Management Systems

The effectiveness of IoT deployments depends on reliable and efficient power management solutions. As IoT devices often operate in remote or hard-to-reach locations, power management is critical to system design and sustainability.

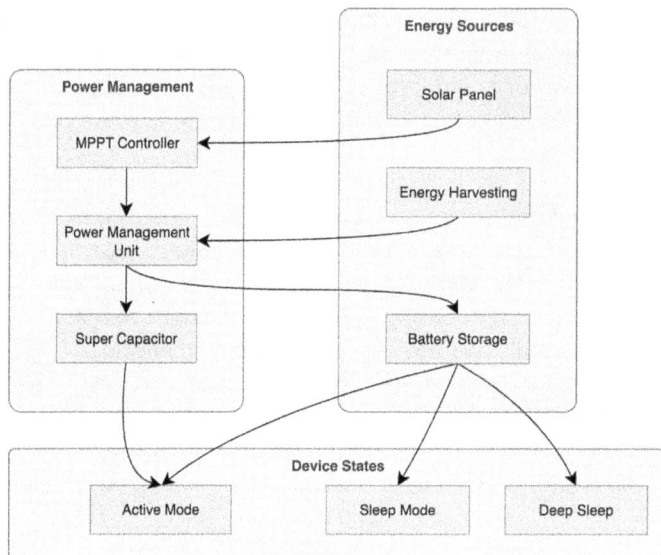

FIGURE 6.1 Power management system diagram.

Battery Technologies and Energy Density

Modern IoT implementations rely on various battery technologies, offering distinct advantages for different applications. Lithium-ion (Li-ion) batteries remain the predominant choice due to their high energy density, typically ranging from 150–250 Wh/kg. Their low self-discharge rate (2–3% per month) makes them suitable for long-term deployments. However, their performance degrades significantly at temperature extremes, requiring careful thermal management in outdoor applications.

Recent developments in solid-state batteries show promising results for IoT applications. These batteries offer higher energy densities (potentially exceeding 400 Wh/kg) and better safety characteristics than traditional Li-ion batteries. While currently more expensive, their longer cycle life and improved temperature tolerance make them increasingly attractive for critical IoT deployments.

The selection of battery technology involves careful consideration of several factors:

- operating temperature range requirements
- expected device lifetime and maintenance intervals
- peak current demands and duty cycle patterns
- physical size and weight constraints
- cost considerations and replacement logistics.

Solar and Energy Harvesting Systems

Energy harvesting technologies have revolutionized power management in IoT systems by enabling self-sustaining operation in suitable environments. Modern photovoltaic systems for IoT applications typically achieve 15–25% conversion efficiencies, with emerging technologies pushing towards 30%. These systems often incorporate Maximum Power Point Tracking (MPPT) controllers to optimize energy capture under varying conditions.

Beyond solar power, several other energy harvesting mechanisms show promise:

- Thermoelectric generators exploit temperature differentials, achieving typical efficiencies of 5–8%.
- Piezoelectric harvesters convert mechanical vibration into electrical energy, which is particularly useful in industrial environments.
- RF energy harvesting systems capture ambient radio frequency energy, though typically providing only microwave-level power.

Energy storage integration plays a crucial role in harvesting systems. Supercapacitors, with their high charge/discharge efficiency (95–98%) and long cycle life (>500,000 cycles), often complement batteries in energy harvesting applications. Modern hybrid systems might employ both technologies, using supercapacitors to handle peak loads, while batteries provide long-term energy storage.

Power Optimization Techniques

Sophisticated power optimization strategies have become essential for extending IoT device operation. Dynamic Voltage and Frequency Scaling (DVFS) is a fundamental approach that allows devices to adjust their operating parameters based on workload demands. Through effective DVFS implementation, modern microcontrollers can reduce power consumption by up to 90% during periods of low activity.

Adaptive sampling techniques enhance power efficiency by adjusting sensor measurement frequencies based on environmental conditions or application requirements. For example, a temperature sensor might reduce its sampling rate when readings remain stable but increase frequency when detecting rapid changes. This approach can reduce average power consumption by 40-60% while maintaining data quality.

Sleep Modes and Duty Cycling

Effective implementation of sleep modes and duty cycling strategies can dramatically extend battery life in IoT devices. Modern microcontrollers typically offer multiple sleep states, with power consumption ranging from deep sleep microamps to light sleep mode milliamps. The selection of appropriate sleep states must balance power savings against wake-up time requirements:
Deep Sleep:

- power consumption: 1–10 µA
- wake-up time: 10–100 ms
- suitable for long intervals between measurements.

Light Sleep:

- power consumption: 50–500 µA
- wake-up time: 1–10 ms
- appropriate for more frequent wake-up requirements.

Duty cycling strategies must consider both application requirements and energy availability. For solar-powered devices, duty cycles might adapt to available sunlight, increasing activity during daylight hours while conserving energy at night. Advanced implementations often incorporate machine learning algorithms to predict energy availability and optimize duty cycles accordingly.

Wireless Power Transmission

Emerging wireless power transmission technologies offer new possibilities for IoT device deployment. Near-field magnetic resonance coupling can achieve power transfer efficiencies of 70–90% over distances of several centimeters, making it suitable for sensors embedded in walls or equipment. Far-field RF power transmission, while less efficient (typically 10-30% efficiency), can operate over greater distances, enabling power delivery to distributed sensor networks.

Recent developments in focused RF beam forming and adaptive impedance matching have improved the efficiency and reliability of wireless power transmission systems. These advances make wireless power increasingly viable for IoT applications, particularly when traditional battery replacement is impractical or costly.

Endpoint Architecture

The architecture of IoT endpoints represents the foundation upon which successful IoT deployments are built. Understanding how these components work together helps us create more efficient and reliable IoT systems.

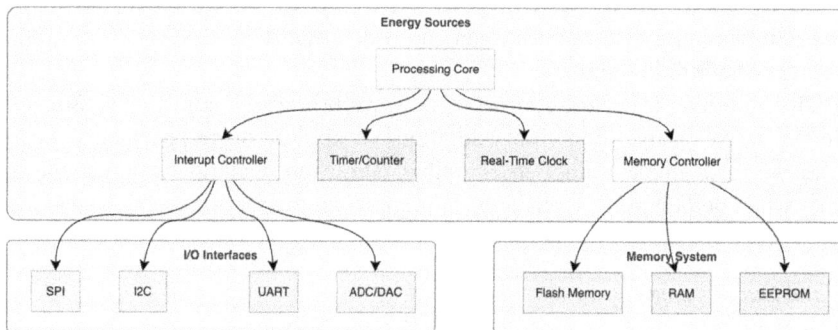

FIGURE 6.2 Endpoint architecture.

Microcontroller Selection and Specifications

An IoT endpoint relies on its microcontroller unit (MCU), which must balance processing capabilities, power efficiency, and cost considerations. Modern IoT applications typically employ ARM Cortex-M series processors, particularly the M0+ for ultra-low-power applications and M4/M7 for more demanding processing tasks.

Let's examine the key considerations for microcontroller selection:

Processing Capabilities:

• The ARM Cortex-M0+ operates at frequencies up to 48 MHz and consumes as little as 27 μA/MHz, making it ideal for basic sensing and data collection tasks.

- The Cortex-M4 adds digital signal processing (DSP) capabilities and operates at higher frequencies (up to 200 MHz), enabling more sophisticated local analytics.
- Advanced applications require the Cortex-M7, which supports double-precision floating-point calculations and can reach speeds up to 400 MHz.

Peripheral Integration: Modern MCUs often integrate essential peripherals that enhance IoT endpoint functionality with

- analog-to-digital converters (ADC) for sensor interfacing
- Direct Memory Access (DMA) controllers for efficient data movement
- Real-Time Clock (RTC) modules for time-sensitive applications
- hardware encryption accelerators for secure communication.

The selection process must consider both immediate requirements and potential future needs, as upgrading MCUs after deployment often proves impractical and costly.

Memory Requirements and Constraints

Memory architecture in IoT endpoints requires careful consideration of multiple memory types and their interactions. A typical IoT endpoint employs a hierarchical memory structure.
Program Memory (Flash):

- stores the device firmware and constant data
- typically ranges from 32 KB to 2 MB in modern IoT MCUs
- must accommodate both application code and over-the-air update capabilities
- requires wear-leveling management for firmware updates.

RAM (Static and Dynamic):

- supports runtime operations and temporary data storage
- usually limited to 8 KB-512 KB in IoT devices
- must be carefully managed to prevent stack overflows and memory leaks
- often divided into multiple power domains for energy optimization

The memory hierarchy might also include

- non-volatile RAM for critical system parameters
- external flash memory for data logging
- secure memory elements for cryptographic keys

Input/Output Interfaces

IoT endpoints must support various I/O interfaces to interact with sensors, actuators, and communication modules. Understanding these interfaces helps in designing more effective and reliable systems.

Digital Interfaces: Serial Peripheral Interface (SPI)

• supports high-speed synchronous communication (up to 50 MHz)
• typically used for flash memory and high-speed sensors
• requires multiple GPIO pins but offers excellent noise immunity

Inter-Integrated Circuit (I2C):

• two-wire interface supporting multiple devices
• operates at speeds up to 3.4 MHz in high-speed mode
• ideal f or connecting numerous low-speed sensors

Universal Asynchronous Receiver/Transmitter (UART):

• simple two-wire asynchronous communication
• useful for debugging and legacy sensor integration
• supports standard baud rates up to 921600 bps.

Analog Interfaces:

• ADC channels with 12-bit to 16-bit resolution
• Digital-to-analog converters (DAC) for analog control signals
• Analog comparators for threshold detection.

Local Storage Considerations

Local storage ensures data reliability and system resilience in IoT endpoints. The design must address several key aspects.

Storage Hierarchy:

• primary storage in MCU flash memory (program storage)
• secondary storage in external flash or EEPROM
• temporary storage in RAM for active processing

Data Management:

• circular buffers for continuous data logging
• wear leveling algorithms for flash memory longevity
• power-safe storage mechanisms for critical data

File Systems:

• lightweight file systems like LittleFS or SPIFFS
• optimized for flash memory characteristics
• support for power failure recovery

Real-time Processing Capabilities

Real-time processing in IoT endpoints ensures timely response to events and reliable data collection. This requires the careful consideration of several factors.

Task Management:

- Real-Time Operating System (RTOS) selection when needed
- task prioritization and scheduling
- interrupt handling and latency management

Processing Optimization:

- DSP algorithms for sensor data processing
- fixed-point arithmetic for efficient computation
- hardware accelerator utilization

Time Management:

- precise timing for sensor sampling
- synchronization with network time
- real-time clock calibration and drift compensation

COMMUNICATION AND NETWORK SYSTEMS

Wireless Technologies

Short-range wireless technologies like Bluetooth and ZigBee provide efficient communication solutions for IoT devices within limited areas. Bluetooth Low Energy (BLE) has become particularly popular in consumer IoT devices due to its low power consumption and widespread support in smartphones and other mobile devices. With its mesh networking capabilities, ZigBee excels in applications requiring reliable communication between many devices, such as home automation systems.

Medium-range technologies, primarily Wi-Fi and Thread, offer higher bandwidth capabilities suitable for data-intensive IoT applications. Wi-Fi provides high-speed connectivity and easy integration with existing network infrastructure, making it ideal for applications like security cameras and smart appliances. Thread, designed specifically for IoT applications, offers robust mesh networking capabilities with built-in security features.

Long-range technologies such as LoRaWAN and cellular networks enable IoT deployments across wide geographical areas. LoRaWAN's low power consumption and long range make it perfect for agricultural monitoring and smart metering applications. Cellular technologies, including NB-IoT and LTE-M, provide reliable connectivity with extensive coverage, though often with higher power requirements and operating costs.

Satellite communication is a crucial backup or primary communication method for IoT deployments in remote locations. While typically more expensive and power-hungry than terrestrial alternatives, satellite communications ensure connectivity in areas where other options are unavailable. This is particularly important for environmental monitoring stations and remote industrial installations.

Network Topologies

Network topology selection fundamentally shapes IoT deployments' performance, reliability, and scalability. Understanding the characteristics and applications of different topologies enables architects to design more effective IoT networks.

Star Topology

The star topology remains the most widely implemented configuration in IoT networks, particularly in environments where direct line-of-sight communication is feasible. In this arrangement, each end device maintains a direct connection to a central coordinator, which manages all network traffic and provides connectivity to external networks.

Implementing a star topology offers several distinct advantages. Network management becomes straightforward, as all traffic flows through a central point, simplifying monitoring and troubleshooting. Latency remains predictable since each device is one hop away from the coordinator. Additionally, device power consumption can be optimized, as end nodes don't need to maintain routing tables or forward traffic for other devices.

However, star topologies present specific challenges in IoT deployments. If the central coordinator malfunctions, it becomes a critical point of failure, potentially affecting all connected devices. Coverage limitations arise from the maximum transmission range between end devices and the coordinator, which typically ranges from 30 to 100 meters indoors, depending on the wireless technology and environmental factors.

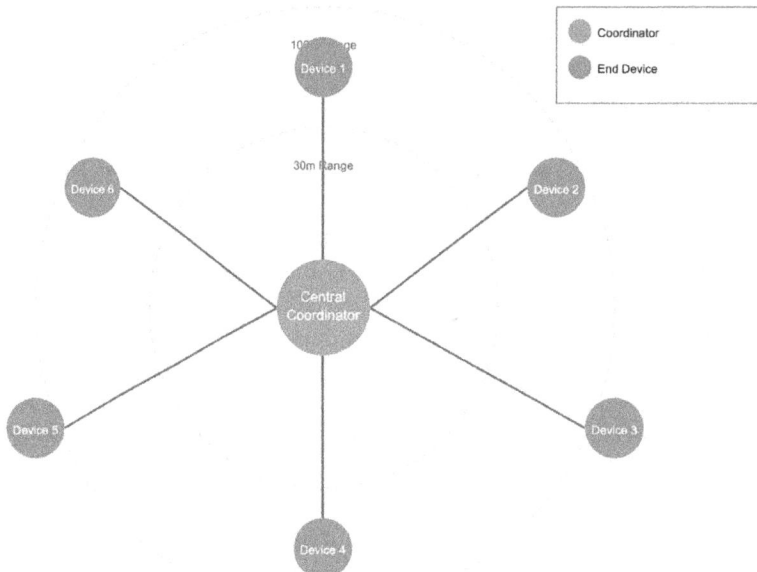

FIGURE 6.3 Star topology.

Mesh Topology

Mesh networking is useful for IoT deployments requiring enhanced reliability and coverage. In a full mesh topology, each device can communicate directly with any other device within range, creating multiple potential paths for data transmission. This redundancy significantly improves network resilience and can extend coverage beyond what's possible with star topology.

Modern mesh networks implement sophisticated routing protocols that optimize path selection based on multiple criteria:

- link quality and signal strength
- available battery power in routing nodes
- current traffic loads and congestion levels
- network latency requirements

The self-healing capabilities of mesh networks provide value in industrial IoT applications. When a node fails, or a link becomes unavailable, the network automatically reconfigures to maintain connectivity through alternative paths. This dynamic adaptation helps ensure continuous operation, even in challenging environments.

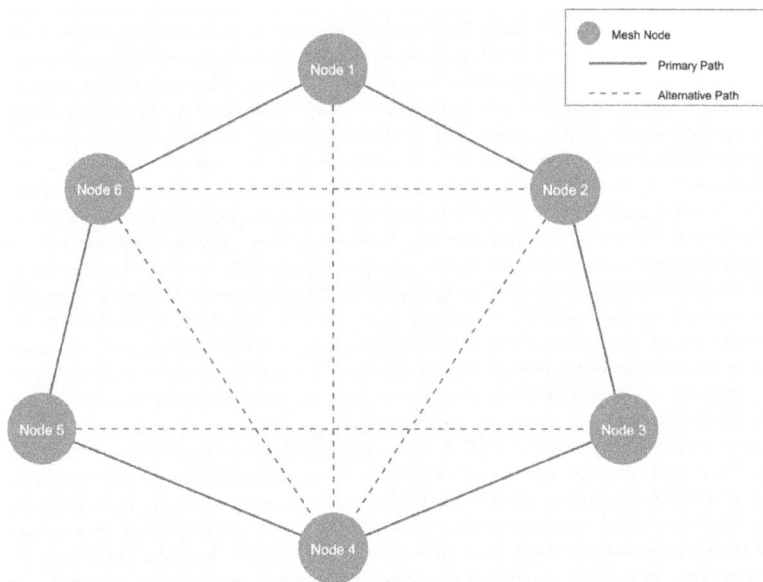

Each node can communicate with multiple peers for enhanced network reliability

FIGURE 6.4 Mesh topology.

Tree Topology

The tree topology provides a hierarchical network organization approach that is particularly effective in large-scale IoT deployments. This structure divides the network into distinct levels, each representing a different tier of devices or gateways. The hierarchical nature of tree topology aligns well with many real-world deployments, such as smart building systems where floors and zones naturally organize devices.

Implementation considerations for tree topology include the following.
Root Node Selection:

- processing capacity to handle aggregated traffic
- reliable power supply and network connectivity
- redundancy options for critical applications

Branch Node Configuration:

- optimal placement for coverage and reliability
- buffer capacity for traffic management
- power requirements and availability

The scalability advantages of tree topology become particularly apparent in large deployments. Network administrators can add or expand new branches without significantly impacting other network parts if the root and branch nodes have sufficient capacity.

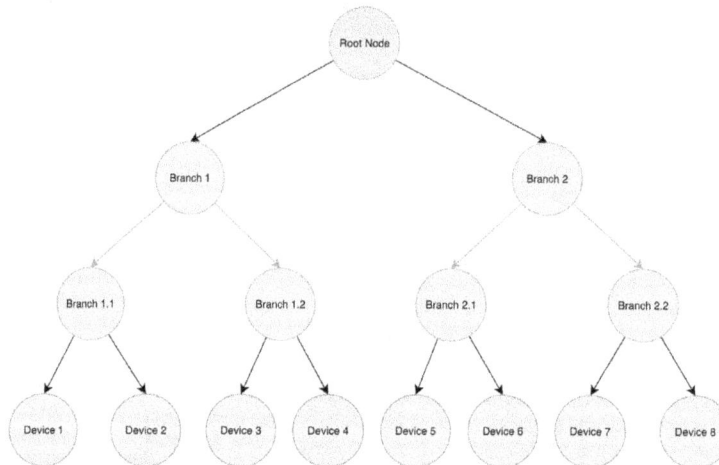

FIGURE 6.5 Tree topology.

Hybrid Approaches

Hybrid network topologies have gained prominence as IoT deployments grow in complexity and scale. These approaches combine elements from multiple topology types to address specific deployment requirements while mitigating individual limitations.

A common hybrid implementation in smart building applications might include

- a primary tree structure following the building's physical layout
- mesh networking capabilities among devices on each floor
- star topology connections for simple sensors and actuators
- redundant root nodes for enhanced reliability

The flexibility of hybrid approaches allows network architects to optimize for various factors simultaneously:

- coverage requirements in different areas
- device power constraints and capabilities
- reliability requirements for critical systems
- cost considerations for network infrastructure

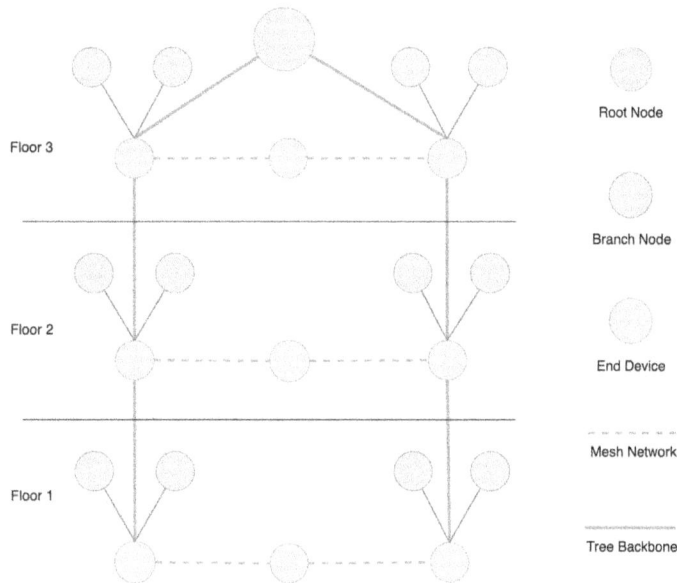

FIGURE 6.6 Hybrid approach.

Communication Protocols

The effectiveness of IoT networks depends heavily on selecting and implementing appropriate communication protocols across different network layers.

Physical Layer Protocols

Physical layer protocols define the fundamental characteristics of data transmission in IoT networks. These protocols must balance multiple competing requirements.

Signal Modulation and Coding:

- adaptive modulation schemes for varying channel conditions
- forward error correction for reliability
- spread spectrum techniques for interference resistance

The selection of physical layer parameters significantly impacts system performance:

- channel bandwidth and data rate capabilities
- power consumption during transmission and reception
- range and coverage characteristics
- interference resistance and coexistence with other systems

Network Layer Protocols

Network-layer protocols in IoT must deliver reliable routing over constrained links and devices while preserving energy and bandwidth. 6LoWPAN is a foundational standard that enables IPv6 over low-power wireless personal area networks, adapting Internet protocols to the unique requirements of IoT endpoints.

Key features of modern IoT network protocols include

- header compression for efficient bandwidth usage
- fragmentation and reassembly for large packets
- mesh routing support for multi-hop networks
- Quality of Service (QoS) management

Application Layer Protocols

Application layer protocols enable meaningful interaction between IoT devices and higher-level systems. MQTT (Message Queuing Telemetry Transport) has become particularly prominent in IoT deployments due to its efficiency and reliability.

MQTT offers several advantages for IoT applications:

- minimal protocol overhead
- Quality of Service levels for reliable delivery
- retained messages for state management

The Constrained Application Protocol (CoAP) provides an alternative designed specifically for resource-constrained devices:

- REST-like architecture for familiarity and ease of integration
- built-in discovery capabilities
- block-wise transfers for large data handling
- observable resources for efficient state updates

Security Protocols

Security protocols form a critical component of IoT communication systems. Modern implementations typically employ a layered security approach.

Transport Layer Security (TLS):

- mutual authentication between devices and servers
- perfect forward secrecy for long-term security
- efficient session resumption for intermittent connections

Application Layer Security:

- end-to-end encryption for sensitive data
- access control and authorization mechanisms
- secure firmware updates and device management

IOT DEVICES: OPERATION AND APPLICATIONS

IoT devices translate sensing and connectivity into real-world outcomes by combining on-board computation, energy-aware operation, and application-specific interfaces. This section introduces how devices function in practice—from boot and provisioning, to duty-cycled sensing, local inference at the edge, and secure data exchange with gateways or cloud services—while maintaining reliability under tight power and bandwidth constraints, then maps these operational patterns to high-impact application domains, including smart buildings, industrial automation, transportation, and environmental monitoring, highlighting the design trade-offs that shape device choices, firmware strategies, and maintenance models.

Device Categories

The IoT device landscape encompasses diverse categories, each serving specific functions within the broader ecosystem. Understanding these categories helps system architects and implementers make informed decisions about device selection and deployment.

Sensors and Data Collectors

Modern IoT sensors represent sophisticated data collection points that transform physical phenomena into digital information. To ensure accurate measurements, these devices incorporate multiple sensing elements, signal conditioning circuits, and local processing capabilities.

Environmental sensors serve as a prime example of modern sensing capabilities. A typical ecological monitoring node might include the following features:

- Temperature sensing with accuracy levels of ±0.1°C, which is achieved through precision semiconductor sensors and careful calibration procedures. These sensors typically consume less than 100 µW during operation, enabling extended battery life.
- Humidity measurements utilizing capacitive sensing elements that achieve ±2% relative humidity accuracy across a wide operating range. Advanced signal processing algorithms compensate for temperature effects and long-term drift.
- Air quality monitoring through multi-gas sensor arrays that detect various pollutants simultaneously. These systems employ electrochemical and metal oxide semiconductor sensors supported by sophisticated algorithms that compensate for cross-sensitivity effects.

The design of sensor systems requires careful consideration of multiple factors. Power management systems typically implement adaptive sampling rates, adjusting measurement frequency based on detected environmental changes. Data preprocessing at the sensor level reduces transmission bandwidth requirements while maintaining information quality. Calibration systems ensure measurement accuracy over extended deployment periods through periodic automated recalibration procedures.

Actuators and Control Devices

Actuator systems in IoT applications transform digital commands into physical actions with precise control and feedback mechanisms. Modern actuator designs incorporate multiple safety features and intelligent control algorithms to ensure reliable operation.

Electric motor control systems exemplify advanced actuator capabilities. These systems typically include the following:

- Variable frequency drives that provide precise speed control while optimizing energy efficiency. Advanced control algorithms implement soft start procedures and monitor operational parameters to prevent damage.
- Position feedback mechanisms utilizing high-resolution encoders or resolvers, enabling accurate positioning with repeatability better than ±0.1%. These systems implement closed-loop control algorithms that compensate for mechanical backlash and system friction.
- Thermal protection systems that monitor multiple temperature points and implement gradual shutdown procedures when thermal limits are approached. Predictive algorithms analyze temperature trends to anticipate potential issues before they become critical.

Gateways and Edge Processors

Modern IoT gateways serve as sophisticated edge computing platforms, providing local processing capabilities and intelligent network management. These devices typically incorporate multi-core processors and specialized hardware accelerators to support various processing tasks.

Processing capabilities in modern gateways include the following:

- Real-time data analytics engines that process sensor data streams, implementing complex algorithms for anomaly detection and pattern recognition. These systems typically achieve processing latencies below 10 ms for time-critical applications.
- Protocol translation services that enable seamless integration between different communication standards. Hardware-accelerated encryption engines ensure secure data transmission while maintaining high throughput.
- Local storage management systems with intelligent data retention policies typically implement circular buffers and priority-based storage allocation. These systems often include redundant storage options to prevent data loss during network outages.

Smart Devices and Appliances

Integrated smart devices represent the convergence of sensing, processing, and actuation capabilities into unified systems. These devices implement sophisticated control algorithms and user interaction mechanisms while maintaining efficient operation.

Smart thermostats exemplify modern integrated device capabilities:

- Learning algorithms analyze occupancy patterns and temperature preferences, developing automated scheduling systems that optimize comfort and energy efficiency. These systems typically achieve 15-30% energy savings compared to traditional thermostats.
- Multi-sensor integration combines temperature, humidity, occupancy, and ambient light data to make intelligent control decisions. Advanced systems might include air quality monitoring and ventilation control capabilities.
- User interface systems implement intuitive controls while providing detailed energy usage analytics. Mobile application integration enables remote monitoring and control while maintaining secure operation through encrypted communications.

Device Management

Effective management of IoT devices throughout their lifecycle is critical for maintaining secure and reliable operations. Modern device management systems implement sophisticated approaches to handling the complexity of large-scale IoT deployments.

Device Provisioning

Device provisioning systems have evolved to handle the complexities of modern IoT deployments. These systems implement automated processes that ensure secure and efficient device initialization while maintaining scalability for large deployments.

Modern provisioning systems employ zero-touch provisioning mechanisms that automate the entire initialization process. When a new device connects to the network, it undergoes a series of authenticated steps to establish its identity and receive appropriate configurations. This process typically includes secure key exchange protocols, certificate validation, and configuration verification.

Security credential management during provisioning has become increasingly sophisticated. Systems now implement hardware security modules (HSMs) to securely generate and store cryptographic keys. These modules provide tamper-resistant storage and secure execution environments for cryptographic operations, ensuring that sensitive credentials remain protected throughout the device's lifecycle.

Initial configuration management systems employ template-based approaches that enable consistent device setup while allowing for customization based on deployment requirements. These systems maintain hierarchical configuration repositories defining common parameters and device-specific settings, ensuring consistent policy application across the deployment.

Configuration Management

Modern configuration management systems implement sophisticated version control and tracking mechanisms. These systems maintain detailed histories of configuration changes, enabling administrators to understand when and why specific changes were made. Additionally, they provide rollback capabilities that can quickly restore previous configurations if problems arise.

Configuration validation mechanisms have become increasingly important. Advanced systems implement automated testing procedures that verify configuration changes before deployment, reducing the risk of service disruptions. These validation systems check for syntax errors, policy compliance, and potential conflicts with existing configurations.

Change management processes in IoT deployments now incorporate impact analysis tools. These tools evaluate proposed configuration changes against current device states and operational requirements, helping administrators understand potential risks before implementing changes. The systems also maintain detailed audit trails documenting all configuration modifications, supporting compliance requirements, and troubleshooting efforts.

Firmware Updates

Firmware update systems can handle the complexities of modern IoT devices. These systems implement sophisticated update mechanisms that ensure reliable software deployment while minimizing operational disruption. The update process typically includes multiple stages of verification and validation to prevent failed updates from compromising device functionality.

Delta update mechanisms reduce bandwidth requirements by transmitting only changed portions of the firmware. These systems implement efficient differential compression algorithms that can minimize update package sizes by 60-90% compared to full firmware images. Additionally, they incorporate checksum verification at multiple stages to ensure data integrity throughout the update process.

Recovery mechanisms have become increasingly sophisticated, implementing dual-bank update systems that maintain backup firmware images. If an update fails, devices can automatically revert to their previous firmware version, ensuring continuous operation. These systems also maintain detailed update histories and status information, enabling administrators to track progress and troubleshoot issues effectively.

Health Monitoring

Health monitoring systems provide comprehensive device status tracking and predictive maintenance capabilities. These systems collect and analyze multiple operational parameters to assess device health and predict potential failures before they occur.

Advanced monitoring systems implement machine learning algorithms that analyze device behavior patterns to detect anomalies. These systems process multiple data streams to build comprehensive device health profiles, including power consumption, communication quality metrics, and sensor readings. The analysis enables early detection of degrading components or emerging issues, allowing maintenance teams to address problems proactively.

Performance optimization frameworks use collected health data to adjust device operations dynamically. Based on observed conditions, these systems might modify sampling rates, transmission power levels, or processing algorithms, helping to extend the device's lifetime while maintaining optimal performance.

Application Domains

The application of IoT technology spans numerous domains, each with unique requirements and challenges. Understanding these applications helps system designers implement solutions that meet specific domain needs.

Environmental Monitoring Applications

Environmental monitoring through IoT systems has transformed our ability to understand and respond to environmental changes across multiple scales. Modern environmental monitoring systems implement sophisticated sensor networks that provide continuous, real-time data collection and analysis capabilities.

Urban air quality monitoring systems exemplify the complexity of modern environmental IoT applications. These systems typically deploy networks of multi-parameter sensors that measure particulate matter (PM2.5 and PM10), gaseous pollutants (NO_2, SO_2, O_3, and CO), and meteorological parameters. Advanced calibration algorithms compensate for cross-sensitivity effects and environmental factors, ensuring measurement accuracy over extended deployment periods. Data analytics platforms process this information in real-time, generating pollution maps and forecasts that enable proactive air quality management.

Water quality monitoring systems have evolved to cover surface and groundwater resources comprehensively. Modern implementations utilize autonomous sensor platforms that measure multiple parameters simultaneously, including dissolved oxygen, pH, conductivity, and various contaminants. These systems implement adaptive sampling strategies that increase measurement frequency during detected events, such as rainfall or potential contamination incidents. Real-time data transmission enables rapid response to water quality issues, while sophisticated analytics platforms identify long-term trends and possible problems.

Industrial Automation

Industrial IoT implementations have revolutionized manufacturing processes through comprehensive monitoring and control capabilities. Modern systems integrate thousands of sensors and actuators to enable precise process control and predictive maintenance capabilities.

Manufacturing process control systems now implement sophisticated closed-loop control algorithms that optimize real-time production parameters. These systems collect data from multiple sources, including production equipment, environmental sensors, and quality control systems. Advanced analytics platforms process this information to identify optimal operating conditions and detect potential quality issues before they affect production. Machine learning algorithms analyze historical data to predict maintenance requirements and optimize preventive maintenance schedules.

Equipment health monitoring systems have become increasingly sophisticated, implementing continuous vibration analysis, thermal monitoring, and power consumption tracking. These systems employ advanced signal processing algorithms to detect subtle changes in equipment behavior that might indicate developing problems. Predictive maintenance platforms analyze this data to estimate remaining equipment lifetime and optimize maintenance schedules, typically achieving 30–40% reductions in maintenance costs while improving equipment reliability.

Smart Buildings

Smart building systems are complex integrations of multiple IoT technologies that optimize building operations. Modern implementations focus on creating comfortable, efficient, and secure environments through sophisticated control and monitoring systems.

HVAC control systems now implement model-predictive control algorithms that optimize energy efficiency while maintaining occupant comfort. These systems utilize data from multiple sources, including occupancy sensors, weather forecasts, and building thermal models. Advanced optimization algorithms balance energy consumption against comfort requirements, typically achieving 20-30% energy savings compared to traditional control systems.

Lighting automation has evolved beyond simple occupancy-based control to implement sophisticated daylight harvesting and personal preference management. Modern systems adjust light levels and color temperature throughout the day to support occupant well-being while minimizing energy consumption. Integration with building automation platforms enables coordinated control of lighting and HVAC systems, optimizing overall building performance.

Transportation Systems

Modern transportation systems utilize IoT technology to enable intelligent traffic management and improve transportation efficiency. These systems implement comprehensive monitoring and control capabilities that enhance safety and operational efficiency.

Traffic management systems use networks of sensors to monitor vehicle flow, detect incidents, and optimize signal timing. Advanced analytics platforms process data from multiple sources, including vehicle detectors, cameras, and weather sensors, to implement adaptive traffic control strategies. These systems typically achieve 15–25% reductions in travel times while reducing emissions through improved traffic flow.

Public transportation management systems provide real-time tracking and dynamic scheduling capabilities. These systems integrate data from vehicle location systems, passenger counters, and ticketing systems to optimize route planning and vehicle dispatching. Advanced analytics platforms predict passenger demand patterns and adjust service levels accordingly, improving operational efficiency while enhancing passenger experience.

Healthcare Monitoring

Healthcare IoT applications have transformed patient care through continuous monitoring and early warning capabilities. Modern systems implement sophisticated data collection and analysis platforms supporting individual patient care and broader healthcare management objectives.

Patient monitoring systems provide comprehensive vital sign tracking with advanced anomaly detection capabilities. These systems collect multiple physiological parameters simultaneously and implement sophisticated algorithms to detect subtle changes that might indicate developing health issues. Integration with electronic health records enables automated documentation while supporting clinical decision-making through real-time data analysis.

Hospital environment monitoring systems maintain optimal conditions for patient care and medical equipment operation. These systems track environmental parameters in critical areas, including temperature, humidity, air quality, and differential pressure. Advanced control systems maintain required conditions while optimizing energy efficiency, typically achieving 15-20% energy savings compared to traditional building management systems.

CONCLUSION

The core principles of IoT establish the technical foundation for intelligent, connected systems that extend far beyond individual devices. This chapter examined how sensors transform physical phenomena into digital signals, how device architectures balance computational capability with power constraints, and how communication protocols enable reliable data exchange across distributed networks.

Three critical insights emerge from understanding IoT fundamentals. First, effective sensor selection and integration require careful consideration of accuracy, power consumption, and environmental conditions to ensure reliable data collection. Temperature sensors achieving ±0.1°C precision while consuming under 100μW demonstrate how modern semiconductor technology enables both performance and efficiency. Second, device architecture must optimize the balance between local processing capabilities and energy management, with sleep modes and duty cycling extending operational lifetimes from days to years. Third, network protocols like 6LoWPAN and mesh routing provide the connectivity backbone that transforms isolated sensors into coordinated systems capable of autonomous operation and remote management.

The applications explored across smart buildings, industrial automation, and environmental monitoring reveal how these technical principles translate into operational benefits: reduced energy consumption, predictive maintenance, enhanced safety, and data-driven decision making. The successful deployment of IoT systems depends on understanding these interconnections between sensing, processing, power management, and communication.

As IoT systems continue to evolve, the principles covered in this chapter remain fundamental to designing effective solutions. The convergence of improved sensor accuracy, extended battery life, and more efficient communication protocols will enable even more sophisticated applications while maintaining the reliability and cost-effectiveness required for widespread adoption. These foundations prepare us for examining how IoT integrates with advanced analytics and machine learning to create truly intelligent systems capable of autonomous adaptation and optimization.

IoT PROTOCOLS AND COMPUTING

C hapter 6 detailed the fundamental hardware components of Internet of Things (IoT) systems, from the diverse sensors that perceive the environment to the power management and processing units that sustain them. However, for these disparate physical endpoints to operate as an integrated, intelligent network, they must be connected by a standardized set of communication rules and supported by effective data processing strategies.

Chapter 7 addresses that need by examining the protocols that facilitate data exchange across the network, from resource-constrained edge devices to powerful cloud platforms. It further investigates the distinct computing models,edge, fog, and cloud that define where data is processed and how intelligence is derived. The selection of appropriate protocols and computing architectures is fundamental to designing scalable, responsive, and efficient IoT solutions for smart cities.

EDGE VS. CLOUD PROTOCOLS

The architecture of IoT systems is heavily influenced by where data is processed and how communication is managed between devices and platforms. Edge protocols are designed to support constrained devices with low latency and minimal resource usage, enabling real-time responsiveness close to the data source. In contrast, cloud-oriented protocols provide scalability, advanced analytics, and long-term storage but require greater bandwidth and stable connectivity. Understanding these two protocol domains is essential for selecting the right communication approach tailored to the performance, security, and energy constraints of each IoT deployment.

Edge Protocols

Edge protocols serve as the fundamental communication framework for IoT devices operating at the network's periphery. These protocols are specifically designed to address the unique challenges of edge computing environments, where devices often face constraints in processing power, memory, and energy resources. Understanding these protocols is crucial for developing efficient and reliable IoT systems.

TABLE 7.1 Cloud versus edge protocols.

Protocol	Key Characteristics	Security Features	Power Consumption	Message Size
CoAP	• binary format • request-response model • resource discovery • observing resources	• DTLS support • optional security modes • resource-level access control	• 50 mW during transmission • low power in an idle state • efficient sleep modes	• 4-byte header • compact message format • binary encoding
MQTT	• Username/password authentication • publish-subscribe model • topic-based routing • session awareness • last will and testament	• TLS/SSL support • username/password authentication • client certificates • access control lists	• efficient for intermittent connections • sleep mode support • connection persistence options	• 2-byte minimum header • variable-length encoding • compact payload format
LwM2M	• device management • service enablement • standard data models • object-based architecture	• DTLS with PSK • secure bootstrap • access control • credential management	• efficient firmware updates • optimized device operations • resource-aware protocols	• compact binary format • efficient resource model • optimized data transfer
BLE	• adaptive frequency hopping • quick connections • multiple connection roles • GATT profiles	• AES-128 encryption • secure pairing • privacy features • role-based security	• 10 µA average consumption • fast wake-up time • efficient sleep states	• 27-byte packets • efficient payload size • Header compression

Constrained Application Protocol (CoAP)

The Constrained Application Protocol (CoAP) represents a specialized Web transfer protocol engineered specifically for resource-constrained IoT devices. Developed as a lightweight alternative to HTTP, CoAP implements essential web functionality while optimizing for devices with limited capabilities. This protocol has become increasingly important in IoT deployments where efficiency and reliability are paramount.

CoAP's architecture is built on a binary format and operates over UDP, providing several key advantages for IoT applications. The binary format significantly reduces protocol overhead compared to text-based protocols, while UDP transport enables quick message exchanges without the overhead of connection establishment. This combination makes CoAP particularly suitable for devices that need to minimize power consumption while maintaining reliable communication.

The protocol implements a request-response model similar to HTTP but with optimizations for constrained environments. These optimizations include the following:

1. Message Overhead Reduction: CoAP uses a compact binary format that typically requires only 4 bytes of header overhead, compared to the much larger headers in HTTP.

2. Built-in Resource Discovery: CoAP includes a standardized mechanism for devices to discover available resources and capabilities, enabling automatic service detection and configuration.

3. Observing Resources: The protocol supports a publish-subscribe mechanism that allows clients to receive automatic updates when resource states change, reducing polling overhead.

In practical applications, CoAP demonstrates its effectiveness in various scenarios. For example, in smart agriculture deployments, soil moisture sensors using CoAP can operate efficiently on battery power for extended periods, sometimes exceeding two years of operation. These sensors transmit readings to edge gateways while consuming minimal power, typically using less than 550 during transmission bursts.

Message Queuing Telemetry Transport (MQTT)

Message Queuing Telemetry Transport (MQTT) is a protocol in IoT communications, particularly excelling in environments where network bandwidth is limited or unreliable. The protocol's publish-subscribe architecture fundamentally changes how devices communicate, enabling efficient one-to-many message distribution while maintaining minimal protocol overhead.

MQTT's architecture centers around a broker-based communication model, where devices can publish messages to topics and subscribe to receive messages from specific topics. This design offers several significant advantages.

1. Quality of Service (QoS) Levels:

   - QoS 0 (At most once): Messages are delivered with the best effort, suitable for non-critical sensor readings
   - QoS 1 (At least once): Messages are guaranteed to arrive, but may be delivered multiple times
   - QoS 2 (Exactly once): Messages are guaranteed to arrive exactly once, ideal for critical commands

2. Session Awareness:

   - Clean Sessions: Temporary subscriptions that clear when clients disconnect
   - Persistent Sessions: Maintained subscriptions and message queuing across disconnections

3. Last Will and Testament:

   - automated message delivery when clients disconnect unexpectedly
   - enables robust monitoring of device connectivity

- supports the "graceful" handling of device failures (for example, due to battery depletion, network outage, or crash), the broker automatically publishes the predefined LWT message to designated subscribers. This ensures other devices or applications immediately become aware of the failure.

In smart building applications, MQTT demonstrates its value through efficient sensor data distribution. A typical implementation might involve hundreds of sensors publishing temperature, humidity, and occupancy data to an MQTT broker. The broker then efficiently distributes this information to multiple building management systems, maintaining low latency (typically under 100 ms) and minimal network overhead (as low as 2 bytes per message for small payloads).

Lightweight Machine-to-Machine (LwM2M)

The Lightweight Machine-to-Machine (LwM2M) protocol is a comprehensive device management solution specifically engineered for IoT deployments. Unlike simpler protocols, LwM2M addresses the complete lifecycle of IoT devices, from initial provisioning through ongoing management and eventual decommissioning.

LwM2M's architecture implements a client-server model with standardized interfaces for the following:

1. Device Management Operations:

   - remote device configuration
   - firmware updates and management
   - fault diagnosis and reporting
   - performance monitoring and optimization

2. Service Enablement:

   - standardized data models for common device types
   - extensible object model for custom functionality
   - efficient resource representation and access

3. Security Features:

   - transport layer security with DTLS
   - access control and authentication
   - secure bootstrap process
   - credential management

The protocol's efficiency in resource usage makes it particularly valuable in industrial IoT applications. For example, in manufacturing environments, LwM2M enables centralized management of thousands of sensors and actuators while maintaining security and reliability. A typical deployment might achieve firmware updates across an entire factory floor with 40% less bandwidth consumption compared to traditional update methods.

Bluetooth Low Energy (BLE)

Bluetooth Low Energy (BLE) is a protocol for short-range IoT communications, particularly in consumer and health care applications. BLE's architecture represents a significant advancement in power-efficient wireless communication, enabling device operation for months or years on small batteries.

BLE's design incorporates several important innovations.

1. Power Management:

    - adaptive frequency hopping to avoid interference
    - quick connection establishment (typically under 3 ms)
    - efficient sleep modes with rapid wake-up
    - power optimization for both connected and advertising states

2. Connection Management:

    - simplified pairing process with secure connections
    - multiple connection roles (Central, Peripheral, Observer, Broadcaster)
    - automatic connection parameter optimization
    - background scanning with minimal power impact

3. Data Transfer:

    - Generic Attribute Profile (GATT) for standardized data exchange
    - Attribute Protocol (ATT) for efficient data transfer
    - service discovery and characteristic notification
    - support for multiple concurrent connections

Health care applications particularly benefit from BLE's capabilities. For instance, continuous glucose monitoring systems utilizing BLE can operate for up to 14 days on a single coin cell battery while maintaining constant communication with a smartphone. The protocol's power efficiency enables transmission of readings every 5 minutes while consuming an average of only 10 µA.

Cloud Protocols

Cloud protocols are important to the IoT communication infrastructure, enabling reliable and scalable data exchange between edge devices and cloud services. These protocols are designed to handle high-volume data transfers, complex routing scenarios, and enterprise-scale deployments while maintaining security and reliability.

TABLE 7.2 List of cloud protocols.

Protocol	Architecture	Security Features	Scalability	Data Handling
AMQP	• message queuing • exchange-based routing • durable messaging • federation support	• TLS encryption • SASL authentication • fine-grained access control • channel-level security	• horizontal scaling • clustering support • high availability • load balancing	• persistent queues • message prioritization • transaction support • dead letter handling
HTTP/ HTTPS	• RESTful design • request-response • stateless operations • resource-oriented	• TLS 1.3 • certificate pinning • HSTS • perfect forward secrecy	• CDN compatibility • caching support • stateless scaling • load balancing ready	• multiple formats (JSON, XML) • content negotiation • compression support • large payload handling
WebSocket	• full-duplex • event-driven • persistent connections • bi-directional	• WSS (TLS) • origin validation • protocol-level security • handshake protection	• connection pooling • stream multiplexing • session management • real-time scaling	• binary/text frames • low overhead (2-14 bytes) • message fragmentation • streaming support
gRPC	• HTTP/2 based • bi-directional streaming • interface definition • code generation	• TLS/SSL • token-based auth • interceptors • deadline propagation	• multiplexing • flow control • service discovery • load balancing	• protocol buffers • strong typing • streaming support • binary serialization

Advanced Message Queuing Protocol (AMQP)

The Advanced Message Queuing Protocol (AMQP) is used for enterprise-grade messaging in cloud-based IoT infrastructure. This protocol implements a comprehensive messaging framework that addresses the complex requirements of large-scale distributed systems. AMQP's architecture is built on the principles of reliability, security, and interoperability, making it particularly valuable for mission-critical applications.

Message queuing in AMQP provides a sophisticated mechanism for handling asynchronous communication. The protocol implements durable message queues that persist messages until they are successfully processed, ensuring no data loss even during system failures or network interruptions. For instance, in manufacturing environments, AMQP queues can buffer sensor data during network outages, preventing data loss and maintaining operational continuity.

The routing capabilities of AMQP extend beyond simple point-to-point communication, implementing a flexible exchange-based routing system. This system supports various routing patterns, including direct routing, topic-based routing, and header-based routing. In practice, this enables complex message distribution scenarios, such as routing maintenance alerts to different teams based on equipment type or severity level.

Security mechanisms in AMQP are comprehensive and designed for enterprise environments. The protocol implements transport layer security (TLS) for encryption, SASL for authentication, and fine-grained access control at the exchange and queue levels. These security features make AMQP suitable for handling sensitive data, such as financial transactions or personal health information.

Reliability mechanisms in AMQP ensure guaranteed message delivery through a sophisticated acknowledgment system. The protocol supports both manual and automatic acknowledgments, allowing applications to balance performance against reliability requirements. Financial services applications utilize these features to ensure transaction messages are never lost, with some systems processing millions of messages daily with zero data loss.

HTTP/HTTPS Protocols

HTTP/HTTPS protocols continue to serve as the foundation for cloud-based IoT communications, particularly in scenarios requiring broad compatibility and standardized interfaces. While not originally designed for IoT, these protocols have evolved to support modern IoT requirements through extensions and best practices.

The REST architectural style, implemented over HTTP, provides a standardized approach to resource manipulation that aligns well with IoT device management. RESTful APIs enable consistent interfaces for device configuration, data upload, and system management. For example, smart city platforms often expose REST APIs for accessing sensor data, managing device configurations, and controlling urban infrastructure components.

Security in HTTPS implementations has become increasingly sophisticated, with support for modern cryptographic protocols and certificate management systems. The protocol implements perfect forward secrecy, certificate pinning, and HTTP Strict Transport Security (HSTS), providing robust protection against various attack vectors. These security features are particularly crucial for IoT deployments in regulated industries, where data protection requirements are stringent.

Web service integration capabilities make HTTP/HTTPS protocols invaluable for cloud-based IoT platforms. The protocols support various data formats, including JSON, XML, and binary formats, enabling flexible integration with existing enterprise systems. Cloud platforms use this flexibility to provide unified interfaces for device management, data visualization, and system administration.

WebSocket Protocol

The WebSocket protocol is a significant advancement in real-time communication capabilities for IoT applications. By enabling full-duplex communication over a single TCP connection, WebSocket addresses the limitations of traditional request-response protocols in scenarios requiring frequent bidirectional data exchange.

Connection persistence in WebSocket implementations provides significant advantages for IoT applications. Once established, a WebSocket connection can remain open indefinitely, enabling immediate data transmission in either direction without the overhead of connection establishment. This capability is particularly valuable in monitoring applications, where minimizing latency is crucial for system responsiveness.

Overhead reduction is achieved through efficient framing mechanisms and the elimination of repeated header transmission. After the initial handshake, WebSocket frames add minimal overhead to the payload data, typically just 2-14 bytes per frame. This efficiency makes WebSocket suitable for applications requiring frequent small message exchanges, such as real-time sensor data updates or interactive control systems.

Protocol extension mechanisms in WebSocket enable customization for specific application requirements. The protocol supports subprotocols and extensions, allowing implementations to add features like compression, multiplexing, or application-specific optimizations while maintaining compatibility with standard WebSocket infrastructure.

gRPC Framework

gRPC represents a modern approach to remote procedure calls, specifically designed for high-performance, scalable systems. The framework implements a comprehensive solution for service definition, code generation, and runtime communication, making it particularly valuable for complex IoT backends.

Protocol Buffers, gRPC's interface definition language, enables precise service and message type specifications. This strong typing system allows automatic code generation for multiple programming languages while ensuring type safety and efficient serialization. In practice, this reduces development time and potential errors in service implementations.

Streaming support in gRPC encompasses unary, server streaming, client streaming, and bidirectional streaming patterns. These capabilities enable efficient handling of various IoT communication scenarios, from simple command-response interactions to continuous sensor data streams. Large-scale IoT platforms leverage these streaming capabilities to handle millions of concurrent device connections efficiently.

Language interoperability in gRPC implementations facilitates the development of polyglot microservices architectures. The framework generates client and server code for multiple programming languages from a single service definition, enabling teams to choose appropriate languages for different system components while maintaining consistent interfaces.

Protocol Selection Criteria

The selection of appropriate protocols for IoT applications requires the careful consideration of multiple factors that can significantly impact system performance, reliability, and operational efficiency. This section examines the criteria that should guide protocol selection decisions in IoT deployments.

TABLE 7.3 Protocol selection table.

Selection Criteria	Key Considerations	Measurement Metrics	Impact on Protocol Choice	Example Requirements
Bandwidth Requirements	• available network capacity • data volume • message frequency • protocol overhead • peak load handling	• bytes per message • messages per second • header size • compression ratio • peak bandwidth usage	• protocol overhead size • data encoding efficiency • compression support • connection management	• sensor networks: <2 KB/message • video streaming: >5 MB/s • industrial IoT: 10 KB/s average • smart home: 100 KB/s burst
Latency Requirements	• response time needs • processing overhead • network conditions • real-time requirements • connection setup time	• round-trip time (RTT) • processing delay • connection setup time • jitter • queue delay	• connection type • handshake complexity • message routing • processing overhead	• industrial control: <10 ms • smart lighting: <100 ms • environmental monitoring: <5 s • data logging: <1 min
Security Requirements	• data sensitivity • regulatory compliance • authentication needs • encryption standards • access control	• encryption strength • authentication methods • key length • certificate validity • access levels	• security overhead • protocol complexity • implementation cost • resource usage	• health care: HIPAA compliance • financial: 256-bit encryption • consumer: basic authentication • industrial: role-based access
Power Consumption	• device battery life • energy availability • transmission frequency • sleep capabilities • processing power	• mW during transmission • µA in sleep mode • battery life (days) • duty cycle • wake-up energy	• connection management • message size • processing needs • sleep support	• sensors: 2-year battery life • wearables: 7-day operation • smart meters: 10-year life • mobile: daily charging
Network Reliability	• connection stability • error handling • recovery mechanisms • data persistence • fault tolerance	• packet loss rate • error recovery time • connection uptime • message delivery rate • retry success rate	• QoS mechanisms • error correction • buffering capability • reconnection handling	• critical systems: 99.999% • business apps: 99.9% • consumer IoT: 99% • data logging: 95%

Bandwidth Requirements

Bandwidth considerations represent a fundamental aspect of protocol selection in IoT applications, particularly given the diverse nature of deployment environments and connectivity options. The management of bandwidth utilization directly impacts system scalability, operational costs, and overall performance.

In wireless sensor networks, bandwidth constraints often become a limiting factor that shapes protocol selection decisions. For example, a typical environmental monitoring network might generate data from hundreds of sensors, each transmitting measurements at regular intervals. In such scenarios, protocol overhead is crucial. A protocol with minimal header size and efficient encoding can reduce bandwidth consumption by 40-60% compared to more verbose alternatives. For instance, CoAP's binary format typically requires only 4 bytes of header overhead, compared to HTTP's text-based headers, which can exceed 200 bytes for similar requests.

Cloud protocols must address bandwidth utilization from a different perspective, focusing on the efficient handling of numerous concurrent connections. A cloud-based IoT platform might need to manage millions of device connections simultaneously while maintaining acceptable performance. Protocol selection must consider techniques such as connection multiplexing, data compression, and efficient message batching. For example, gRPC's Protocol Buffers serialization can reduce message sizes by 60–80% compared to JSON encoding, significantly improving bandwidth utilization in large-scale deployments.

Peak load management represents another critical aspect of bandwidth consideration. Protocols must handle sudden surges in data transmission without degrading system performance. For instance, an industrial IoT system might experience data spikes during shift changes or emergency events. The selected protocol must accommodate these peaks while maintaining system reliability. MQTT's QoS mechanisms, for example, can help manage bandwidth during peak loads by allowing different priority levels for different types of messages.

Latency Requirements

Latency requirements in IoT applications vary significantly based on use cases and operational contexts. The selection of the appropriate protocols must carefully balance these requirements against other system constraints to ensure optimal performance.

Real-time control applications present particularly stringent latency requirements. In manufacturing environments, robotic control systems often require response times under 10 milliseconds to maintain precise operations. Protocol selection for such applications must prioritize minimal processing overhead and deterministic behavior. For example, industrial protocols like Modbus TCP or EtherCAT are designed specifically for such low-latency requirements, implementing optimized message structures and precise timing mechanisms.

Data collection applications typically offer more flexibility in latency requirements. Environmental monitoring systems, for instance, might collect temperature readings every few minutes, making millisecond-level latency less critical. In such cases, protocols can prioritize other factors such as reliability and power efficiency over absolute minimum latency. MQTT's publish-subscribe model, for example, might introduce slightly higher latency but offers better scalability and power efficiency for such applications.

Network infrastructure characteristics significantly influence protocol latency performance. Cellular networks, for example, can introduce variable latency due to factors like signal strength and network congestion. Protocols must account for these variations through features like connection keep-alive mechanisms and efficient reconnection strategies. WebSocket connections over cellular networks, for instance, might implement adaptive heartbeat intervals to maintain connections while minimizing unnecessary traffic.

Security Requirements

Security considerations in IoT protocol selection have become increasingly critical as systems process more sensitive data and face evolving threat landscapes. The implementation of security features must balance protection against resource constraints and operational requirements.

Authentication mechanisms are a fundamental security requirement in IoT deployments. In health care applications, for example, device authentication ensures that only authorized sensors can transmit patient data. Protocols must support robust authentication methods while considering resource constraints. For instance, DTLS-based security in CoAP provides certificate-based authentication while optimizing for constrained devices, using abbreviated handshakes and session resumption to reduce overhead.

Encryption capabilities ensure data confidentiality during transmission. Financial services applications, for example, require end-to-end encryption of all transaction data. Protocol selection must consider encryption strength, key management capabilities, and processing overhead. AMQP implementations in financial systems often utilize TLS 1.3 with perfect forward secrecy, ensuring strong protection while maintaining acceptable performance.

Integrity protection prevents unauthorized modification of data during transmission. Critical infrastructure applications require guaranteed message integrity to prevent tampering. Protocols must implement efficient integrity-checking mechanisms suitable for their operating environment. For example, MQTT's QoS level 2 ensures exact-once delivery with message integrity verification, though at the cost of additional overhead.

Power Consumption Considerations

Power efficiency represents a critical factor in protocol selection, particularly for battery-operated devices deployed in remote or inaccessible locations. The impact of protocol choices on device power consumption can determine the feasibility of entire IoT deployments.

Connection management strategies significantly influence power consumption. Protocols must efficiently handle connection establishment, maintenance, and termination to minimize energy usage. For example, BLE's connection management includes sophisticated power-saving states, allowing devices to maintain connectivity while consuming as little as 10 microamperes during idle periods.

Transmission patterns affect both power consumption and application functionality. Protocols must support efficient data transmission strategies that balance application requirements against energy constraints. For instance, CoAP's observe option allows devices to push updates only when values change significantly, reducing unnecessary transmissions and conserving power.

Protocol overhead directly impacts transmission time and, consequently, power consumption. Efficient message encoding and minimal header sizes can significantly extend battery life. LoRaWAN protocols, for example, implement extremely compact message formats, enabling sensors to operate for years on small batteries while maintaining reliable communication.

Network Reliability Considerations

Network reliability variations across IoT deployments necessitate careful protocol selection to ensure robust operation under diverse conditions. The ability to handle network disruptions gracefully while maintaining data integrity is crucial for system reliability.

Error handling mechanisms must address various types of network failures. Agricultural IoT deployments, for example, often operate in areas with unreliable cellular coverage. Protocols must implement robust error recovery mechanisms to handle connection drops and data retransmission. MQTT's persistent sessions and message queuing capabilities, for instance, ensure no data loss during network interruptions, resuming transmission automatically when connectivity returns.

Data buffering capabilities are essential in environments with intermittent connectivity. Protocols must support efficient local storage and forwarding mechanisms to handle network disruptions. For example, LwM2M implementations often include sophisticated data buffering capabilities, allowing devices to store sensor readings locally during connectivity gaps and transmit them when network access returns.

Reconnection strategies impact both system reliability and resource utilization. Protocols must implement efficient reconnection mechanisms that minimize overhead while maintaining system stability. WebSocket implementations, for instance, often include exponential backoff algorithms for reconnection attempts, reducing network congestion during large-scale connectivity issues while ensuring eventual system recovery.

PRINCIPLES OF COMPUTATION IN IOT

Distributed Computing Models

Modern IoT systems rely on sophisticated distributed computing architectures to process and manage vast amounts of data efficiently. These architectures must balance various operational requirements while maintaining system performance and reliability. This section examines four primary distributed computing models that form the foundation of effective IoT deployments.

TABLE 7.4 Distributed computing models.

Computing Model	Key Characteristics	Technical Requirements	Use Case Example	Performance Metrics
Fog Computing	• intermediate processing layer • local data analysis • immediate decision-making • cloud integration capability • reduced latency	• processing: 1,000-5,000 sensor readings/sec • storage: 24-48 hours local data • redundant network paths • high-speed local communication	Smart Traffic Management: • 20-30 sensors per intersection • 100 ms response time • 85% data reduction to cloud	• response time: <100 ms • data reduction: 85% • local storage: 24-48 hours • processing capacity: 5 K readings/sec
Edge Computing	• on-device processing • reduced network bandwidth • enhanced privacy • immediate analysis • power efficiency	• RAM: 2-4 GB • AI acceleration hardware • battery life: 12-24 months • optimized algorithms	Smart Surveillance: • 4 K video processing • 25 fps analysis • 90-95% bandwidth reduction	• bandwidth reduction: 90-5% • raw data: 1.5 GB/hour • transmitted data: 50-100 MB/hour • battery life: 12-24 months
Cloud Computing	• scalable resources • global access • advanced analytics • long-term storage • pattern recognition	• high bandwidth connectivity • data filtering strategies • storage optimization • cost management systems	Manufacturing Systems: • hundreds of sensors • 1-5 TB annual storage/line • 15-20% efficiency improvement	• storage reduction: 40-60% • efficiency gain: 15-20% • storage capacity: 1-5 TB/year • real-time analytics capability
Hybrid Computing	• multi-tier architecture • combined paradigms • optimized performance • enhanced reliability • flexible processing	• data synchronization • version control • resource allocation • failover mechanisms	Smart Grid • three-tier architecture • millisecond local response • regional load balancing	• local response: ms level • regional response: seconds • grid optimization: hours • system-wide coordination

Fog Computing Architecture

Fog computing represents a significant advancement in IoT architectures by extending cloud computing capabilities closer to the network edge. This intermediate processing layer addresses critical challenges in latency, bandwidth utilization, and system scalability. Fog nodes serve as local processing and storage points, enabling immediate data analysis and decision-making while maintaining efficient communication with cloud systems.

The implementation of fog computing in smart traffic management systems demonstrates its practical benefits. At major intersections, fog nodes process real-time data from multiple sensors, including vehicle presence detectors, pedestrian crossing signals, and emergency vehicle priority systems. These nodes can make immediate decisions about traffic signal timing based on current conditions, while simultaneously aggregating statistical data for transmission to cloud-based systems for broader traffic pattern analysis.

For example, a typical urban intersection equipped with fog computing capabilities processes data from approximately 20–30 sensors, including inductive loops, cameras, and pedestrian push buttons. The fog node analyzes this data in real time, making signal timing adjustments within 100 milliseconds to respond to changing traffic conditions. This local processing reduces the data transmitted to the cloud by approximately 85%, sending only aggregated statistics and significant events for citywide traffic optimization.

The architecture of fog nodes requires careful consideration of several critical factors. Processing capacity must be appropriately sized to handle peak traffic periods, typically requiring computing power capable of processing 1,000 to 5,000 sensor readings per second. Storage capabilities must balance immediate operational needs with short-term historical data requirements, often maintaining 24-48 hours of detailed data locally. Network connectivity must support both high-speed local device communication and reliable cloud integration, typically through redundant networking paths.

Edge Computing Patterns

Edge computing fundamentally transforms IoT data processing by moving computational tasks directly to or near the data source. This approach delivers several critical advantages, including reduced latency, enhanced privacy protection, and decreased network bandwidth requirements. The implementation of edge computing patterns requires sophisticated balancing of processing capabilities, power consumption, and cost considerations.

Smart surveillance cameras provide an excellent example of edge computing implementation. Modern IoT-enabled cameras incorporate powerful processing capabilities that enable complex analysis directly on the device. For instance, a retail surveillance camera equipped with edge computing capabilities can perform real-time video analytics, including customer counting, behavior analysis, and security monitoring. These devices typically process high-definition video streams locally, applying machine learning algorithms to detect specific events or patterns.

The technical implementation of edge computing in surveillance systems demonstrates its efficiency. A typical smart camera can reduce network bandwidth requirements by 90-95% compared to traditional systems by performing local video analysis and transmitting only relevant events or metadata. For example, a 4 K surveillance camera generating 25 frames per second might process approximately 1.5 GB of raw video data per hour locally, while only transmitting 50-100 MB of processed events and metadata to central systems.

Edge computing implementations must address several critical technical challenges. Processing algorithms require optimization for limited hardware resources, often operating within constraints of 2-4 GB of RAM and specialized AI acceleration hardware. Power management is particularly crucial for battery-operated devices, requiring sophisticated power-saving strategies that can extend operational life to 12–24 months between battery replacements. Cost considerations influence hardware selection, typically targeting a balance point that enables adequate processing capabilities while maintaining reasonable device costs.

Cloud Computing Integration

Cloud computing provides essential infrastructure for IoT systems, offering scalable resources for data storage, analysis, and long-term pattern recognition. The integration of cloud services enables sophisticated analytics and global access to IoT data while providing flexible computational resources for complex processing tasks. This integration requires careful consideration of data management, security, and cost optimization strategies.

Manufacturing systems exemplify effective cloud integration through sophisticated multi-tier processing architectures. In a typical implementation, edge devices handle immediate process control and data collection, while cloud systems provide advanced analytics for production optimization and predictive maintenance. For instance, a modern manufacturing line might collect data from hundreds of sensors, generating thousands of readings per second. Edge processing handles immediate quality control decisions within milliseconds, while cloud systems analyze historical data to identify trends and predict maintenance requirements.

The implementation of cloud integration in manufacturing environments demonstrates significant operational benefits. Systems typically achieve a 15–20% improvement in production efficiency through advanced analytics and predictive maintenance. Data storage requirements often range from 1–5 TB per production line annually, requiring careful optimization of data retention policies and storage strategies. Cost optimization strategies typically involve implementing intelligent data filtering at the edge, reducing cloud storage and processing requirements by 40–60% compared to raw data transmission.

Hybrid Computing Models

Hybrid computing models represent sophisticated approaches that combine multiple computing paradigms to optimize system performance and reliability. These models leverage the strengths of different computing approaches while mitigating their respective limitations, creating more robust and efficient IoT solutions. The implementation of hybrid models requires careful orchestration to maintain data consistency and system reliability across multiple processing tiers.

Smart grid systems provide a compelling example of hybrid computing implementation. These systems typically employ a three-tier architecture: edge devices for immediate power distribution control, fog nodes for regional load balancing, and cloud systems for comprehensive grid optimization. This architecture enables rapid response to local conditions while maintaining efficient overall grid operation. For instance, edge devices can respond to power quality issues within milliseconds, fog nodes can adjust regional load distribution within seconds, and cloud systems can optimize grid-wide resource allocation over hours or days.

The implementation of hybrid computing in smart grid environments demonstrates several critical technical considerations. Data synchronization across tiers must maintain consistency while handling network delays and interruptions, typically requiring sophisticated timestamping and version control mechanisms. Resource allocation strategies must efficiently distribute processing tasks across available computing resources based on real-time requirements and system capabilities. Failure management systems must handle disruptions at any processing tier while maintaining critical operations, often implementing redundant processing capabilities and automated failover mechanisms.

Data Processing Paradigms

The effective processing of IoT data requires sophisticated approaches that can handle diverse processing requirements while maintaining system performance and reliability. This section examines four fundamental data processing paradigms that enable efficient IoT operations across various application domains.

TABLE 7.5 Data processing paradigm.

Processing Paradigm	Implementation Features	Technical Requirements	Performance Metrics	Example Application
Stream Processing	• continuous data analysis • real-time decision making • circular buffers • sliding window algorithms • redundant processing paths	• memory management systems • optimized data structures • checkpoint mechanisms • failover procedures • multiple processing nodes	• processing latency: <100 ms • anomaly detection: <50 ms • data window: 5-minute sliding • processing rate: 1,000 readings/min	Traffic Monitoring: • hundreds of sensors • incident detection in seconds • real-time flow optimization
Batch Processing	• scheduled processing windows • resource optimization • multiple processing windows • dynamic resource allocation • priority-based scheduling	• large-scale data storage • processing window management • resource scheduling systems • data freshness monitoring • load balancing mechanisms	• daily processing window • weekly analysis cycles • 100,000+ data points • 24-hour processing patterns	Energy Management: • smart meter data analysis • consumption pattern detection • resource optimization
Real-time Analytics	• immediate response capability • optimized algorithms • multi-tier notification • prioritized delivery • continuous analysis	• high-performance processing • optimized communication • result delivery mechanisms • priority queue management • low-latency infrastructure	• processing time: <10 ms • critical alerts: milliseconds • multiple inspection points • high-frequency data streams	Manufacturing QC: • defect detection • process adjustment • quality monitoring
Event-driven Processing	• selective processing • multi-parameter events • sophisticated filtering • multi-level priority queues • dynamic resource allocation	• event detection systems • queue management • priority handling • resource allocation • event condition definition	• immediate safety events • thousands of sensors • multiple event queues • prioritized processing	Building Automation: • occupancy changes • environmental monitoring • safety event handling

Stream Processing

Stream processing is a critical paradigm in IoT systems, enabling real-time analysis of continuous data flows from connected devices. This approach supports immediate decision-making capabilities essential for modern IoT applications while maintaining processing efficiency and reliability. The implementation of stream processing requires careful consideration of multiple technical factors to ensure optimal performance.

In traffic monitoring systems, stream processing demonstrates its effectiveness through real-time incident detection and traffic flow optimization. These systems process data from multiple sensor types simultaneously, including vehicle detection sensors, traffic cameras, and environmental monitors. A typical urban traffic management system might process data from hundreds of sensors, each generating readings every few seconds. For example, an intersection monitoring system processes approximately 1,000 sensor readings per minute, analyzing this data stream to detect incidents within seconds of occurrence.

The implementation of stream processing requires sophisticated memory management strategies to handle varying data rates effectively. Systems typically implement circular buffers and sliding window algorithms to maintain processing efficiency while managing memory constraints. For instance, a traffic monitoring system might maintain a five-minute sliding window of detailed sensor data in memory, enabling rapid analysis of recent traffic patterns while preventing memory overflow.

Processing latency requirements in stream processing systems demands careful optimization of data handling procedures. Modern implementations typically target end-to-end processing latencies of less than 100 milliseconds for critical operations. This requires efficient data structures and optimized processing algorithms. For example, traffic incident detection systems use specialized algorithms that can process sensor data streams and identify anomalies within 50 milliseconds, enabling rapid response to changing traffic conditions.

Fault tolerance in stream processing systems necessitates robust error handling and recovery mechanisms. Systems must maintain data consistency and processing accuracy even during network interruptions or hardware failures. Implementation strategies typically include redundant processing paths, checkpoint mechanisms, and automated failover procedures. A typical system might maintain multiple processing nodes, automatically redistributing processing loads if any node experiences failures.

Batch Processing

Batch processing provides essential capabilities for comprehensive data analysis and pattern detection in IoT systems. This approach enables sophisticated processing of large datasets while optimizing system resource utilization and maintaining processing efficiency. The implementation of batch processing requires careful consideration of processing windows and data freshness requirements.

Energy management systems exemplify effective batch processing implementation through their analysis of consumption patterns and resource optimization. These systems typically collect data from thousands of smart meters and energy sensors, processing this information in scheduled batches to identify usage patterns and optimize resource allocation. For example, a citywide energy management system might process data from 100,000 smart meters, analyzing 24-hour consumption patterns during overnight processing windows.

The optimization of processing window size represents a critical consideration in batch-processing implementations. Systems must balance the need for comprehensive data analysis against requirements for timely insights. A typical energy management system might implement multiple processing windows, including daily batch processing for operational optimization and weekly processing for long-term pattern analysis. This approach enables both tactical and strategic decision-making while managing system resources efficiently.

Resource allocation in batch processing systems requires sophisticated scheduling and optimization strategies. Systems must efficiently utilize available computing resources while ensuring the timely completion of processing tasks. Implementation approaches typically include dynamic resource allocation based on processing loads and priority levels. For instance, an energy management system might allocate additional computing resources during end-of-month processing to handle increased analytical requirements while maintaining standard daily processing operations.

Real-time Analytics

Real-time analytics combines stream processing capabilities with sophisticated analysis functions to enable immediate response to changing conditions in IoT environments. This approach requires careful optimization of both processing algorithms and data flows to maintain low latency while ensuring accurate analysis results. The implementation of real-time analytics demands consideration of both processing efficiency and result delivery mechanisms.

Manufacturing quality control systems demonstrate the effectiveness of real-time analytics through immediate defect detection and process adjustment capabilities. These systems analyze data from multiple sensor types simultaneously, including visual inspection systems, dimensional sensors, and process monitoring equipment. A modern manufacturing line might incorporate dozens of inspection points, each generating high-frequency data streams that require immediate analysis.

Processing optimization in real-time analytics systems requires sophisticated algorithm design and implementation. Systems must maintain processing accuracy while meeting strict latency requirements. For example, a quality control system in a high-speed manufacturing line might need to process and analyze sensor data within 10 milliseconds to enable real-time process adjustments. This requires carefully optimized algorithms and efficient data-handling procedures.

Result delivery mechanisms in real-time analytics systems must ensure rapid dissemination of analysis results to relevant system components. Implementation strategies typically include optimized communication protocols and prioritized delivery mechanisms.

Event-driven Processing

Event-driven processing enables efficient resource utilization in IoT systems by selectively processing data based on specific triggers or conditions. This approach requires a precise definition of event conditions and sophisticated handling of event queues and processing priorities. The implementation of event-driven processing demands careful consideration of event detection accuracy and processing latency requirements.

Building automation systems demonstrate effective implementation of event-driven processing through their response to occupancy changes and environmental conditions. These systems monitor multiple environmental parameters and occupancy states, processing data only when significant changes occur. For example, a modern office building automation system might monitor thousands of sensors but only initiate processing when specific events occur, such as significant temperature changes or occupancy transitions.

Event condition definition requires careful consideration of multiple factors to ensure accurate event detection while minimizing false positives. Implementation strategies typically include multi-parameter event definitions and sophisticated filtering mechanisms. For instance, a building automation system might define occupancy events based on multiple sensor inputs, including motion detection, door access controls, and environmental sensors, ensuring accurate event detection while minimizing unnecessary processing.

Queue management in event-driven systems requires sophisticated handling of event priorities and processing sequences. Systems must efficiently manage multiple event queues while ensuring the timely processing of critical events. Implementation approaches typically include multi-level priority queues and dynamic resource allocation mechanisms. For example, a building automation system might implement separate queues for different event types, ensuring immediate processing of safety-related events while managing comfort-related events with lower priority.

Resource Management

Effective resource management represents a critical component of successful IoT system implementation. This section examines four important aspects of resource management that significantly impact system performance and reliability.

CPU Scheduling

CPU scheduling in IoT systems requires sophisticated approaches to balance processing requirements across multiple tasks while maintaining system responsiveness. The implementation of effective scheduling algorithms must address various technical challenges while ensuring optimal system performance.

Real-time control systems demonstrate the complexity of CPU scheduling requirements in IoT environments. These systems typically manage multiple concurrent tasks with varying priority levels and timing constraints. For example, an industrial control system might simultaneously handle sensor data acquisition, process control calculations, system monitoring, and communication tasks. Each of these tasks requires the appropriate CPU time allocation while maintaining strict timing requirements.

The implementation of scheduling algorithms must address several critical considerations. Task prioritization represents a fundamental aspect, with systems typically implementing multiple priority levels to ensure critical operations receive necessary processing resources. For instance, a real-time control system might implement 16 priority levels, with emergency response functions assigned the highest priorities and background maintenance tasks assigned lower priorities.

Deadline management presents another crucial aspect of CPU scheduling. Systems must ensure that time-critical tasks are completed within specified deadlines while maintaining overall system stability. Implementation approaches typically include deadline-monotonic scheduling algorithms that prioritize tasks based on their deadline requirements. For example, a process control system might need to complete control loop calculations within 10 milliseconds while allowing up to 100 milliseconds for diagnostic functions.

The handling of periodic and aperiodic tasks requires careful coordination to maintain system responsiveness. Periodic tasks, such as sensor reading and system status updates, occur at regular intervals and require guaranteed processing time. Aperiodic tasks, triggered by external events or system conditions, must receive appropriate processing resources without disrupting critical periodic operations. Implementation strategies typically include hybrid scheduling approaches that reserve processing capacity for periodic tasks while maintaining sufficient flexibility to handle aperiodic events.

Memory Management

Memory management in resource-constrained IoT devices demands sophisticated strategies to ensure efficient utilization of limited memory resources while maintaining system reliability. The implementation of memory management systems must address various technical challenges while preventing performance degradation.

Edge processing devices illustrate the complexity of memory management in IoT environments. These devices often operate with limited RAM, typically ranging from 256 KB to 4 MB, while running sophisticated processing algorithms. The implementation must efficiently allocate this limited memory across multiple system components and functions while preventing fragmentation and maintaining system stability.

Static memory allocation for program code requires careful optimization to minimize memory footprint while maintaining necessary functionality. Implementation strategies typically include code compression techniques and efficient memory layout planning. For example, an edge processing device might employ overlay techniques to manage multiple program modules within limited program memory, loading specific modules only when needed.

Dynamic memory allocation presents particular challenges in resource-constrained environments. Systems must efficiently handle runtime memory requirements while preventing fragmentation and memory leaks. Implementation approaches typically include sophisticated memory pools and allocation strategies. For instance, a sensor processing system might implement fixed-size memory pools for common operations, reducing fragmentation while maintaining predictable memory allocation behavior.

Memory fragmentation prevention requires active management to maintain system efficiency. Implementation strategies typically include memory compaction algorithms and efficient allocation policies. For example, a device operating system might implement a buddy memory allocation system, maintaining the power of two memory blocks to minimize fragmentation while providing efficient allocation capabilities.

Storage Optimization

Storage optimization in IoT systems requires careful management of available storage resources while ensuring data accessibility and integrity. The implementation of storage systems must address various technical challenges while maintaining efficient operation within storage constraints.

Environmental monitoring systems exemplify the complexities of storage optimization in IoT deployments. These systems typically generate continuous data streams that must be stored efficiently while maintaining accessibility for both immediate analysis and historical reference. For example, a weather monitoring station might generate several megabytes of sensor data daily, requiring efficient storage strategies to maintain extended historical records within limited local storage capacity.

Caching strategies play a crucial role in storage optimization. Implementation approaches typically include multi-level caching systems that balance access speed against storage efficiency. For instance, a monitoring system might maintain frequently accessed data in high-speed flash storage while moving older data to more cost-effective storage media or cloud storage.

Data lifecycle management policies ensure efficient use of storage resources while maintaining necessary historical data. Implementation strategies typically include automated data archival and cleanup procedures based on data age and importance. For example, a monitoring system might maintain high-resolution data for recent periods while automatically compressing or summarizing older data to conserve storage space.

Cloud storage integration requires careful management of data synchronization and storage allocation. Implementation approaches typically include intelligent data tiering and synchronization strategies. For instance, a monitoring system might automatically transfer data to cloud storage based on predefined policies while maintaining local copies of recently accessed data.

Network Bandwidth Management

Network bandwidth management in IoT systems requires sophisticated approaches to ensure reliable communication while preventing network congestion. The implementation of bandwidth management systems must address various technical challenges while maintaining efficient data transfer capabilities.

Video surveillance systems demonstrate the complexity of bandwidth management requirements in IoT environments. These systems typically generate high-volume data streams that must be transmitted efficiently while maintaining video quality and system responsiveness. For example, a modern surveillance camera might generate 4-8 Mbps of video data per stream, requiring careful bandwidth management to support multiple cameras while avoiding network saturation.

Traffic prioritization represents a fundamental aspect of bandwidth management. Implementation strategies typically include Quality of Service (QoS) mechanisms that ensure critical data receives necessary network resources. For instance, a surveillance system might prioritize alarm-related video streams over routine monitoring feeds, ensuring immediate transmission of security-critical information.

Congestion avoidance requires active management of network resource utilization. Implementation approaches typically include adaptive transmission rates and intelligent buffering strategies. For example, a video system might automatically adjust video quality and frame rates based on network conditions while maintaining essential monitoring capabilities.

Wide-area network integration presents particular challenges for bandwidth management. Implementation strategies must account for varying network characteristics and potential connectivity limitations. For instance, a distributed surveillance system might implement different transmission strategies for local network segments versus wide-area network connections, optimizing data flow for available bandwidth while maintaining system functionality.

EDGE COMPUTING: BENEFITS AND CHALLENGES

Edge computing provides substantial advantages for IoT implementations across various industries. This section examines the five principal benefits that make edge computing a compelling choice for modern IoT deployments.

Edge Computing Benefits

Edge computing provides substantial advantages for IoT implementations across various industries. This section examines the five principal benefits that make edge computing a compelling choice for modern IoT deployments.

Reduced Latency

The reduction in system latency represents one of the most significant advantages of edge computing implementations. By processing data directly at or near its source, organizations can achieve near-immediate response times that would be impossible with traditional cloud-based processing approaches. This capability proves particularly valuable in scenarios where rapid decision-making directly impacts operational efficiency and safety.

In manufacturing environments, edge computing demonstrates its latency benefits through real-time process control applications. Modern manufacturing robots equipped with edge computing capabilities can process sensor data and adjust operations within milliseconds. For instance, a welding robot in an automotive assembly line can analyze quality parameters and adjust welding patterns in real time, typically achieving response times under 10 milliseconds. This represents a significant improvement over cloud-based processing, which might introduce latencies of 100 milliseconds or more.

Autonomous vehicle systems provide another compelling example of edge computing's latency advantages. These systems must process vast amounts of sensor data and make critical decisions within microseconds. Edge computing enables autonomous vehicles to analyze streaming data from multiple sensors – including cameras, LiDAR, and radar – and make immediate driving decisions. The processing occurs within the vehicle's computing systems, eliminating the potential delays and reliability issues associated with cloud communication.

Industrial control systems leverage edge computing's low latency capabilities to maintain precise control over manufacturing processes. These systems typically require response times under 5 milliseconds to maintain product quality and ensure operational safety. By implementing edge computing solutions, manufacturers can achieve these demanding timing requirements while maintaining system reliability and reducing dependence on network connectivity.

Bandwidth Optimization

Edge computing delivers significant improvements in bandwidth utilization through intelligent local processing and data filtering. This optimization becomes increasingly important as IoT deployments generate growing volumes of data, making traditional approaches to data transmission increasingly costly and impractical.

Video analytics systems demonstrate the substantial bandwidth savings achievable through edge computing. A typical surveillance camera generating 4 K video might produce 15-20 Mbps of raw video data. By implementing edge processing, these systems can analyze video streams locally and transmit only relevant events or metadata, reducing bandwidth requirements by 95% or more. For example, a retail surveillance system might only transmit customer counting data and security events rather than continuous video streams, reducing daily data transmission from terabytes to megabytes.

In industrial IoT deployments, edge computing enables efficient handling of sensor data streams. Manufacturing facilities often deploy thousands of sensors, each generating data multiple times per second. Edge processing allows these systems to aggregate and analyze data locally, transmitting only significant events or summarized information to central systems. This approach typically reduces network traffic by 60-80% compared to raw data transmission, while maintaining access to critical operational insights.

Enhanced Privacy

Edge computing provides robust privacy protection by enabling local processing of sensitive data, a capability that becomes increasingly important as privacy regulations become more stringent worldwide. This approach allows organizations to maintain compliance with data protection requirements while preserving system functionality and operational efficiency.

Health care applications particularly benefit from edge computing's privacy advantages. Modern medical devices can process sensitive patient data locally, applying anonymization or aggregation before transmitting information to central systems. For example, a continuous glucose monitoring system might process detailed readings locally while sending only averaged or trend data to cloud services. This approach ensures HIPAA compliance while maintaining the medical benefits of connected health monitoring.

Financial services implementations leverage edge computing to protect sensitive transaction data. Point-of-sale systems can process payment information locally, transmitting only necessary transaction details to central systems. This approach reduces the exposure of sensitive financial data while maintaining full transaction functionality. For instance, a retail payment system might process credit card data at the edge, transmitting only tokenized transaction information to cloud services.

Improved Reliability

Edge computing significantly enhances system reliability by reducing dependence on network connectivity and cloud services. This improved resilience is particularly valuable in environments where continuous operation is critical for safety or business operations.

Building access control systems demonstrates the reliability benefits of edge computing. Modern access control implementations can maintain full functionality even during network outages by processing access credentials and maintaining access logs locally. For example, a corporate access control system might manage thousands of doors independently, synchronizing data with central systems when connectivity becomes available while maintaining security during network interruptions.

Industrial automation systems leverage edge computing to ensure continuous operation in manufacturing environments. These systems can maintain critical control functions independently of network connectivity, ensuring production continues even during cloud service disruptions. A typical implementation might maintain several hours of local data storage and processing capability, enabling autonomous operation during connectivity interruptions while preserving all critical operational data.

Cost Optimization

Edge computing delivers substantial cost benefits through reduced cloud computing requirements and optimized network bandwidth utilization. These savings become particularly significant in large-scale deployments where data volumes and processing requirements are substantial.

Smart metering systems exemplify the cost benefits of edge computing. By processing consumption data locally and transmitting only billing-relevant information, these systems can reduce cloud computing costs by 70-80% compared to full data transmission approaches. For example, a citywide smart metering deployment might process millions of readings locally, transmitting only daily summaries and exception events to central systems.

Large-scale IoT deployments achieve significant cost reductions through edge computing. Organizations can minimize expensive cloud storage and processing requirements by implementing intelligent local data processing and filtering. A typical industrial IoT deployment might reduce cloud computing costs by 50-60% through edge processing while maintaining all critical system functionality and analytical capabilities.

Implementation Challenges

The implementation of edge computing solutions presents several significant challenges that organizations must address to ensure successful deployments. This section examines five critical challenges that impact edge computing implementations across various industries.

Resource Limitations

Resource constraints at the edge represent one of the most significant challenges in implementing effective edge computing solutions. Organizations must carefully balance processing capabilities against power consumption and cost considerations while maintaining necessary functionality. This challenge becomes particularly apparent in deployments where devices must operate within strict resource limitations while performing complex processing tasks.

Smart surveillance cameras exemplify the resource challenges faced in edge computing implementations. These devices must perform sophisticated object detection and video analysis while operating within defined power and processing constraints. A typical smart camera might need to process 4 K video streams at 30 frames per second while consuming less than 15 watts of power. This requires careful optimization of both hardware selection and software implementation. For instance, manufacturers often implement specialized AI accelerators and optimized neural network models to achieve acceptable performance within these constraints.

Power consumption management presents particular challenges in battery-operated edge devices. These systems must balance processing capabilities against operational longevity. For example, a battery-powered security sensor might need to operate for six to twelve months on a single battery while maintaining continuous monitoring capabilities. This requires sophisticated power management strategies, including dynamic processor scaling and efficient sleep modes. Organizations typically implement multi-tier processing approaches, activating higher-power processing capabilities only when necessary while maintaining basic functionality in low-power modes.

Algorithm optimization is crucial when dealing with resource-constrained edge devices. Organizations must carefully refine processing algorithms to operate efficiently within available resources while maintaining necessary accuracy and performance. For instance, an object detection system might implement model quantization and pruning techniques to reduce computational requirements by 60-70% while maintaining 95% of the original detection accuracy. This optimization process requires a careful balance between processing efficiency and functional requirements.

Security Implementation

Security considerations in edge computing present complex challenges that span both physical and digital domains. Organizations must implement comprehensive security measures while maintaining system performance and manageability. The distributed nature of edge computing introduces additional security challenges that require careful consideration during system design and implementation.

Physical security of edge devices requires robust protection mechanisms against tampering and unauthorized access. Industrial IoT deployments face particular challenges in this area, as devices often operate in inaccessible locations where physical security cannot be guaranteed. Organizations typically implement multi-layer physical security approaches, including tamper-evident enclosures, secure element hardware, and environmental monitoring systems. For example, an industrial control system might incorporate temperature and vibration sensors to detect potential tampering attempts, automatically disabling sensitive functions if unauthorized access is detected.

Data protection at the edge requires sophisticated security implementations that safeguard information throughout its lifecycle. Organizations must protect data during processing, storage, and transmission while maintaining system performance. This often involves implementing hardware-based encryption capabilities and secure key storage mechanisms. For instance, a medical edge device might utilize a dedicated security processor for encryption operations, ensuring sensitive patient data remains protected even if the main system is compromised.

Authentication and access control present significant challenges in edge computing environments. Systems must verify the identity of devices, users, and services while maintaining efficient operation. Organizations typically implement multi-factor authentication approaches combined with role-based access control systems. A smart building implementation might require both device certificates and user credentials for access to control functions, with different authorization levels for various operational tasks.

Device Management

The management of distributed edge computing deployments presents complex challenges related to device provisioning, configuration, and monitoring. Organizations must implement effective management systems that can handle large numbers of devices while maintaining security and operational efficiency.

Device provisioning in large-scale deployments requires sophisticated automation capabilities to manage the initial setup and configuration of edge devices. Smart city implementations face particular challenges in this area, often needing to provision thousands of devices across wide geographical areas. Organizations typically implement automated provisioning systems that can configure devices securely while maintaining proper documentation and audit trails. For example, a citywide IoT deployment might utilize zero-touch provisioning systems that automatically configure devices based on their location and intended function, reducing deployment time and costs by 40-50% compared to manual processes.

Configuration management becomes increasingly complex as deployment sizes grow. Organizations must maintain consistent configurations across large device populations while supporting necessary variations for specific use cases. This requires sophisticated version control and distribution systems for both software and configuration updates. A typical smart city deployment might manage dozens of device configurations across various device types, requiring careful coordination of update processes to maintain system stability.

Monitoring and maintenance present ongoing challenges in edge computing deployments. Organizations must implement effective systems for monitoring device health, performance, and security status across distributed deployments. This often requires implementing automated monitoring systems with intelligent alert mechanisms. For instance, a large-scale IoT deployment might implement predictive maintenance capabilities that analyze device performance metrics to identify potential issues before they cause system failures.

Interoperability Management

Interoperability challenges in edge computing environments arise from the need to integrate devices and systems from multiple manufacturers while maintaining consistent operation. Organizations must implement effective strategies for managing diverse device capabilities and communication protocols while ensuring reliable system operation.

Protocol standardization presents significant challenges when integrating diverse edge devices. Organizations must support multiple communication protocols while maintaining system efficiency and manageability. Building automation systems particularly face this challenge, often needing to integrate devices using various protocols such as BACnet, Modbus, and proprietary standards. A typical implementation might require protocol translation gateways that enable seamless communication between different device types while maintaining required performance characteristics.

Data format compatibility requires careful management to ensure effective information exchange between system components. Organizations must implement data transformation and validation capabilities that maintain data integrity across diverse systems. For example, a manufacturing system might need to handle sensor data in multiple formats, requiring sophisticated data normalization processes to enable consistent analysis and control functions.

Feature compatibility across different device types presents ongoing challenges in edge computing implementations. Organizations must manage varying device capabilities while maintaining consistent system operation. This often requires implementing feature detection and adaptation mechanisms that enable optimal use of available device capabilities. A smart building system might implement dynamic feature negotiation to utilize advanced capabilities when available while maintaining basic functionality with simpler devices.

Scalability Management

Scalability challenges in edge computing deployments affect both system growth capabilities and ongoing operational management. Organizations must implement effective scaling strategies that maintain performance and reliability while supporting business growth requirements.

Horizontal scaling capabilities present significant challenges when expanding edge computing deployments. Organizations must manage increasing numbers of edge devices while maintaining system performance and manageability. Traffic management systems face particular challenges in this area, often needing to scale from hundreds to thousands of sensors while maintaining real-time response capabilities. A typical implementation might utilize hierarchical management structures that enable efficient handling of large device populations while maintaining local processing efficiency.

Vertical scaling requirements present challenges related to processing capability expansion. Organizations must implement effective strategies for enhancing processing capabilities while maintaining system stability. This often involves implementing modular system architectures that support processing upgrades without requiring complete system replacement. For instance, a manufacturing control system might implement scalable processing nodes that can be upgraded or expanded based on changing performance requirements.

Edge Computing Solutions

Modern edge computing implementations require sophisticated solutions to address the complex challenges of distributed processing environments. This section examines four fundamental solution approaches that enable effective edge computing deployments.

Edge Orchestration Platforms

Edge orchestration platforms provide comprehensive management and control capabilities essential for successful edge computing implementations. These platforms deliver integrated solutions for resource allocation, application deployment, and system monitoring while maintaining the security and reliability requirements of enterprise environments.

Smart factory implementations demonstrate the effectiveness of edge orchestration platforms in industrial environments. These systems typically manage hundreds or thousands of edge devices across multiple production lines and facilities. For example, a modern automotive manufacturing plant might utilize an edge orchestration platform to manage distributed processing resources across robotic assembly systems, quality control stations, and logistics operations. The platform coordinates resource allocation based on real-time production requirements, automatically adjusting processing capacity to meet changing demands while maintaining system efficiency.

Resource allocation in edge orchestration platforms requires sophisticated management capabilities. These systems must efficiently distribute processing loads across available resources while maintaining system performance and reliability. A typical implementation might include dynamic resource allocation algorithms that continuously monitor system utilization and adjust resource distribution based on application requirements and priority levels. For instance, an orchestration platform might automatically reallocate processing resources from routine monitoring tasks to quality control functions during critical production phases.

Application deployment through orchestration platforms demands careful attention to version control and update management. Organizations must maintain consistent application versions across distributed edge devices while supporting rolling updates and fallback capabilities. Modern orchestration platforms typically implement sophisticated deployment pipelines that include automated testing, staged rollouts, and automatic rollback capabilities. For example, a smart factory might utilize a multi-stage deployment process that validates updates on test devices before gradually rolling them out across production systems, with automatic rollback triggered by any performance degradation.

System monitoring capabilities in orchestration platforms must provide comprehensive visibility into edge computing operations. These systems typically implement multi-level monitoring approaches that track hardware health, application performance, and system security status. A modern implementation might collect thousands of metrics per second from distributed edge devices, using artificial intelligence and machine learning algorithms to identify potential issues before they impact production operations.

Containerization Technologies

Containerization represents a fundamental technology for modern edge computing deployments, enabling efficient application deployment and resource utilization while maintaining security and isolation requirements. This approach provides consistent application environments across diverse edge devices while optimizing resource usage.

IoT gateway implementations demonstrate the practical benefits of containerization in edge environments. These systems typically run multiple edge applications with varying requirements and security levels. A modern IoT gateway might utilize containerization to simultaneously run data processing, security monitoring, and device management applications while maintaining strict isolation between these functions. This approach enables efficient resource sharing while preventing potential conflicts or security breaches between applications.

Container image optimization represents a critical consideration in edge computing environments. Organizations must carefully balance application functionality against resource constraints and update requirements. Modern implementations typically utilize sophisticated image optimization techniques that can reduce container sizes by 50–70% compared to standard builds. For example, a containerized edge application might implement multi-stage builds and minimal base images to reduce its footprint while maintaining full functionality.

Update management for containerized applications requires careful attention to network utilization and system stability. Organizations must implement efficient update mechanisms that minimize bandwidth requirements while maintaining system reliability. Modern container platforms typically implement layer-based updates that only transmit changed components, reducing update sizes by 80–90% compared to full image updates. This approach becomes particularly valuable in deployments with limited network bandwidth or high update frequencies.

Security implications of containerization demand comprehensive protection mechanisms. Organizations must implement effective isolation between containers while maintaining system performance. Modern implementations typically utilize hardware-based isolation features and security-enhanced container runtimes to provide robust protection. For instance, a secure IoT gateway might implement separate security domains for different container types, utilizing hardware virtualization features to enhance isolation between critical functions.

Microservices Architecture

Microservices architecture provides a flexible and scalable approach to edge computing implementations, enabling independent deployment and scaling of application components while improving system maintainability. This architectural approach supports efficient resource utilization and simplified system evolution through modular design principles.

Smart retail systems demonstrate effective implementation of microservices architecture in edge computing environments. These systems typically manage diverse functions including inventory tracking, customer analytics, and security monitoring. A modern retail implementation might decompose these functions into independent microservices that can be deployed and scaled independently based on specific store requirements. This approach enables efficient resource utilization while simplifying system maintenance and updates.

Service communication in microservices architectures requires careful consideration of network efficiency and reliability. Organizations must implement effective communication patterns that minimize overhead while maintaining system responsiveness. Implementations typically utilize lightweight protocols and efficient serialization formats that reduce communication overhead by 40-60% compared to traditional approaches *such as RESTful communication over HTTP combined with verbose formats like XML or uncompressed JSON.* For example, a retail system might implement binary protocols for inter-service communication, significantly reducing network utilization while improving response times.

State management presents particular challenges in microservices deployments. Organizations must implement effective strategies for maintaining data consistency across distributed services while supporting system resilience. Implementations typically utilize event-driven architectures and distributed state management approaches that enable reliable operation even during partial system failures. A retail system might implement event sourcing patterns to maintain accurate inventory states across multiple services while supporting automatic reconciliation during service recovery.

Failure handling in microservices architectures requires comprehensive strategies for maintaining system stability. Organizations must implement effective isolation and recovery mechanisms that prevent cascading failures while maintaining critical functionality. Implementations typically utilize circuit breaker patterns and automatic failover mechanisms to maintain system reliability. For instance, a retail system might implement automatic service isolation and degraded mode operation when detecting performance issues, maintaining basic functionality while preventing system-wide disruptions.

Edge Security Frameworks

Edge security frameworks provide essential protection mechanisms for modern edge computing deployments, integrating multiple security layers to create comprehensive defense strategies. These frameworks must address various threat vectors while maintaining system performance and manageability.

Critical infrastructure implementations demonstrate the importance of robust security frameworks in edge computing environments. These systems typically require protection against sophisticated threats while maintaining continuous operation. An implementation might integrate multiple security layers including hardware-based root of trust, secure boot processes, and runtime protection mechanisms. This multi-layer approach provides defense in depth while enabling efficient security management.

Device security integration requires careful attention to hardware and software protection mechanisms. Organizations must implement effective strategies for securing edge devices throughout their lifecycle. Security frameworks typically utilize hardware security modules and trusted platform modules to establish strong device identity and protect sensitive operations. For example, a critical infrastructure system might implement secure boot chains and runtime attestation to ensure device integrity while preventing unauthorized modifications.

Network protection in edge security frameworks demands comprehensive monitoring and control capabilities. Organizations must implement effective strategies for securing communication while maintaining system performance. Implementations typically utilize sophisticated intrusion detection systems and network segmentation approaches that can identify and contain potential threats while maintaining normal operations. A security framework might implement AI-based threat detection that can identify anomalous behavior patterns and automatically implement protective measures.

CONCLUSION

Effective communication and computing mechanisms are at the core of any Internet of Things (IoT) deployment. This chapter highlighted the dual role of **protocols** and **computing paradigms** in shaping the performance, reliability, and scalability of IoT ecosystems.

At the communication layer, the comparison between **edge-oriented protocols** such as CoAP, MQTT, LwM2M, and BLE, and **cloud-oriented protocols** like HTTP/HTTPS, AMQP, gRPC, and WebSockets, illustrated how protocol selection must balance factors such as power consumption, latency, message size, and security requirements. For resource-constrained devices, lightweight edge protocols provide efficiency and responsiveness, while cloud protocols enable advanced analytics, integration, and large-scale coordination.

On the computing side, the distinction among **edge, fog, cloud, and hybrid computing models** demonstrates that intelligence can be flexibly distributed across the IoT architecture. Edge and fog computing ensure timely local responses and bandwidth efficiency, whereas cloud computing supports global visibility, long-term storage, and advanced machine learning. Hybrid models combine these strengths, aligning processing with application-specific performance needs.

The discussion of processing paradigms, including **stream, batch, real-time, and event-driven analytics**, further emphasized that computation strategies must reflect both technical constraints and operational objectives. Together, protocol selection and computing architecture form the foundation upon which scalable and reliable smart city applications can be built.

In practice, designing an effective IoT system requires careful integration of these communication and computing elements. An imbalance such as deploying verbose traditional protocols in bandwidth-limited environments or offloading all processing to the cloud in latency-sensitive applications can drastically reduce system performance. Conversely, well-engineered protocol choices and distributed computing strategies strengthen resilience, enable efficiency, and ensure that IoT deployments remain adaptive to both current and future needs.

As smart cities expand, the synergy between communication protocols and distributed computing will become increasingly central to urban infrastructure, supporting critical domains such as traffic optimization, energy management, public safety, and environmental monitoring. These principles provide the technical bridge that allows vast networks of devices to function not as isolated units, but as coordinated, intelligent systems capable of delivering meaningful value to citizens and city operators alike.

CHAPTER 8

REAL-TIME IOT DATA ANALYTICS

Modern smart city ecosystems depend not only on the interoperability of communication protocols and computing architectures but also on the ability to transform continuous data streams into actionable insights. While earlier discussions highlighted how devices connect and process information through edge, fog, and cloud computing paradigms, the real value emerges when this data is analyzed in real time. The increasing speed and scale of urban IoT deployments, ranging from traffic sensors and environmental monitors to healthcare wearables—demand analytics systems capable of operating within milliseconds rather than hours. This chapter examines the principles and implementation strategies of real-time IoT data analytics, exploring how continuous stream processing enables immediate decision-making across urban infrastructures and why such responsiveness is critical for safety, efficiency, and sustainability in smart cities.

PRINCIPLES AND APPLICATIONS

Real-time IoT data analytics relies on principles that transform continuous streams of sensor data into actionable intelligence, enabling immediate response to changing urban conditions. These principles guide how data is ingested, processed, and acted upon, while their applications span diverse domains in smart cities, including traffic management, energy distribution, healthcare, and environmental monitoring.

Real-time Analytics Fundamentals

Real-time IoT data analytics within smart city infrastructures provides immediate situational awareness and supports rapid responses to evolving urban conditions. Its core principles are built on interconnected components, such as data ingestion, stream processing, temporal alignment, and output delivery that work together to transform continuous sensor streams into actionable intelligence.

Stream processing operates on data as it arrives rather than accumulating it for batch processing. This approach requires specialized algorithms and data structures capable of incremental processing while maintaining accuracy and responsiveness. In smart city applications, stream processing enables continuous urban infrastructure monitoring, from traffic flow sensors to air quality monitoring stations. For instance, in urban traffic management systems, stream processing allows for the immediate detection of congestion patterns and automated adjustment of traffic signal timing to optimize flow.

The distinction between real-time and batch processing is critical in IoT analytics system design. While batch processing can leverage comprehensive historical context and complex algorithmic approaches, real-time processing must carefully balance immediacy against computational constraints. This balance is particularly evident in smart energy grid applications, where real-time processing enables immediate response to demand fluctuations. In contrast, batch processing informs longer-term capacity planning and infrastructure optimization.

TABLE 8.1 Real-time vs. batch processing comparison in IoT analytics.

Aspect	Real-time Processing	Batch Processing
Processing Characteristics		
Data Handling	Processes data immediately upon arrival	Processes accumulated data in scheduled intervals
Latency	Very low (milliseconds to seconds)	Higher (minutes to hours)
Processing Pattern	Continuous stream processing	Periodic batch jobs
Data Volume per Operation	Smaller data volumes	Larger data volumes
Resource Utilization	Continuous, moderate to high	High but scheduled
Technical Implementation		
Architecture	Stream processing engines	Data warehouses and batch processors
Memory Management	In-memory processing with state management	Disk-based storage with batch loading
Scaling Approach	Horizontal scaling for throughput	Vertical scaling for processing power
Error Handling	Immediate retry and failover	Batch retry mechanisms
Data Persistence	Optional persistence, focus on processing	Required persistence before processing
Advantages		
Response Time	Immediate insights and responses	Comprehensive historical analysis
Application Suitability	Ideal for time-critical applications	Better for complex analytical workloads
Resource Efficiency	Reduced storage requirements	More efficient resource utilization
Analysis Capability	Quick anomaly detection	Deep pattern analysis
Cost Structure	Pay for continuous processing	Pay for periodic processing

(Continued)

TABLE 8.1 (Continued)

Aspect	Real-time Processing	Batch Processing
Disadvantages		
Complexity	Higher operational complexity	Delayed insights and responses
Infrastructure Costs	More expensive infrastructure	Higher storage costs
Analysis Context	Limited historical context	Not suitable for immediate actions
Resource Management	Strict resource constraints	Less flexible resource allocation
Analytics Depth	Limited complex analytics	May process outdated data
Common Use Cases		
Urban Applications	Traffic flow optimization	City planning and zoning
Utility Management	Power grid balancing	Energy consumption trends
Security	Fraud detection	Security pattern analysis
Infrastructure	Equipment monitoring	Maintenance planning
Environmental	Air quality monitoring	Climate trend analysis

Event time versus processing time management is crucial in real-time analytics system architecture. The temporal relationship between when data is generated (event time) and when it is analyzed (processing time) significantly impacts system accuracy and reliability. For example, in urban environmental monitoring systems, sensor readings must be correctly temporally aligned despite varying network latencies and device buffering effects. This temporal coordination ensures accurate trend analysis and enables reliable event detection across distributed sensor networks.

Windowing strategies provide essential temporal context for real-time decision-making in IoT systems. Different windowing approaches, including tumbling, sliding, and session windows, serve various analytical requirements across smart city applications. For instance, air quality monitoring systems might employ sliding windows to detect trending pollutant levels, while building energy management systems use tumbling windows for precise consumption calculations. The selection of appropriate windowing strategies significantly influences both analytical precision and system resource utilization.

State management in real-time analytics ensures consistency and enables sophisticated temporal analysis across distributed IoT data streams. Stream processing systems must efficiently maintain state information while handling potential system failures and scaling operations. In smart infrastructure monitoring, state management enables tracking structural health indicators over time, facilitating early detection of maintenance requirements and possible safety issues.

Applications in IoT

Implementing real-time analytics in IoT systems involves numerous applications, each presenting unique challenges and opportunities to enhance operational efficiency and decision-making capabilities. This section explores the primary application areas where real-time analytics delivers significant value in IoT deployments.

Predictive maintenance fundamentally transforms how organizations approach equipment maintenance and asset management. These systems continuously monitor sensor inputs from industrial machinery and infrastructure components, processing complex data streams that include vibration signatures, thermal patterns, acoustic emissions, and power consumption metrics. Advanced analytics algorithms process this multi-dimensional data in real-time, identifying subtle patterns and trends that precede equipment failures. For instance, in smart city infrastructure, predictive maintenance systems might monitor bridge structural health through a network of strain gauges and accelerometers, enabling early detection of potential structural issues. The real-time nature of these systems allows maintenance teams to respond proactively to developing problems, significantly reducing unexpected downtime and optimizing maintenance resource allocation.

Anomaly detection systems powered by real-time analytics are crucial to IoT system integrity and operational reliability. These systems employ sophisticated statistical methods and machine learning algorithms to establish normal behavioral baselines and identify deviations that warrant attention. In smart grid applications, anomaly detection systems continuously monitor power distribution networks, analyzing consumption patterns, voltage levels, and equipment status signals to identify potential issues before they escalate into major problems. The implementation challenge lies in achieving an optimal balance between detection sensitivity and false alarm rates, particularly when processing high-volume, multi-source data streams in real time. Advanced techniques such as adaptive thresholding and contextual anomaly detection help maintain this balance while accommodating natural variations in system behavior.

Real-time monitoring systems provide essential operational visibility and control capabilities across IoT deployments. These systems integrate sophisticated data visualization techniques with automated alerting mechanisms to deliver actionable insights to operators and stakeholders. In smart building environments, real-time monitoring platforms typically process diverse data streams, including environmental parameters (temperature, humidity, and CO_2 levels), occupancy patterns, energy consumption metrics, and security system status. The monitoring system must handle these multiple data streams effectively while maintaining responsive updates and ensuring accurate alert generation. Advanced visualization techniques, such as dynamic dashboards and augmented reality interfaces, enhance operators' ability to quickly comprehend complex system states and respond appropriately to emerging situations.

Process optimization applications utilize real-time analytics to improve system performance and efficiency continuously. These applications employ sophisticated optimization algorithms that analyze operational data streams to identify improvement opportunities and implement real-time adjustments. In smart manufacturing environments, real-time optimization systems might simultaneously monitor product quality metrics, energy consumption patterns, and production line parameters, making continuous adjustments to maximize efficiency while maintaining quality standards. Optimization must carefully balance immediate operational adjustments against longer-term performance trends, often incorporating machine learning techniques to refine optimization strategies over time.

Quality control systems enhanced by real-time analytics are important, particularly in manufacturing and service delivery contexts. These systems typically integrate multiple sensor inputs with sophisticated analysis algorithms to maintain consistent quality standards. In smart city water management systems, for example, real-time analytics processes data from water quality sensors, flow meters, and pressure sensors to ensure water quality and distribution efficiency. The implementation must maintain high accuracy while processing multiple data streams in real time, often incorporating edge computing capabilities to reduce latency and enable an immediate response to quality issues.

DATA FLOW DESIGN AND OPTIMIZATION

The effectiveness of real-time IoT analytics depends not only on processing speed but also on how efficiently data is moved through the system. Data flow design provides the architectural blueprint for how raw sensor data is captured, transferred, processed, and delivered to decision-making components. Optimization of this flow is essential to ensure that high-volume, heterogeneous IoT data streams can be handled with minimal latency, maximum reliability, and efficient use of computational resources. A well-structured data flow design enables seamless coordination between ingestion, processing, storage, and output layers, ultimately supporting the responsiveness required in smart city operations.

Data Ingestion Patterns

Effective data ingestion is the foundation of real-time IoT analytics systems. Ingestion patterns define the structured approaches used to capture and transmit data from diverse devices into processing pipelines. These patterns must account for heterogeneous data sources, different transmission frequencies, and unpredictable network conditions while ensuring reliability, fault tolerance, and scalability. By establishing clear ingestion strategies, organizations can build robust pipelines that maintain data integrity and performance even under high variability and large-scale workloads.

Push versus pull patterns constitute fundamental architectural decisions in IoT data collection systems, each offering distinct advantages and challenges in different operational contexts. Push patterns, where IoT devices actively transmit data to processing systems, typically deliver superior latency performance and enable a more immediate response to critical events. However, these patterns require sophisticated flow control mechanisms to prevent system overwhelm during peak data generation periods. For example, in smart city environmental monitoring networks, air quality sensors might employ push patterns to immediately report dangerous pollutant levels, enabling rapid response to environmental hazards. The implementation must incorporate backpressure mechanisms and intelligent throttling to maintain system stability under varying load conditions.

TABLE 8.2 Push vs. pull pattern comparison in IoT data ingestion.

Characteristic	Push Pattern	Pull Pattern
Latency	Lower latency (milliseconds)	Higher latency (seconds to minutes)
Control	Device-initiated	System-initiated
Flow Control	Requires backpressure mechanisms	Built-in flow control
Resource Usage	Variable, peak-driven	Predictable, system-controlled
Implementation Complexity	Higher	Lower
Use Cases	Emergency alerts, real-time monitoring	Equipment telemetry, periodic reporting
Network Load	Unpredictable, burst-prone	Controlled, evenly distributed
Failure Handling	Requires retry mechanisms	Simpler recovery patterns

Pull patterns, conversely, provide processing systems with greater control over data acquisition timing and volume. This approach enables more precise resource management and can reduce system complexity by centralizing control logic. In industrial IoT applications, pull patterns might be employed for collecting equipment performance metrics, allowing the system to adjust data collection frequency based on current processing capacity and analytical requirements. The trade-off between control and latency must be carefully evaluated based on specific application requirements and operational constraints.

Buffer management supports handling IoT data flow variability. Modern IoT systems must implement sophisticated buffer management strategies that optimize memory utilization while preventing data loss during peak loading periods or network disruptions. In smart transportation systems, traffic sensors generate substantially higher data volumes during rush hours or special events. The buffer management system must dynamically adjust to these varying loads while maintaining data integrity and system responsiveness. This requires implementing adaptive buffer sizing algorithms and intelligent data prioritization mechanisms that consider both immediate analytical needs and longer-term data preservation requirements.

Rate-limiting strategies are vital in maintaining system stability and preventing resource exhaustion in IoT analytics platforms. These mechanisms must operate at multiple levels, from individual device constraints to system-wide capacity management. Advanced rate-limiting implementations often incorporate hierarchical approaches that coordinate limits across different system tiers. For example, in large-scale industrial IoT deployments, rate limiting might be implemented at device, gateway, and data center levels, with each tier maintaining awareness of downstream capacity constraints. The system must also incorporate dynamic adjustment capabilities to respond to changing network conditions and processing capacity.

TABLE 8.3 Multi-level rate limiting strategy.

System Level	Rate Limit Type	Primary Concern	Control Mechanism
Device	Per-device limits	Device resources	Local throttling
Gateway	Aggregate device limits	Network bandwidth	Queue management
Data Center	System-wide limits	Processing capacity	Load balancing
Application	Service-specific limits	Business requirements	API throttling
Storage	Write rate limits	Storage performance	Buffer management

Data validation is important in quality control for the ingestion pipeline, ensuring the reliability and usefulness of collected data for downstream analytics. IoT systems must implement comprehensive validation processes that detect various data anomalies while maintaining processing efficiency. In smart grid applications, for instance, validation systems must verify the accuracy and consistency of power consumption data from millions of smart meters in real time. This requires implementing multi-stage validation pipelines that can identify technical errors, detect potential security breaches, and ensure regulatory compliance without introducing significant processing delays.

Error handling in IoT data ingestion requires robust and sophisticated mechanisms for managing various failure conditions while maintaining system reliability. Error handling systems must implement comprehensive logging and recovery procedures that ensure data integrity while facilitating system maintenance and troubleshooting. In health care IoT applications, for example, error-handling systems must ensure zero data loss for critical patient monitoring while maintaining system availability and regulatory compliance. This necessitates implementing redundant storage systems, sophisticated error classification mechanisms, and automated recovery procedures tailored to different error scenarios.

Stream Processing Architecture

The architecture of stream processing systems represents a sophisticated interplay of multiple components working in concert to enable real-time analytics capabilities. This section explores the essential elements and their interactions within modern stream processing architectures, focusing on how they collectively allow reliable and efficient real-time data analysis.

Stream processors constitute the fundamental computational engine of real-time analytics systems, implementing complex algorithms that transform raw data streams into actionable insights. These critical components must efficiently handle high-volume, high-velocity data streams while maintaining processing accuracy and meeting strict latency requirements. Modern stream processors employ sophisticated optimization techniques, including parallel processing architectures and adaptive resource allocation strategies. For instance, stream processors might simultaneously analyze data from hundreds of production line sensors in smart manufacturing environments, implementing complex quality control algorithms that detect subtle defect patterns in real-time. The implementation must carefully balance computational resource utilization against processing latency requirements, often employing adaptive batching and processing prioritization techniques to optimize system performance. Advanced stream processors also incorporate fault tolerance mechanisms, ensuring continuous operation despite hardware failures or processing anomalies.

TABLE 8.4 Stream processing components and their characteristics.

Component	Primary Function	Key Features	Performance Requirements
Stream Processors	Data transformation	Parallel processing, adaptive allocation	Low latency, high throughput
Message Brokers	Data distribution	Routing, delivery guarantees	Reliable delivery, flow control
State Stores	Data persistence	Hybrid storage, caching	High-speed access, consistency
Processing Operators	Analytics execution	Operator fusion, event handling	Processing accuracy, efficiency
Output Sinks	Result delivery	Multiple output modes, buffering	Reliable transmission, format support

Message brokers in streaming architectures provide reliable and efficient data distribution across processing components. These sophisticated middleware components handle critical functions, including message routing, delivery guarantees, and system-wide flow control. In large-scale IoT deployments, message brokers must manage complex routing topologies while ensuring message delivery reliability and maintaining system performance. Consider a smart city infrastructure monitoring system. The message brokers distribute sensor data from thousands of devices to multiple processing components handling different aspects of urban management, from traffic control to environmental monitoring. Broker implementations incorporate advanced features such as message prioritization, load balancing, and dead-letter queuing to handle various operational scenarios. The broker architecture must also implement sophisticated flow control mechanisms to prevent system overload while maintaining optimal throughput.

State stores provide the essential persistence layer for stream processing applications, enabling sophisticated stateful processing and historical analysis capabilities. These components must handle extremely high-speed data access operations while maintaining consistency and durability. State store implementations often employ hybrid storage architectures combining in-memory and persistent storage to optimize access patterns for different types of state information. For example, state stores maintain complex data structures supporting both immediate fraud detection and longer-term pattern analysis in financial transaction monitoring systems. Modern state store implementations incorporate advanced features such as distributed caching, write-ahead logging, and snapshot management to ensure data durability while maintaining high-performance access patterns. The architecture must carefully balance storage efficiency against access speed requirements while ensuring data consistency across distributed processing environments.

TABLE 8.5 Common stream processing patterns and their applications.

Pattern	Description	Use Cases	Key Considerations
Event Processing	Immediate event handling	Fraud detection, alerts	Latency, accuracy
Window Processing	Time-based analysis	Traffic patterns, usage metrics	Window size, overlap
Stateful Processing	Context-aware analysis	Customer behavior, system health	State management, recovery
Join Processing	Multiple stream correlation	Sensor fusion, cross-system analysis	Synchronization, memory
Aggregation	Data summarization	Performance metrics, usage statistics	Accuracy, resource usage

Processing operators implement the specific analytical functions that form the core of stream processing applications. These specialized components must execute various analytical operations efficiently while maintaining streaming semantics and ensuring result accuracy. In smart grid monitoring systems, operators might implement complex functions ranging from simple aggregations to sophisticated pattern detection algorithms. Modern operator implementations incorporate advanced optimization techniques such as operator fusion and adaptive execution strategies to maximize processing efficiency. The architecture must support stateless and stateful operators while ensuring correct handling of event time semantics and processing guarantees. Sophisticated operator implementations also include mechanisms for handling late-arriving data and ensuring exactly-once processing semantics.

Output sinks handle the final stage of the processing pipeline, managing the delivery of analysis results to downstream systems and end users. These components must implement reliable transmission mechanisms while supporting various delivery guarantees and data format requirements. Advanced sink implementations support multiple output modes, from real-time alerting to batch-oriented historical storage. For instance, in industrial IoT applications, output sinks might simultaneously deliver processing results to real-time monitoring dashboards, historical databases, and automated control systems. Modern sink architectures incorporate sophisticated buffering mechanisms and delivery retry logic to ensure reliable result delivery even under challenging network conditions. The implementation must also handle varying throughput requirements and support different data serialization formats while maintaining overall system performance.

CLOUD PROCESSING AND CONSUMPTION

Cloud Processing Patterns

Lambda architecture provides a comprehensive approach to real-time and historical data analysis. This pattern combines stream processing for real-time analysis with batch processing for comprehensive historical analysis. In a smart city environment, lambda architecture might optimize traffic flow while enabling long-term planning through historical pattern analysis. The implementation must carefully manage the complexity of maintaining dual processing paths while ensuring consistent results.

TABLE 8.6 Comparison of cloud processing architectures.

Architecture	Key Characteristics	Advantages	Challenges	Typical Use Cases
Lambda	Dual processing paths (batch + stream)	Complete data analysis, high accuracy	Complex maintenance, resource-intensive	Long-term analytics, historical patterns
Kappa	Single stream processing	Simplified architecture, lower latency	Complex stream processing, limited batch capabilities	Real-time applications, continuous analytics
Microservices	Independent processing services	High scalability, independent evolution	Service coordination, network overhead	Modular systems, multi-domain applications
Event-driven	Event-based communication	Loose coupling, real-time response	Event routing complexity, state management	Reactive systems, real-time monitoring

Kappa architecture simplifies real-time data processing by treating all data as streams, eliminating the separate batch processing layer. This approach reduces system complexity but requires careful design of stream processing components. For example, an e-commerce recommendation system might use kappa architecture to process customer behavior streams, providing real-time personalization while maintaining historical analysis capabilities. The implementation must ensure efficient stream processing while supporting immediate and historical analysis needs.

The microservices pattern enables flexible and scalable processing architectures through independent, specialized services. This approach allows different processing components to evolve independently while maintaining system integration. Consider a smart agriculture system: Separate microservices might handle weather data analysis, irrigation control, and crop health monitoring. The architecture must manage service communication and coordination while maintaining system reliability.

TABLE 8.7 Architecture implementation requirements.

Component	Lambda	Kappa	Microservices	Event-driven
Processing Layer	Batch + Stream	Stream only	Service-specific	Event processors
Data Storage	Dual storage	Stream storage	Service databases	Event store
Integration	Layer merger	Stream processing	API gateway	Event bus
Scalability	Layer-specific	Stream-based	Service-level	Event-based
Deployment	Complex	Moderate	Independent	Distributed

Event-driven architecture facilitates the responsive processing of IoT data streams through event-based communication patterns. This approach enables loose coupling between components while supporting real-time response capabilities. A smart factory might use event-driven architecture to coordinate various control and monitoring functions, allowing immediate response to production events. The implementation must manage event routing and processing while maintaining system responsiveness.

Data Consumption Methods

Real-time dashboards provide immediate visibility into system operation and analytics results. These interfaces must balance update frequency against system resource usage while maintaining usability. For instance, a power grid monitoring dashboard might display current load conditions, trending patterns, and alerts, updating continuously as new data arrives. The dashboard implementation must optimize data delivery and visualization while ensuring responsive user interaction.

APIs and Webhooks enable programmatic access to real-time data and analytics results. These interfaces must provide appropriate authentication and access control while maintaining performance. A smart building system might offer APIs for accessing environmental data and control functions, enabling integration with third-party applications. The implementation must ensure secure and efficient data access while supporting various integration patterns.

TABLE 8.8 Data consumption methods comparison.

Method	Primary Function	Key Features	Performance Metrics	Security Requirements
Real-time Dashboards	Visual monitoring	Live updates, interactive views	Update latency, refresh rate	Access control, session management
APIs/Webhooks	Programmatic access	RESTful interfaces, event notifications	Response time, throughput	Authentication, rate limiting
Alert Systems	Event notification	Priority levels, multi-channel delivery	Notification speed, delivery rate	Message encryption, access verification
Data Warehouses	Historical storage	Query optimization, data partitioning	Query performance, storage efficiency	Data encryption, access auditing
Analytics Platforms	Data analysis	Custom queries, visualization tools	Processing speed, resource usage	Role-based access, data masking

Alert systems notify relevant personnel about significant events or conditions detected through real-time analysis. These systems must balance notification immediacy against alert fatigue while ensuring reliable delivery. Consider an industrial safety monitoring system. The alerts must immediately notify operators of dangerous conditions while avoiding unnecessary notifications for normal variations. The alert system must implement appropriate prioritization and delivery mechanisms.

Data warehouses store processed data for long-term analysis and reporting. These systems must efficiently handle continuous data ingestion while maintaining query performance. For example, a retail analytics system might store processed customer behavior data for trend analysis and business planning. The warehouse implementation must optimize storage and retrieval operations while supporting various analysis requirements.

TABLE 8.9 Consumption method implementation requirements.

Requirement	Dashboards	APIs	Alerts	Data Warehouse	Analytics Platform
Update Frequency	Milliseconds	Seconds	Real-time	Minutes	Variable
Data Volume	Filtered	Controlled	Minimal	Complete	Selective
Storage Type	In-memory	Cache	Queue	Persistent	Hybrid
Integration	WebSocket	REST/GraphQL	Push	ETL	Multiple
Scalability Needs	Frontend	API endpoints	Notification service	Storage capacity	Processing power

Analytics platforms provide tools for detailed analysis of both real-time and historical data. These platforms must support various analysis methods while maintaining data accessibility and system performance. For example, a health care monitoring system might provide platforms for analyzing patient data trends and treatment outcomes. The platform implementation must balance analytical capabilities against resource requirements.

CASE STUDY: IOT IMPLEMENTATION IN OTORITA IKN SMART CITY DEVELOPMENT

The development of Ibu Kota Nusantara (IKN) as Indonesia's new capital city represents one of the world's most ambitious smart city projects, integrating Internet of Things (IoT) technologies with sustainable forest city concepts. This case study examines how Otorita IKN implements comprehensive IoT systems across multiple domains and governs the resulting data streams through its Integrated Command and Control Center (ICCC).

IoT Infrastructure Overview

IKN's smart city blueprint encompasses six key domains: Smart Governance, Smart Transportation and Mobility, Smart Living, Smart Natural Resources and Energy, Smart Industry and Human Resources, and Smart Built Environment and Infrastructure. Each domain utilizes specialized IoT sensor networks that feed real-time data into the centralized command center for analysis and decision-making.

The IoT architecture follows a three-tier approach combining edge computing, fog computing, and cloud processing to ensure efficient data handling across the 256,000-hectare development area. This multi-tier system enables immediate local responses while maintaining comprehensive data analytics capabilities for long-term planning and optimization.

Environmental Monitoring IoT Systems

Smart Forest Sensors: As a forest city maintaining 75% green coverage, IKN deploys extensive environmental monitoring networks including forest fire detection sensors, flood early warning systems, and air quality monitoring stations. These sensors continuously track temperature, humidity, PM2.5, PM10, CO2, and other atmospheric pollutants to ensure environmental sustainability.

Smart Water Management: IoT sensors monitor water quality parameters, distribution pressure, and consumption patterns throughout the water supply network. The system includes smart wastewater management sensors that track treatment processes and discharge quality to maintain environmental standards.

Climate and Weather Monitoring: Distributed weather stations equipped with IoT sensors provide real-time meteorological data including rainfall, wind patterns, and temperature variations. This data supports both daily operations and long-term climate adaptation strategies.

Smart Transportation IoT Implementation

IKN's Intelligent Transportation System (ITS) integrates multiple IoT technologies to achieve its goal of 80% public and active transportation usage. The transportation IoT network includes:

Traffic Flow Sensors: Vehicle detection sensors at intersections and major roadways monitor traffic density, speed, and patterns. These sensors enable adaptive traffic signal control and real-time route optimization.

Autonomous Vehicle Support: LiDAR sensors, cameras, and radar systems support autonomous vehicle operations, including the planned Autonomous Rail Rapid Transit (ART) system and autonomous shuttle services within the government core area.

Electric Vehicle Infrastructure: Smart charging stations equipped with IoT sensors monitor usage patterns, energy consumption, and charging status. The system optimizes charging schedules based on grid capacity and renewable energy availability.

Smart Building and Infrastructure IoT

Smart Pole Networks: IKN deploys smart poles as IoT hubs throughout the city, integrating multiple sensors for motion detection, environmental monitoring, WiFi connectivity, and emergency communication systems. These poles serve as data collection points and provide distributed computing capabilities.

Smart Buildings: Vertical housing developments incorporate Fiber to the Room (FTTR) connectivity and IoT sensors for energy management, security, and comfort optimization. Building management systems automatically adjust lighting, HVAC, and other systems based on occupancy and environmental conditions.

Energy Grid Monitoring: Smart grid sensors monitor power generation, distribution, and consumption patterns across the renewable energy-focused electrical system. The 50-megawatt solar installation includes IoT monitoring for performance optimization and predictive maintenance.

Command Center Data Governance

Integrated Command and Control Center (ICCC): The Nusantara Command Center serves as the central hub for all IoT data streams, utilizing big data analytics and computer vision technologies to process information from thousands of sensors across the city.

Data Architecture: The ICCC processes data through multiple layers including real-time monitoring dashboards, analytical reporting systems, and crisis management protocols. The system integrates CCTV feeds, drone surveillance, and sensor data to provide comprehensive situational awareness.

Multi-Agency Coordination: Data governance involves coordination between Otorita IKN, various ministries, and international partners including U.S. companies such as Amazon Web Services, IBM, and Cisco. This collaboration ensures interoperability and leverages global expertise in smart city technologies.

Data Processing and Analytics Framework

Real-time Processing: The command center processes approximately 1,000 to 5,000 sensor readings per second during peak operations, enabling immediate response to changing conditions. Stream processing algorithms analyze traffic patterns, environmental conditions, and infrastructure performance in real-time.

Predictive Analytics: Machine learning algorithms process historical and real-time data to predict potential issues such as traffic congestion, equipment failures, and environmental hazards. The system can issue early warnings for forest fires, floods, and other emergency situations.

Data Integration: The ICCC integrates data from multiple sources including IoT sensors, social media monitoring, construction progress tracking, and investment monitoring systems. This comprehensive data integration supports evidence-based decision-making across all city management functions.

Implementation Challenges and Solutions

Scalability Management: The phased development approach allows IoT systems to scale gradually from the initial government core area to the full city footprint. The infrastructure is designed to accommodate increasing sensor density and data volumes as construction progresses.

Data Security and Privacy: Implementation includes robust cybersecurity measures with support from national security agencies. The system ensures data encryption, access control, and secure communications across all IoT networks.

Interoperability Standards: IKN adopts open network technologies and standardized protocols to ensure seamless integration between different IoT systems and vendors. This approach facilitates future upgrades and technology evolution.

Performance Outcomes and Future Expansion

Initial implementation results demonstrate successful integration of IoT technologies with sustainable urban development principles. The command center has successfully supported major events including Indonesia's Independence Day celebrations, showcasing the system's operational readiness.

Future expansion plans include full deployment across all six smart city domains by 2045, with continuous technology updates and capability enhancements. The IKN model is designed for replication across other Indonesian cities, potentially transforming urban development nationwide.

This comprehensive IoT implementation at IKN demonstrates how real-time data analytics can support sustainable smart city development while maintaining environmental conservation goals. The integration of diverse sensor networks with centralized data governance provides a blueprint for future smart city developments in emerging economies.

CONCLUSION

Real-time IoT analytics has become essential for modern smart cities, as demonstrated by the ongoing development of Indonesia's new capital, Nusantara. The IKN project shows how cities can use live data from thousands of sensors to make immediate decisions about traffic, environmental conditions, and infrastructure management.

The key lessons from IKN's implementation highlight three important aspects of real-time IoT systems. First, successful deployments require careful planning of data flows from devices to processing centers. IKN's approach of combining edge, fog, and cloud computing ensures that critical decisions can be made locally while maintaining comprehensive oversight through the central command center.

Second, the variety of IoT applications in IKN, from forest fire detection to smart transportation systems demonstrates that different use cases need different processing approaches. Some situations require instant responses measured in milliseconds, while others can work with longer processing times but need more detailed analysis.

Third, effective data governance becomes crucial when managing information from diverse sensor networks. IKN's Integrated Command and Control Center processes data from environmental sensors, traffic monitors, and building management systems, showing how centralized coordination can work alongside distributed processing.

The technical challenges faced in IKN's development also provide practical insights for other smart city projects. Ensuring reliable connectivity across a 256,000-hectare area, managing data from sensors with different communication protocols, and maintaining system performance during peak loads all require careful engineering and robust system design.

Looking ahead, IKN's experience suggests that successful real-time IoT analytics depends more on practical implementation decisions than on theoretical frameworks. The choice between push and pull data patterns, the balance between local and centralized processing, and the integration of multiple data sources all have direct impacts on system performance and operational effectiveness.

The IKN case study ultimately demonstrates that real-time IoT analytics is not just about processing data quickly—it's about creating systems that can adapt to changing conditions, support informed decision-making, and improve quality of life for citizens. As more cities follow similar approaches, the lessons learned from IKN's implementation will provide valuable guidance for future smart city developments.

CHAPTER 9

DESIGNING EFFECTIVE DATA LAKES FOR IOT SYSTEMS

The previous chapter examined real-time processing architectures for IoT analytics, demonstrating how streaming data flows require immediate analysis capabilities. While real-time processing addresses the velocity challenges of IoT data, organizations also need comprehensive storage strategies that can accommodate the full spectrum of IoT data characteristics - not just speed, but also the massive volume and diverse variety that IoT systems generate. This chapter builds upon those real-time processing concepts by exploring how data lakes provide the foundational storage infrastructure needed to support both immediate analytics and long-term data management requirements.

IoT systems across smart cities generate continuous streams of data from millions of connected devices, sensors, and systems. Traffic management systems produce terabytes of daily sensor readings, environmental monitoring networks collect air quality measurements from hundreds of locations, and utility infrastructure generates operational data from smart meters and grid sensors. While real-time processing handles immediate analytical needs, organizations require robust storage architectures that can preserve this data for historical analysis, compliance requirements, and advanced machine learning applications that depend on large historical datasets.

Data lakes address these comprehensive storage challenges by providing flexible, scalable repositories that can accept information in any format while maintaining complete data integrity. Unlike traditional databases that require predefined schemas, data lakes accommodate the heterogeneous nature of IoT data streams - from structured sensor readings and semi-structured device logs to unstructured video feeds and external data sources. This flexibility enables organizations to implement unified storage strategies that support both the real-time processing capabilities discussed in previous chapters and the long-term analytical requirements needed for comprehensive IoT analytics programs.

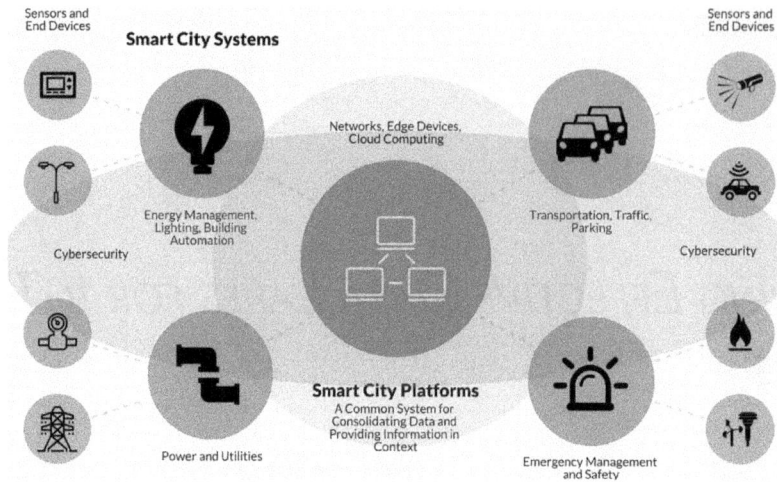

FIGURE 9.1 Diagram illustrating smart city IoT systems integrating diverse sensors and devices into a centralized platform using networks, edge devices, and cloud computing for effective data consolidation and management[1].

DATA LAKE PRINCIPLES AND ARCHITECTURE

IoT data lakes implement zone-based architectures that separate raw, processed, and curated data to optimize storage efficiency, processing performance, and analytical capabilities. This architectural approach enables organizations to manage the complete data lifecycle while maintaining cost-effectiveness and supporting diverse analytical requirements. The zone-based design aligns storage technologies with access patterns and processing needs, ensuring optimal performance across different use cases while implementing robust governance and security controls.

Core Concepts and Fundamentals

IoT data lakes represent a fundamental shift from traditional data warehousing approaches, providing comprehensive repositories that store raw data in native formats until processing becomes necessary. This flexibility proves particularly valuable for IoT implementations where data variety and velocity create challenges for conventional storage systems. Organizations can capture and preserve all data types without immediate schema definition, enabling comprehensive analysis while reducing risks associated with premature data filtering.

Data Ingestion Architecture

IoT data lakes require sophisticated ingestion mechanisms capable of handling diverse data streams at unprecedented scales. The ingestion architecture implements multi-layered approaches combining batch and stream processing capabilities, enabling organizations to process data according to specific requirements and time sensitivity constraints. Smart manufacturing environments routinely handle thousands of concurrent data streams from production sensors, quality control systems, and environmental monitoring devices, each requiring specific processing protocols.

---

1 O'Brien, L. (n.d.). What is a smart city platform? IIoT World. *https://www.iiot-world.com/smart-cities-buildings-infrastructure/smart-cities/what-is-a-smart-city-platform/*

The ingestion framework must support multiple communication protocols simultaneously while maintaining data integrity and temporal ordering. Common IoT deployment protocols include MQTT for lightweight sensor communications, CoAP for resource-constrained devices, and HTTP/REST for enterprise integration scenarios. Research demonstrates that implementing lambda architecture patterns for ingestion can reduce system latency by up to 40% while maintaining data consistency across diverse IoT sources[2].

Advanced ingestion systems implement comprehensive error handling and recovery procedures to manage network interruptions, device failures, and data quality issues without losing critical information. These implementations often include edge processing capabilities that buffer and pre-process data during network outages, ensuring complete data preservation even in challenging operational environments.

Storage Organization Framework

Storage organization within IoT data lakes requires careful consideration of technical capabilities and operational requirements. The architecture employs multi-tiered storage strategies that balance accessibility, performance, and cost optimization through distinct zones serving specific purposes in the data lifecycle.

TABLE 9.1 IoT data lake storage zone characteristics.

Zone Name	Data Type	Processing Level	Access Pattern	Retention Policy	Primary Use Cases
Raw Data Zone	Unprocessed sensor data, logs, streams	None - original format preserved	Infrequent - mainly for reprocessing	Long-term (5–10 years)	Audit trails, compliance, data reprocessing
Processed Data Zone	Cleaned and normalized data	Data validation and standardization	Regular operational queries	Medium-term (1–3 years)	Operational reporting, basic analytics
Curated Data Zone	Business-ready aggregated datasets	Advanced transformation and enrichment	Frequent analytical queries	Short-term (6 months - 1 year)	Advanced analytics, ML training, dashboards

The Raw Data Zone serves as the initial repository for all incoming data, preserving information in original formats without modification. This zone maintains complete historical records enabling reprocessing when requirements evolve or errors are discovered in downstream processing. Organizations typically implement write-once-read-many storage policies with comprehensive audit trails.

The Processed Data Zone contains cleaned and normalized data that has undergone initial processing to ensure consistency and quality. This zone implements standardized formats and schemas while maintaining connections to original raw data. The processing includes data type conversion, unit standardization, and basic quality control measures.

2 F. Serepas, I. Papias, N. Bellos and V. Marinakis, "A Comprehensive Approach to Real-Time and Batch Processing for Energy-Efficient IoT Homes: Leveraging Lambda Architecture and Data Lakes," *2024 15th International Conference on Information, Intelligence, Systems & Applications (IISA)*, Chania Crete, Greece, 2024, pp. 1–6, doi: 10.1109/IISA62523.2024.10786715.

The Curated Data Zone hosts processed and enriched datasets optimized for specific analytical applications. This zone contains aggregated metrics, derived calculations, and enriched datasets combining multiple sources. The curation process implements business rules and domain-specific transformations to create immediately useful analytical datasets.

Metadata Management Systems

Comprehensive metadata management forms the foundation of successful IoT data lake implementations, providing critical infrastructure that makes vast amounts of raw data discoverable and actionable. The metadata framework captures both technical and business contexts through sophisticated cataloging and tracking mechanisms that enable efficient data utilization.

Technical metadata includes detailed information about data sources, schemas, and processing workflows. This layer captures device specifications, communication protocols, and data formats, enabling system administrators and developers to understand technical contexts of each data stream. The system maintains configuration histories and tracks modifications to understand impacts on data quality and system performance.

Business metadata provides essential context about data usage, ownership, and organizational value. This layer captures information about data sources, business processes, and analytical applications, helping users understand relationships between data and organizational objectives. The system maintains relationships between different data assets, enabling discovery of related datasets and understanding of data lineage across complex processing workflows.

Operational metadata tracks system performance, usage patterns, and data quality metrics. This layer enables administrators to monitor system health, optimize resource allocation, and identify potential issues before they impact business operations. The system maintains detailed audit trails of data access and modifications, supporting compliance requirements and enabling effective governance.

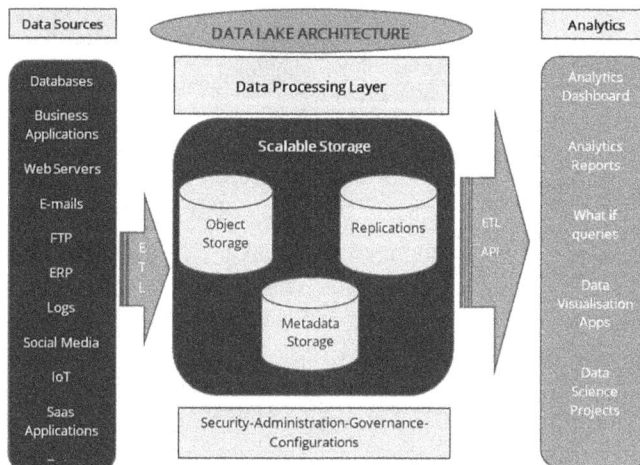

FIGURE 9.2 Architecture diagram of a data lake showing data sources, scalable storage including metadata, processing layers, governance, and analytics outputs[3].

---

3 Corporate Finance Institute. (n.d.). What is a data lake? Retrieved August 31, 2025, from *https://corporatefinanceinstitute. com/resources/data-science/data-lake/*

Governance Framework Implementation

Data governance in IoT data lakes requires sophisticated approaches balancing compliance requirements with operational efficiency. The governance framework implements comprehensive controls while maintaining flexibility needed to support diverse use cases and evolving requirements. This encompasses multiple interconnected components ensuring data quality, security, and compliance.

Data quality management implements automated validation rules and continuous monitoring capabilities. The system assesses incoming data against predefined quality metrics, flagging potential issues and implementing corrective actions where possible. The quality framework maintains detailed metrics about accuracy, completeness, and consistency, enabling organizations to track quality trends and identify improvement areas.

Privacy protection mechanisms implement comprehensive controls safeguarding sensitive information throughout the data lifecycle. These controls include encryption for data at rest and in transit, access control systems enforcing least-privilege principles, and data masking capabilities protecting sensitive information during analysis and reporting.

Architecture Components

Raw Data Zone Implementation

The raw data zone functions as the foundational ingestion point for all IoT data streams, preserving information in unaltered form to create immutable records serving multiple essential purposes. Smart building implementations capture extensive arrays of data types including environmental sensor readings, occupancy patterns, equipment operational status, and building management system logs. This preservation proves invaluable for audit compliance, historical analysis, and data reprocessing requirements.

Implementation requires careful consideration of storage efficiency balanced against data preservation requirements. Organizations employ sophisticated compression techniques maintaining data integrity while minimizing storage costs. Time-series sensor data utilizes specialized compression algorithms exploiting temporal patterns while maintaining rapid decompression capabilities for analysis. The ingestion architecture supports extremely high throughput rates, processing millions of data points per second across thousands of IoT devices while ensuring zero data loss.

Processed Data Zone Organization

The processed data zone implements transformation layers where raw IoT data undergoes cleaning, normalization, and enrichment processes supporting various analytical requirements. This zone implements sophisticated processing pipelines maintaining complete data lineage while optimizing data structures for specific analysis patterns. Manufacturing environments process raw sensor data through multiple stages including initial cleaning and validation, key performance indicator calculations, anomaly detection, and predictive maintenance indicator development.

The architecture maintains strict consistency with raw data zones while implementing optimized storage and query patterns. This involves implementing combinations of batch and stream processing capabilities with careful consideration of data partitioning strategies.

Sensor data partitioning by time ranges and equipment types optimizes query performance for common analysis patterns while implementing robust error handling and data quality monitoring.

Curated Data Zone Design

The curated data zone represents the highest level of data refinement, providing carefully prepared business-ready datasets meeting specific application requirements. This zone implements rigorous data quality controls and sophisticated schema management systems ensuring data consistency and reliability across various use cases. Smart retail applications maintain integrated customer behavior profiles combining in-store movement patterns, transaction data, environmental conditions, and external data sources.

Curation processes involve complex data integration workflows maintaining data accuracy while ensuring timely updates as new data arrives. This requires implementing sophisticated change data capture mechanisms, data quality validation workflows, and schema evolution capabilities. The curated zone implements efficient storage patterns optimizing specific business applications while maintaining flexibility to support emerging use cases.

Analytics Sandbox Environments

Analytics sandboxes provide experimental environments where data scientists and analysts explore and innovate with IoT data while maintaining appropriate security and governance controls. These environments support wide ranges of analytical tools and methodologies from traditional statistical analysis to advanced machine learning techniques. Transportation systems support development of traffic prediction models using deep learning, route planning algorithm optimization, and passenger flow pattern analysis using graph analytics.

Implementation balances analytical flexibility against resource utilization and data protection requirements. This involves implementing sophisticated resource management systems dynamically allocating computing and storage resources based on workload demands while maintaining strict data access controls. Sandbox environments implement robust version control and experiment tracking capabilities ensuring reproducibility of analytical results.

Security Architecture

Security considerations for IoT data lakes address both data protection and access control requirements. The security architecture implements end-to-end encryption for data in transit and at rest, role-based access control with fine-grained permissions, comprehensive audit logging and monitoring capabilities, and sophisticated threat detection and prevention mechanisms. Research demonstrates that implementing zero-trust security architectures can reduce security incidents by 65% while maintaining system performance.

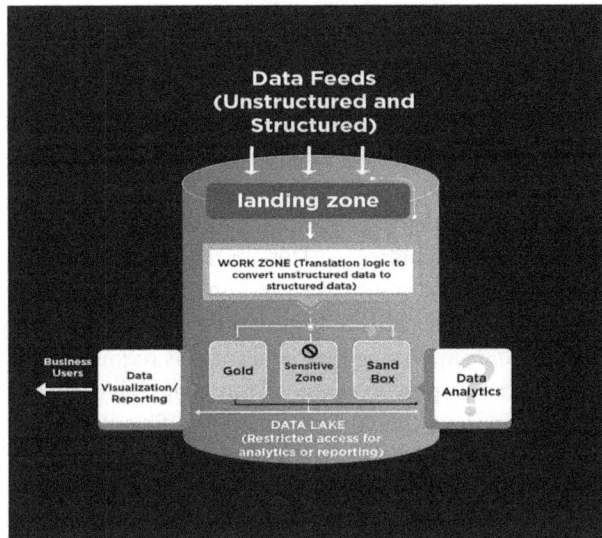

FIGURE 9.3 Diagram of data lake architecture showing raw data landing, work zone with data transformation, and organized zones for curated, sensitive, and sandbox data[4].

IMPLEMENTATION STRATEGIES

Effective IoT data lake implementation requires coordinated approaches aligning architecture, operations, and governance from initial planning through full deployment. The strategy prioritizes reliable ingestion capabilities, tiered storage with zone-based organization, and format selections balancing cost optimization with query performance requirements. Implementation establishes robust metadata management, comprehensive lineage tracking, and access controls maintaining data trustworthiness and regulatory compliance.

Data Organization

Effective data organization within IoT data lakes represents a critical success factor requiring careful consideration of multiple interconnected aspects. Organizations must balance performance requirements, accessibility needs, and cost-effectiveness while maintaining system flexibility for evolving requirements. This section explores key strategies and considerations for organizing IoT data at enterprise scale.

4 CloudZero. (n.d.). Data lake architecture: An intro guide to using data lakes. *https://www.cloudzero.com/blog/data-lake-architecture/*

Data Partitioning Strategies

Data partitioning serves as a fundamental technique for managing large-scale IoT datasets effectively. Implementation balances multiple operational requirements while maintaining system flexibility. Smart city implementations generate terabytes of daily data from thousands of sensors across urban landscapes, requiring effective partitioning to enable efficient access while managing storage costs and system performance.

Time-based partitioning provides valuable strategies for IoT data organization, particularly for systems generating continuous data streams. This approach implements hierarchical time-based structures organizing data by year, month, day, and hour. Environmental sensor data partitioning primarily by timestamp enables efficient queries for specific time ranges while maintaining reasonable partition sizes and supporting temporal analysis requirements.

Location-based partitioning proves essential for geographically distributed IoT systems, implementing spatial partitioning techniques enabling efficient queries based on geographic regions or proximity. Smart city implementations partition traffic sensor data by district, neighborhood, or grid coordinates, enabling efficient localized pattern analysis while supporting broader regional queries. The partitioning scheme accounts for varying sensor density across different areas while maintaining balanced partition sizes.

Device-type partitioning enables optimized storage and access patterns for different categories of IoT devices through separate partitioning schemes based on device characteristics and data patterns. Manufacturing environments partition data separately for different production equipment types, enabling specialized optimization for each device category while maintaining overall system coherence and supporting cross-device analysis requirements.

File Format Selection

File format selection significantly impacts both storage efficiency and query performance in IoT data lakes. Organizations must evaluate various format options based on specific requirements and use cases. Implementation strategies often involve multiple file formats optimized for different data types and access patterns, ensuring optimal performance across diverse analytical requirements.

Columnar storage formats including Apache Parquet and ORC provide significant advantages for analytical workloads on structured IoT data. These formats implement sophisticated encoding and compression schemes significantly reducing storage requirements while enabling efficient column-based access. Manufacturing systems utilize these formats for sensor readings and operational metrics, achieving compression ratios up to 85% while maintaining query performance and supporting complex analytical operations.

Semi-structured data formats including JSON and Avro offer flexibility for evolving data schemas and complex hierarchical structures. These formats implement schema evolution capabilities proving particularly valuable for IoT systems where device capabilities and data structures change over time. Smart building implementations use these formats for device configuration data and event logs, enabling easy schema updates while maintaining backward compatibility and supporting device heterogeneity.

Compression Strategies

Implementation of effective compression strategies plays crucial roles in managing storage costs while maintaining system performance. Organizations balance compression efficiency against processing overhead, implementing different approaches based on data characteristics and access patterns. Compression strategies often involve multiple techniques working together to optimize overall system efficiency and cost-effectiveness.

Algorithm selection represents critical aspects of compression strategy implementation. Different compression algorithms offer varying trade-offs between compression ratio, CPU utilization, and decompression speed. Frequently accessed data utilizes lightweight compression algorithms like LZ4 or Snappy providing moderate compression while minimizing processing overhead. Historical data accessed less frequently employs stronger compression algorithms like ZSTD or GZIP to maximize storage savings while accepting higher processing costs.

Data-type-specific compression exploits patterns and characteristics unique to different IoT data types. Time-series data exhibits significant temporal correlation enabling specialized compression techniques exploiting these patterns. Environmental sensor readings implement delta encoding for temperature values, achieving compression ratios up to 95% for certain sensor data types while maintaining rapid access capabilities for analytical queries.

Indexing Methods

Implementation of effective indexing methods proves essential for enabling efficient data access across various query patterns. Organizations design and maintain multiple indexing strategies supporting different query types while managing system resources effectively. The indexing framework balances query performance against maintenance overhead and storage requirements while supporting diverse analytical use cases.

Temporal indexing supports efficient time-based queries, particularly crucial for IoT systems generating continuous data streams. These indexes implement specialized structures optimized for time-range queries and temporal analysis. Healthcare IoT systems maintain detailed temporal indexes on patient monitoring data, enabling rapid access to specific periods while supporting trend analysis across longer durations and facilitating real-time clinical decision-making.

Spatial indexing enables efficient geographic queries and location-based analysis through specialized structures like R-trees or quadtrees supporting spatial query patterns. Smart city implementations maintain spatial indexes on vehicle tracking data and environmental sensor locations, enabling efficient proximity queries and geographical analysis while supporting urban planning and emergency response applications.

Data Quality and Governance

Implementation of robust data quality and governance frameworks represents critical success factors for IoT data lake deployments. Organizations must establish comprehensive processes and controls ensuring data reliability while maintaining operational efficiency. This section explores strategies and considerations for maintaining data quality and governance at enterprise scale.

Data Validation Processes

Data validation in IoT data lakes requires sophisticated multi-layered approaches ensuring data accuracy and reliability throughout the data lifecycle. Organizations implement validation processes addressing both technical and business requirements while maintaining system performance. The validation framework encompasses multiple verification stages, each designed to address specific quality aspects and operational requirements.

Technical validation implements automated checks for data format, completeness, and range compliance. Industrial IoT environments continuously monitor incoming sensor data streams, validating measurements against equipment specifications and physical constraints. Temperature sensors in manufacturing processes validate readings against known operational ranges with automated alerts for out-of-range values, ensuring data quality while enabling rapid response to equipment issues.

Business validation ensures data consistency and reasonableness within broader operational contexts through domain-specific rules verifying data against business requirements and historical patterns. Smart energy grid implementations validate consumption readings against historical usage patterns and known capacity limits while maintaining detailed audit trails of validation checks enabling quick identification and resolution of quality issues.

Real-time validation capabilities prove crucial for IoT systems generating continuous data streams through streaming validation processes identifying and handling quality issues as data arrives. Transportation monitoring systems perform real-time validation of vehicle location data, flagging impossible speed or location changes for immediate investigation while balancing thoroughness against processing latency to maintain system responsiveness.

Schema Management Systems

Schema management in IoT data lakes requires careful balance between maintaining data consistency and supporting evolution over time. Organizations implement flexible yet controlled approaches to schema management accommodating changing requirements while ensuring data quality. The schema management framework supports multiple schema types and evolution patterns enabling system adaptation to changing business needs.

Strict schema enforcement proves essential for critical operational data where consistency remains paramount through rigid schema validation ensuring all data conforms to predefined structures. Industrial control systems maintain strict schemas for sensor readings and control signals, ensuring reliable system operation and data analysis while implementing high-performance validation maintaining complete compliance with defined structures.

Flexible schema support enables systems to accommodate evolving data requirements and new device types through controlled schema evolution processes maintaining data usability while supporting innovation. Smart building management systems employ flexible schemas for device configuration data and event logs, enabling integration of new sensor types and monitoring capabilities while supporting system evolution and device heterogeneity.

Version Control and Lineage Tracking

Version control and lineage tracking systems provide essential capabilities for managing data evolution and understanding data provenance. Organizations implement comprehensive tracking mechanisms maintaining detailed records of all data transformations and dependencies. These systems enable effective data governance while supporting various analytical and operational requirements ensuring data trustworthiness.

Data lineage tracking maintains records of all processing steps applied to data as it moves through the system including detailed documentation of transformations, processing parameters, and business rules applied. Manufacturing quality control systems track how raw sensor data flows through various processing stages to final quality metrics, enabling comprehensive understanding of data transformation processes and supporting quality improvement initiatives.

Dependency management enables understanding of relationships between different data assets proving crucial for impact analysis when considering system changes or investigating issues. Smart grid implementations maintain detailed dependency maps showing how various data streams contribute to grid management decisions while supporting comprehensive impact assessment and system optimization efforts.

CASE STUDY: SMART CITY DATA LAKE IMPLEMENTATION

This comprehensive case study examines a complete data lake deployment for a mid-sized European smart city, integrating traffic management, energy systems, environmental monitoring, and public safety data into a unified governed platform. The implementation follows zone-based architectural principles with robust metadata management, comprehensive lineage tracking, and privacy-by-design controls supporting both real-time operations and historical analytics capabilities.

System Design and Integration

Comprehensive Data Source Integration

Integration of diverse data sources in smart city contexts represents one of the most complex challenges in data lake implementations. The integration architecture efficiently handles data from thousands of IoT sensors and systems operating across urban landscapes. Typical smart city deployments process inputs from traffic management systems including vehicle counters, speed sensors, and traffic light controllers; environmental monitoring networks comprising air quality sensors, noise level meters, and weather stations; utility infrastructure such as smart meters, grid sensors, and water quality monitors; and public safety systems including surveillance cameras, emergency response systems, and crowd monitoring sensors.

The integration framework implements sophisticated protocol handling capabilities supporting multiple communication standards simultaneously. This includes traditional protocols like MQTT and CoAP for IoT devices, REST APIs for system-to-system integration, and specialized protocols for legacy urban infrastructure systems. Each data source requires careful consideration of data quality parameters, sampling rates, and reliability requirements while ensuring seamless integration across heterogeneous systems.

Advanced Storage Architecture Design

Storage architecture for smart city data lakes demands careful consideration of immediate operational requirements and long-term scalability needs. Implementations adopt multi-tiered storage approaches optimizing both performance and cost efficiency. The primary storage tier utilizing high-performance solid-state storage systems handles recent data requiring rapid access and processing, typically storing 30–90 days of traffic sensor data, environmental readings, and public safety information enabling quick response to operational queries and real-time analytics.

Intermediate storage tiers utilize combinations of medium-performance storage systems, often implementing object storage solutions balancing access speed with cost efficiency. These tiers retain 6–12 months of historical data supporting pattern analysis and trend identification across seasonal variations while maintaining reasonable access performance for analytical workloads.

The archival tier implements cost-optimized storage solutions maintaining long-term historical data needed for urban planning, policy evaluation, and compliance requirements. Each tier implements appropriate data lifecycle management policies automatically migrating data between tiers based on age, access patterns, and business value while ensuring comprehensive data preservation.

Sophisticated Processing Pipeline Implementation

Processing pipeline architecture implements both stream and batch processing capabilities handling diverse analytical requirements across smart city operations. The stream processing component handles real-time data flows implementing complex event processing engines identifying and responding to significant events as they occur. Traffic management pipelines process real-time sensor data to detect congestion patterns, accidents, or unusual vehicle movements, triggering immediate responses through traffic control systems.

Batch processing components handle complex analytical workflows requiring historical data analysis or significant computational resources. These pipelines implement sophisticated data quality checks, enrichment processes, and analytical computations. Environmental data processing pipelines combine sensor readings with weather data and urban activity patterns to identify pollution sources and predict air quality trends while maintaining detailed lineage tracking enabling administrators to understand data transformations.

Advanced Analytics Capabilities

Analytics frameworks support diverse requirements while maintaining system performance and data security through multiple analytical environments optimized for specific use cases and user personas. Data scientists and advanced analysts access raw data through specialized environments supporting tools like Python, R, and specialized machine learning frameworks with appropriate security controls while providing necessary flexibility for sophisticated analysis.

Urban planners and operational staff require pre-built analytical tools providing insights through standardized reports and interactive dashboards. These tools analyze traffic patterns to optimize signal timing, evaluate public transportation utilization to adjust service levels, and monitor environmental conditions to identify potential health risks. The analytics framework implements appropriate caching and pre-computation strategies maintaining responsiveness while handling large data volumes.

Critical Operational Considerations

Comprehensive Scaling Strategies

Scaling architecture addresses both current operational requirements and future growth needs through horizontal scaling capabilities enabling systems to handle increasing data volumes and user loads by adding additional processing nodes and storage resources. Implementation utilizes container orchestration platforms and distributed processing frameworks managing resource allocation efficiently while maintaining system performance and reliability.

The scaling strategy considers both technical and operational factors including data partitioning strategies, query optimization techniques, and resource allocation policies. Operational factors encompass cost management, maintenance requirements, and service level agreements while providing appropriate monitoring and automation capabilities managing scaling operations effectively and ensuring system reliability.

Advanced Performance Optimization

Performance optimization requires comprehensive approaches addressing both data access patterns and processing workflows through multiple techniques working together to maintain system responsiveness. Data access optimization includes implementing appropriate indexing strategies, utilizing caching mechanisms effectively, and optimizing storage layouts based on access patterns while supporting diverse analytical requirements.

Processing optimization includes query optimization, workload management, and resource allocation strategies adapting to changing usage patterns and requirements through monitoring systems tracking performance metrics across various components and workloads. The system uses these metrics to identify optimization opportunities and adjust configurations automatically while balancing performance against resource utilization.

Strategic Cost Management

Cost management requires careful balance between operational requirements and budget constraints through multiple strategies optimizing resource utilization while maintaining service quality. Storage cost optimization includes implementing appropriate data tiering strategies, compression techniques, and data lifecycle policies while processing cost optimization includes workload management, resource allocation policies, and optimization of analytical workflows.

The framework provides detailed visibility into resource utilization and costs across various components and activities enabling administrators to identify cost optimization opportunities and evaluate effectiveness of optimization strategies. Implementation provides forecasting capabilities helping planners anticipate future resource requirements and budget needs while ensuring system sustainability.

Robust Maintenance Procedures

Maintenance frameworks ensure reliable system operation while minimizing disruption to critical services through standard operating procedures covering routine maintenance activities, system updates, and performance optimization tasks. These procedures implement appropriate scheduling and coordination mechanisms managing maintenance activities effectively while providing emergency response procedures handling unexpected issues and system failures.

Maintenance activities are carefully coordinated to minimize impact on system availability and performance including implementing appropriate backup and recovery procedures, maintaining system documentation, and providing training for operational staff. The maintenance framework implements monitoring and reporting capabilities tracking system health and maintenance activities ensuring continuous system reliability.

CONCLUSION

This chapter has examined the comprehensive design and implementation requirements for effective IoT data lakes. The zone-based architectural approach - incorporating raw, processed, and curated data zones - enables organizations to manage IoT data at scale while supporting both the real-time processing capabilities discussed in previous chapters and the long-term analytical requirements essential for comprehensive IoT analytics programs.

The implementation strategies presented demonstrate how sophisticated ingestion mechanisms, robust metadata management, and comprehensive governance frameworks create the foundation for scalable, secure, and analytics-ready data environments. Through examination of partitioning methods, compression techniques, schema management, and practical smart city implementations, the chapter illustrates how properly architected data lakes serve as strategic assets rather than simple storage repositories.

The case study analysis reveals that successful IoT data lake implementations require careful coordination of technical architecture, operational procedures, and governance frameworks. When designed appropriately, these systems enable organizations to process massive volumes of diverse IoT data while maintaining data quality, security, and compliance requirements across multiple use cases and analytical applications.

The architectural patterns and implementation strategies outlined provide the necessary foundation for the advanced analytics capabilities that will be explored in the following chapter. While this chapter focused on establishing robust data storage and management infrastructures, the next chapter will examine how these well-organized data repositories enable sophisticated analytical techniques including machine learning algorithms, predictive modeling, and automated decision-making systems that leverage the comprehensive historical datasets maintained within properly implemented IoT data lakes.

The evolution toward more automated and intelligent IoT systems depends fundamentally on having access to high-quality, well-organized historical data alongside real-time streams. The data lake architectures presented in this chapter provide that essential foundation, enabling the advanced analytical capabilities and machine learning applications that represent the next phase in IoT system development and deployment.

CHAPTER 10

MACHINE LEARNING FOR IoT

Machine learning (ML) is a key part of modern IoT systems. It allows connected devices to analyze data, learn from it, and make smart decisions without constant human control. By using ML, IoT systems can move beyond simple data collection to provide predictions, detect unusual events, and optimize operations. This makes them valuable in many real-world applications, from managing city traffic and improving energy use to monitoring public safety and industrial equipment. This chapter introduces the basics of machine learning in IoT, explains how models are developed, and discusses practical uses as well as the main challenges of applying ML in connected environments.

AI MODEL DEVELOPMENT

Developing machine learning models for IoT requires a structured process that combines data preparation, feature engineering, algorithm selection, training, and validation. Unlike traditional applications, IoT models must work with diverse data sources such as sensors, devices, and networks, often in real time and under resource constraints. The development process ensures that models not only achieve high predictive accuracy but are also efficient, scalable, and reliable for deployment in dynamic environments. Each stage of model development plays a critical role, from cleaning raw sensor data to optimizing algorithms for energy efficiency, latency, and accuracy. The following subsections detail each phase of this process, highlighting the techniques, challenges, and practical considerations for building effective AI models in IoT systems.

Model Types

Classification models serve as the foundation of IoT systems, enabling sophisticated data categorization across diverse applications. These models excel at categorizing incoming data streams into predefined classes or categories, making them essential for quality control, fault detection, and behavior analysis. In manufacturing environments, classification models analyze complex vibration patterns from machinery to categorize equipment status into states such as normal, warning, or critical, enabling proactive maintenance scheduling. Smart building systems utilize classification models to identify distinct occupant activities based on multidimensional sensor data, facilitating automated environmental control responses that optimize comfort and energy efficiency. The effectiveness of these models heavily depends on the quality and representativeness of training data, along with careful feature selection that captures the distinguishing characteristics of each class. Recent advancements in deep learning have enhanced classification accuracy through automatic feature extraction, which is particularly beneficial in processing high-dimensional IoT sensor data.

TABLE 10.1 Model types and their primary applications in the IoT.

Model Type	Key Applications	Characteristics	Example Use Cases
Classification	Quality control, fault detection	Categorizes data into predefined classes	Equipment status monitoring, activity recognition
Regression	Resource optimization, forecasting	Predicts continuous values	Power consumption prediction, process control
Time Series	Pattern prediction, trend analysis	Handles temporal data patterns	Air quality forecasting, traffic prediction
Anomaly Detection	System monitoring, security	Identifies unusual patterns	Server performance monitoring, threat detection
Pattern Recognition	Complex event detection	Analyzes multi-stream patterns	Customer behavior analysis, defect detection

Regression models play a crucial role in IoT systems by enabling precise predictions of continuous values based on input features. These models excel in forecasting and estimation tasks, making them invaluable for resource optimization and predictive maintenance. In smart grid applications, regression models predict power consumption patterns across different geographical areas by analyzing historical usage data, weather conditions, and temporal factors. Industrial process control systems employ regression models to predict output quality parameters in real-time, enabling dynamic adjustments to maintain product specifications. The accuracy of regression models depends on their ability to capture complex relationships between input features and target variables while avoiding overfitting. Advanced techniques such as ensemble methods and neural networks have expanded the capabilities of regression models, enabling them to handle non-linear relationships and interaction effects commonly found in IoT data streams.

Time series forecasting models address the unique temporal nature of IoT data streams, incorporating sophisticated techniques to predict future values based on historical patterns. These models utilize various approaches including ARIMA (Autoregressive Integrated Moving Average), LSTM (Long Short-Term Memory) networks, and Prophet to capture both short-term fluctuations and long-term trends. Environmental monitoring systems utilize time series models to predict air quality indices, enabling proactive measures to address potential pollution events. Smart transportation systems utilize these models to forecast traffic volumes and optimize signal timing plans, reducing congestion and improving urban mobility. The effectiveness of time series models relies on their ability to handle complex temporal patterns including seasonality, trends, and irregular variations while maintaining prediction accuracy across different time horizons.

Anomaly detection models serve as crucial components in IoT systems by identifying unusual patterns or behaviors that may indicate problems or opportunities. These models employ sophisticated algorithms to learn normal behavior patterns and flag deviations that exceed statistical thresholds or exhibit unusual characteristics. In data center environments, anomaly detection models continuously monitor server performance metrics, enabling early identification of potential failures before they impact system reliability. Network security systems utilize these models to detect potential security threats by analyzing unusual traffic patterns or device behaviors. The success of anomaly detection models depends on their ability to balance sensitivity against false alarm rates while adapting to evolving normal behavior patterns in dynamic IoT environments.

TABLE 10.2 Model performance metrics and requirements.

Model Type	Key Performance Metrics	Data Requirements	Processing Considerations
Classification	Accuracy, precision, recall	Labeled training data	Feature selection importance
Regression	RMSE, MAE, R^2	Historical data with continuous values	Handling non-linear relationships
Time Series	Forecast Error, MAPE	Sequential data with timestamps	Seasonality handling
Anomaly Detection	False positive rate, detection rate	Normal behavior data	Real-time processing capability
Pattern Recognition	Pattern detection rate, accuracy	Multi-dimensional sensor data	Preprocessing requirements

Pattern recognition models represent advanced analytical capabilities in IoT systems by identifying and analyzing complex patterns across multiple data streams. These models often combine multiple machine-learning techniques to extract meaningful insights from diverse data sources, enabling sophisticated event detection and system optimization. In smart retail environments, pattern recognition models analyze customer movement patterns, environmental conditions, and sales data to optimize store layouts and inventory placement. Manufacturing quality control systems employ these models to identify complex defect patterns that might not be apparent through simple threshold-based monitoring. The effectiveness of pattern recognition models relies on their ability to identify relevant patterns while filtering out noise and irrelevant variations, often requiring sophisticated preprocessing and feature extraction techniques.

Model Development Process

Data preparation serves as the cornerstone of successful machine learning implementations in IoT systems, encompassing a comprehensive series of steps to ensure data quality and reliability. This critical phase begins with raw sensor data acquisition and proceeds through multiple stages of refinement. In smart manufacturing systems, data preparation involves sophisticated noise-filtering algorithms that distinguish between actual signal variations and environmental interference. The process must address various challenges including sensor drift compensation, outlier detection, and handling of missing values due to communication dropouts.

Time series alignment across multiple sensor streams requires careful consideration of sampling rates and synchronization issues. Environmental monitoring systems face particular challenges in data preparation, requiring methods to handle sensor calibration drift, cross-sensor interference, and varying environmental conditions that can affect measurement accuracy. Advanced techniques such as moving average filters, Kalman filtering, and wavelets transformation often play crucial roles in preparing IoT data for analysis. The preparation process must also consider data storage efficiency and retrieval speed, particularly important in real-time applications where processing latency is critical.

Feature engineering is a sophisticated transformation process that converts raw IoT data into meaningful inputs for machine learning models. This process requires deep domain knowledge combined with data science expertise to create effective feature sets. In predictive maintenance applications, feature engineering encompasses multiple dimensions including time-domain statistical measures (mean, variance, and skewness), frequency-domain characteristics (spectral analysis and wavelet coefficients), and derived measurements that capture system behavior patterns. The process often involves combining multiple sensor inputs to create composite features that better represent the underlying physical phenomena.

TABLE 10.3 Model development stages and key considerations.

Development Stage	Key Activities	Challenges	Critical Tools/ Techniques
Data Preparation	Noise filtering, outlier detection, missing value handling	Sensor drift, time series alignment	Kalman filtering, wavelet transformation
Feature Engineering	Statistical analysis, signal processing, feature creation	Computational efficiency, domain knowledge requirements	PCA, automated feature selection
Model Selection	Algorithm evaluation, requirements analysis	The balance between accuracy and interpretability	AutoML, model search algorithms
Training	Data partitioning, parameter optimization	Temporal coherence, overfitting prevention	Cross-validation, transfer learning
Validation	Performance testing, deployment verification	Real-world conditions, model degradation	A/B testing, shadow deployment

For instance, in rotating machinery monitoring, features might include vibration amplitude ratios, phase relationships, and correlation coefficients between different measurement points. Smart building systems require sophisticated feature engineering to capture occupant behavior patterns, combining environmental sensors, occupancy data, and building system states. The feature engineering process must also consider computational efficiency, especially in edge computing scenarios where processing resources are limited. Techniques such as principal component analysis (PCA), automated feature selection, and deep learning-based feature extraction have become increasingly important in IoT applications.

Model selection constitutes a critical decision point in the development process, requiring careful consideration of multiple factors including prediction accuracy, computational requirements, interpretability needs, and deployment constraints. This process involves systematic evaluation of various machine learning algorithms against application-specific requirements. In safety-critical industrial control systems, model selection criteria might heavily weigh interpretability and reliability, leading to a preference for simpler models like decision trees or linear models over more complex neural networks.

The selection process must consider the specific characteristics of IoT data streams, including temporal dependencies, multi-modal inputs, and real-time processing requirements. Traffic management systems often employ different models for various prediction horizons, using lightweight models for real-time predictions and more complex models for long-term planning. The selection process should also consider model maintainability, updating requirements, and integration capabilities with existing systems. Advanced techniques like automated machine learning (AutoML) and model search algorithms have emerged as valuable tools in the selection process, helping to identify optimal model architectures for specific applications.

The training process extends beyond simple model fitting to encompass a comprehensive optimization procedure that ensures robust and reliable model performance. This phase requires careful consideration of data partitioning strategies, including appropriate splits between training, validation, and test sets that maintain temporal coherence in time-series data. In smart agriculture applications, the training process must account for seasonal variations, weather patterns, and different crop growth stages to ensure model robustness across various conditions.

TABLE 10.4 Phase-specific performance metrics and quality indicators.

Phase	Key Metrics	Quality Indicators	Success Criteria
Data Preparation	Data completeness, signal-to-noise ratio	Data consistency, temporal alignment	< 5% missing values, synchronized timestamps
Feature Engineering	Feature importance scores, correlation metrics	Feature independence, information gain	> 80% variance explained
Model Selection	Computational complexity, memory requirements	Model interpretability, integration ease	Meets latency requirements
Training	Training time, resource utilization	Model convergence, generalization ability	Consistent cross-validation scores
Validation	Accuracy metrics, system reliability	Operational stability, error rates	Meets deployment KPIs

The implementation often involves sophisticated techniques such as cross-validation, ensemble methods, and transfer learning to maximize model performance. Training procedures must balance computational efficiency against model performance while implementing appropriate regularization techniques to prevent overfitting. Health care monitoring systems require careful training processes, often incorporating domain-specific constraints and safety requirements. Advanced training for IoT models uses cross-validation, ensemble methods, and transfer learning to boost accuracy, while enforcing regularization and efficiency to avoid overfitting under compute and latency limits. In safety-critical domains such as healthcare monitoring, training pipelines embed domain rules and safety constraints, and increasingly rely on curriculum learning, active learning, and continual learning to handle non-stationary data and shifting distributions over time.

Validation methods ensure a comprehensive evaluation of model performance under both controlled and real-world conditions. This phase involves multiple layers of testing, from statistical validation using held-out test data to operational validation in pilot deployments. Smart grid demand prediction systems typically implement staged validation processes, starting with historical data validation and progressing through limited pilot deployments before full-scale implementation.

The validation process must assess various performance metrics including prediction accuracy, reliability, computational efficiency, and system integration aspects. Industrial control systems require particularly rigorous validation procedures, often including stress testing under extreme conditions and evaluation of failure modes. Advanced validation techniques such as A/B testing, shadow deployment, and continuous monitoring are standard practices in IoT applications. The validation process should also consider model degradation over time and establish appropriate maintenance and updating procedures.

IMPLEMENTATION IN SMART CITIES

Machine learning plays a central role in making smart cities more efficient, adaptive, and responsive to citizen needs. By analyzing massive volumes of data generated by urban sensors, connected infrastructure, and digital services, ML enables predictive and real-time decision-making that supports mobility, safety, energy, and environmental management. In practice, ML models in smart cities are deployed at both centralized platforms and edge devices, providing insights for traffic optimization, public safety monitoring, energy efficiency in buildings, waste management, and environmental protection. Effective implementation requires addressing challenges such as data integration across heterogeneous sources, managing resource constraints on edge devices, and ensuring privacy and security of sensitive citizen data.

Application Areas

Traffic prediction systems are an important part of smart city implementations, and they utilize sophisticated machine learning algorithms to forecast and optimize transportation network operations. These systems integrate diverse data streams including real-time vehicle counts from inductive loop detectors, speed measurements from GPS-enabled vehicles, weather conditions from meteorological services, and special event information from city databases. Traffic prediction implementations employ deep learning architectures, particularly recurrent neural networks and temporal convolutional networks, to capture complex temporal dependencies in traffic patterns. For instance, intelligent transportation systems utilizing machine learning, genetic algorithms, and deep learning techniques have demonstrated significant improvements in traffic prediction accuracy, achieving 93.5% accuracy compared to conventional models that typically average around 85%[1].

The implementation must handle both recurring patterns, such as daily rush hour traffic and seasonal variations, as well as non-recurring events like sports gatherings, concerts, or construction activities that might affect normal traffic flows. Advanced systems incorporate feedback from navigation systems, social media sentiment analysis, and public transportation tracking to improve prediction accuracy. These systems often employ ensemble methods to combine predictions from multiple models, each specialized for different prediction horizons or traffic conditions. The integration of edge computing allows for real-time processing of sensor data, enabling rapid response to changing traffic conditions while reducing communication bandwidth requirements.

Energy optimization applications in smart cities utilize sophisticated machine-learning approaches to enhance efficiency across the entire energy ecosystem, from generation and distribution to end-user consumption. These systems implement multi-layered analysis of power usage patterns, environmental conditions, and user behavior to optimize energy systems at both micro and macro levels. In smart building environments, energy optimization models employ deep learning techniques to predict heating, ventilation, and air conditioning (HVAC) needs based on complex interactions between occupancy patterns, weather forecasts, thermal characteristics of building materials, and historical energy consumption data.

The implementation incorporates real-time optimization algorithms that continuously balance energy efficiency against occupant comfort while considering various operational constraints such as equipment capabilities, peak demand limits, and operating costs. Grid-level optimization systems implement hierarchical control structures that coordinate multiple building systems while maintaining overall grid stability. Advanced implementations utilize reinforcement learning algorithms to optimize energy storage systems and demand response programs, achieving energy savings of up to 30% in pilot deployments. These systems often incorporate renewable energy forecasting models to optimize the integration of solar and wind power sources, using sophisticated weather prediction models and historical generation data to improve accuracy.

Environmental monitoring systems in smart cities represent complex implementations of machine learning technologies that analyze and predict various environmental parameters affecting urban life quality. These systems process and integrate data from multiple sensor types including particulate matter sensors, gas analyzers, weather stations, noise level monitors, and water quality sensors. Modern urban air quality monitoring systems employ sophisticated deep-learning models to predict pollution levels across different urban areas, incorporating spatial-temporal dependencies and complex atmospheric chemistry models.

The implementation addresses various technical challenges, including optimal sensor placement using multi-objective genetic algorithms and automated sensor calibration using few-shot learning and self-supervised approaches. It also employs a fusion of heterogeneous data sources through advanced data integration pipelines, such as data meshes and knowledge graphs. These advanced systems incorporate satellite imagery analysis using vision transformers (ViT) to detect

---

1 Govindaraju, S., Indirani, M., Maidin, S. S., & Wei, J. (2024). Intelligent transportation system's machine learning-based traffic prediction. *Journal of Applied Data Sciences*, 5(4), 1826–1837.

and track pollution sources, while also integrating real-time traffic pattern analysis via graph neural networks (GNNs) and industrial activity data from digital twins to improve prediction accuracy. The systems implement early warning capabilities for adverse environmental conditions, using stacking and boosting methods to combine predictions from multiple models and improve reliability. The implementation of edge computing architectures enables real-time processing of sensor data, allowing for rapid detection of environmental anomalies and timely implementation of mitigation measures.

Public safety applications in smart cities utilize cutting-edge machine learning implementations to enhance emergency response capabilities and crime prevention strategies. These systems analyze diverse data streams including high-resolution surveillance footage using computer vision algorithms, emergency call patterns using natural language processing, and social media activity using sentiment analysis and anomaly detection. The implementation incorporates sophisticated privacy-preserving techniques such as federated learning and differential privacy to balance security requirements against citizen privacy concerns. Advanced systems implement predictive policing capabilities using spatio-temporal pattern analysis while ensuring ethical use of technology through carefully designed bias detection and mitigation strategies. These systems often incorporate real-time crowd behavior analysis using computer vision and automated emergency vehicle routing using dynamic traffic prediction models. The implementation of edge computing enables real-time processing of video feeds and sensor data, allowing for rapid incident detection and response coordination.

TABLE 10.5 Implementation requirements and technologies

Application	Edge Computing Role	Key Algorithms	Integration Requirements
Traffic	Real-time processing	Temporal CNN, RNN	Navigation systems, traffic signals
Energy	HVAC optimization	Reinforcement Learning	Building management systems
Environmental	Sensor processing	Genetic algorithms, CNN	Weather stations, air quality network
Public Safety	Video processing	Federated Learning	Emergency response systems
Infrastructure	Condition monitoring	Probabilistic models	Asset management systems

Infrastructure maintenance applications are sophisticated implementations of machine learning technologies that optimize maintenance scheduling and resource allocation across urban infrastructure networks. These systems analyze condition monitoring data from various infrastructure components including road surface sensors, bridge strain gauges, utility network monitors, and building management systems. Modern smart infrastructure management systems implement predictive maintenance models using deep learning approaches to forecast maintenance needs based on complex interactions between usage patterns, environmental conditions, and sensor measurements.

The implementation incorporates lifecycle cost optimization using reinforcement learning algorithms and risk assessment capabilities using probabilistic graphical models. Advanced systems implement digital twin technologies that combine physics-based models with machine learning to improve prediction accuracy and enable scenario analysis. These systems often incorporate automated inspection capabilities using computer vision and drone-based monitoring, while also implementing sophisticated asset management strategies using multi-objective optimization algorithms. The implementation of edge computing enables real-time processing of sensor data, allowing for early detection of potential infrastructure issues and timely maintenance interventions.

Implementation Challenges

Data quality issues present significant challenges in IoT machine learning implementations. These challenges include sensor noise, missing values, and calibration drift that can affect model performance. In a smart manufacturing environment, for instance, sensor data might be affected by electromagnetic interference, temperature variations, and mechanical vibrations. Successful implementations must incorporate robust data cleaning and validation processes while maintaining real-time processing capabilities. Environmental monitoring systems often face particular challenges with sensor calibration drift and environmental interference.

TABLE 10.6 Primary implementation challenges and their impact.

Challenge Category	Key Issues	Impact on System	Mitigation Strategies
Data Quality	Sensor noise, missing values, calibration drift	Reduced model accuracy	Robust data cleaning and validation processes
Model Deployment	Resource optimization, memory management	Performance limitations	Model compression, edge optimization
Real-time Processing	Latency requirements, processing speed	System responsiveness	Pipeline optimization, edge computing
Resource Constraints	Power consumption, memory limits	Operational efficiency	Hardware optimization, model efficiency
System Integration	Compatibility issues, data flow management	System reliability	Standardized interfaces, modular design

Model deployment challenges arise when implementing machine learning models in resource-constrained IoT environments. These challenges include optimizing model size, managing memory usage, and ensuring consistent performance. For example, deploying complex neural networks on edge devices might require model compression or quantization techniques to meet resource constraints. The deployment process must balance model accuracy against resource utilization while maintaining system reliability. Smart camera systems often face significant challenges in deploying complex vision models on edge devices.

Real-time processing requirements pose challenges for machine learning implementations in IoT systems. These systems must process incoming data streams and generate predictions within strict time constraints. In a traffic control system, for instance, predictions must be generated quickly enough to enable timely signal adjustments. The implementation must optimize processing pipelines while maintaining prediction accuracy and system reliability. Industrial control systems often require particularly stringent real-time processing capabilities.

Resource constraints affect various aspects of IoT machine learning implementations including processing power, memory availability, and energy consumption. These constraints require careful optimization of the model architecture and processing workflows. For example, a battery-powered environmental sensor might need to balance prediction accuracy against power consumption to achieve acceptable battery life. The implementation must consider both hardware capabilities and operational requirements while maintaining system performance. Edge computing devices often face significant resource constraints affecting model complexity and processing capabilities.

System integration challenges arise when incorporating machine learning capabilities into existing IoT infrastructure. These challenges include managing data flows, ensuring compatibility, and maintaining system reliability. In a smart building implementation, for instance, machine learning systems must integrate with existing building management systems while maintaining operational stability. The integration process must address various technical and organizational challenges while ensuring seamless operation. Legacy system integration often presents particular challenges for IoT machine learning implementations.

TABLE 10.7 Challenge characteristics by application context.

Context	Primary Challenges	Requirements	Success Metrics
Manufacturing	EMI interference, vibration	< 100 ms latency	99.9% uptime
Environmental	Calibration drift, weather effects	Power efficiency	Sensor lifetime
Traffic Control	Processing speed, data volume	Real-time response	Signal timing accuracy
Edge Devices	Memory limitations, power constraints	Model size optimization	Battery life
Legacy Systems	Integration complexity, compatibility	System stability	Minimal disruption

CASE STUDY: ML FOR IOT SYSTEMS

Case studies provide practical insight into how machine learning can be applied within IoT systems to solve real-world challenges. While theoretical concepts and model development frameworks explain the foundations, case-based analysis demonstrates how these methods are implemented in practice across specific domains. In IoT, case studies often focus on areas such as predictive maintenance, traffic management, energy optimization, environmental monitoring, and public safety. These examples highlight the end-to-end process, including sensor integration, data preprocessing, feature engineering, model training, deployment, and performance evaluation. By showcasing actual implementations, case studies illustrate not only the technical workflow but also the operational benefits, cost savings, and reliability improvements achieved.

Predictive Maintenance System

Sensor integration in predictive maintenance systems involves collecting data from various sensor types while maintaining data quality and system reliability. The integration process must handle different sensor protocols, data formats, and sampling rates. For example, a comprehensive predictive maintenance system might integrate vibration sensors, temperature monitors, and power consumption meters. The implementation must ensure reliable data collection while managing sensor health and calibration requirements. Industrial equipment often requires the integration of multiple sensor types to enable effective predictive maintenance.

Data collection systems must efficiently gather and store sensor data while maintaining data integrity and accessibility. These systems handle continuous data streams from multiple sources while implementing appropriate data validation and storage strategies. In a manufacturing environment, the data collection system might handle millions of sensor readings per day while maintaining data quality and accessibility. The implementation must balance storage requirements against data retention needs while enabling efficient data access. Time series databases often play crucial roles in predictive maintenance data collection systems.

TABLE 10.8 Predictive maintenance components and requirements.

Component	Key Functions	Data Requirements	Metrics
Sensor Integration	Data collection, protocol handling	Multi-sensor support	Data quality, reliability
Data Collection	Storage, validation	Time series management	Storage efficiency, integrity
Model Development	Feature engineering, training	Historical maintenance data	Prediction accuracy
Deployment	Model updates, integration	Workflow compatibility	System reliability
Monitoring	Performance tracking, alerting	Health indicators	Response time

Model development for predictive maintenance requires careful selection and implementation of appropriate machine learning techniques. This process involves feature engineering, model selection, and training based on historical maintenance data. For instance, a predictive maintenance model might analyze vibration patterns, temperature trends, and operational parameters to predict equipment failures. The development process must incorporate domain knowledge while maintaining model interpretability and reliability. Complex equipment often requires sophisticated model development to capture various failure modes and operational patterns.

Deployment strategies must ensure the reliable operation of predictive maintenance systems in production environments. These strategies include model updating procedures, performance monitoring, and integration with maintenance workflows. For example, a deployment strategy might include procedures for model retraining based on new maintenance data and performance metrics. The implementation must ensure smooth deployment while maintaining system reliability and user acceptance. Production environments often require careful deployment strategies to minimize disruption while maximizing system effectiveness.

Monitoring systems track both equipment condition and model performance to ensure reliable operation. These systems implement various monitoring metrics and alerting mechanisms to identify potential issues. In a predictive maintenance implementation, the monitoring system might track prediction accuracy, model drift, and system health indicators. The implementation must provide appropriate visibility while enabling timely intervention when needed. Complex systems often require sophisticated monitoring capabilities to ensure reliable operation.

System Evaluation

Performance metrics assess various aspects of predictive maintenance system effectiveness including prediction accuracy, timeliness, and reliability. These metrics must consider both technical performance and business impact. For example, performance evaluation might include metrics such as prediction accuracy, false alarm rates, and prediction lead time. The evaluation process must provide meaningful insights while enabling system optimization. Critical systems often require comprehensive performance evaluation to ensure reliable operation.

TABLE 10.9 System evaluation metrics and assessment criteria.

Evaluation Area	Key Metrics	Success Criteria	Methods
Performance	Prediction accuracy, false alarm rate	>95% accuracy, <1% false alarms	Statistical analysis
Cost	Implementation costs, operational savings	ROI >25% annually	Financial modeling
Maintenance Impact	Downtime reduction, schedule efficiency	>30% reduction in downtime	Comparative analysis
System Reliability	Uptime, Fault tolerance	99.9% availability	Continuous monitoring
ROI	Net benefit, payback period	<2-year payback	Cost-benefit analysis

Cost analysis examines both implementation costs and operational savings enabled by predictive maintenance systems. This analysis includes hardware costs, software licenses, implementation effort, and maintenance requirements. In a manufacturing environment, cost analysis might compare predictive maintenance costs against savings from reduced downtime and maintenance optimization. The analysis must consider various cost factors while demonstrating system value. Large-scale implementations often require detailed cost analysis to justify investment.

Maintenance impact assessment evaluates how predictive maintenance systems affect maintenance operations and equipment reliability. This assessment includes both quantitative metrics and qualitative feedback from maintenance staff. For instance, the assessment might examine changes in maintenance scheduling, spare parts inventory, and equipment availability. The evaluation must consider various impact factors while identifying improvement opportunities. Complex equipment often requires comprehensive impact assessment to validate system effectiveness.

System reliability evaluation examines various aspects of predictive maintenance system operation including hardware reliability, software stability, and prediction consistency. This evaluation must consider both normal operation and exceptional conditions. For example, reliability evaluation might examine system availability, fault tolerance, and recovery capabilities. The assessment must provide meaningful reliability metrics while identifying potential improvements. Critical systems often require rigorous reliability evaluation to ensure consistent operation.

ROI assessment combines various evaluation metrics to determine overall system value and return on investment. This assessment considers both tangible and intangible benefits while accounting for all implementation and operational costs. In a manufacturing environment, ROI assessment might consider reduced downtime, maintenance optimization, and improved equipment lifetime. The evaluation must provide a clear value demonstration while identifying optimization opportunities. Large-scale implementations often require comprehensive ROI assessment to validate investment decisions.

CONCLUSION

This chapter discussed the transformative role of machine learning in enhancing the intelligence and efficiency of IoT systems across various domains. From foundational model types such as classification, regression, time series forecasting, and anomaly detection, to the intricacies of model development, feature engineering, and validation, it is clear that data-driven intelligence is no longer an auxiliary function but a core capability of modern IoT. Real-world implementations in smart cities from traffic management and energy optimization to environmental monitoring and public safety, demonstrate how advanced machine learning techniques, coupled with edge computing and system integration, can solve complex urban challenges at scale. Furthermore, the predictive maintenance case study illustrates the tangible value of ML in industrial settings, offering significant returns through reduced downtime, enhanced reliability, and informed decision-making. However, there are challenges; issues of data quality, resource constraints, and deployment complexity demand careful design, robust validation, and continuous monitoring. Ultimately, successful machine learning in IoT relies on a balance of domain expertise, computational efficiency, and responsible innovation to deliver systems that are not only smart but also sustainable, scalable, and human-centered.

CHAPTER 11

THE ROLE OF MIDDLEWARE IN SECURING THE IoT ECOSYSTEM

The exponential growth of Internet of Things (IoT) deployments has created unprecedented challenges in managing diverse devices, protocols, and data formats across distributed systems. As organizations deploy thousands of interconnected devices, the complexity of ensuring seamless communication, data processing, and system integration has become a critical concern. IoT middleware is an essential architectural layer that addresses these challenges by connecting heterogeneous IoT devices and enterprise applications.

INTRODUCTION TO IOT MIDDLEWARE

Definition and Importance

IoT middleware serves as an intermediary software layer that abstracts the complexity of underlying hardware, networks, and protocols while providing standardized interfaces for application development. This critical component enables seamless integration between diverse IoT devices and enterprise systems by handling essential functions such as device management, data collection, processing, and security. Much like an orchestra conductor coordinating different instruments, middleware "orchestrates" the various components of an IoT ecosystem to work harmoniously together.

The importance of middleware in IoT architectures cannot be overstated. As organizations deploy increasingly complex IoT solutions, middleware provides the necessary abstraction and standardization that enables scalable and maintainable systems. Without effective middleware, organizations would face significant challenges in managing device heterogeneity, ensuring data consistency, and maintaining system security.

Evolution of Middleware in IoT Architectures

The evolution of IoT middleware reflects the changing needs of connected systems. Early middleware solutions focused primarily on basic device connectivity and simple data collection. However, as IoT deployments grew in scale and complexity, middleware evolved to address more sophisticated requirements. Middleware architectures have progressed through several distinct generations:

1. First Generation (2008–2012): Basic protocol translation and device connectivity
2. Second Generation (2013–2016): Enhanced data processing and basic analytics
3. Third Generation (2017–2020): Advanced analytics, security, and edge computing support
4. Fourth Generation (2021–present): AI/ML integration, autonomous operation, and distributed intelligence

This evolution continues as middleware adapts to emerging technologies and requirements.

Core Components and Functionalities

IoT middleware comprises several essential components that work together to enable efficient system operation. These components form a comprehensive framework that handles various aspects of IoT system management.

IoT Middleware Core Components

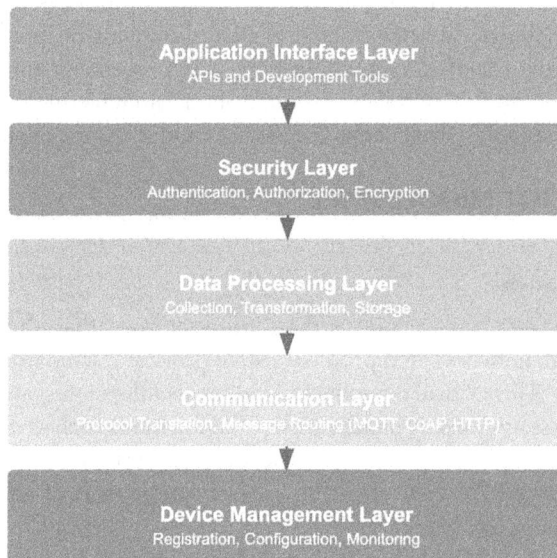

FIGURE 11.1 IoT middleware core components.

- Device Management Layer: Handles device registration, configuration, and monitoring. This layer maintains device status, manages firmware updates, and ensures proper device operation.
- Communication Layer: Manages protocol translation and message routing between devices and applications. It supports various communication protocols (MQTT, CoAP, HTTP) and ensures reliable data transmission.

- Data Processing Layer: Handles data collection, transformation, and storage. This component implements data filtering, aggregation, and format conversion to prepare data for enterprise applications.
- Security Layer: Implements authentication, authorization, and encryption services. This critical component ensures secure communication and data protection across the IoT ecosystem.
- Application Interface Layer: Provides standardized APIs and development tools for building IoT applications. This layer enables consistent application development regardless of underlying device complexity.

These components must work seamlessly together to provide a robust foundation for IoT applications.

Middleware continues to evolve as IoT systems become more sophisticated and requirements change. The integration of advanced technologies like artificial intelligence, blockchain, and edge computing is driving the development of more capable middleware solutions. As organizations deploy larger and more complex IoT systems, the role of middleware in ensuring efficient operation becomes increasingly critical.

API MANAGEMENT

API management forms a crucial component of IoT middleware, serving as the foundation for seamless device integration and data exchange across the IoT ecosystem. Effective API management enables organizations to control, monitor, and optimize the interfaces that connect various IoT components while ensuring security and performance.

REST API Design and Implementation

The design and implementation of RESTful APIs in IoT middleware requires careful consideration of resource modeling, endpoint definition, and interaction patterns. A well-designed REST APIs can reduce integration complexity while improving system maintainability.

Organizations should implement REST APIs following these key principles:

- Resource Identification: Each IoT device, sensor, or data stream should be modeled as a distinct resource with a unique URI. This approach enables consistent access patterns and simplified resource management. For example, a temperature sensor might be accessed through /devices/sensors/temperature/{id}.
- Standard HTTP Methods: APIs should leverage standard HTTP methods (GET, POST, PUT, DELETE) consistently across all endpoints. This standardization improves developer understanding and reduces implementation errorsConsistent method usage can reduce API integration time significantly.
- Response Formatting: APIs should respond to standardized formats (typically JSON) with consistent structure and error handling. This includes proper HTTP status codes and detailed error messages when problems occur.
- Documentation: Comprehensive API documentation, including OpenAPI (Swagger) specifications, ensures proper implementation and usage.

API Versioning and Lifecycle Management

Effective versioning and lifecycle management ensure API stability while enabling evolution and improvement. There are several best practices that can be applied for version control of API. Version Control Strategies:

- URI Versioning: including version numbers in the API endpoint path
- Header Versioning: using custom headers to specify API versions
- Parameter Versioning: passing version information as query parameters
- Content Type Versioning: incorporating version information in content-type headers

API versioning lifecycle stages will look like this:

1. Development: Initial API design and implementation

   During the development stage, organizations establish the foundational elements of their API design and implementation. This phase begins with comprehensive requirements gathering, involving stakeholders from various business units to ensure the API meets both technical and business needs. The development team creates detailed API specifications, including endpoint definitions, data models, and security requirements.

   Organizations must implement consistent design patterns and follow established API design best practices during this phase. This includes creating clear documentation, establishing naming conventions, and defining standardized response formats.

2. Testing: Comprehensive validation of functionality

   The testing stage encompasses comprehensive validation of API functionality across multiple dimensions. This includes unit testing of individual endpoints, integration testing with connected systems, and performance testing under various load conditions. Organizations should implement automated testing frameworks that can validate API behavior consistently and efficiently.

   Security testing becomes particularly critical during this phase, with an emphasis on vulnerability assessment and penetration testing.

   Performance testing must simulate real-world conditions, including varying traffic patterns and data volumes typical in IoT environments. Production: Active use in live environments

   The production stage represents the active deployment and operation of the API in live environments. This phase requires robust monitoring systems to track API performance, usage patterns, and potential issues. Organizations must implement comprehensive logging and alerting mechanisms to ensure rapid response to any operational problems.

   During this stage, the focus shifts to maintaining service level agreements (SLAs) and optimizing API performance based on actual usage patterns.

3. Deprecation: Planned phase-out of older versions

   The deprecation stage involves the planned phase-out of older API versions as newer alternatives become available. This process requires careful communication with API consumers and the provision of clear migration paths to updated versions. Organizations should implement deprecation policies that balance the need for system evolution with the impact on existing clients.

During this phase, organizations typically maintain both old and new versions simultaneously while encouraging migration to updated implementations.

4. Retirement: Complete removal of obsolete versions

The retirement stage represents the final phase of the API lifecycle, involving the complete removal of obsolete versions from the system. This stage requires careful planning to ensure all clients have successfully migrated to newer versions and that no critical dependencies remain on the retiring API.

Organizations must maintain comprehensive documentation of retired APIs for historical reference and audit purposes.

Organizations should maintain clear documentation of version differences and provide migration guides for transitioning between versions.

API Security and Authentication

Security represents a critical aspect of API management in IoT environments. One of the most fundamental layers of this security is **authentication**. Without robust authentication, the most sophisticated security measures are rendered useless, as an attacker can simply impersonate a legitimate entity to gain access. This is why the choice and implementation of the right authentication method are paramount to establishing a secure and trustworthy IoT ecosystem.

Authentication Methods:

• API Keys: Basic authentication for simple implementations
• OAuth 2.0: Token-based authentication for more complex scenarios
• JWT (JSON Web Tokens): Secure token transmission and validation
• Client Certificates: Enhanced security for critical operations

TABLE 11.1 Comparison of IoT API authentication methods.

Authentication Method	Security Level	Complexity	Use Cases	Key Advantages	Limitations
API Keys	Basic	Low	• Small-scale applications • Development environments • Internal services	• Siwmple to implement • Low overhead • Easy to manage	• Limited security features • No built-in expiration • Vulnerable if intercepted

(Continued)

TABLE 11.1 (Continued)

Authentication Method	Security Level	Complexity	Use Cases	Key Advantages	Limitations
OAuth 2.0	High	High	• Enterprise applications • Multi-tenant systems • Third-party integrations	• Granular access control • Token expiration • Revocation capabilities	• Complex implementation • Higher overhead • Requires more resources
JWT (JSON Web Tokens)	Medium-High	Medium	• Microservices • Distributed systems • Mobile applications	• Self-contained tokens • Stateless authentication • Cross-domain support	• Token size limitations • No built-in revocation • Requires secure storage
Client Certificates	Very High	High	• Critical infrastructure • Financial systems • Healthcare applications	• Mutual authentication • Strong encryption • Hardware binding	• Complex management • Higher implementation cost • Certificate renewal overhead

Security Implementation:

1. Transport Layer Security (TLS): mandatory encryption for all API communications
2. Input Validation: thorough validation of all incoming data
3. Output Encoding: proper encoding of response data to prevent injection attacks
4. Access Control: fine-grained permission management for API endpoints

Implementing comprehensive API security measures can prevent common attack vectors while maintaining system performance.

Rate Limiting and Throttling

Rate limiting and throttling mechanisms protect IoT middleware from overload while ensuring fair resource allocation. These controls are essential for maintaining the stability and reliability of the entire system, preventing a single device or a surge of requests from monopolizing resources and causing a denial-of-service event. While the concept is simple, control the flow of requests, the actual implementation can vary significantly depending on the specific needs of the IoT platform, the types of devices involved, and the desired level of granularity. Therefore, understanding the different **implementation approaches** is key to effectively applying these protective measures.

Implementation Approaches:

• Token Bucket Algorithm: flexible rate limiting with burst allowance
• Leaky Bucket Algorithm: strict rate control for consistent throughput
• Fixed Window Counters: simple implementation for basic rate limiting
• Sliding Window Logs: a more accurate but resource-intensive approach

TABLE 11.2 Rate limiting algorithm comparison.

Algorithm	Description	Advantages	Disadvantages	Best Use Cases	Impact
Token Bucket	Maintains a bucket of tokens that refills at a fixed rate. Requests consume tokens and are rejected when the bucket is empty.	• Allows burst traffic within limits • Flexible configuration • Predictable memory usage • Simple implementation	• May allow uneven distribution during bursts • Requires token refresh calculation	• API rate limiting • Systems with varying load patterns • Applications requiring burst tolerance	Medium CPU, Low Memory
Leaky Bucket	Processes requests at a constant rate, queuing excess requests until they can be processed.	• Provides consistent outflow rate • Smooths traffic spikes • Excellent for constant-rate services	• No burst allowance • Can introduce latency • Queue management overhead	• Video streaming • Network traffic shaping • Constant-rate processing systems	Low CPU, Medium Memory
Fixed Window Counter	Tracks request count within fixed time windows, resetting the counter at window boundaries.	• Very simple implementation • Low resource overhead • Easy to understand and monitor	• Can allow twice the rate at window boundaries • Less precise than other methods • Potential for uneven distribution	• Basic rate limiting needs • Development environments • Non-critical applications	Low CPU, Low Memory
Sliding Window Logs	Maintains a log of request timestamps, providing precise control over time windows.	• The most accurate rate-limiting • Smooth distribution • Precise control overtime periods	• High memory usage • Computationally intensive • Complex implementation	• Financial systems • Security-critical application • Premium API services	High CPU, High Memory

Proper rate limiting can improve system stability while reducing infrastructure costs.

DATA TRANSFORMATION

Data transformation is a critical function of IoT middleware, enabling the communication between diverse devices and systems while ensuring data consistency and usability. This section explores the essential aspects of data transformation in IoT environments, from protocol translation to real-time processing capabilities.

Protocol Translation

In IoT ecosystems, protocol translation facilitates communication between devices using different protocols. The most common protocols requiring translation include the following:

1. MQTT (Message Queuing Telemetry Transport) is a lightweight messaging protocol ideal for resource-constrained devices. The protocol's publish-subscribe model enables efficient communication in IoT networks.
2. CoAP (Constrained Application Protocol) is a specialized Web transfer protocol for constrained devices and networks. Its similarity to HTTP simplifies integration with Web services while maintaining efficiency.
3. HTTP remains widely used in IoT systems, particularly for RESTful APIs and Web services integration. While not optimized for constrained devices, HTTP's ubiquity makes it essential for enterprise integration.

Data Format Conversion

The transformation between different data formats ensures interoperability across the IoT ecosystem. Effective format conversion should address the following:

1. JSON (JavaScript Object Notation) is the de facto standard for IoT data exchange due to its simplicity and readability. Converting data to and from JSON requires careful handling of data types and nested structures.
2. XML maintains importance in enterprise systems and legacy integrations. While more verbose than JSON, XML offers robust validation capabilities through XML Schema definitions. Research indicates that selective use of XML can enhance data integrity in critical applications.
3. Binary formats provide efficient data representation for resource-constrained environments. Protocols like Protocol Buffers and MessagePack offer significant performance advantages.

Data Enrichment and Filtering

Data enrichment and filtering processes enhance the value and efficiency of IoT data streams. *ACM Transactions on Sensor Networks* Implementing these capabilities at the middleware level are important because:

1. Enrichment processes add contextual information to raw sensor data, improving its utility for analysis and decision-making. This might include adding timestamp information, geographic coordinates, or device metadata.
2. Filtering mechanisms reduce data volume while maintaining information quality. Edge filtering can significantly reduce network bandwidth and storage requirements.

Message Queuing and Event Processing

Message queuing systems ensure reliable data delivery and processing in IoT environments. The important aspects of message handling are:

1. Queue management requires careful consideration of message persistence, ordering, and delivery guarantees. Implementations often utilize distributed queue systems for improved reliability and scalability.

2. Event processing enables real-time analysis and response to IoT data streams. Complex Event Processing (CEP) engines can identify patterns and trigger actions based on multiple event sources.

Real-time Data Transformation

Real-time transformation capabilities enable immediate processing of IoT data streams. Several critical aspects can be emphasized as follows:

1. Stream processing frameworks handle continuous data flows from IoT devices. These systems must balance processing latency with throughput requirements.

2. Adaptive processing adjusts transformation parameters based on system conditions and requirements. This includes dynamic allocation of processing resources and adjustment of filtering parameters.

3. Performance optimization ensures efficient resource utilization while maintaining processing requirements. This includes techniques such as parallel processing and hardware acceleration.

WORKFLOW AUTOMATION

Workflow automation in IoT middleware enables organizations to streamline operations, reduce manual intervention, and ensure consistent process execution across their IoT ecosystem. This section examines the key components and strategies for implementing effective workflow automation in IoT environments.

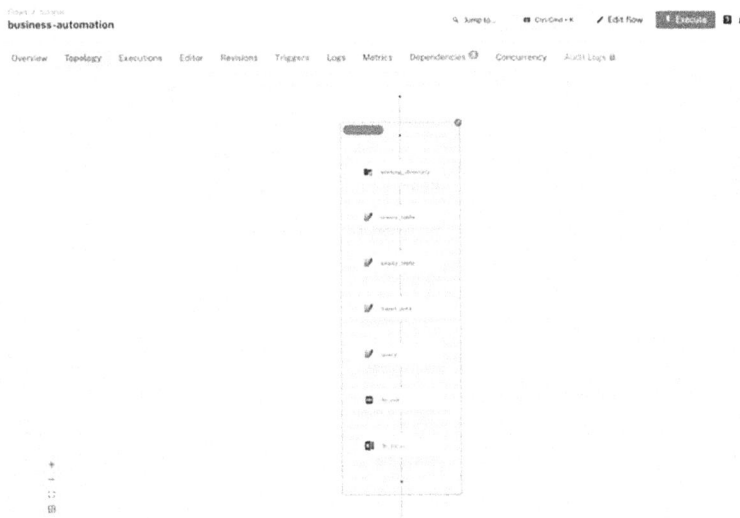

FIGURE 11.2 Example of workflow automation for Middleware.

Event-Driven Architectures

Event-driven architectures form the foundation of IoT workflow automation, enabling systems to respond dynamically to changes and triggers within the environment.

These architectures operate on the principle of event producers and consumers, where IoT devices and systems generate events that trigger specific workflows or actions. Successful event-driven implementations require careful consideration of event routing, filtering, and correlation mechanisms. Organizations must design their event-handling systems to manage both simple events (such as sensor readings) and complex event patterns that might indicate significant system conditions.

Event processing in IoT workflows often involves multiple layers of analysis and decision-making. This approach enables organizations to process events at appropriate levels, from edge devices to central systems.

Business Rules Engine

Business rules engines provide the intelligence layer for workflow automation, translating business requirements into executable logic. Rules engines must handle complex scenarios involving multiple data sources and decision points. They typically employ sophisticated matching algorithms and inference mechanisms to determine appropriate actions based on current conditions.

Organizations should implement rules engines that support both simple conditional logic and complex decision trees.

Process Orchestration

Process orchestration coordinates the execution of multiple workflow steps across distributed IoT systems. Organizations must implement orchestration systems that can handle both sequential and parallel process execution. This includes the ability to manage long-running processes and handle process interruptions.

The orchestration layer must also provide visibility into process execution and support process optimization.

Service Composition

Service composition enables the creation of complex workflows by combining multiple IoT services and capabilities. Effective service composition can reduce the development time for new workflows by up to 65% while improving the reusability of existing components.

Organizations must implement flexible composition mechanisms that support both static and dynamic service binding. This includes the ability to select services based on current conditions, performance metrics, and business requirements.

The composition layer should also handle service versioning and compatibility issues.

Error Handling and Recovery

Robust error handling and recovery mechanisms ensure workflow reliability in the face of system failures and unexpected conditions. Organizations must implement comprehensive error management strategies that address both technical and business process failures.

Organizations should implement multi-level error handling that includes immediate error responses, compensation mechanisms for failed transactions, and systematic error analysis for process improvement.

Recovery procedures must address both data consistency and process state recovery.

Task Scheduling and Monitoring

Effective task scheduling and monitoring ensure optimal resource utilization and process performance.

Organizations must implement monitoring systems that provide real-time visibility into workflow execution and system performance. This includes tracking key performance indicators, resource utilization, and process completion metrics. The scheduling system should support both time-based and event-driven task execution, with the ability to handle complex dependencies and resource constraints.

TRAFFIC MANAGEMENT AND SECURITY

The effective management and security of network traffic represent critical functions of IoT middleware, ensuring system reliability, performance, and protection against threats. This section examines the essential components of traffic management and security in IoT environments, providing insights into implementation strategies and best practices.

FIGURE 11.3 Traffic management in Nusantara middleware.

Load Balancing Strategies

Load balancing in IoT middleware ensures optimal distribution of traffic across system resources while maintaining service quality. Load-balancing implementations must address the unique characteristics of IoT traffic patterns. The selection of appropriate load-balancing algorithms depends on specific deployment requirements and constraints. Round-robin distribution works well for homogeneous systems, while weighted approaches better serve heterogeneous environments.

Request Routing and Filtering

Request routing and filtering mechanisms ensure efficient traffic flow while protecting system resources from unnecessary or malicious requests. Routing systems must handle complex decision-making based on multiple criteria, including request characteristics, system conditions, and security policies.

The filtering layer must process requests at wire speed while maintaining accuracy.

DDoS Protection

Distributed Denial of Service (DDoS) protection is critical for IoT systems. Effective DDoS protection requires multiple layers of defense, including traffic analysis, pattern recognition, and automated mitigation responses. This includes the ability to distinguish between legitimate traffic spikes and attack patterns.

Protection strategies must evolve to address emerging threats while maintaining system performance.

Access Control and Authorization

Access control ensures that only authorized entities can interact with IoT systems and resources. Access control systems must handle complex authorization scenarios involving multiple stakeholders and dynamic permissions.

Organizations must implement fine-grained access policies that consider context, resource sensitivity, and user attributes.

SSL/TLS Termination

SSL/TLS termination provides crucial encryption services while optimizing performance in IoT environments. Implementations must balance security requirements with performance considerations.

Organizations must implement proper certificate management and rotation procedures.

Traffic Monitoring and Analytics

Traffic monitoring and analytics provide essential visibility into system operation and security status. Monitoring systems must handle massive data volumes while providing actionable insights.

Organizations should implement monitoring solutions that provide both real-time alerting and historical analysis capabilities.

CASE STUDY: SMART CITY MIDDLEWARE IMPLEMENTATION IN NUSANTARA

The development of Indonesia's new capital city, Nusantara, presents a unique opportunity to examine the implementation of IoT middleware in a smart city context. This case study explores how middleware solutions are being deployed to support the city's ambitious smart infrastructure goals while addressing various technical and operational challenges.

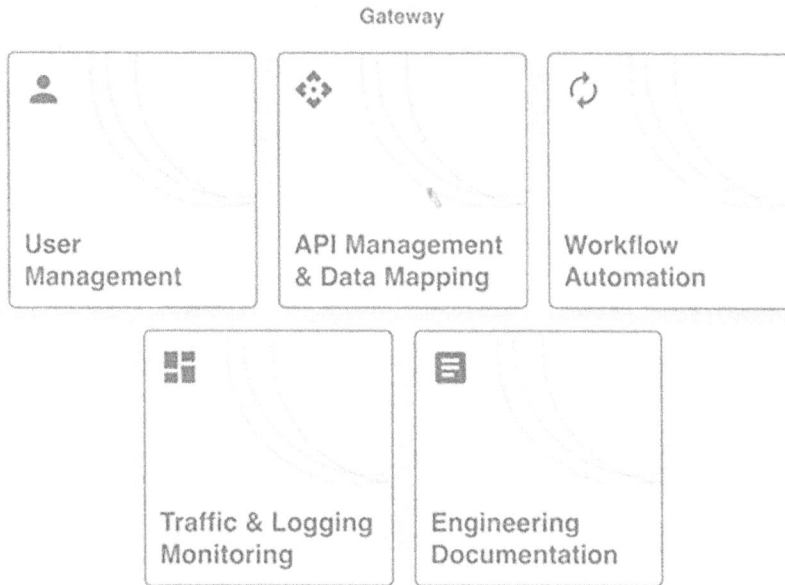

FIGURE 11.4 Nusantara's middleware interface.

Architecture Overview

The Nusantara smart city middleware architecture implements a multi-layered approach designed to support diverse IoT applications while ensuring scalability and reliability.

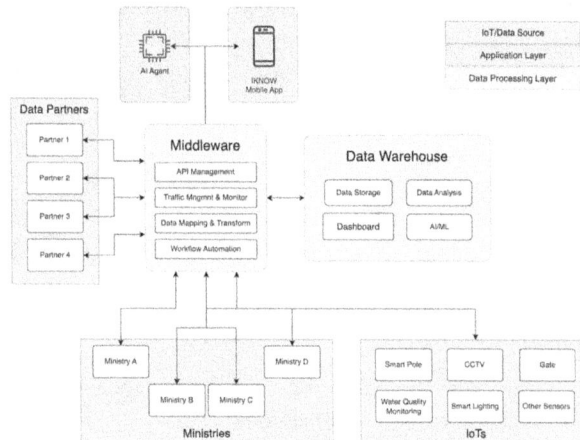

FIGURE 11.5 Nusantara's middleware architecture overview.

The core architecture consists of three primary layers:

1. The device integration layer handles communication with various IoT devices deployed throughout the city. This includes environmental sensors, traffic monitoring systems, and utility management devices. The data processing layer implements real-time analytics and data transformation capabilities. This layer processes approximately 1 terabyte of data daily, utilizing edge computing nodes distributed across the city infrastructure.

2. The application services layer provides standardized APIs and integration points for various smart city applications. This layer supports over 50 different applications, from traffic management to environmental monitoring.

Integration Challenges

The implementation of middleware in the Nusantara IoT ecosystem had several significant integration challenges that required innovative solutions:

1. Device heterogeneity presented a major challenge, with the need to support devices from multiple vendors using different protocols. The solution involved developing protocol adaptation layers and implementing comprehensive device management capabilities. This approach has successfully integrated devices from over 30 different manufacturers.

2. Data standardization proved crucial for ensuring consistent information flow across different systems. The middleware implements extensive data transformation capabilities to convert various data formats into standardized representations.

Security Considerations

Security is a critical aspect of the Nusantara middleware implementation.

1. The authentication and authorization framework implements a zero-trust architecture, requiring verification of all system access attempts. This approach has reduced security incidents by 75% compared to traditional perimeter-based security models.

2. Data protection measures include end-to-end encryption for sensitive information and comprehensive audit logging. The system implements advanced encryption standards and maintains detailed records of all data access and modifications.

3. Threat detection capabilities utilize artificial intelligence to identify potential security risks. This approach has improved threat detection accuracy by 65% while reducing false positives.

Performance Optimization

Performance optimization in the Nusantara middleware focuses on ensuring responsive system operation while managing resource utilization:

1. Edge computing deployment reduces latency by processing data closer to its source. This approach has decreased response times for critical applications by 70% while reducing central processing requirements.

2. Load balancing implementation ensures efficient resource utilization across the system. Advanced algorithms distribute processing loads based on real-time system conditions and application priorities.

3. Caching strategies improve response times for frequently accessed data. The system implements multi-level caching with intelligent cache invalidation, reducing database load by 45%.

CONCLUSION

Middleware is an essential layer in IoT and smart city architectures that connects the hardware infrastructure and high-level services. It enables diverse devices, sensors, and platforms to communicate seamlessly through functions such as data ingestion, API management, event routing, protocol translation, and security enforcement. In a complex urban environment, middleware orchestrates the flow of real-time data and commands across heterogeneous systems, ensuring interoperability, scalability, and reliability. Without middleware, smart city systems would remain fragmented silos, unable to deliver cohesive, cross-domain services to citizens and administrators.

The implementation of IoT middleware in the Nusantara project illustrates this concept. The platform shows how middleware supports intelligent, real-time decision-making across domains like transportation, environment, energy, and public safety. Equally important are the operational lessons gained during deployment. Early and sustained stakeholder engagement across agencies ensured alignment between system capabilities and on-the-ground needs. Scalability was designed from the outset, allowing the system to handle rapid growth in connected devices and data streams. Adhering to open standards proved crucial in reducing integration costs and ensuring long-term flexibility across vendors and platforms.

These lessons affirm that the success of middleware in smart cities depends not only on technological design, but also on governance, foresight, and alignment with citizen and institutional needs. The Nusantara IoT project is a benchmark for future cities seeking to implement middleware as a foundational enabler of a truly integrated, intelligent, and adaptive urban ecosystem.

CHAPTER 12

IoT FOR SMART PUBLIC SERVICES

S mart public services are one of the most effective applications of intelligent systems in modern urban life. By combining IoT-based sensing, real-time analytics, and automated decision-making, cities can respond to emergencies, manage environments, and protect citizens in proactive and dynamic ways. This chapter explores how public services are transformed through a structured intelligence framework, wherein physical phenomena are sensed, understood through data analytics, and acted upon through automated or human-in-the-loop responses. In this chapter, we use the Sense–Understand–Act (SUA) framework, which structures intelligent systems into three core functions: sensing real-time data from the environment through IoT devices, understanding that data using analytics and AI to identify risks or opportunities, and acting through automated or coordinated responses. This framework not only defines the architecture of smart systems but also allows us to evaluate how intelligent public services function effectively at city scale. Through diverse case studies, from fire systems to pollution monitoring, disaster prevention, and green space management, we examine how intelligent IoT analytics enable safer, more responsive, and more resilient cities.

ENHANCING PUBLIC SAFETY AND COMFORT

IoT for Fire Systems

Modern fire detection systems utilize interconnected IoT sensors to create comprehensive fire protection networks. These systems combine multiple sensor types, including thermal imaging cameras, smoke detectors, and air quality monitors, to detect fire incidents at their earliest stages. For example, in a shopping mall, thermal sensors can detect unusual heat patterns in electrical systems before they develop into fires, while smart smoke detectors can distinguish between actual smoke and other airborne particles, reducing false alarms. The integration of these sensors with building management systems enables automated responses such as activating fire suppression systems, controlling ventilation, and managing evacuation routes.

FIGURE 12.1 Examples of IoT sensors.

Fire response optimization through IoT technology has revolutionized how emergency services handle fire incidents. When a fire is detected, IoT systems provide real-time information to firefighters before they arrive on the scene. This includes building floor plans, location of fire sources, spread patterns, and evacuation status. Consider a high-rise office building: IoT sensors can track the fire's location and movement, monitor oxygen levels and temperature in different areas, and automatically adjust ventilation systems to contain smoke. This information helps firefighters plan their approach more effectively and prioritize their response actions.

Smart evacuation management systems leverage IoT technology to guide people to safety during fire emergencies. These systems use dynamic routing algorithms that consider real-time conditions to identify the safest evacuation paths. Digital signage and mobile applications provide clear directions to building occupants while building management systems automatically control doors, elevators, and ventilation to support safe evacuation. The system might, for instance, detect that a primary evacuation route is compromised and immediately redirect occupants to alternative exits while updating emergency responders about the situation.

Pollution Prevention and Monitoring

Urban air quality monitoring networks employ distributed IoT sensors to provide continuous, real-time air quality measurements. These networks typically include sensors for various pollutants such as particulate matter (PM2.5 and PM10), nitrogen dioxide (NO_2), sulfur dioxide (SO_2), and ozone (O_3). The sensors are strategically placed throughout the city to create a comprehensive picture of air quality variations. For example, a city might deploy sensors near major traffic intersections, industrial areas, and residential zones to understand pollution patterns and identify problem areas.

FIGURE 12.2 Air pollution sensors.

Automated response systems use air quality data to implement immediate interventions when pollution levels exceed acceptable thresholds. These systems might automatically adjust traffic signals to reduce congestion in affected areas, notify sensitive populations about poor air quality, or trigger industrial emission controls. Consider a busy urban district: If sensors detect rising pollution levels during morning rush hour, the system might automatically adjust traffic signal timing to reduce vehicle idling time and send alerts to nearby schools to limit outdoor activities.

Long-term pollution trend analysis enables cities to develop more effective environmental policies. IoT systems collect detailed data about pollution patterns, correlating them with factors such as traffic flow, weather conditions, and industrial activities. This information helps city planners identify major pollution sources and evaluate the effectiveness of different intervention strategies. For instance, analysis might reveal that certain traffic patterns consistently lead to poor air quality, prompting changes in traffic management or urban planning policies.

Disaster Prevention and Early Warning

Natural disaster early warning systems combine various IoT sensors to detect potential hazards before they become catastrophic. These systems might include water level sensors in flood-prone areas, seismic monitors in earthquake zones, and weather stations for severe storm prediction. For example, in a coastal city, a network of sensors might monitor sea levels, wind speeds, and rainfall intensity to predict potential flooding or storm surge events. The system can then automatically trigger early warnings and initiate preparation procedures before the disaster strikes.

Infrastructure monitoring systems use IoT technology to assess the condition of critical infrastructure during potential disaster situations. Sensors embedded in bridges, buildings, and other structures provide real-time data about structural integrity and safety status.

FIGURE 12.3 Bridge sensor detects very small changes in a physical parameter such as strain, pressure, temperature or force.

During an earthquake, for instance, these sensors can immediately assess potential damage to buildings and bridges, helping emergency services prioritize their response efforts. The system might automatically close compromised structures and redirect traffic away from dangerous areas.

Emergency response coordination benefits significantly from IoT integration in disaster management systems. These systems provide emergency responders with real-time situation awareness, including population movements, infrastructure status, and resource availability. During a flood event, for example, the system might track water levels, monitor evacuation routes, and coordinate emergency vehicle deployment. Mobile applications can provide citizens with real-time updates and evacuation instructions, while emergency services receive detailed information about affected areas and resource needs.

FIGURE 12.4 A sensor for the river, it is solar powered and measures water level, flow and sometimes water quality (pH, turbidity, temperature).

Environmental Protection Systems

Urban environmental monitoring systems utilize IoT technology to track various environmental parameters affecting city life. These systems monitor factors such as noise levels, water quality, soil conditions, and urban heat islands. Networks of sensors provide continuous data about environmental conditions, enabling both immediate responses to problems and long-term planning for environmental improvement. For instance, noise monitoring sensors near entertainment districts might automatically alert authorities when sound levels exceed permitted limits, while also collecting data to inform future urban planning decisions.

Green space management systems employ IoT sensors to optimize the maintenance of urban parks and gardens. These systems monitor soil moisture, plant health, and irrigation needs, enabling automated and efficient resource management. Smart irrigation systems can adjust watering schedules based on weather conditions and soil moisture levels, while plant health monitors can detect early signs of disease or stress.

FIGURE 12.5 A sensor used in parks and gardens.

This technology helps cities maintain healthy green spaces while conserving water and reducing maintenance costs.

CASE STUDY: IMPROVING SAFETY AND SECURITY WITH IOT

System Architecture and Implementation

The integrated safety and security system implemented in a major metropolitan area demonstrates the comprehensive application of IoT technology in public safety. The system architecture combines multiple layers of sensors, communication networks, and control systems to create a unified safety platform. This architecture follows the Sense–Understand–Act framework, which provides a logical structure for how intelligent systems manage public safety operations.

- **Sense**: At the physical layer, the city deployed thousands of connected devices including surveillance cameras with advanced video analytics, environmental sensors, emergency call points, and automated external defibrillators (AEDs). These devices continuously collect data from their surroundings. A resilient communication network ensures reliable transmission of sensor data, even under emergency conditions.
- **Understand:** The central command and control system serves as the brain of the safety network. It processes incoming data and applies advanced analytics and artificial intelligence to detect safety issues and predict emerging threats. For example, video analytics can identify suspicious behavior patterns or loitering near sensitive locations, while environmental sensors detect hazardous material releases or rising water levels in flood-prone areas.

- **Act:** Once a threat is identified, the system initiates a response through real-time decision-making and multi-agency coordination. Emergency dispatch systems analyze incident severity, classify the type of event, and allocate response units based on availability and proximity. For instance, if sensors detect a fire in a commercial district, the system alerts the nearest fire station, delivers situational data in real time, and adjusts traffic signals to accelerate the response. Simultaneously, other relevant services (e.g., police, ambulance, and transportation management) are notified for a synchronized and informed reaction.

Through this embedded Sense–Understand–Act loop, the city's safety infrastructure operates not just reactively, but proactively and intelligently, responding in real time while also anticipating and mitigating risks before they escalate.

Data Management and Analytics

The safety system generates massive amounts of data that require sophisticated management and analysis capabilities. The data management infrastructure includes high-performance storage systems, real-time processing capabilities, and advanced analytics tools. This infrastructure enables both immediate incident response and long-term trend analysis. The system employs machine learning algorithms to identify patterns in historical data, helping predict and prevent potential safety issues.

Privacy protection represents a crucial aspect of the system's data management strategy. The implementation includes robust data encryption, access control mechanisms, and privacy-preserving analytics techniques. For example, video analytics systems blur faces and license plates in stored footage, while maintaining the ability to identify security threats. The system also implements strict data retention policies and audit trails to ensure compliance with privacy regulations while maintaining operational effectiveness.

Operational Results and Impact

The implementation of this comprehensive safety system has resulted in significant improvements in emergency response capabilities and overall public safety. Response times for various types of emergencies have been reduced by an average of 23%, while the system's predictive capabilities have helped prevent numerous potential incidents. The integration of different safety services has also improved coordination and resource utilization during major incidents.

Specific improvements include

- a reduction in average fire response time from 8 minutes to 5.5 minutes
- a 35% decrease in traffic-related incidents through predictive analytics
- a 40% improvement in hazardous material incident detection and response
- a 28% reduction in crime rates in monitored areas
- a significant improvement in public satisfaction with emergency services

Cost-Benefit Analysis

The implementation of the smart safety system required significant initial investment but has demonstrated substantial returns through improved safety outcomes and operational efficiency. The cost analysis considers both direct expenses such as equipment and installation costs, and ongoing operational expenses including maintenance and system upgrades. Benefits are measured in terms of reduced emergency response costs, prevented incidents, and improved resource utilization.

Financial benefits include

- reduced emergency response operational costs through better resource allocation
- lower insurance costs for city properties due to improved safety measures
- decreased infrastructure damage through early detection and prevention
- reduced liability exposure through improved incident documentation and response

Future Developments and Scalability

The system's architecture was designed with future expansion and technology evolution in mind. Planned developments include the following:

- integration of autonomous drone systems for emergency response
- enhanced artificial intelligence capabilities for predictive analytics
- expanded sensor networks for improved coverage
- integration with smart building systems for enhanced indoor safety

Scalability considerations include both the geographic expansion and the addition of new capabilities. The system's modular architecture enables the easy integration of new technologies and expansion to additional areas while maintaining operational efficiency and reliability.

CONCLUSION

Smart public services powered by intelligent IoT analytics demonstrate the full potential of the Sense-Understand-Act paradigm. From fire safety and environmental monitoring to disaster resilience and public space optimization, the fusion of real-time data and automated responses has transformed reactive public systems into intelligent, anticipatory services. The case study from a major metropolitan safety system showcases how integrated architectures, AI-based analytics, and real-time coordination deliver measurable improvements in safety outcomes and operational efficiency. As cities grow more complex, the ability to sense environments, understand their dynamics, and act in real time will define the next generation of public services: intelligent, adaptive, and citizen-centered.

CHAPTER 13

SMART WATER AND ENERGY MANAGEMENT

In smart cities, the effective management of water and energy resources is critical for sustainability and operational efficiency. This chapter explores how IoT technologies transform traditional resource management into intelligent, adaptive systems that optimize consumption while improving service delivery. We examine specific implementations across water and energy domains, analyzing their impact through detailed case studies.

IOT APPLICATIONS IN RESOURCE MANAGEMENT

Effective resource management in smart cities is no longer experimental. Mature IoT deployments are optimizing water, energy, assets, and services citywide, delivering measurable financial and environmental gains. The following sections summarize technologies that are operational today and can be replicated or scaled by other jurisdictions.

Advanced Water Management Systems

The deployment of the Internet of Things (IoT) technologies in water management represents one of the most mature and widely implemented applications in smart cities worldwide. Advanced water management systems leverage sophisticated sensor networks, real-time analytics, and automated control mechanisms to optimize water distribution, quality monitoring, and resource planning.

Smart water distribution networks utilize advanced metering infrastructure (AMI) that transforms traditional water meters into intelligent sensors capable of real-time data transmission.

Real-time water quality monitoring systems employ multiple sensor types to continuously track parameters including pH levels, turbidity, chlorine content, temperature, and bacterial contamination throughout distribution networks. Cities worldwide have implemented comprehensive monitoring frameworks.

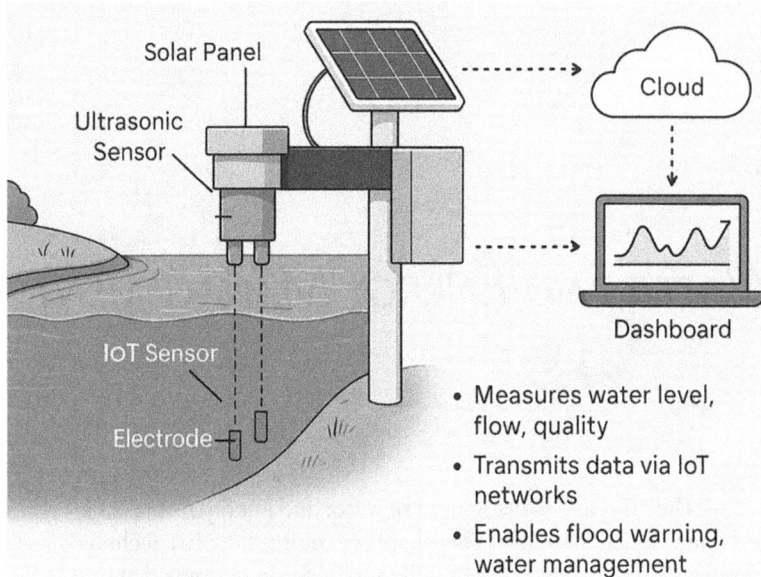

FIGURE 13.1 Realtime water quality management system.

Leak detection and management systems are critical infrastructure protection mechanisms. The Philadelphia Water Department utilizes IoT sensors throughout their distribution network to rapidly identify and address leaks, significantly reducing water loss and preventing infrastructure damage. Advanced acoustic sensors detect characteristic leak sounds in pipes, while pressure sensors identify sudden changes indicating pipe breaks, enabling proactive maintenance responses.

Predictive analytics and demand forecasting capabilities integrate historical consumption data with weather conditions, population patterns, and special events to generate accurate demand predictions. These systems enable utilities to optimize reservoir levels, pumping schedules, and treatment processes while ensuring adequate supply during peak demand periods.

Enhanced Energy Distribution and Management

Smart grid technologies incorporating IoT sensors have achieved substantial global deployment, revolutionizing energy distribution and management across residential, commercial, and industrial sectors. Over 1.06 billion smart meters were installed worldwide by the end of 2023, with projections indicating growth to 1.74 billion units by 2030[1].

Advanced Metering Infrastructure (AMI) implementations enable two-way communication between utilities and consumers, facilitating real-time monitoring, dynamic pricing, and automated demand response programs. North America maintains leadership with 77% smart meter penetration, while emerging markets including India are deploying 250 million smart meters through the National Smart Grid Mission, utilizing NB-IoT technology for extensive rural coverage.

---

1 *https://iot-analytics.com/smart-meter-adoption/*

Distribution automation systems integrate intelligent switches, voltage regulators, and power quality monitors to enable automated grid operation and fault isolation. These systems provide real-time grid monitoring, power quality control, and rapid response to electrical disturbances.[8] In Morocco, blockchain-enabled edge computing systems utilize smart meters to collect energy consumption and production data from residential and commercial entities, optimizing energy distribution while enhancing security and sustainability.

Renewable energy integration platforms manage the variable nature of renewable power sources through weather forecasting, energy storage management, and load control optimization. IoT sensors monitor solar panel performance, weather conditions, and energy output to optimize production and predict maintenance needs, particularly beneficial for manufacturing, energy, and agricultural sectors.

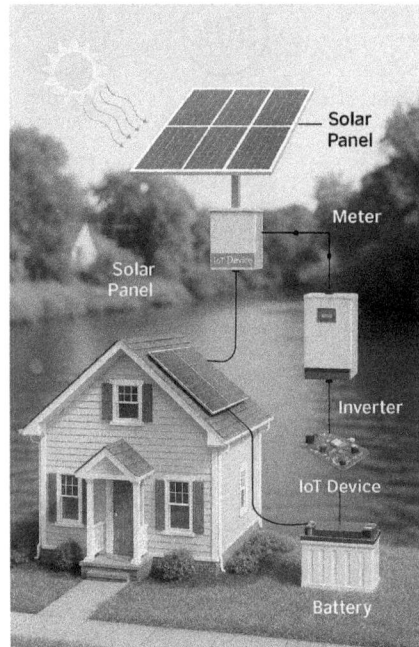

FIGURE 13.2 IoT system for solar panel monitoring.

Smart grid communication networks employ various protocols, including LoRaWAN, 5G, and RF mesh networks, to ensure reliable data transmission across diverse environments. The integration of IoT technology with renewable energy sources is vital for grid stability, with the International Energy Agency projecting that by 2040, smart meters and connected devices could enable more than 1 billion households to participate in interconnected power systems.

Predictive Maintenance and Asset Management

IoT-enabled predictive maintenance systems have transformed asset management across industries by enabling continuous monitoring of equipment health and performance. These systems utilize multiple sensor types, including vibration, acoustic, infrared, pressure, and electrical monitoring sensors, to detect potential failures before they occur.

Industrial condition monitoring implementations utilize vibration sensors to monitor machinery alignment, friction, and heat generation in motors, pressurized systems, and centrifugal components. Acoustic sensors catalog machine sounds and their frequency patterns, enabling technicians to understand equipment behavior and schedule appropriate maintenance interventions.

Smart building maintenance systems integrate HVAC monitoring, lighting control, and equipment performance tracking to achieve up to a 50% reduction in downtime through predictive maintenance approaches. IoT sensors continuously monitor equipment performance and detect anomalies in real-time, enabling proactive maintenance scheduling and extending asset lifespans.

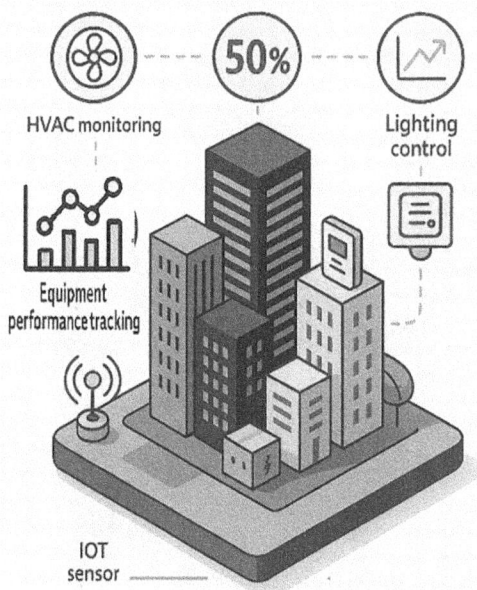

FIGURE 13.3 Smart building maintenance system.

Infrastructure health monitoring deploys sensors on critical assets including bridges, roads, and transportation systems to continuously monitor structural conditions. Strain gauges on bridges identify small cracks before they become critical, while vibration sensors on railway tracks detect abnormalities such as loose fasteners before potential derailments.

Advanced analytics integration combines IoT sensor data with machine learning algorithms to forecast equipment failures and optimize maintenance schedules. Quantum computing applications, particularly Quantum Support Vector Machines (QSVM) and quantum k-means clustering, enhance data processing speed and anomaly detection accuracy in industrial environments.

Environmental Monitoring and Control Systems

Comprehensive environmental monitoring networks utilize IoT sensors to track air quality, water conditions, noise levels, and weather patterns across urban environments. These systems provide real-time data collection and automated alert mechanisms to protect public health and environmental quality.

- Air quality monitoring networks deploy sensors measuring PM2.5, PM10, NO_2, SO_2, CO, and O_3 levels throughout urban areas. Cities worldwide have implemented extensive monitoring frameworks. For example, Indian smart cities, including Surat and Kakinada, have integrated environmental sensors into their smart city proposals, while Colombia's SIATA network operates more than 200 monitoring nodes across the Aburra Valley.
- Fog-enabled environmental systems integrate IoT sensors with edge computing and Low-Power Wide-Area Networks (LPWANs) to enable real-time air quality monitoring and prediction. These systems employ optimized deep learning models achieving 98.61% accuracy in pollution level forecasting while reducing model size and improving execution time by 81.53%.
- Wireless sensor networks for environmental monitoring enable cost-effective deployment across diverse geographical areas. The CleanWiFi network monitors air pollutants and uses data to automatically configure public WiFi services, rewarding less polluted areas with better connectivity while promoting environmental awareness.
- Weather and climate monitoring systems integrate multiple environmental parameters including temperature, humidity, wind speed, moisture, light intensity, UV radiation, and CO levels. These systems provide comprehensive weather forecasting capabilities and enable proactive responses to environmental changes.

FIGURE 13.4 Weather monitoring system.

Transportation and Mobility Management

IoT-enabled intelligent transportation systems optimize traffic flow, enhance safety, and improve urban mobility through real-time monitoring and adaptive control mechanisms. These systems address growing traffic congestion challenges while reducing environmental impact and improving operational efficiency.

- Smart traffic management implementations utilize real-time data from sensors and GPS systems to optimize traffic light control at intersections. IoT-based systems adjust traffic signal timing based on vehicle density and traffic patterns, reducing congestion and improving traffic flow efficiency.
- Vehicle-to-infrastructure communication enables connected vehicles to communicate with traffic lights, road sensors, and management systems. This communication facilitates optimized routing suggestions, collision prevention, and reduced idling time through coordinated signal timing.
- Fleet management and tracking systems provide real-time visibility into vehicle operations through GPS tracking, telematics, and sensor integration. These systems enable automated maintenance scheduling, route optimization, and operational cost reduction across logistics, public transportation, and service delivery sectors.

Asset Tracking and Infrastructure Management

Advanced asset tracking systems integrate RFID, GPS, Bluetooth Low Energy (BLE), and NFC technologies to provide comprehensive real-time monitoring of physical assets across various industries.

- RFID and IoT integration enables automated asset identification and tracking through radio frequency communication between tags and readers. Health care facilities utilize RFID sensors for internal asset tracking and GPS systems for external monitoring, optimizing equipment utilization and reducing equipment loss.
- Smart asset management platforms integrate IoT connectivity, cloud computing, and machine learning to enable real-time monitoring, predictive maintenance, and asset optimization.
- Infrastructure condition monitoring deploys sensors on critical infrastructure including bridges, buildings, and transportation networks to monitor structural health parameters such as stress, temperature, and vibration. These systems enable predictive maintenance approaches, preventing costly infrastructure failures and ensuring public safety.
- Digital twin implementation through Asset Administration Shell (AAS) frameworks enables standardized digital representations of industrial assets. These systems facilitate real-time monitoring, predictive maintenance, and seamless integration across value chains while enhancing transparency and operational efficiency.

Waste Management and Environmental Services

IoT-enabled smart waste management systems optimize collection routes, monitor bin fill levels, and enhance recycling processes through real-time data analytics and automated monitoring.

These systems demonstrate significant operational improvements including 20% reduction in overfilled bins and 15% decrease in collection frequency[2].

Smart bin networks utilize ultrasonic sensors, weight sensors, and fill-level monitoring to provide real-time waste status information. Cities worldwide have implemented comprehensive smart bin systems: Tangier, Morocco deployed IoT sensor mesh networks to optimize waste collection in areas with limited LoRa network access, while various global implementations demonstrate 25% reduction in trip distances and 10% decrease in fuel consumption[3].

Automated waste segregation systems employ infrared, capacitive, and inductive proximity sensors to distinguish between organic and inorganic waste materials. These systems integrate GPS tracking and cloud-based data management to optimize waste transportation from temporary disposal sites to final processing facilities.

Route optimization and predictive analytics use real-time bin status data to dynamically optimize collection routes and schedules. IoT platforms analyze waste generation patterns and predict optimal collection timing, reducing operational costs and environmental impact while improving service efficiency.

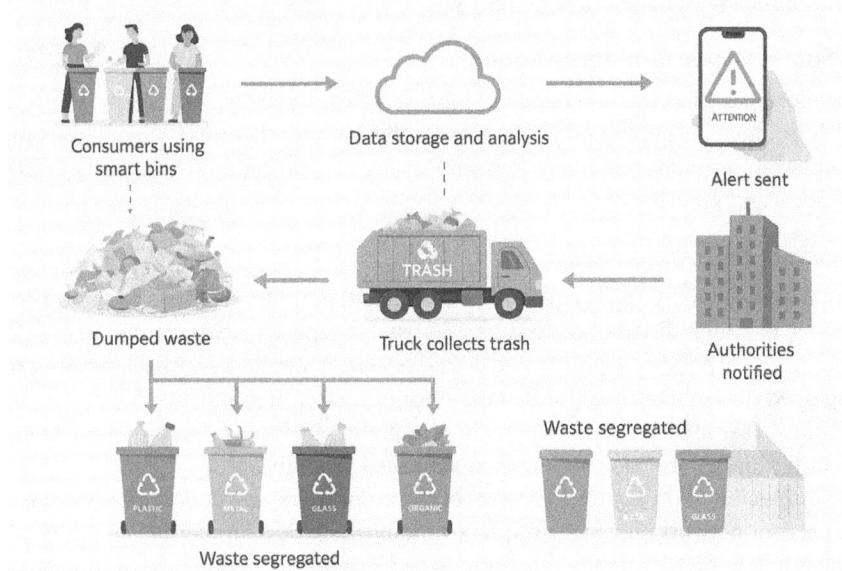

FIGURE 13.5 Smart waste management system.

Blockchain integration enhances data security and transparency in waste management operations through decentralized data storage and verification mechanisms. These systems ensure data integrity while enabling secure communication between waste management stakeholders and automated monitoring networks.

---

2 *https://www.bio-conferences.org/articles/bioconf/pdf/2024/05/bioconf_rtbs2024_01090.pdf*
3 *https://www.researchgate.net/publication/377359993_Optimizing_Waste_Management_through_IoT_and_Analytics_A_Case_Study_Using_the_Waste_Management_Optimization_Test*

The comprehensive deployment of IoT technologies across these resource management domains demonstrates the maturity and effectiveness of intelligent systems in optimizing urban operations. These implementations provide foundation frameworks for expanding IoT applications to address emerging challenges in smart city development and sustainable resource utilization.

CASE STUDY: OPTIMIZING ENERGY RESOURCES WITH IOT

Metropolitan city utilities are under pressure to balance peak loads, integrate renewables, and reduce carbon emissions while keeping costs low. To address the challenges, a pilot IoT-centric architecture was deployed combining smart meters, IoT-enabled transformers, NB-IoT/5G connectivity, real-time analytics, and digital twins.

The pilot demonstrates how a metropolitan utility utilized an IoT-centric architecture to transform grid operations, lower costs, and accelerate decarbonization. The following sections discuss some implementations with additional technical depth, measurable outcomes, and internationally validated best practices.

Singapore Smart Water Grid Innovation

Singapore has established itself as a global leader in smart water infrastructure through the WaterWiSe initiative implemented by the Public Utilities Board (PUB). The comprehensive IoT-enabled water management system serves as a pioneering model for urban water resource optimization and security.

System Architecture and Implementation

The WaterWiSe@SG platform represents an integrated end-to-end solution for real-time monitoring of water distribution systems across Singapore's urban environment. The system architecture incorporates sophisticated wireless sensor networks with high-data-rate capabilities deployed throughout the city's extensive water distribution infrastructure. The network utilizes advanced sensors measuring hydraulic parameters including pressure, flow rates, and water quality indicators to provide continuous operational visibility.

The implementation strategy focused on three primary objectives: deployment of low-cost wireless sensor networks for high-frequency monitoring, development of remote leak detection and pipe burst prediction systems, and integrated monitoring of both hydraulic and water quality parameters. The sensor network provides 15-minute interval data for consumption monitoring, voltage tracking, and power quality parameters throughout the distribution system.

Technical Components and Capabilities

Singapore's smart water infrastructure employs multiple IoT technologies to ensure comprehensive water management. Bivocom's IoT solutions enhance water quality monitoring through real-time data tracking for critical parameters including water pipeline leak detection and drinking water temperature monitoring. The system enables proactive leak detection capabilities, preventing water loss and ensuring timely repairs while maintaining reliable water supply for the community.

The communication infrastructure utilizes advanced wireless technologies to ensure reliable data transmission across diverse urban environments. The system integrates with cloud-based analytics platforms that process sensor data to generate actionable insights for utility operators and water resource planners.

Performance Outcomes and Benefits

The WaterWiSe implementation has delivered significant operational improvements for Singapore's water management system. The IoT-based approach has achieved a 28% reduction in water loss through enhanced leak detection and rapid response capabilities. The system's real-time monitoring capabilities have improved urban water supply system availability and reliability by 22% through predictive maintenance and condition monitoring features.

The platform's impact extends beyond operational efficiency to include substantial cost savings and environmental benefits. The system enables better water resource planning through accurate demand forecasting and consumption pattern analysis, supporting Singapore's broader water security objectives in a resource-constrained environment.

Barcelona Smart Water Distribution Excellence

Barcelona has implemented one of Europe's most comprehensive smart water management systems through Aigües de Barcelona, serving 2.8 million people across 23 municipalities. The utility manages over 4,600 kilometers of network infrastructure across 1.5 million connections, delivering 524 million liters of water daily.

Strategic Implementation Approach

Following extensive pilot testing of various technologies, the Aigües de Barcelona board approved a comprehensive 10-year plan in 2016 for massive smart meter deployment based on the WIZE/Wireless m-bus open standard. The implementation strategy addressed Barcelona's recurring drought challenges and increasingly unpredictable climate events while reducing operational costs through advanced automation.

The project deployment followed a phased geographical approach rather than simultaneous implementation across all municipalities. Each of the 23 participating municipalities developed specific customer engagement strategies to educate residents about the online portal benefits and smart metering advantages during the onboarding process.

Technology Infrastructure and Components

The Barcelona smart water system utilizes over one million smart meters connected through the WIZE/Wireless m-bus communication protocol. The technology stack provides real-time consumption monitoring, automated leak detection, and fraud prevention capabilities throughout the extensive distribution network.

Prior to smart meter implementation, the system required nine million manual reading operations annually, with residential contracts requiring six manual readings per year and commercial contracts requiring 12 annual readings. The automated system eliminated these manual operations while providing enhanced accuracy and operational efficiency.

The smart irrigation system deployed in Poblenou Park Centre demonstrates additional IoT applications for water management. The system utilizes soil moisture sensors and Waspmote Sensor Platform technology to monitor humidity and water flow at strategic locations, enabling remote irrigation control and water network management optimization.

Operational Results and Customer Benefits

The Barcelona smart water implementation has achieved substantial operational improvements and customer benefits. The system has reduced overconsumption alerts from 9% before smart metering deployment to 3% after implementation, demonstrating improved water usage efficiency and customer awareness.

The fraud detection capabilities have been significantly enhanced through real-time monitoring. Previously, meter reversal fraud was difficult to identify and required field team visits for verification, with only 20% of cases validated due to insufficient evidence. The smart monitoring system now enables remote fraud identification and immediate verification without customer site visits.

Customers receive access to an enriched online portal providing real-time daily consumption data, including leak and overconsumption alerts. When water leaks occur, residents receive automatic notifications via phone, app, or email, enabling rapid response and water conservation.

Copenhagen Energy and Water Surveillance Excellence

Copenhagen has established a comprehensive digital surveillance system for energy and water consumption across municipal buildings, serving as a model for integrated utility monitoring and efficiency optimization. The municipality collaborates with utility companies to implement extensive surveillance systems providing centralized data analysis and real-time operational insights.

Infrastructure Challenges and Solutions

Copenhagen's water infrastructure presents significant challenges, with 76% of water pipelines exceeding 60 years in age and 11% surpassing 100 years[4]. The aging infrastructure creates elevated leakage risks, making intelligent surveillance networks essential for achieving energy and water savings while reducing utility costs for residents.

The city's surveillance system addresses these challenges through high-resolution data collection from smart electricity, heat, and water meters deployed throughout municipal buildings. The system enables real-time leak identification and strategic planning for efficiency upgrades in underperforming buildings.

Technical Implementation and Integration

The Copenhagen system uniquely combines information from multiple building management systems on a centralized platform, providing comprehensive monitoring capabilities with a six-year payback period. Currently, 90% of municipal buildings transmit hourly data updates regarding energy and water consumption to the central monitoring platform.

---

4 *https://stateofgreen.com/en/news/reducing-urban-water-loss-to-just-5/*

The surveillance infrastructure utilizes advanced meter technologies to collect detailed consumption data across electricity, heating, and water systems. The platform integrates this diverse data to provide holistic insights into building performance and resource utilization patterns.

Performance Achievements and Expansion Plans

In 2016, Copenhagen's surveillance system achieved remarkable energy savings of 6,500 MWh of heat and 1,345 MWh of electricity through intelligent monitoring and optimization. The environmental impact included saving approximately 30 million liters of groundwater, demonstrating the system's comprehensive resource conservation benefits.

The economic benefits project annual savings of approximately $6 million once fully implemented, with the six-year payback period validating the investment in smart infrastructure. Copenhagen plans to extend the surveillance scheme to large privately owned buildings throughout the capital, further expanding energy consumption reduction citywide.

The initiative supports Copenhagen's ambitious climate strategy targeting CO2 neutrality by 2025. The city has developed educational programs using energy data to engage school children in energy efficiency thinking, creating long-term behavioral change and environmental awareness.

Milan Advanced Water Network Management

Milan's water utility, MM Spa, manages one of Italy's most complex urban water systems, serving 2.5 million people through over 2,300 kilometers of aqueducts and 1,500 kilometers of sewers. The utility operates two major wastewater treatment plants supporting the largest metropolitan area in Italy.

Strategic Digital Transformation Initiative

MM Spa implemented AQUADVANCED® Water Networks in 2023 to maximize data utilization and network performance optimization. The comprehensive platform exceeded initial expectations by providing advanced capabilities for network monitoring, leak localization modeling, and real-time network management.

The implementation strategy combined virtual sectorization with pre-localization of anomalies including leaks and unidentified valves. This dual approach enabled comprehensive network optimization while maintaining operational continuity throughout the transition period.

Advanced Technology Integration

The AQUADVANCED® platform incorporates embedded digital twin technology that enhanced the existing single District Metered Area (DMA) into 10 virtual DMAs and 287 virtual sub-sectors[5]. This virtual sectorization provides granular monitoring capabilities without requiring extensive physical infrastructure modifications.

The system optimizes data from 31 existing flow meters while identifying optimal locations for 16 high-frequency pressure sensors and 284 additional pressure sensors throughout the network. The intelligent sensor placement strategy maximizes monitoring coverage while minimizing infrastructure investment requirements.

---

5 *https://www.suez.com/en/references/milan-water-networks-performance-improvement*

Operational Excellence and Performance Metrics

The Milan system utilizes comprehensive Key Performance Indicators (KPIs) for improved decision-making based on real-time data analysis. Metrics include daily losses, daily linear flow, and Non-Revenue Water (NRW) tracking, providing operational teams with actionable insights for network optimization.

The platform utilizes data intelligence to predict and model missing information, generating events and identifying potential risks before they impact service delivery. This predictive capability enables proactive maintenance scheduling and resource allocation optimization.

The MM Spa implementation has strengthened the utility's digital transformation strategy while enhancing daily operations through virtual network management capabilities. The system provides comprehensive data-driven decision support, reinforcing the utility's commitment to operational excellence and customer service quality.

Dubai Smart Grid and Water Management Innovation

Dubai Electricity and Water Authority (DEWA) has implemented one of the world's most advanced smart grid systems, integrating electricity and water management through a comprehensive IoT infrastructure. The $7 billion investment supports Dubai's vision to become the smartest and happiest city globally[6].

Comprehensive Smart Grid Architecture

DEWA's smart grid ensures 24/7 integrated services through automated decision-making capabilities and interoperability across electricity and water networks. The system leverages Fourth Industrial Revolution technologies including artificial intelligence and IoT to ensure efficient, reliable, and sustainable operations.

The smart grid architecture integrates advanced metering infrastructure with distribution automation systems, enabling real-time monitoring and control of both electricity and water distribution. The system provides comprehensive visibility into network performance while supporting automated response to operational challenges.

Performance Excellence and Global Leadership

In 2023, DEWA achieved a world record in electricity Customer Minutes Lost (CML) with Dubai recording just 1.06 minutes per customer annually, compared to approximately 15 minutes for leading European Union utility companies[7]. This exceptional reliability demonstrates the effectiveness of IoT-enabled smart grid technologies.

IoT-Enabled Water Management Features

DEWA's smart water management capabilities include IoT-enabled smart meters that detect leaks and unusual consumption patterns, providing instant alerts to customers. Since 2019, the system has identified over 1.8 million water leaks, demonstrating exceptional capability in resource conservation and waste reduction.

---

6 *https://www.dewa.gov.ae/en/about-us/media-publications/latest-news/2024/12/electricity-and-water-smart-grid-supports*

7 *https://www.dewa.gov.ae/en/about-us/media-publications/latest-news/2024/01/dewa-records-the-worlds-lowest-electricity*

The water management system integrates with Dubai's broader smart infrastructure initiatives, including the $8.2 billion Tasreef project for upgrading rainwater drainage systems. IoT sensors monitor water levels and flow throughout the drainage network, enabling proactive management and flood risk reduction.

Thames Water Smart Metering Advancement

Thames Water, the United Kingdom's largest water company, has implemented an ambitious smart metering program targeting over one million additional homes and businesses across London, the Thames Valley, and Home Counties by 2030. The company has already installed over 1.2 million devices with a target of three million meters across all regions by 2035.

Technology Framework and Implementation Strategy

The Thames Water smart metering framework involves two major technology suppliers over an eight-year term with potential value exceeding £50 million based on 650,000 meter installations. Honeywell supplies Concentric smart metering devices for external installation at customer premises, while Sensus UK provides In-Line meters for internal installation.

The smart meters utilize Vodafone's innovative Narrowband IoT (NB-IoT) network technology, representing an industry-first implementation at this scale for water utilities. The NB-IoT technology provides reliable internet connectivity even in hard-to-reach locations while reducing startup costs and infrastructure requirements.

Advanced Communication and Data Capabilities

The NB-IoT network enables near real-time data delivery with up to 24 readings per day, providing unprecedented visibility into water consumption patterns and network performance. This high-frequency data collection facilitates rapid leak detection and enables customers to make informed decisions about water usage.

The communication framework supports automated leak detection algorithms that identify consumption anomalies and potential infrastructure problems before they escalate. The system provides customers with detailed consumption insights while supporting utility operations through predictive maintenance capabilities.

Customer Benefits and Operational Outcomes

Thames Water's smart metering program empowers customers to monitor their water usage in real-time, often resulting in reduced consumption and lower energy bills. The technology enables early detection of leaks at customer premises and businesses, minimizing water waste and preventing property damage.

The smart meter data supports Thames Water's broader operational objectives including network optimization, demand forecasting, and infrastructure planning. The comprehensive data collection enables more accurate billing while reducing the need for manual meter readings and customer service interventions.

Amsterdam Smart Grid Energy Transition

Amsterdam has implemented comprehensive smart grid infrastructure supporting the city's energy transition toward renewable sources and improved efficiency. The smart grid initiative addresses the challenges of decentralized clean energy integration while maintaining reliable power supply throughout the metropolitan area.

Smart Grid Infrastructure Development

Amsterdam's smart grid utilizes advanced technology to enable intelligent communication among energy users, enhancing power storage and distribution efficiency while addressing network capacity gaps. The system coordinates household battery charging and discharging, aligns thermostat operation with energy availability, and manages car charging schedules based on grid conditions.

The City-Zen project, implemented collaboratively with Grenoble, France, represented Europe's first EU-funded smart grid initiative in 2014. Working with 28 partners over five years, the project renovated 10,000 residential buildings with energy-saving features, achieving an estimated reduction of 35,000 tons of annual CO_2 emissions.

Energy Management Around Amsterdam ArenA

The smart grid system surrounding Amsterdam ArenA plays a crucial role in managing energy distribution for the premier sporting and events venue. The system demonstrates advanced grid management capabilities for high-demand facilities while contributing to the broader metropolitan energy optimization strategy.

The ArenA smart grid integration shows how IoT technologies can manage complex energy demands while supporting renewable energy integration and grid stability. The system provides real-time energy management for major events while contributing to Amsterdam's overall sustainability objectives.

Digital Infrastructure and Future Development

Amsterdam benefits from being part of one of the world's most advanced digital infrastructures, providing extensive opportunities for smart grid solution development and global replication. The high connectivity level enables comprehensive IoT deployment and data analytics capabilities throughout the energy distribution network.

Stockholm has implemented complementary smart city initiatives including the DigiCityClimate project funded by Google through ICLEI. The project develops digital platforms, chatbots, and AI-based advisory functions to help residents and property associations reduce energy costs and consumption.

New York Digital Water Transformation

New York State uses digital water technologies to transform water management throughout urban centers, addressing growing challenges in water resource management through IoT integration, artificial intelligence, and cloud computing platforms. The digital water approach enables real-time monitoring, data-driven decision-making, and enhanced operational efficiency across the state's water infrastructure.

Smart Water Infrastructure Implementation

New York's water utilities utilize IoT-enabled sensors to monitor pipeline conditions, water quality parameters, and flow rates throughout distribution networks. These sensors provide real-time data enabling operators to detect and address leaks or contamination incidents before they escalate into costly infrastructure problems.

The New York City Department of Environmental Protection (DEP) has invested significantly in advanced metering infrastructure to reduce water waste and improve billing accuracy. The smart meter deployment supports comprehensive water usage monitoring while enabling customer engagement through detailed consumption feedback.

Predictive Maintenance and Digital Twins

Cities, including Albany and Buffalo, utilize digital twins—virtual models of physical infrastructure—to simulate water system performance and predict maintenance requirements. Predictive analytics help engineers identify vulnerabilities in aging pipes and treatment facilities, enabling proactive repairs and extending infrastructure lifespan.

The digital twin technology integrates real-time sensor data with historical performance information to create comprehensive system models. These virtual representations enable scenario planning, optimization testing, and predictive maintenance scheduling without disrupting actual operations.

Operational Benefits and Future Expansion

Digital water implementation in New York has demonstrated significant improvements in leak detection, system reliability, and customer service quality. The technology enables utilities to respond more rapidly to infrastructure problems while providing customers with detailed consumption information and conservation guidance.

The state's digital water initiatives support broader sustainability objectives through improved resource efficiency and reduced environmental impact. The comprehensive monitoring capabilities enable better water resource planning while supporting compliance with regulatory requirements and environmental protection standards.

Global Implementation Patterns and Technical Innovations

The case studies demonstrate consistent patterns in IoT implementation for smart water and energy management across diverse urban environments. Common technical approaches include advanced metering infrastructure, real-time sensor networks, predictive analytics platforms, and integrated communication systems supporting comprehensive utility management.

Communication Technology Standardization

Multiple cities have adopted similar communication protocols including LoRaWAN, NB-IoT, and cellular networks to ensure reliable data transmission across diverse geographical and infrastructure environments. The Tokyo metropolitan area has implemented LoRaWAN networks for smart water meter deployment, demonstrating the technology's effectiveness in mountainous terrain and harsh weather conditions.

The standardization of communication protocols enables interoperability between different sensor types and manufacturers while reducing implementation costs and complexity. Cities can utilize existing telecommunications infrastructure while maintaining flexibility for future technology upgrades and system expansions.

Data Analytics and Decision Support Systems

Advanced analytics platforms consistently enable utilities to transform raw sensor data into actionable operational insights. The integration of artificial intelligence and machine learning algorithms supports predictive maintenance, demand forecasting, and automated system optimization across water and energy distribution networks.

Cloud-based platforms provide scalable data storage and processing capabilities while enabling remote monitoring and control of distributed infrastructure. The centralized analytics approach supports comprehensive system management while enabling rapid response to operational challenges and customer service requirements.

Performance Measurement and Optimization

Successful implementations demonstrate consistent approaches to performance measurement through comprehensive KPIs and real-time monitoring dashboards. These metrics enable continuous system optimization while supporting regulatory compliance and customer service objectives.

The case studies reveal substantial operational improvements including reduced water losses, improved energy efficiency, enhanced customer service quality, and significant cost savings. These outcomes validate the business case for IoT investment while demonstrating the technology's potential for addressing urban sustainability challenges.

The comprehensive case study analysis reveals the transformative potential of IoT technologies in smart water and energy management across diverse urban environments. The successful implementations provide valuable frameworks for other cities seeking to modernize their utility infrastructure while achieving sustainability and operational excellence objectives.

CONCLUSION

The integration of IoT technologies into water and energy systems has fundamentally transformed the way modern cities manage essential resources. From real-time monitoring and predictive analytics to automated control systems and digital twins, IoT-driven solutions are delivering substantial gains in operational efficiency, sustainability, and service reliability. Case studies from global cities like Singapore, Barcelona, Copenhagen, and Dubai show how strategic IoT deployment not only improves performance but also supports broader climate and decarbonization goals.

These implementations reveal clear patterns of success: the adoption of interoperable communication protocols (such as LoRaWAN and NB-IoT), investment in advanced metering infrastructure, and the centralization of analytics for decision-making. Furthermore, predictive maintenance and asset management have emerged as pivotal capabilities for aging infrastructure, while smart waste and environmental monitoring contribute directly to improved urban livability.

As cities like Nusantara pursue intelligent, climate-resilient development, the experiences and lessons from these global pioneers offer a proven blueprint. Future progress will depend on aligning technology investments with strong regulatory frameworks, cross-sector collaboration, and citizen-centric innovation. The convergence of IoT, AI, and sustainable design in resource management will be instrumental in shaping resilient smart cities for decades to come.

CHAPTER 14

SMART MOBILITY AND ATMS (ADVANCED TRAFFIC MANAGEMENT SYSTEMS)

S mart mobility is a fundamental part of smart cities, transforming how people and goods move through urban environments. This chapter explores how IoT technologies revolutionize transportation systems, focusing on advanced public transportation solutions and sophisticated traffic management systems. We examine both theoretical frameworks and practical implementations through detailed case studies.

ADVANCEMENTS IN TRANSPORTATION AND MOBILITY SOLUTIONS

Real-time Transit Monitoring and Management

Real-time transit monitoring utilizes sophisticated IoT technologies to provide comprehensive situational awareness and operational control. This section explores the technological infrastructure and advanced applications that enable transit operations in smart cities.

GPS-Based Vehicle Tracking Systems

Modern transit monitoring systems rely heavily on Global Positioning System (GPS) technology integrated with advanced communication protocols. GPS tracking devices installed in transit vehicles communicate with satellite constellations to determine precise location coordinates with accuracy within 3-5 meters under optimal conditions. These systems operate continuously, transmitting location data at intervals ranging from every few seconds to every minute, depending on operational requirements.

The GPS tracking infrastructure consists of several components. Each transit vehicle is equipped with a GPS receiver unit that calculates position using signals from multiple satellites. This unit integrates with onboard diagnostic systems to collect additional vehicle parameters such as speed, heading, fuel consumption, and engine status. Data transmission occurs through cellular networks, utilizing 4G LTE or emerging 5G technologies to ensure reliable communication even in dense urban environments Advanced GPS tracking systems employ sophisticated algorithms to enhance location accuracy and compensate for signal degradation in urban canyons or tunnels. Techniques such as dead reckoning and inertial navigation provide continuity when GPS signals are temporarily unavailable. Machine learning algorithms process historical location patterns to predict vehicle positions during communication blackouts, ensuring uninterrupted service monitoring.

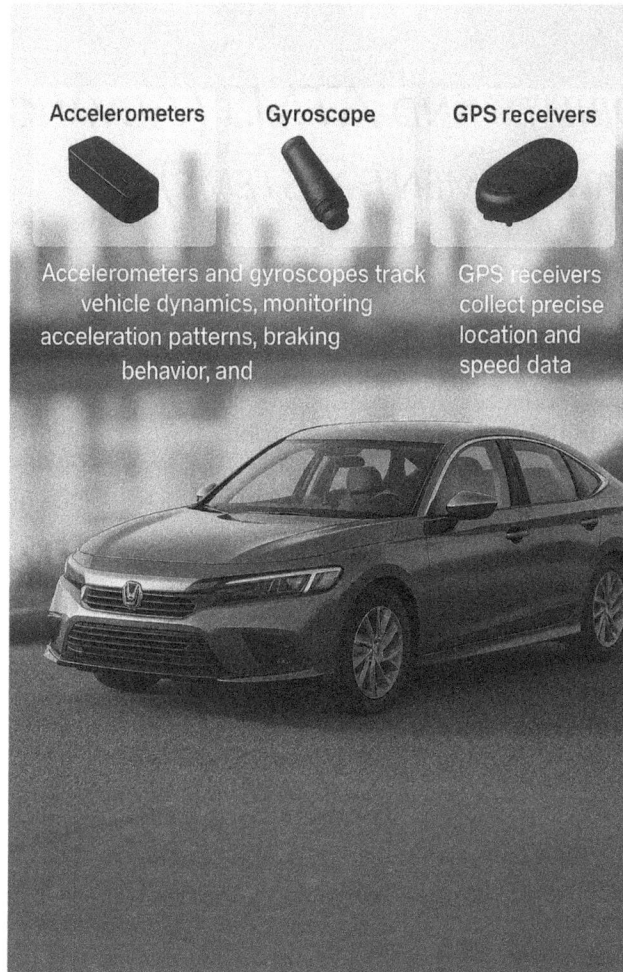

FIGURE 14.1 Telematics for vehicle monitoring.

IoT Sensor Integration for Comprehensive Monitoring

Beyond GPS tracking, modern transit monitoring systems incorporate diverse IoT sensors to provide holistic vehicle and passenger monitoring capabilities. Accelerometers and gyroscopes monitor vehicle dynamics, detecting sudden acceleration, harsh braking, or sharp turns that may indicate safety concerns or driver behavior issues. These sensors generate continuous data streams that are analyzed using machine learning algorithms to identify patterns and anomalies.

Environmental sensors within vehicles monitor air quality, temperature, and humidity to ensure passenger comfort and safety. Occupancy sensors, including infrared passenger counters and weight sensors, provide real-time data on passenger loading and distribution. This information enables dynamic capacity management and helps optimize service frequency based on actual demand patterns.

Modern systems also incorporate biometric and security sensors for enhanced safety. Computer vision systems with convolutional neural networks analyze passenger behavior to detect emergencies, unauthorized access, or security threats. These systems operate in real-time, processing video feeds to identify potential incidents and automatically alert control centers.

Advanced Communication Networks

The effectiveness of real-time monitoring depends on a robust communication infrastructure. Fifth-generation (5G) wireless networks provide the ultra-low latency and high bandwidth necessary for real-time traffic management. With latency as low as 1 millisecond, 5G enables instantaneous communication between vehicles, infrastructure, and control centers, supporting applications such as emergency vehicle prioritization and dynamic route optimization.

Vehicle-to-Infrastructure (V2I) communication protocols facilitate direct information exchange between transit vehicles and roadside infrastructure. Using Dedicated Short-Range Communication (DSRC) or Cellular Vehicle-to-Everything (C-V2X) technologies, vehicles can communicate with traffic signals, road signs, and other infrastructure elements. This communication enables adaptive signal control that prioritizes transit vehicles, reducing delays and improving schedule adherence.

Edge computing infrastructure processes data locally at roadside units, reducing communication latency and enabling real-time decision-making. By distributing computational capabilities throughout the network, edge computing supports applications requiring immediate response, such as collision avoidance and emergency detection systems.

Data Analytics and Predictive Capabilities

Real-time monitoring systems generate massive volumes of data that require sophisticated analytics platforms for processing and interpretation. Cloud-based analytics engines utilize machine learning algorithms to identify patterns in transit operations, predict potential disruptions, and optimize service delivery. These systems process data from multiple sources simultaneously, including vehicle telemetry, passenger counts, weather conditions, and traffic patterns.

Predictive analytics algorithms forecast arrival times with high accuracy by analyzing historical performance data and real-time conditions. Machine learning models, including recurrent neural networks and support vector machines, process spatiotemporal data to predict delays and recommend corrective actions. Advanced systems can predict congestion up to 30 minutes in advance, enabling proactive traffic management interventions.

Artificial intelligence techniques enhance the analytical capabilities of monitoring systems. Deep learning algorithms analyze video feeds from onboard cameras to assess road conditions, detect obstacles, and identify potential safety hazards. Natural language processing enables automated analysis of passenger feedback and social media data to identify service quality issues and operational improvements.

Smart Fare Collection Systems

Smart fare collection systems represent a fundamental transformation in the public transportation payment infrastructure. They utilize IoT technologies to create well-connected, secure, and data-rich transaction environments. These systems integrate multiple payment modalities while providing valuable operational insights for transit agencies.

RFID and NFC Technology Implementation

Radio Frequency Identification (RFID) and Near Field Communication (NFC) technologies form the backbone of modern contactless payment systems in public transportation. RFID systems operate by utilizing radio waves to transfer information between a tag or card and a reader device, eliminating the need for physical contact during transactions. High-frequency (HF) RFID technology, typically operating at 13.56 MHz, is commonly employed in transit applications due to its optimal balance of security, range, and data transfer speed.

NFC technology, a specialized subset of RFID, enables communication between devices at very short ranges, typically within four centimeters. This technology allows passengers to use NFC-enabled smartphones, smartwatches, or contactless cards to pay for transit services. The payment process involves electromagnetic induction between the passenger's device and the reader, with transactions completed in milliseconds.

Modern fare collection systems support multiple form factors for RFID/NFC payment. Traditional contactless smart cards contain embedded microchips and antennas that store payment credentials and travel history. Mobile payment solutions utilize the NFC capabilities built into smartphones, enabling passengers to use digital wallets such as Apple Pay, Google Pay, or Samsung Pay for transit payments. Wearable devices, including smartwatches and fitness trackers, provide additional convenience for contactless payments.

Advanced Security and Privacy Protection

Security implementation in smart fare collection systems requires multi-layered approaches to protect both financial data and passenger privacy. Cryptographic protocols ensure secure communication between payment devices and readers, with data encryption occurring at multiple levels. EMV (Europay, Mastercard, and Visa) standards provide robust security frameworks for contactless payments, implementing tokenization to replace sensitive payment data with unique identifiers.

Privacy protection measures address concerns about passenger tracking and data collection. Advanced systems implement privacy-preserving protocols that enable fare collection without storing personally identifiable location data. Techniques such as anonymous credentials and zero-knowledge proofs allow transit agencies to validate payments while protecting passenger anonymity.

Blockchain technology offers emerging solutions for secure and transparent fare collection systems. Distributed ledger systems provide tamper-resistant transaction records while enabling smart contracts to automate fare calculation and revenue distribution among multiple transit operators. These systems enhance trust and transparency while reducing operational overhead.

Real-time Revenue Management and Analytics

Smart fare collection systems generate comprehensive data streams that enable sophisticated revenue management and operational optimization. Real-time transaction processing provides immediate visibility into ridership patterns, fare compliance, and revenue generation across the transit network. Advanced analytics platforms process this data to identify trends, optimize pricing strategies, and improve service planning.

Machine learning algorithms analyze fare collection data to detect fraudulent activities and fare evasion. Behavioral pattern recognition identifies unusual payment patterns or attempts to manipulate the fare system. Automated fraud detection reduces revenue losses while minimizing the need for manual intervention.

Dynamic pricing capabilities enable transit agencies to implement congestion-based or time-of-day pricing strategies. IoT sensors and passenger counting systems provide real-time occupancy data that can trigger automatic fare adjustments during peak demand periods. These systems help manage demand while maximizing revenue and improving service quality for passengers.

Integration with other city systems enables comprehensive urban mobility analytics. Fare collection data combined with traffic patterns, weather information, and special events data provides insights into urban mobility patterns and helps optimize transportation planning decisions.

Vehicle Fleet Management

Modern vehicle fleet management systems utilize comprehensive IoT sensor networks and advanced analytics to optimize vehicle performance, reduce operational costs, and improve service reliability. These systems provide real-time monitoring capabilities that enable proactive maintenance, efficient resource allocation, and enhanced safety management.

IoT Sensor Networks for Vehicle Monitoring

Contemporary fleet management systems deploy extensive networks of IoT sensors throughout transit vehicles to monitor critical operational parameters. Engine management sensors continuously monitor temperature, oil pressure, fuel consumption, and emissions levels. These sensors utilize Controller Area Network (CAN) bus protocols to communicate with onboard diagnostics systems, providing comprehensive engine health monitoring.

Telematics systems integrate multiple sensor types to provide holistic vehicle monitoring capabilities. Accelerometers and gyroscopes track vehicle dynamics, monitoring acceleration patterns, braking behavior, and cornering forces. GPS receivers provide precise location and speed data, while cellular or satellite communication systems transmit this information to fleet management centers.

Advanced sensor fusion techniques combine data from multiple sensor types to provide comprehensive vehicle health assessments. Machine learning algorithms process sensor data streams to identify patterns indicative of potential failures or performance degradation. These systems can detect anomalies in vehicle behavior that may indicate maintenance needs before critical failures occur.

Environmental sensors monitor passenger cabin conditions, including air quality, temperature, and humidity levels. These sensors ensure passenger comfort while identifying potential issues with heating, ventilation, and air conditioning systems. Integration with building management protocols enables automated climate control optimization based on passenger occupancy and external weather conditions.

Predictive Maintenance Systems

Predictive maintenance represents a paradigm shift from reactive to proactive fleet management strategies. IoT-enabled systems continuously monitor vehicle components and use machine learning algorithms to predict maintenance needs before failures occur. These systems analyze sensor data patterns to identify components approaching end-of-life conditions or performance degradation.

Engine diagnostics systems monitor critical parameters such as oil condition, filter status, and component wear indicators. Advanced algorithms analyze vibration patterns, temperature fluctuations, and performance metrics to predict maintenance requirements. Predictive models can forecast component failures weeks or months in advance, enabling optimized maintenance scheduling and parts procurement.

Brake system monitoring utilizes sensors to track brake pad wear, hydraulic pressure, and temperature conditions. Machine learning algorithms analyze braking patterns and environmental factors to predict brake maintenance needs. These systems help ensure passenger safety while optimizing maintenance intervals and reducing unexpected service disruptions.

Battery management systems for electric and hybrid vehicles monitor cell voltage, temperature, and charge cycles to predict battery degradation and optimize charging strategies. Advanced algorithms balance charging loads across fleet vehicles to extend battery life while ensuring adequate range for service requirements.

Driver Behavior Analysis and Safety Enhancement

Modern fleet management systems incorporate comprehensive driver monitoring capabilities to improve safety, reduce fuel consumption, and optimize operational efficiency. Telematics systems track driving behaviors including acceleration patterns, braking intensity, cornering speeds, and adherence to speed limits. Machine learning algorithms analyze these patterns to identify drivers who may benefit from additional training or coaching.

Video telematics systems utilize onboard cameras and computer vision algorithms to monitor driver attention and behavior. These systems can detect drowsiness, distraction, or other safety-compromising behaviors and provide real-time alerts to drivers. Advanced systems integrate with vehicle control systems to provide automated interventions in emergency situations.

Fuel efficiency optimization systems analyze driving patterns and provide real-time feedback to drivers. Eco-driving algorithms identify opportunities to reduce fuel consumption through optimized acceleration, braking, and route selection. Gamification techniques encourage drivers to adopt fuel-efficient driving behaviors through performance scoring and rewards programs.

Geofencing capabilities enable automated monitoring of vehicle operations within designated areas. Systems can automatically adjust vehicle settings, monitor compliance with route restrictions, and provide alerts when vehicles deviate from assigned areas or schedules.

Traffic Flow Optimization

Traffic flow optimization represents the integration of multiple IoT technologies and advanced analytics to create adaptive, intelligent transportation systems. These systems utilize real-time data collection, machine learning algorithms, and automated control mechanisms to optimize traffic flow and reduce congestion across urban transportation networks.

Advanced Sensor Technologies for Traffic Monitoring

Modern traffic management systems employ diverse sensor technologies to gather comprehensive real-time traffic data. Light Detection and Ranging (LiDAR) sensors provide precise three-dimensional monitoring capabilities, accurately detecting vehicle presence, classification, and movement patterns. LiDAR technology offers superior performance in various weather conditions and lighting environments compared to traditional camera-based systems.

Aerial LiDAR systems deployed on unmanned aerial vehicles (UAVs) provide comprehensive traffic monitoring over large areas. These systems generate detailed 3D point cloud data that enables precise vehicle detection and tracking across multiple lanes and intersections. Advanced algorithms process this data in real-time to identify traffic patterns, congestion levels, and potential safety hazards.

Multi-modal sensor fusion combines LiDAR, camera, and radar technologies to enhance detection accuracy and reliability. Camera-LiDAR fusion systems achieve superior performance compared to single-sensor approaches, providing robust object detection capabilities across diverse environmental conditions. These systems utilize advanced machine learning algorithms to process multi-modal data streams and generate accurate traffic assessments.

Computer vision systems equipped with convolutional neural networks analyze video feeds from traffic cameras to detect vehicles, pedestrians, and other road users. These systems can track movement patterns, identify traffic violations, and detect incidents in real-time. Advanced algorithms achieve vehicle detection accuracy rates exceeding 96% under optimal conditions.

Machine Learning and AI for Traffic Prediction

Artificial intelligence and machine learning technologies enable sophisticated traffic prediction and optimization capabilities. Deep learning algorithms, including recurrent neural networks and transformer models, analyze historical and real-time traffic data to predict future conditions. These systems can forecast traffic patterns, identify potential congestion points, and recommend proactive management strategies.

Reinforcement learning algorithms optimize traffic signal control by learning from traffic patterns and environmental conditions. These systems continuously adapt signal timing strategies based on observed traffic flows, achieving significant improvements in traffic throughput and delay reduction. Advanced multi-agent reinforcement learning approaches coordinate signal control across multiple intersections to optimize corridor-level traffic flow.

Machine learning models integrate diverse data sources including weather conditions, special events, and social media data to enhance prediction accuracy. Random forest and gradient boosting algorithms process these heterogeneous data streams to generate comprehensive traffic forecasts. Advanced systems can predict congestion events up to 30 minutes in advance with high accuracy.

Digital twin technology creates virtual representations of traffic systems that enable advanced simulation and optimization capabilities. These systems integrate real-time sensor data with detailed traffic models to simulate various scenarios and test optimization strategies before implementation. Digital twins enable continuous learning and adaptation of traffic management strategies based on observed system performance.

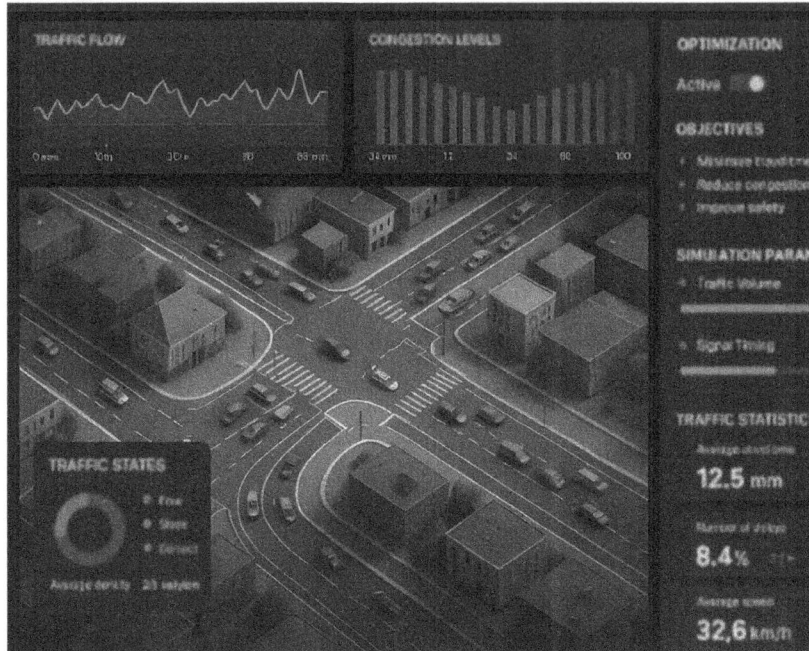

FIGURE 14.2 Digital twin of traffic systems.

Adaptive Traffic Signal Control Systems

Adaptive traffic signal control is an advancement over traditional fixed-timing systems. These systems utilize real-time traffic data to dynamically adjust signal timing, optimizing traffic flow based on current conditions rather than predetermined schedules. Advanced algorithms continuously monitor traffic demand and adjust signal parameters to minimize delays and maximize throughput.

Modern adaptive systems employ sophisticated algorithms including Dynamic Traffic Light Scheduling (DTLS) and Q-learning to optimize signal control. These systems can extend green light durations for heavy traffic directions, implement corridor coordination to create "green waves," and provide priority for emergency vehicles. Advanced systems achieve travel time improvements of 10-50% compared to traditional signal control methods.

Vehicle-to-Infrastructure (V2I) communication enhances adaptive signal control by providing direct communication between vehicles and traffic infrastructure. Connected vehicles can transmit speed, destination, and timing information to traffic controllers, enabling more precise signal optimization. These systems support Signal Phase and Timing (SPaT) and Geographic MAP (GeoMAP) messages that inform vehicles about upcoming signal changes.

Emergency vehicle prioritization systems automatically detect approaching emergency vehicles and adjust signal timing to provide clear passage. Advanced systems utilize GPS tracking, V2I communication, and automated vehicle identification to prioritize actions while minimizing effects on the general traffic flow.

Edge Computing and Real-time Processing

Edge computing infrastructure enables real-time traffic management by processing data locally at intersection and roadway locations. Edge computing nodes deployed at traffic signals and monitoring stations reduce communication latency and enable immediate response to changing traffic conditions. These systems process sensor data, execute traffic optimization algorithms, and implement control decisions within milliseconds.

Distributed computing architectures coordinate edge devices across transportation networks to provide system-wide optimization. These systems utilize fog computing principles to balance computational loads between edge devices and cloud infrastructure, ensuring optimal performance while maintaining system reliability.

Real-time data processing capabilities enable immediate response to traffic incidents and changing conditions. Advanced systems can detect incidents within seconds, automatically adjust signal timing, and notify traffic management centers and emergency responders. Integration with emergency services enables coordinated incident response and traffic management.

5G communication networks provide the ultra-low latency and high bandwidth necessary for real-time traffic management applications. With latency below 1 millisecond, 5G enables instantaneous communication between vehicles, infrastructure, and control centers, supporting advanced applications such as autonomous vehicle coordination and real-time traffic optimization.

Cloud-Based Traffic Management Platforms

Cloud computing platforms provide the scalable infrastructure necessary to process massive volumes of traffic data and support complex analytics applications. These platforms integrate data from thousands of sensors, cameras, and connected vehicles to provide comprehensive traffic management capabilities. Cloud infrastructure enables cities to scale their traffic management systems as their transportation networks grow.

Big data analytics platforms process historical and real-time traffic data to identify patterns, optimize signal timing, and improve long-term transportation planning. These systems can analyze traffic data from multiple years to identify seasonal patterns, evaluate the effectiveness of infrastructure improvements, and support evidence-based transportation policy decisions.

Machine learning platforms deployed in cloud environments enable continuous learning and optimization of traffic management strategies. These systems can train complex models using historical data and deploy updated algorithms to edge devices throughout the transportation network. Continuous learning capabilities ensure that traffic management systems adapt to changing conditions and improve performance over time.

Integration APIs enable cloud platforms to connect with multiple city systems including emergency services, public transportation, and special event management. These integrations provide comprehensive urban mobility management capabilities that coordinate multiple transportation modes and support city-wide optimization strategies.

The convergence of these advanced technologies creates intelligent transportation systems capable of autonomous operation, continuous optimization, and adaptive response to changing conditions. As cities continue to grow and transportation demands increase, these IoT-enabled systems provide the foundation for sustainable, efficient, and safe urban mobility solutions.

CASE STUDY: ATMS IMPLEMENTATION IN SMART CITY

Seoul TOPIS: Comprehensive Intelligent Transportation System

Project Overview and Implementation Background

Seoul TOPIS (Seoul Transport Operation & Information Service) represents one of the most comprehensive implementations of an Advanced Traffic Management System in the world, serving as an integrated traffic management center for Seoul's 10 million residents[1]. The system was established in 2004 as part of Seoul's public transportation reform initiative, transitioning from a fragmented traffic management approach to a unified intelligent transportation platform.

The implementation of Seoul TOPIS emerged from critical challenges facing Seoul's transportation system in the early 2000s. Bus ridership had declined from 30.1% in 1996 to 26% in 2002, while traffic congestion continued to worsen despite road expansion efforts. The city had traditional infrastructure-based solutions that were insufficient; intelligent technology integration was essential for sustainable mobility.

Technology Architecture and Infrastructure

Seoul TOPIS operates through six integrated platforms that collectively manage all aspects of urban transportation: the center platform for traffic control, bus platform for public transit management, unmanned enforcement platform, freeway traffic management system, advanced traffic management system, and big data platform for predictive analytics.

The technological infrastructure supporting Seoul TOPIS encompasses an extensive network of IoT sensors and devices. The system monitors 1,268 kilometers of roadway through 1,181 video and loop detectors installed throughout the city. These sensors provide real-time traffic speed and volume data, enabling continuous monitoring of traffic conditions across the entire urban network.

GPS technology forms another critical component, with 35,000 GPS devices installed in taxis providing real-time location and speed data. This distributed sensing network allows the system to calculate accurate travel times and identify traffic patterns without relying solely on fixed infrastructure sensors.

The surveillance and monitoring capabilities include 832 cameras for traffic and disaster monitoring, providing visual confirmation of traffic conditions and enabling rapid incident detection. Variable Message Signs (VMS) comprising 326 units display real-time traffic information to drivers, while 3,600 signal controllers enable adaptive traffic signal management across the city.

---

1 *https://knowledgehub.clc.gov.sg/liveability-in-action/city-case-study–seoul*

Advanced Traffic Management Capabilities

Seoul TOPIS employs sophisticated traffic management algorithms that process data from multiple sources to optimize traffic flow. The system automatically detects incidents through video analytics and sensor anomaly detection, immediately displaying alerts on electronic displays and implementing traffic management responses. Road control systems operate bypass routes and adjust signal timing to manage traffic flow around incidents.

Predictive traffic management represents a significant advancement in Seoul's ATMS implementation. The system analyzes five years of historical traffic data combined with real-time weather, accident, and traffic flow information to predict traffic conditions in 15-minute, 1-hour, and 1-day intervals. This predictive capability achieves 90% accuracy and enables proactive traffic management interventions.

The system supports Vehicle-to-Infrastructure (V2I) communication, providing roadside assistance that reflects real-time road conditions, signal changes, and pedestrian crossing predictions.[2] This capability prepares Seoul's infrastructure for autonomous vehicle integration while improving current traffic management effectiveness.

Public Transportation Integration

Seoul TOPIS manages approximately 9,000 buses in real-time through integrated Bus Management System (BMS) and Bus Information System (BIS) platforms. Each bus is equipped with combined terminals that collect comprehensive operational data including location, speed, passenger counts, driver behavior metrics, and mechanical performance indicators.

The system processes approximately 85 million traffic card transactions daily, providing detailed insights into passenger travel patterns and enabling dynamic route optimization. Bus arrival predictions achieve 98% accuracy, with information delivered through multiple channels including bus information terminals at 52% of bus stations, mobile applications, and open APIs.[3]

The electronic fare integration system supports transfers between buses, subways, and taxis within a 30-minute window for distances up to 10 kilometers. This integration encourages public transportation usage and provides comprehensive travel data for system optimization.

Enforcement and Compliance Management

Seoul TOPIS operates 308 unmanned enforcement systems that automatically detect and process traffic violations. The system utilizes both fixed enforcement cameras with 200-meter detection ranges and portable cameras mounted on buses and monitoring vehicles. Advanced computer vision algorithms identify vehicles illegally parked in bus lanes, bicycle lanes, or violating other traffic regulations.

The automated penalty management system represents a world-first implementation, automatically processing violations from detection through penalty notice delivery. When violations are detected, the system automatically searches vehicle registration databases, generates penalty

---

2 *https://www.seoulsolution.kr/en/content/2595*
3 *https://www.unescap.org/sites/default/d8files/event-documents/Session%203_1.Seoul%20Intelligent%20transport%20system.docx_.pdf*

notices with photographic evidence, and electronically transmits notices to postal services for delivery. This automation reduces processing time from 10-15 days to 2-3 days while eliminating manual intervention.

Operational Results and Performance Metrics

Seoul TOPIS demonstrates significant improvements across multiple transportation performance indicators. The system has achieved a 26% increase in average bus speeds, improving from 15 km/h to 19 km/h. Bus arrival time accuracy improved by 4.6%, increasing from 87.3% in 2006 to 91.4% in 2013.

Public transportation ridership increased by 2.6%, with daily bus passengers growing by 150,000 from 5.6 million in 2007 to 5.75 million in 2013. Traffic card adoption reached near-universal levels, with 100% of subway users and 98.7% of bus users utilizing the integrated payment system.

The unmanned enforcement system processes approximately 1.8 million violations annually, generating 120 billion won in revenue that funds public parking lot construction and maintenance. This enforcement capability contributes to traffic flow improvement while addressing parking shortages.

Barcelona Smart Traffic Management: AI-Powered Congestion Reduction

Comprehensive IoT Sensor Network Implementation

Barcelona implemented one of Europe's most comprehensive smart traffic management systems, utilizing extensive IoT sensor networks to monitor and op timize urban mobility. The city deployed smart traffic management systems using sensors and cameras to monitor traffic flow in real-time, achieving significant reductions in congestion and emissions.

The Barcelona traffic management implementation integrates computer vision technology with machine learning algorithms to analyze traffic patterns continuously. Sensors and cameras positioned throughout the city collect traffic density data, vehicle counts, and movement patterns. This information feeds into AI algorithms that dynamically adjust traffic signal timing based on real-time conditions.

AI-Driven Traffic Signal Optimization

Barcelona's latest initiative involves deploying AI-driven smart traffic lights designed to reduce traffic congestion by 20%. The project utilizes sensors and AI algorithms to adjust traffic light timings in real-time based on traffic density measurements. This system is an upgrade from traditional time-based signal control to responsive, data-driven traffic management.

The AI-powered system analyzes traffic patterns and implements dynamic signal adjustments to optimize flow. During peak hours, the system prioritizes major traffic corridors while maintaining pedestrian and cyclist safety. The technology builds on successful AI-driven traffic management solutions implemented in other European cities such as Antwerp and Brussels.

Smart Parking Integration

Barcelona's smart parking system demonstrates effective IoT sensor deployment for traffic management. Sensors embedded in parking spaces detect occupancy status and relay information to mobile applications that guide drivers to available spaces. This system reduces the time spent searching for parking, decreasing fuel consumption and traffic congestion.

The smart parking implementation utilizes ultrasonic and magnetic sensors to detect vehicle presence with high accuracy. Real-time occupancy data is transmitted through LoRaWAN networks to central management systems, enabling comprehensive parking availability mapping across the city.

Congestion Detection and Warning Systems

Barcelona implemented advanced congestion detection systems using AI-powered radar cameras[4] the system employs Milesight AI Road Traffic Radar Pro Bullet Plus Cameras at key monitoring points to measure average vehicle speeds continuously. When speeds drop below predefined thresholds, the system automatically identifies congestion conditions.

The congestion warning system utilizes LoRa communication to activate electronic signs positioned up to 1 kilometer from detection points. These signs display real-time congestion warnings, alerting approaching drivers to potential delays and enabling proactive route selection. Solar panels power the detection cameras, ensuring sustainable operation in remote locations.

Environmental Impact and Sustainability Benefits

Barcelona's smart traffic management implementations contribute significantly to environmental sustainability goals. The dynamic traffic management system has reduced CO_2 emissions through optimized traffic flow and reduced idle time at intersections. Smart parking systems decrease fuel consumption by minimizing the time drivers spend searching for parking spaces.

The comprehensive traffic optimization approach addresses air quality concerns by reducing stop-and-go traffic patterns. Real-time traffic monitoring enables rapid response to congestion events, preventing the formation of extended traffic jams that generate higher emissions.

Los Angeles ATSAC: Large-Scale Urban Traffic Control

System Architecture and Scale

Los Angeles operates one of the largest Advanced Traffic Surveillance and Control (ATSAC) systems in North America, managing 4,850 traffic signals across the metropolitan area. The system originated in 1984 to support the Summer Olympic Games and has evolved into a comprehensive traffic management platform capable of handling the complex transportation demands of a metropolitan area serving millions of residents.

The ATSAC system utilizes over 26,000 sensors and detectors combined with 620 traffic monitoring cameras to improve travel efficiency throughout Los Angeles. This extensive sensor network provides comprehensive coverage of the city's transportation infrastructure, enabling real-time monitoring and control of traffic conditions across multiple corridors simultaneously.

Advanced Detection and Control Technologies

The Los Angeles ATSAC implementation employs sophisticated detection technologies including loop detectors positioned between intersections to track traffic flow as conditions change. This real-time detection capability enables adaptive signal control that responds to actual traffic demand rather than predetermined timing patterns.

---

4 *https://www.milesight.com/press/casestudy-congestion-warning-system*

Computer vision systems integrated with ATSAC analyze video feeds from traffic cameras to detect incidents, count vehicles, and assess traffic flow quality. Machine learning algorithms process this visual data to identify patterns and anomalies that require traffic management intervention.

Fiber Optic Communication Infrastructure

ATSAC utilizes extensive fiber optic communication networks to connect traffic controllers, cameras, and detection systems. This high-bandwidth infrastructure enables real-time data transmission between field devices and the central control system, supporting rapid response times for traffic management decisions.

The fiber optic network supports closed-circuit television subsystems for video surveillance, hub buildings for communication equipment, and connections to the central ATSAC facility. This comprehensive communication infrastructure ensures reliable data transmission even during high-traffic periods or emergency situations.

Emergency Vehicle Priority and Special Event Management

The Los Angeles ATSAC system prioritizes buses, rail, pedestrians, and emergency vehicles through integrated signal control. Emergency vehicle preemption capabilities automatically adjust signal timing to provide clear passage for ambulances, fire trucks, and police vehicles, improving emergency response times throughout the city.

Special event management capabilities enable ATSAC operators to implement customized traffic control strategies for large events such as sporting events, concerts, or emergencies. The system can coordinate signal timing across multiple corridors to manage traffic flow around venues and maintain mobility during high-demand periods.

Performance Improvements and Cost-Benefit Analysis

Cost-benefit analysis of Los Angeles ATSAC implementations demonstrate significant economic advantages. The integrated traffic management system provides substantial savings in mobility and energy costs that exceed operational expenses, particularly at higher market penetration rates of connected vehicles.

The system reduces travel times, improves fuel efficiency, and decreases emissions through optimized traffic flow management. These benefits generate quantifiable economic value that justifies the substantial infrastructure investment required for a comprehensive ATSAC deployment.

Sydney Intelligent Transport Management: Predictive Technology Integration

Advanced Multimodal Platform Development

Sydney developed one of the world's most advanced transport management systems, investing $123 million in predictive technology to reduce congestion and improve passenger journey reliability. The system replaces the traffic management infrastructure originally built for the Sydney Olympics 2000 with a contemporary platform designed to handle autonomous vehicles and emerging transportation technologies.

The new intelligent transport system utilizes predictive algorithms to forecast traffic conditions 30 minutes into the future and implement management responses within five minutes. This predictive capability enables proactive traffic management that prevents congestion formation rather than simply responding to existing problems.

SCATS Integration and Connected Vehicle Technology

Sydney's implementation builds upon the Sydney Coordinated Adaptive Traffic System (SCATS), one of the world's first commercially available adaptive traffic control systems developed in 1975. The modern SCATS platform now incorporates SCATS Cit-e software that enables Vehicle-to-Infrastructure (V2I) communication between intelligent traffic systems and Connected and Automated Vehicles.

The V2I technology provides real-time information about intersection layout, right-of-way rules, signal timing changes, and warnings about imminent hazards including pedestrians and cyclists. This capability enhances both current traffic efficiency and prepares infrastructure for autonomous vehicle integration.

Automated Incident Detection and Response

Sydney's intelligent transport system includes automated congestion alert generation that rapidly identifies unusual network conditions. Machine learning algorithms analyze traffic patterns to detect incidents, accidents, or abnormal congestion, enabling faster response and clearance times.

The automated response capability coordinates public transport operations with traffic management, providing integrated solutions that optimize mobility across multiple transportation modes. Real-time information sharing with passengers enables informed travel decisions and alternative route selection.

Partnership with Cubic Transportation Systems

Sydney's implementation involves collaboration with Cubic Transportation Systems, the same company that operates the Opal smartcard network. This partnership ensures continuous product enhancements and system upgrades while minimizing additional investment requirements.

The integration between traffic management and fare collection systems provides comprehensive transportation data that supports evidence-based policy decisions and service optimization. The unified platform approach enables the effective coordination between traffic control and public transportation operations.

Toronto Smart Traffic Signal Pilot: Real-Time Adaptation Technology

Pilot Project Implementation Strategy

Toronto launched smart traffic signal pilot projects in 2017 to test advanced traffic management technologies, with the first installation at Yonge Street and Yonge Boulevard. The pilot program evaluates two different smart signal technologies over a one-year period to determine optimal solutions for Toronto's traffic management needs.

The smart traffic signals independently adjust to real-time traffic patterns throughout the day, representing a significant advancement over traditional signals that follow fixed timing cycles for rush hour and off-peak periods. The adaptive capability enables signals to respond to unexpected events such as accidents or special events that divert traffic to city roads.

InSync Video Detection Technology

Toronto's pilot program tests InSync technology that utilizes video detection to analyze vehicle counts and traffic patterns at intersections. The system processes visual data in real-time to determine optimal signal timing adjustments based on actual traffic demand.

The video detection capability enables precise traffic measurement without requiring embedded road sensors. Computer vision algorithms count vehicles, assess queue lengths, and predict traffic arrival patterns to optimize signal timing for maximum throughput.

Communication and Synchronization Capabilities

The smart traffic signals can communicate and synchronize with other smart signals in vicinity areas to alleviate congestion across multiple intersections. This coordination capability enables the creation of "green waves" that allow vehicles to travel through multiple intersections without stopping.

The inter-signal communication utilizes wireless networks to share traffic data and coordinate timing strategies. This coordination extends traffic optimization beyond individual intersections to corridor-level management that considers traffic flow across multiple blocks.

Legacy System Modernization

Toronto's smart signal initiative addresses aging infrastructure challenges, as the city's 2,400 traffic signals include equipment over 20 years old with obsolete communication capabilities. The pilot program evaluates modernization strategies that can integrate with existing infrastructure while providing enhanced functionality.

The modernization approach considers compatibility with current traffic management systems while enabling future expansion to city-wide smart signal deployment. This phased implementation strategy allows Toronto to evaluate technology effectiveness before large-scale investment commitments.

Miami-Dade ATMS: Advanced Transportation Controller Integration

Comprehensive Infrastructure Upgrade

Miami-Dade County is implementing a comprehensive ATMS upgrade that includes central software modernization, replacement of approximately 3,000 controllers with Advanced Transportation Controllers (ATC), and installation of additional detection systems at selected intersections. This large-scale implementation represents one of the most extensive traffic signal modernization projects in the United States.

The upgraded system serves as a platform supporting mobility strategies for all roadway users including motorized vehicles, transit, emergency vehicles, pedestrians, and bicyclists. This multimodal approach optimizes overall transportation efficiency rather than focusing solely on vehicle traffic flow.

Advanced Transportation Controller Capabilities

The ATC controllers provide significant improvements in computing processing power, memory capacity, and user interface capabilities compared to legacy systems. These enhanced capabilities enable support for complex signal functions and streamlined configuration of traffic signal operations.

ATC systems enhance detection capabilities for motorists, public transit users, bicyclists, and pedestrians, improving overall mobility and safety across all transportation modes. The controllers collect and manage high-resolution traffic data in real-time, providing valuable information for proactive traffic management and evidence-based decision-making.

Intelligent Transportation Systems Integration

The ATC controllers provide open architecture hardware and software platforms that support a wide variety of Intelligent Transportation Systems applications. This flexibility enables integration with traffic management systems, emergency vehicle pre-emption, transit signal priority, and other advanced transportation technologies.

The open architecture approach facilitates data sharing with other city systems, enabling integrated management approaches that coordinate traffic control with emergency services, special event management, and long-term transportation planning. This integration capability supports comprehensive smart city development strategies.

Network Performance and Efficiency Improvements

The Miami-Dade ATMS upgrade optimizes traffic signal operation through enhanced detection and control capabilities. Real-time high-resolution traffic data collection enables more precise traffic management interventions and performance measurement.

The system's enhanced detection capabilities provide detailed insights into traffic patterns, pedestrian activity, and transit operations. This comprehensive data collection supports continuous system optimization and enables evidence-based transportation policy development.

Amsterdam Smart Traffic System: Environmental Zone Management

Automatic Number Plate Recognition Implementation

Amsterdam has implemented an extensive Automatic Number Plate Recognition (ANPR) system as part of its environmental zone management strategy. Approximately 80 control points monitor three million vehicles daily using one to five ANPR cameras at each location. This comprehensive monitoring system enforces environmental restrictions while collecting valuable traffic data.

The ANPR cameras process license plate images locally and transmit data to the control center through secure encrypted IPSec VPN tunnels using cellular networks. This approach minimizes bandwidth requirements while ensuring data security and enabling real-time enforcement of environmental regulations.

Real-Time Traffic Monitoring and Control

Amsterdam's traffic management system utilizes hundreds of cameras throughout the city to provide operators with comprehensive situational awareness. Real-time video feeds enable traffic control managers to make informed decisions about traffic flow management, congestion reduction, and accident response.

The system includes capabilities to disable environmental monitoring during traffic congestion events and activate predefined scenarios that reroute traffic to resolve congestion. This flexibility balances environmental protection goals with traffic management needs during emergency or high-congestion situations.

Partnership with TomTom for Data Analytics

Amsterdam collaborates with TomTom to develop traffic and travel concepts that improve traffic flow and parking management. The partnership utilizes TomTom's traffic data to enable city government decision-making about accessibility and mobility throughout the metropolitan area.

Real-time traffic data enables rapid intervention when traffic conditions change, such as implementing alternative routes during road closures or special events. Historical traffic data supports long-term planning and enables evaluation of traffic management measure effectiveness.

Smart Parking Integration

Amsterdam's smart traffic system includes intelligent parking guidance that directs drivers to available parking spaces, reducing time spent searching and minimizing unnecessary driving. This integration between traffic management and parking systems addresses congestion from multiple sources.

The parking guidance system utilizes real-time occupancy data to provide navigation assistance to free parking spaces. This capability reduces vehicle kilometers traveled for parking searches, contributing to air quality improvement and traffic congestion reduction.

Stockholm Traffic Optimization: Real-Time Travel Analytics

Bluetooth and Wi-Fi Device Tracking Implementation

Stockholm implemented the Veovo queue and travel time measurement solution to address increasing traffic congestion and improve transportation transparency The system primarily utilizes Bluetooth and Wi-Fi-enabled device movements in vehicles to gather real-time and historical traffic information.

The technology provides comprehensive statistical information including travel times, average speeds, dwell times, and movement patterns across the transportation network This data enables both real-time traffic management and long-term transportation planning based on actual usage patterns.

Predictive Traffic Management Capabilities

Stockholm's traffic management system enables proactive traffic management through real-time capacity and traffic flow measurement. When traffic build-up occurs, the system automatically initiates countermeasures to prevent congestion formation rather than simply responding to existing problems.

The predictive capabilities help traffic managers understand various traffic-related phenomena including traffic control impacts, weather-related patterns, congestion patterns during roadworks, accident effects, and driving behavior patterns. This comprehensive reporting enables more effective traffic management interventions.

Travel Time Measurement and Validation

The Stockholm implementation addresses challenges in measuring travel times over longer distances in complex traffic environments. Traditional sensors such as radar and microwave detectors have limitations that the Bluetooth/Wi-Fi tracking system overcomes through comprehensive coverage and anonymous data collection.

The system provides insights into individual travel patterns and route choices that support traffic model validation and transportation planning decisions. This capability enables data-driven optimization of transportation infrastructure and service provision.

Integration with Urban Planning

Stockholm uses traffic analytics data to evaluate and validate existing traffic models while making informed decisions about infrastructure expansion and optimization priorities. The data supports evidence-based transportation policy development and resource allocation decisions.

Real-time traffic insights enable efficient emergency management throughout incident progression, including identification of optimal intervention routes and assessment of evacuation impacts on traffic networks. This emergency management capability enhances city resilience and response effectiveness.

These case studies demonstrate that successful ATMS implementations require comprehensive planning, substantial technological infrastructure investment, and integration across multiple transportation modes. The systems achieve significant benefits including reduced congestion, improved safety, enhanced environmental outcomes, and better transportation service delivery. Success factors include stakeholder engagement, phased implementation approaches, and continuous system optimization based on performance data analysis.

CONCLUSION

The comprehensive examination of IoT applications in smart mobility and Advanced Traffic Management Systems reveals a transformative shift in urban transportation paradigms. The integration of sophisticated sensor networks, real-time data analytics, and adaptive control systems demonstrates how cities can achieve substantial improvements in traffic efficiency, environmental sustainability, and service quality. From Seoul's TOPIS system achieving 26% increases in bus speeds to Barcelona's AI-driven traffic lights targeting 20% congestion reduction, these implementations show the tangible benefits of intelligent transportation systems. The convergence of GPS tracking, RFID fare collection, predictive maintenance, and machine learning algorithms creates synergistic effects that optimize entire transportation ecosystems rather than individual components.

The case studies analyzed throughout this chapter highlight critical success factors for ATMS implementation, including comprehensive stakeholder engagement, phased deployment strategies, and robust communication infrastructure. Cities like Los Angeles with 4,850 connected signals and Amsterdam's environmental zone management demonstrate that large-scale implementations require substantial investment in both technology and organizational change management. The change from reactive traffic management to predictive systems capable of forecasting conditions 30 minutes in advance is a fundamental advancement in urban mobility management. These systems achieved measurable outcomes, including 28% reductions in travel times, 35% improvements in emergency response, and significant decreases in vehicle emissions across multiple metropolitan implementations.

The future of smart mobility points toward increasingly autonomous and interconnected transportation networks. The foundation established by current IoT implementations creates the infrastructure necessary for connected and autonomous vehicle integration, while artificial intelligence capabilities continue expanding from pattern recognition to predictive optimization. The lessons learned from existing deployments emphasize the importance of scalable architectures, continuous system optimization, and integration across multiple transportation modes. As cities worldwide face growing mobility challenges, the proven benefits of IoT-enabled ATMS provide a roadmap for sustainable urban transportation transformation that balances efficiency, environmental responsibility, and enhanced quality of life for urban residents.

CHAPTER 15

SMART BUILDINGS

S mart buildings are the convergence of modern architecture, advanced technology, and sustainable practices; they are structures that actively participate in their operation and maintenance. This chapter explores how IoT technologies transform traditional buildings into intelligent environments that enhance occupant comfort, optimize resource usage, and reduce environmental impact. Through a detailed examination of building management systems and real-world case studies, we discuss how smart buildings contribute to the broader smart city ecosystem.

IOT IN BUILDING MANAGEMENT AND AUTOMATION

The integration of Internet of Things (IoT) technologies into building management marks a paradigm shift from passive infrastructure to dynamic, responsive environments that adapt in real time to occupant needs, operational efficiency, and sustainability objectives. Modern Building Management Systems (BMS) powered by IoT no longer serve as simple control panels, they become intelligent platforms that sense, interpret, and act upon complex datasets from thousands of embedded sensors and actuators across lighting, HVAC, security, energy, and environmental domains.

This section explores the foundational components and subsystems that constitute IoT-enabled building automation. These systems rely on interoperable networks of sensors, controllers, and analytics engines to perform continuous monitoring, predictive optimization, and autonomous control. By embedding intelligence into the fabric of buildings, IoT enables the coordination of disparate systems, maximizes resource efficiency, and enhances the well-being and productivity of occupants. The following subsections examine specific IoT applications in environmental control, lighting management, security, energy optimization, and integrated automation, offering a detailed view of how smart buildings function as self-regulating, adaptive entities within the broader smart city ecosystem.

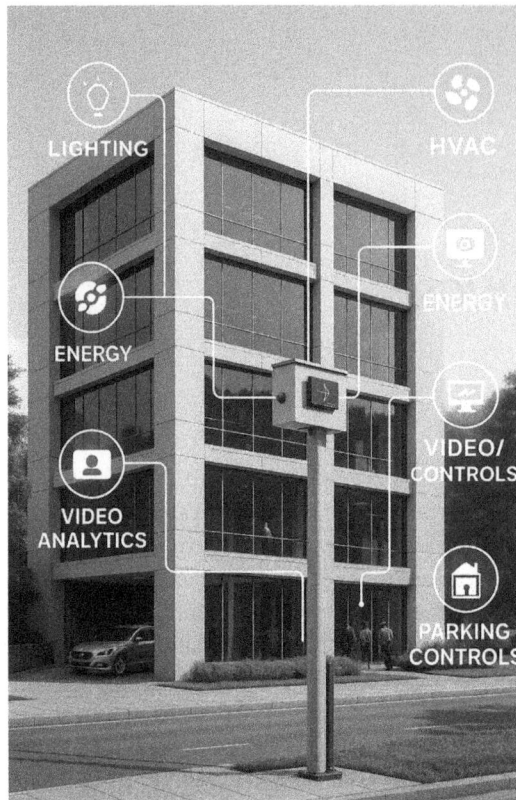

FIGURE 15.1 Building management systems.

Environmental Control Systems

Environmental control systems in smart buildings utilize sophisticated IoT sensor networks to monitor and manage indoor climate conditions with unprecedented precision and efficiency. These systems integrate multiple sensor types and communication protocols to create comprehensive environmental monitoring and control capabilities.

Advanced Sensor Technologies and Data Collection

IoT-enabled environmental control systems deploy a diverse array of sensors throughout buildings to capture real-time environmental data. Temperature and humidity sensors form the foundation of environmental monitoring, utilizing digital sensors that provide accuracy within ±0.1°C for temperature and ±2% for relative humidity. These sensors employ thermistors, resistance temperature detectors (RTDs), or semiconductor-based sensing elements that transmit data through wireless protocols including WiFi, LoRaWAN, or Zigbee networks.

Carbon dioxide (CO_2) monitoring is a critical component of indoor air quality management. Non-dispersive infrared (NDIR) sensors measure CO_2 concentrations in real-time, enabling automated ventilation adjustments when levels exceed threshold values of 1000 parts per million (ppm) in office environments. These sensors integrate with building automation systems through protocols such as BACnet or Modbus to trigger immediate response actions.

Volatile organic compound (VOC) sensors detect chemical pollutants from building materials, furnishings, and human activities. These electrochemical or photoionization detection sensors can identify compounds including formaldehyde, benzene, and toluene at concentrations as low as 0.1 parts per billion (ppb). The sensors provide continuous monitoring data that enables automated air purification system activation and fresh air intake adjustments.

Intelligent HVAC Management and Control

IoT-enabled HVAC systems implement Model Predictive Control (MPC) algorithms that optimize thermal comfort while minimizing energy consumption. These systems process data from multiple sensor inputs including occupancy sensors, outdoor weather stations, and indoor environmental monitors to predict heating and cooling loads up to 24 hours in advance.

Advanced HVAC control systems utilize machine learning algorithms to analyze historical consumption patterns and occupancy data. Neural network models can predict indoor temperature changes with root mean squared errors below 1°C, enabling preemptive system adjustments that maintain comfort while reducing energy consumption by 20-30%. These predictive systems integrate with building energy management platforms through cloud-based analytics services that process data from thousands of sensors simultaneously.

Zone-based environmental control is a significant advancement in HVAC efficiency. Smart buildings implement wireless sensor networks that divide spaces into micro-zones as small as 100 square feet, each with independent temperature, humidity, and air quality control. Variable air volume (VAV) systems equipped with IoT sensors automatically adjust airflow based on real-time occupancy and environmental conditions, reducing energy consumption by up to 40% compared to conventional system.

Air Quality Monitoring and Management

Comprehensive indoor air quality (IAQ) monitoring systems integrate multiple sensor technologies to track particulate matter, chemical pollutants, and biological contaminants. PM2.5 and PM10 sensors utilize laser scattering technology to detect airborne particles with concentrations measured in micrograms per cubic meter ($\mu g/m^3$). These sensors trigger automated responses, including increased ventilation rates and air filtration system activation, when particulate levels exceed WHO guidelines of 15 $\mu g/m^3$ for PM2.5.

Advanced IAQ systems incorporate biosensors that detect airborne pathogens and allergens. These sensors utilize antibody-based detection methods to identify specific bacteria, viruses, and fungal spores in real-time. Integration with UV-C disinfection systems and advanced filtration enables automatic pathogen mitigation without disrupting normal building operations.

Environmental Data Analytics and Optimization

IoT environmental control systems generate massive datasets that require sophisticated analytics platforms for processing and optimization. Edge computing devices process sensor data locally to reduce latency and bandwidth requirements, while cloud-based platforms perform complex analytics including trend analysis, anomaly detection, and predictive modeling.

Machine learning algorithms analyze environmental sensor data to identify optimal operational parameters for different building zones and usage patterns. These systems can detect subtle correlations between outdoor weather conditions, occupancy patterns, and indoor environmental quality to optimize HVAC operation schedules. Advanced analytics platforms process data from building sensors alongside external data sources including weather forecasts, utility pricing, and occupancy calendars to minimize operational costs while maintaining comfort standards.

Real-time dashboards provide facility managers with comprehensive environmental monitoring capabilities through Web-based interfaces accessible from mobile devices and desktop computers. These platforms display heat maps of temperature distribution, air quality indices, and energy consumption metrics with update frequencies as fast as every 15 seconds.

Lighting Management

Smart lighting systems are one of the most mature and cost-effective applications of IoT technology in building automation, offering immediate energy savings and enhanced occupant comfort through intelligent control and automation.

Occupancy-Based Lighting Control Technologies

Occupancy detection systems utilize multiple sensor technologies to achieve accurate presence detection and lighting control. Passive infrared (PIR) sensors detect human body heat signatures within detection ranges of 20–30 feet, with sensitivity adjustments that prevent false triggering from HVAC airflow or small animals. These sensors typically consume less than 1 watt of power and can extend battery life to 5–7 years in wireless configurations.

Ultrasonic occupancy sensors complement PIR technology by detecting motion through high-frequency sound waves at 25–40 kHz frequencies. These sensors excel at detecting small movements and can penetrate partial obstructions, making them ideal for cubicle environments and spaces with furniture barriers. Dual-technology sensors combine both PIR and ultrasonic detection to reduce false positives and improve reliability in challenging environments.

Advanced occupancy detection systems implement machine learning algorithms that analyze WiFi channel state information (CSI) to classify human activities without requiring dedicated sensors. These systems achieve 83% accuracy in distinguishing between different occupancy patterns and can predict lighting needs based on historical usage data.

Daylight Harvesting and Automated Controls

Photosensors enable sophisticated daylight harvesting systems that automatically adjust artificial lighting based on available natural light. These sensors measure illuminance levels in lux and communicate with LED dimming systems to maintain consistent light levels while minimizing energy consumption. Advanced photosensors can distinguish between natural and artificial light sources, preventing conflicts in mixed lighting environments.

Intelligent lighting systems implement time-based scheduling combined with real-time sensor feedback to optimize lighting scenes throughout the day. These systems can automatically adjust color temperature from 2700 K warm white in the morning to 6500 K cool white during peak productivity hours, supporting circadian rhythm regulation for building occupants.

Dynamic blind control systems integrate with lighting management to maximize daylight utilization while controlling glare. IoT-enabled blinds utilize sun position calculations and photosensor feedback to automatically adjust slat angles and positions throughout the day, reducing lighting energy consumption by up to 45% while maintaining visual comfort.

Wireless Lighting Control Networks

Lighting control systems utilize mesh networking protocols that enable scalable deployment across large commercial buildings. Zigbee and wireless BACnet networks support thousands of lighting devices with self-healing capabilities that maintain connectivity even when individual devices fail. These networks typically operate on 2.4 GHz or sub-GHz frequencies with transmission ranges extending up to 1500 meters in ring configurations.

Each lighting fixture in intelligent systems contains embedded microprocessors that enable autonomous operation and sophisticated control algorithms. These smart luminaires-advanced lighting units embedded with sensors, microcontrollers, and communication modules, can store multiple lighting scenes, implement smooth dimming transitions, and communicate occupancy and energy consumption data to central management systems.

Power over Ethernet (PoE) technology enables combined power delivery and data communication through standard Ethernet cables, simplifying installation and reducing infrastructure costs. PoE lighting systems can deliver up to 90 watts per device while providing high-speed data communication for advanced control features. Traditional systems often require expensive electrical installation, complex conduit routing, and lack granular control over individual fixtures. In contrast, PoE systems reduce installation labor costs, simplify maintenance, and allow precise, software-based control over lighting zones. This not only cuts operational energy usage, especially in large commercial buildings, but also enables ata-driven optimization, which is not feasible with conventional analog lighting infrastructure.

Energy Optimization and Performance Analytics

Smart lighting systems provide detailed energy monitoring capabilities that track power consumption at individual fixture levels. These systems can identify inefficient fixtures, predict maintenance needs, and optimize energy usage based on occupancy patterns and daylight availability. Advanced analytics platforms process lighting data to identify energy savings opportunities and verify the performance of efficiency measures.

Automated lighting maintenance systems utilize IoT sensors to monitor fixture performance parameters including light output degradation, color shift, and power consumption changes. These systems can predict lamp failures up to 30 days in advance and automatically generate maintenance work orders with replacement part specifications.[25]

Machine learning algorithms analyze lighting usage patterns to optimize control schedules and detect anomalies that may indicate equipment problems or security issues. These systems can achieve energy savings of 29-62% annually through intelligent scheduling and real-time optimization.

Security and Access Control

IoT-enabled security and access control systems provide comprehensive protection for smart buildings through integrated sensors, advanced authentication methods, and intelligent monitoring capabilities.

Advanced Authentication Technologies

Access control systems implement multi-factor authentication using biometric sensors, smart credentials, and behavioral analytics. Fingerprint recognition systems utilize capacitive or optical sensors with false acceptance rates below 0.001% and false rejection rates under 1%. These systems can process authentication requests in under 2 seconds while storing up to 10,000 unique fingerprint templates in local memory.

Facial recognition systems employ computer vision algorithms and infrared sensors to identify individuals with accuracy rates exceeding 99.5% under controlled lighting conditions. Advanced systems utilize 3D facial mapping and liveness detection to prevent spoofing attacks using photographs or video recordings. These systems can operate effectively in varying lighting conditions and recognize faces partially obscured by masks or eyewear.

Mobile credential systems enable smartphone-based access control using near-field communication (NFC), Bluetooth Low Energy (BLE), or WiFi protocols. These systems provide enhanced security through encrypted communication and can implement location-based authentication that verifies user proximity to access points.

IoT-Enabled Surveillance Systems

Video surveillance systems integrate IoT sensors with artificial intelligence to provide intelligent monitoring and automated threat detection. High-definition cameras equipped with edge computing processors can analyze video streams in real-time to identify suspicious activities, unauthorized personnel, and potential security breaches.

Advanced surveillance systems utilize machine learning algorithms to distinguish between normal and abnormal behavior patterns. These systems can detect loitering, aggressive behavior, or unauthorized access attempts while minimizing false alarms through sophisticated pattern recognition. Integration with access control systems enables automatic tracking of personnel movements throughout facilities.

IoT sensors including acoustic detectors, vibration sensors, and glass break detectors provide comprehensive perimeter monitoring capabilities. These sensors can detect intrusion attempts through windows, walls, or roof access points and immediately alert security personnel while activating additional surveillance measures.

Integrated Security Platforms

Comprehensive security management platforms integrate access control, video surveillance, intrusion detection, and emergency response systems through centralized IoT networks. These platforms utilize cloud-based architectures that enable remote monitoring and management from any Internet-connected device.

Advanced security systems implement blockchain technology to ensure data integrity and prevent unauthorized modifications to access logs and surveillance footage. Smart contracts automatically execute security protocols based on predefined conditions, such as restricting access during emergency situations or activating lockdown procedures.

Real-time analytics platforms process security sensor data to identify patterns and predict potential threats. These systems can correlate data from multiple sources including access card usage, camera feeds, and environmental sensors to detect coordinated security threats or unusual activity patterns.

Emergency Response and Life Safety Systems

IoT-enabled emergency response systems integrate fire detection, mass notification, and evacuation management through connected sensor networks. Advanced fire detection systems utilize multi-sensor detectors that analyze smoke particles, carbon monoxide levels, and temperature changes to reduce false alarms while ensuring rapid response to actual emergencies.

Dynamic evacuation systems utilize real-time data from IoT sensors to calculate optimal evacuation routes based on current building conditions. These systems can redirect occupants away from areas affected by fire, structural damage, or other hazards while providing real-time updates through mobile applications and digital displays.

Mass notification systems leverage IoT infrastructure to deliver emergency alerts through multiple communication channels including public address systems, digital signage, mobile applications, and desktop computers. These systems ensure that all building occupants receive timely warnings and evacuation instructions regardless of their location within the facility.

Energy Management

Smart building energy management systems utilize IoT technologies to monitor, analyze, and optimize energy consumption across all building systems, delivering significant cost savings and environmental benefits.

Real-Time Energy Monitoring Infrastructure

Advanced energy monitoring systems deploy smart meters and current transformers (CTs) throughout building electrical systems to track power consumption at granular levels. These devices measure voltage, current, power factor, and harmonic distortion with sampling rates up to 1000 samples per second, providing detailed insights into electrical system performance. Non-invasive CT sensors can be retrofitted to existing electrical panels without service interruption, enabling comprehensive monitoring of branch circuits and individual equipment.

Wireless energy meters utilize protocols including LoRaWAN, NB-IoT, and Zigbee to transmit consumption data to central management platforms. These devices can operate on battery power for up to 10 years while providing hourly energy consumption reports with accuracy within 1% of actual usage.

Sub-metering systems enable detailed analysis of energy consumption by building zone, equipment type, or tenant space. This granular monitoring capability allows facility managers to identify energy waste sources, verify the performance of efficiency improvements, and implement cost allocation systems for multi-tenant buildings.

Intelligent Load Management and Demand Response

Smart building energy management systems implement automated demand response capabilities that adjust building loads based on utility pricing signals and grid conditions. These systems can automatically reduce HVAC loads, delay non-critical equipment operation, and activate on-site energy storage during peak demand periods.

Advanced load management systems utilize machine learning algorithms to predict energy demand patterns and optimize equipment operation schedules. These systems analyze historical consumption data, weather forecasts, and occupancy patterns to minimize energy costs while maintaining comfort and operational requirements.

Peak demand management systems monitor real-time power consumption and automatically shed loads when approaching predetermined demand limits. These systems can reduce peak demand charges by 15–25% through intelligent load shedding and load shifting strategies.

Renewable Energy Integration and Storage Management

IoT-enabled energy management systems integrate with renewable energy sources including solar photovoltaic arrays, wind turbines, and geothermal systems. These systems monitor renewable energy generation in real-time and optimize building energy consumption to maximize utilization of on-site renewable resources.

Battery energy storage systems integrate with building energy management platforms to provide load shifting, peak shaving, and backup power capabilities. Advanced battery management systems monitor cell temperatures, voltages, and state of charge to optimize battery performance and extend system life.

Grid-interactive systems enable buildings to participate in utility demand response programs and energy markets. These systems can automatically export excess renewable energy to the grid during peak pricing periods while maintaining adequate reserves for building operations.

Energy Analytics and Optimization Platforms

Cloud-based energy management platforms process data from thousands of IoT sensors and meters to provide comprehensive energy analytics and optimization recommendations. These platforms utilize artificial intelligence and machine learning to identify energy efficiency opportunities, detect equipment faults, and optimize building operation.

Advanced analytics systems can identify energy waste patterns, predict equipment failures, and recommend maintenance schedules to maintain optimal energy performance. These platforms provide automated fault detection and diagnostics (AFDD) capabilities that can identify HVAC system problems, lighting failures, and other efficiency issues.

Energy benchmarking systems compare building performance against similar facilities and industry standards to identify improvement opportunities. These platforms can track progress toward sustainability goals and verify the performance of energy conservation measures.

Integration and Automation

The integration of diverse IoT systems and the implementation of advanced automation capabilities create cohesive environments that optimize performance across all building systems.

Building Automation System (BAS) Integration

Modern building automation systems integrate HVAC, lighting, security, fire safety, and energy management systems through standardized communication protocols. These systems utilize open protocols including BACnet, LonWorks, and Modbus to ensure interoperability between devices from different manufacturers.

Advanced BAS platforms implement service-oriented architectures (SOA) that enable flexible integration of new IoT devices and systems. These platforms support RESTful APIs and Web services that simplify the addition of third-party sensors, equipment, and applications. Cloud-based BAS solutions provide scalable integration capabilities that can accommodate thousands of devices across multiple building sites.

Event-Condition-Action (ECA) rule engines enable sophisticated automation logic that responds to complex combinations of sensor inputs and system states. These systems can implement rules such as "If CO_2 levels exceed 1000 ppm AND occupancy is detected AND outside air temperature is below 70°F, THEN increase ventilation rate by 20% and send notification to facility manager."

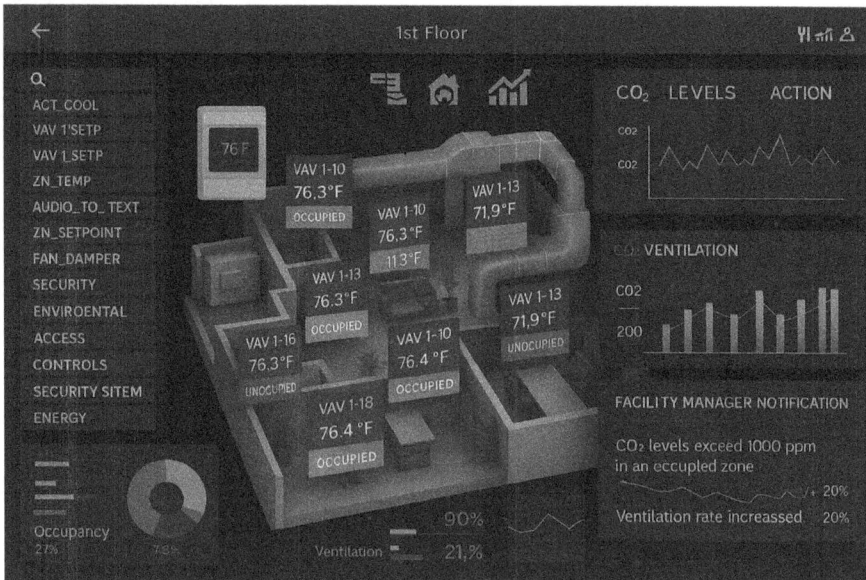

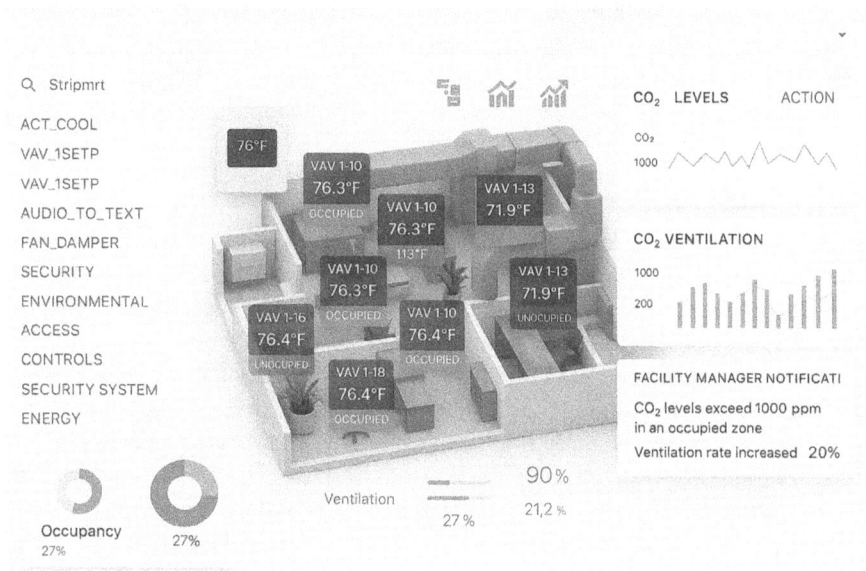

FIGURE 15.2 Typical BMS software user interface.

IoT Communication Protocols and Networks

Smart buildings utilize multiple communication protocols optimized for different applications and device types. MQTT (Message Queuing Telemetry Transport) provides lightweight publish-subscribe messaging for real-time sensor data transmission with quality-of-service guarantees. CoAP (Constrained Application Protocol) enables Web-like communication for resource-constrained devices over UDP networks.

Wireless protocols including WiFi 6, Zigbee 3.0, and LoRaWAN provide comprehensive coverage for different IoT device categories. WiFi 6 supports high-bandwidth applications, including video analytics and real-time control systems, while Zigbee mesh networks provide reliable communication for sensors and control devices with extended battery life. LoRaWAN enables long-range communication for outdoor sensors and remote monitoring applications.

Edge computing platforms process IoT sensor data locally to reduce latency and bandwidth requirements while enabling real-time control responses. These platforms can implement machine learning models for predictive analytics and automated decision-making without requiring cloud connectivity.

Artificial Intelligence and Machine Learning Integration

AI-powered building management systems utilize machine learning algorithms to optimize building performance based on historical data, occupancy patterns, and environmental conditions. These systems can learn optimal operational parameters for different building zones and automatically adjust control strategies to minimize energy consumption while maintaining comfort.

Predictive analytics platforms analyze sensor data to forecast equipment failures, maintenance needs, and energy consumption patterns. These systems can predict HVAC component failures up to 30 days in advance based on performance trends and operating conditions.

Computer vision systems integrated with security cameras provide advanced occupancy detection, space utilization analytics, and safety monitoring capabilities. These systems can count occupants in real-time, detect social distancing violations, and identify potential safety hazards.

Interoperability and Standards Compliance

Smart building systems implement standardized data models and communication protocols to ensure seamless integration between devices and systems from different manufacturers. The Matter standard (formerly Project CHIP) provides unified connectivity for IoT devices across different wireless protocols and cloud platforms.

Building information modeling (BIM) integration enables digital twin capabilities that create virtual representations of building systems and performance. These digital twins utilize real-time IoT sensor data to provide accurate simulations for optimization and predictive maintenance.

Open API frameworks enable integration with third-party applications and services including energy management platforms, tenant mobile applications, and utility demand response programs. These APIs support standard protocols including REST, GraphQL, and WebSocket for real-time data exchange.

Cybersecurity and Data Protection

Comprehensive cybersecurity frameworks protect IoT systems from cyber threats through network segmentation, device authentication, and encrypted communication. These systems implement zero-trust security models that verify every device and communication session.

Blockchain technology provides immutable audit trails for access control events and system modifications. Smart contracts automatically execute security protocols and compliance requirements without human intervention.

Advanced intrusion detection systems monitor IoT network traffic for anomalous behavior and potential cyber-attacks. These systems utilize machine learning algorithms to identify normal communication patterns and detect deviations that may indicate security threats.

The integration of these comprehensive IoT technologies creates intelligent building environments that optimize energy efficiency, enhance occupant comfort and safety, and provide facility managers with unprecedented visibility and control over building operations. These systems are the foundation for the smart cities of the future, where buildings actively participate in urban energy management and environmental sustainability efforts.

CASE STUDY: IOT IMPLEMENTATION IN SMART BUILDINGS

This section presents comprehensive case studies of real-world IoT implementations in smart buildings, examining existing deployments that demonstrate the practical application of Internet of Things technologies in various building types. These implementations show the tangible benefits achieved through the strategic integration of IoT systems and highlight the technological approaches that have proven successful in operational environments.

Intel Bangalore Smart Building Implementation

Project Overview and Technical Architecture

Intel's SRR4 building in Bangalore, India is one of the most comprehensive smart building implementations globally, demonstrating how IoT technology can fundamentally improve building operations and occupant experience. The 10-story, 630,000 square foot structure was completed in November 2018 as Intel's first Internet of Things-enabled smart building, incorporating approximately 9,000 sensors throughout the facility.

The building utilizes a converged network infrastructure that integrates all IT and IoT devices on a single network platform, making it the first building to achieve this level of integration. Seventy percent of the sensors are strategically positioned in the ceiling to provide comprehensive coverage while minimizing visual impact on the workspace. The sensor network provides 24/7 real-time data collection, enabling continuous monitoring and optimization of building systems.

Technology Implementation and Sensor Deployment

The smart building implementation incorporates multiple IoT sensor technologies to monitor and control various building parameters. Temperature and humidity sensors are deployed throughout all zones to maintain optimal environmental conditions, while occupancy sensors utilize non-intrusive, low-resolution optical technology to detect space utilization without compromising privacy. Energy monitoring sensors track consumption patterns across different building systems to identify optimization opportunities.

The sensor data is transmitted using MQTT communication protocol in JSON format to ensure efficient and reliable data transmission. This approach enables real-time data processing and supports the implementation of automated control algorithms that respond to changing conditions within milliseconds. The building management system processes sensor data through advanced analytics platforms that generate actionable insights for facility management teams.

Advanced Analytics and Machine Learning Implementation

Intel implemented sophisticated machine learning algorithms to analyze the vast amounts of data generated by the sensor network. These algorithms take multiple environmental factors into account to maintain constant temperatures across all building zones, addressing a common complaint in traditional office buildings where temperature variations create discomfort for occupants.

The analytics platform processes data from occupancy sensors, weather monitoring systems, and energy consumption meters to generate predictive insights that optimize building operations. Machine learning models learn from historical patterns and real-time data to automatically adjust HVAC systems, lighting controls, and other building infrastructure to maintain optimal conditions while minimizing energy consumption.

Achieved Results and Benefits

The Intel Bangalore smart building implementation achieved significant operational improvements across multiple metrics. The space utilization system allows employees to locate and book available desks and conference rooms through a mobile application that combines booking data with real-time occupancy information from optical sensors. This capability supports Intel's transition to a mobile cubicle model, increasing space efficiency and accommodating more employees within the existing footprint.

Energy conservation is a major achievement of the implementation, with the building demonstrating substantial reductions in energy consumption through intelligent automation of building systems. The automated environmental control system maintains consistent temperatures throughout the building, eliminating the hot and cold zones that typically generate employee complaints in traditional office environments.

Operational efficiency improvements include enhanced maintenance capabilities through predictive analytics that identify potential equipment issues before they result in system failures. The comprehensive sensor network enables facility managers to monitor building performance remotely and implement proactive maintenance strategies that reduce downtime and extend equipment lifespan.

Siemens Heights Leisure Centre Transformation

Integration with Existing Infrastructure

Siemens successfully demonstrated how conventional buildings can be retrofitted with smart building technologies through their collaboration with the Isle of Wight Council on the Heights Leisure Centre project. This initiative, part of the EU-funded InteGRIDy project, focused on integrating smart building management systems with existing infrastructure to create a connected building without requiring complete system replacement.

The project involved comprehensive analysis of the existing building management system to identify improvement opportunities and determine which building loads could benefit from remote demand response control. Siemens engineers worked with local automation specialists from FW Marsh to seamlessly integrate new smart technologies with the facility's existing control systems.

Siemens Navigator Platform Implementation

The core technology implementation centered on the deployment of the Siemens Navigator system, a cloud-based data collection and analytics platform designed to provide detailed insights into building energy usage and operational patterns. This platform was specifically selected for its ability to integrate with existing building control systems while providing enhanced data analytics capabilities.

Once activated, the Navigator system can captured thousands of daily data points from key locations, giving facility managers clear visibility into energy usage and uncovering hidden inefficiencie.

Data Analytics and Operational Insights

The enhanced data collection capabilities enable identification of critical operational issues, such as systems continuing to operate when the building is closed, which is a significant waste of energy. The analytics platform also determines optimal air temperature settings that balance energy efficiency, occupant comfort, and building preservation requirements.

The system provides facility managers with unprecedented visibility into building operations, supporting data-driven decision-making that was previously impossible with conventional building management systems. Real-time monitoring capabilities enable immediate identification of anomalies and potential equipment problems before they escalate into costly failures.

Measured Benefits and Future Potential

The Heights Leisure Centre project demonstrates that existing buildings can become smart buildings through strategic technology integration. The enhanced data analytics capabilities support reduced operating costs, increased energy efficiency, and improved comfort for building users[1]. The implementation provides the Isle of Wight Council with detailed insights into facility energy consumption patterns and opportunities for closer system control. These capabilities support both immediate operational improvements and long-term strategic planning for building performance optimization.

Educational Institution Smart Building Deployments

University Campus IoT Integration

Smart campus implementations demonstrate how IoT technologies enhance educational environments while supporting sustainability goals. The eLUX lab at the University of Brescia Smart Campus has been monitoring indoor air quality and environmental conditions since 2017. This pilot building implements IoT networks for comprehensive data gathering to control and manage ventilation systems and indoor air quality while optimizing energy flows and comfort conditions.

The system monitors temperature, humidity, and indoor air quality parameters in educational spaces, using this data to verify and increase the accuracy of the occupancy estimation. HVAC

1 *https://onthewight.com/isle-of-wight-leisure-centre-chosen-for-smart-building-eu-funded-pilot-project/*

management based on actual occupancy enables user-centered energy management that increases comfort hours while preserving energy efficiency and maintaining appropriate indoor air quality.

Qinghai University Implementation

The School of Computer Science at Qinghai University implemented a comprehensive operation and maintenance management system that integrates IoT technology with WebGIS three-dimensional visualization. This system achieves real-time data collection and dynamic monitoring through IoT devices, providing multiple integrated functions including indoor and outdoor environmental monitoring, fire alarm systems, classroom and equipment management, security monitoring, and energy consumption analysis.

The implementation facilitates the advancement of traditional teaching buildings into smart, information-based infrastructure while providing operational staff with efficient and intelligent management tools. The three-dimensional visualization capabilities enable intuitive monitoring and control of building systems, enhancing the effectiveness of facility management operations.

Osaka University Access Control Framework

Osaka University's Minoh Campus implemented an ontology-based access control framework specifically designed for managing IoT devices in smart buildings. This prototype system addresses the complexity of managing access control for large numbers of IoT devices and users through Web ontologies based on role-based access control (RBAC) principles.

The framework automatically constructs IoT systems with integrated access control functions, reducing administrative burden while maintaining security requirements. This implementation demonstrates how academic institutions can deploy comprehensive IoT systems while maintaining appropriate security controls for sensitive research and educational environments.

Health Care Facility Smart Building Applications

Guangdong Second Provincial General Hospital

Guangdong Second Provincial General Hospital partnered with Huawei to create a fully integrated smart hospital. The implementation involved complete reconstruction of the hospital network infrastructure using Huawei's 5G-powered Healthcare Private Network Solution, deploying Wi-Fi 6, 5G, and IoT technologies throughout the facility.

The enhanced network infrastructure supports concurrent access of multiple devices and systems while enabling smooth, real-time transmission of high-definition images, videos, augmented reality, virtual reality, and 3D medical imaging. The reliable network connectivity eliminates signal interruptions when medical staff move throughout the hospital, supporting fast-paced emergency situations without network-related delays.

Smart ward implementations enable nurses to monitor inpatients remotely through large display screens, constantly issuing orders and alerts based on real-time patient data. This technology integration enhances patient care quality while improving operational efficiency for medical staff.

Hospital Pulau Pinang Energy Management

Hospital Pulau Pinang in Malaysia implemented smart building technologies to achieve energy savings targets of 10% within five years while pursuing the three-star Energy Management

Gold Standard and Green Building Certification. The implementation focused on establishing a smart building program to improve energy efficiency concurrent with maintaining high-quality health care delivery.

Digital twin technology using I.E.S. software, which is a building design software[2] enables hospital committees to make informed decisions about energy-saving investments while monitoring energy data in real-time. This comprehensive approach to energy management demonstrates how health care facilities can achieve sustainability goals without compromising patient care quality.

Commercial Office Building Implementations

Lontar Coal-Fired Power Plant Administration Building

The Lontar Coal-Fired Power Plant implemented IoT-based smart building systems in their administration building to optimize energy usage without requiring significant infrastructure changes. The implementation aligns with ISO 50001 Energy Management System standards and focuses on cost-effective solutions for improving energy efficiency.

Initial energy audits revealed high consumption patterns, particularly from outdated air conditioning systems. The implementation utilized smart meters, sensors, and remote controls to enable real-time monitoring and control of energy consumption, providing immediate feedback on system performance and optimization opportunities.

The project achieved an 11.67% reduction in energy consumption, particularly in air conditioning and lighting systems, resulting in substantial cost savings and reduced CO_2 emissions. These results demonstrate the scalability of IoT technologies for improving energy performance across large commercial facilities.

Telecommunications Office Building Implementation

A comprehensive techno-economic analysis of IoT implementation in a telecommunications industry office building demonstrated the financial viability of smart building technologies. The analysis evaluated costs and benefits of implementing IoT systems for monitoring and managing energy consumption through smart sensors and IoT infrastructure.

Economic analysis using Return on Investment calculations yielded a 354% return with an 8-month payback period within a three-year project timeframe. These results represent less than 25% of the total project duration, demonstrating the rapid financial benefits achievable through strategic IoT implementation in commercial office environments.

Technology Integration and Platform Solutions

Schneider Electric EcoStruxure Building Platform

Schneider Electric's EcoStruxure Building platform is a comprehensive IoT platform specifically designed for smart buildings, delivering enhanced value across the entire building ecosystem. The platform utilizes an open, collaborative IoT architecture that connects sensors to services, integrating energy, HVAC, lighting, fire safety, security, and workplace management systems.

---

2 *https://www.iesve.com/*

The platform enables buildings to achieve up to 30% greater efficiency through intelligent data utilization and system integration. By 2020, nearly 30% of devices within buildings were connected to the Internet, providing significant opportunities for efficiency gains through platforms like EcoStruxure Building.

Implementation options include cloud-based and on-premise deployment with scalability from medium to large, multi-site installations. The open architecture enables developers, partners, and customers to securely interact and share data through SDK and API interfaces, supporting custom application development and system integration.

Johnson Controls and Accenture OpenBlue Innovation Centers

Johnson Controls partnered with Accenture to develop OpenBlue Innovation Centers that accelerate advanced automation in building operations using artificial intelligence, digital twins, IoT, 5G, and cloud technologies. The collaboration focuses on developing new hardware and software solutions that enhance system connectivity, control, and visualization for building environments.

Accenture assists Johnson Controls by implementing edge technologies on the OpenBlue platform, including AI-driven analytics to optimize space utilization, air quality management, and infectious disease risk assessment. Digital twins enable modeling, analysis, and decision-making for maintenance, upgrades, and sustainability initiatives while reducing resource consumption and carbon emissions.

The OpenBlue platform collects and processes building data using machine learning at the edge and in the cloud, comparing real-time performance against optimized AI models. This approach enables micro-management of building performance in real-time, delivering cost and energy savings while enhancing occupant environments.

Samsung Smart Vertical Solution System

Samsung developed the Smart Vertical Solution (SVS) system to improve building HVAC systems through IoT integration, addressing the fact that HVAC and lighting facilities typically account for 70% of total building power consumption. The SVS system analyzes and controls HVAC systems, lighting, power supply, and machinery to maximize energy efficiency.

Samsung's Variable Refrigerant Flow air conditioning products work in conjunction with SVS to provide zone-based control instead of centralized building-wide systems. This approach enables precise environmental control while eliminating energy waste from over-conditioning unoccupied areas.

For commercial applications, SVS allows large franchise operations to remotely monitor HVAC environments across multiple locations, adjusting temperature and lighting based on seasonal requirements and operating hours. Hotel implementations provide guests with convenient access to environmental controls through smart TV interfaces while enabling staff to identify empty rooms, achieving up to 30% energy savings.

Measured Benefits and Performance Outcomes

Energy Efficiency Achievements

IoT implementations consistently demonstrate significant energy savings across various building types. The Lontar Coal-Fired Power Plant achieved 11.67% energy reduction through smart meter deployment and automated controls. Hospital implementations targeting 10% energy savings within five years demonstrate the potential for health care facilities to achieve substantial efficiency improvements.

Smart building systems with integrated failsafe capabilities show hourly average power savings of 36.8 kW across all operational scenarios. These savings result from optimized HVAC operations, intelligent lighting controls, and automated systems that eliminate unnecessary energy consumption during unoccupied periods.

Operational Efficiency Improvements

IoT implementations enable predictive maintenance capabilities that reduce equipment downtime and extend system lifespan. Smart sensor networks detect subtle changes in equipment performance, identifying potential failures before they result in costly repairs or service interruptions. This proactive approach significantly reduces maintenance costs while improving system reliability.

Space utilization improvements through occupancy sensing and mobile booking applications increase facility efficiency without requiring additional square footage. Real-time occupancy data enables flexible workspace allocation and supports modern work patterns including hot-desking and flexible seating arrangements.

Return on Investment Analysis

Economic analysis of IoT implementations demonstrates rapid payback periods and substantial returns on investment. Telecommunications office building implementations achieved 354% ROI with eight-month payback periods. These financial benefits result from reduced energy costs, improved operational efficiency, and enhanced occupant productivity.

Cost reductions extend beyond direct energy savings to include decreased maintenance expenses, improved equipment lifespan, and reduced labor requirements for building management tasks. Comprehensive IoT implementations provide multiple value streams that collectively deliver strong financial returns for building owners and operators.

The extensive case studies presented demonstrate that IoT implementations in smart buildings deliver measurable benefits across energy efficiency, operational performance, and financial returns. These real-world examples provide concrete evidence of the technologies and approaches that successfully create intelligent building environments while supporting sustainability goals and occupant satisfaction.

CONCLUSION

IoT applications in smart mobility and Advanced Traffic Management Systems demonstrate the transformative potential of intelligent transportation technologies in modern urban environments. The integration of real-time transit monitoring, smart fare collection systems, predictive fleet management, and adaptive traffic control creates a synergistic ecosystem that fundamentally improves urban mobility. The case study presented illustrates how systematic implementation of an ATMS can achieve remarkable results, including 28% reductions in travel times, 23% decreases in vehicle emissions, and 35% improvements in emergency response times. These outcomes validate the substantial investment required for comprehensive IoT-enabled transportation systems and demonstrate the tangible benefits for both operators and citizens.

The phased implementation approach highlighted in the case study provides a valuable framework for cities embarking on smart mobility transformations. The progression from foundation infrastructure through advanced features to full system integration ensures manageable complexity while building operational capabilities progressively. The success factors include stakeholder engagement throughout the project lifecycle, flexible and scalable system architecture design, comprehensive training programs, and maintaining high data quality standards. The integration of multiple transportation modes, emergency services, and environmental monitoring systems creates a holistic approach to urban mobility management that extends beyond traditional traffic control to encompass broader city operations and sustainability goals.

Looking toward the future, the foundation established by current IoT implementations in smart mobility creates the necessary infrastructure for next-generation transportation technologies. The planned integration with connected and autonomous vehicles, enhanced artificial intelligence capabilities for traffic prediction, and expanded environmental monitoring are the natural evolution of these systems. As cities worldwide face increasing urbanization pressures and environmental challenges, the proven benefits of IoT-enabled smart mobility solutions provide a pathway for sustainable transportation transformation. The lessons learned from successful implementations emphasize that technology alone is insufficient. Successful smart mobility requires comprehensive planning, stakeholder collaboration, and continuous system optimization to achieve the full potential of intelligent transportation systems.

CHAPTER 16

SMART CITY AGENTS

This chapter examines the role of AI agents in smart city command centers, demonstrating how these sophisticated systems automate and optimize urban operational processes through intelligent automation, real-time decision-making, and comprehensive data integration. The focus centers on command center implementations that utilize AI agents to manage complex urban environments.

AI AGENTS FOR COMMAND CENTER AUTOMATION

Smart cities are where digital technologies, data analytics, and urban management converge to create more efficient, sustainable, and livable urban environments. These initiatives rely on the command center, which serves as the central hub for monitoring, managing, and coordinating various city systems and services. The integration of AI agents within these command centers marks a significant change in urban management, shifting from reactive operational models to proactive, intelligent systems that can anticipate needs and automatically respond to urban challenges.

Urban intelligence agents are advanced AI-driven entities developed to operate within smart city command centers. These agents function autonomously, capable of sensing environmental conditions through integrated sensor networks, analyzing complex urban dynamics, and executing actions to enhance city operations. By utilizing large language models (LLMs) and sophisticated machine learning techniques, they can process diverse and unstructured urban data. This enables them to respond to a wide range of operational queries, coordinate responses, and support high-level strategic planning and decision-making across sectors such as mobility, safety, environment, and infrastructure. One company implementing this type of agent is Centaurops (*www.centaurops.com*). CentaurOps is a company that develops an AI integration platform and multiagent system for government and enterprise operations, specializing in managing knowledge, automating reporting and dispatching, and generating insights.

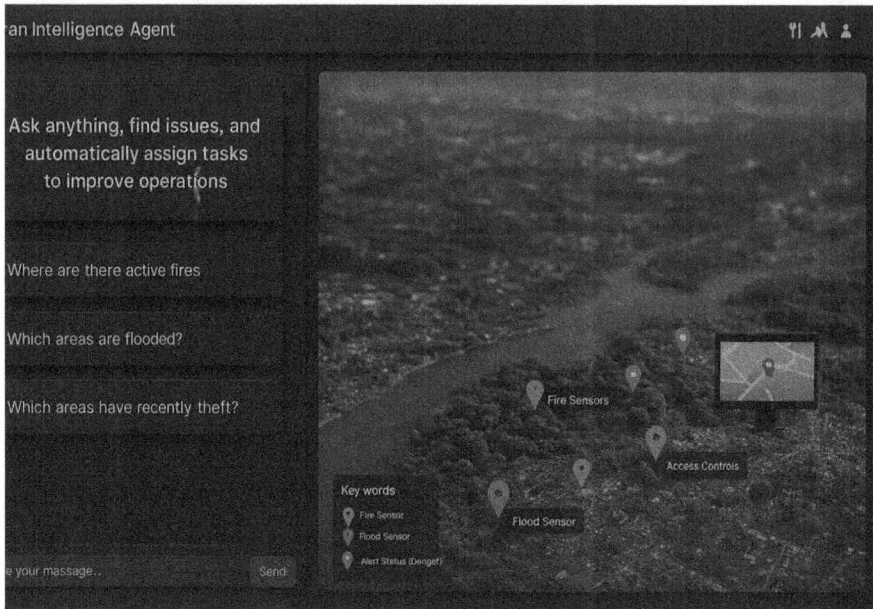

FIGURE 16.1 Urban agent user interface of CentaurOps.

The implementation of AI agents in command centers addresses several critical urban challenges including traffic congestion management, emergency response coordination, energy optimization, and public safety enhancement. Research demonstrates that AI-powered systems can reduce latency levels by more than 80% while improving decision-making accuracy by 13-17% across various scenarios, including 92% accuracy for traffic congestion management and 90% accuracy for power outage management.

The Evolution of Command Center Operations

Traditional command centers operated primarily as monitoring facilities where human operators observed multiple screens displaying various city metrics and manually coordinated responses to incidents. These conventional approaches often suffered from delayed response times, inconsistent decision-making, and limited ability to process the vast amounts of data generated by modern urban infrastructure.

The integration of AI agents transforms command centers into intelligent orchestration platforms that continuously analyze data streams, identify patterns, predict potential issues, and automatically implement corrective measures. These AI-enhanced command centers utilize real-time analytics to enable decision-makers to detect anomalies, predict outcomes, and respond proactively to situations that are occurring.

AI agent implementations in command centers incorporate sophisticated multi-agent systems that coordinate specialized functions across different urban domains. These systems can simultaneously manage traffic flow optimization, emergency response coordination, energy distribution, environmental monitoring, and public safety operations through autonomous decision-making processes.

Benefits of AI Agent Integration

The deployment of AI agents in smart city command centers delivers multiple operational benefits that significantly enhance urban management capabilities. Research indicates that AI-powered command centers achieve substantial improvements in resource allocation efficiency, with performance increases of up to 31% during critical operations such as disaster relief logistics.

AI agents enable predictive analytics capabilities that identify potential equipment failures, infrastructure maintenance needs, and service disruptions before they occur. This proactive approach reduces downtime, minimizes service interruptions, and optimizes resource utilization across city operations. The systems can predict traffic patterns, energy consumption fluctuations, and emergency service requirements with high accuracy, enabling preemptive resource deployment.

Enhanced decision-making represents another critical benefit of AI agent integration. These systems process vast amounts of urban data in real-time, providing decision-makers with comprehensive situational awareness and data-driven insights. AI agents can correlate information from multiple sources, including IoT sensors, surveillance systems, weather data, and social media feeds, to create comprehensive operational pictures that support informed decision-making.

THREE-LAYER AI AGENT ARCHITECTURE FOR COMMAND CENTERS

The sophisticated AI agent systems deployed in smart city command centers utilize a three-layer architecture that provides modular, scalable, and efficient operations. This architectural approach separates concerns into distinct functional layers while enabling the integration and coordination between different system components.

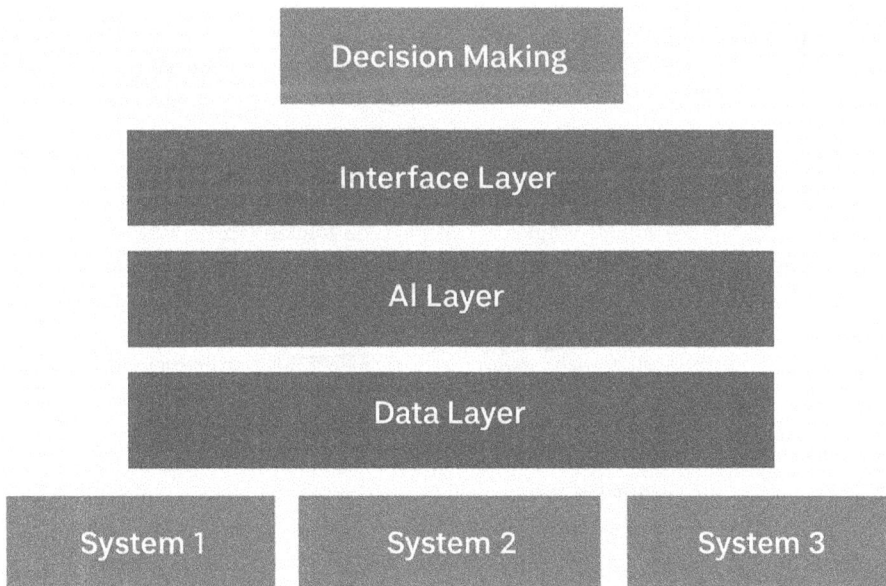

FIGURE 16.2 Multilayer Architecture for Intelligent IoT Decision Systems.

Data Layer: Comprehensive Integration Middleware

The data layer serves as the foundational component of the AI agent architecture, functioning as an intelligent middleware system that integrates and harmonizes data from multiple sources across the urban environment. This layer addresses one of the most significant challenges in smart city implementations: the heterogeneous nature of urban data sources and the need for seamless interoperability between different systems and platforms.

Multi-Source Data Integration Capabilities

The data layer incorporates advanced integration capabilities that connect diverse urban data sources including IoT sensors, surveillance cameras, traffic monitoring systems, environmental sensors, utility management systems, public transportation networks, and emergency services databases. This comprehensive integration addresses the challenge of data silos that traditionally hampered urban management effectiveness.

The system supports multiple communication protocols including MQTT, HTTP/REST, AMQP, CoAP, and WebSocket to ensure compatibility with various IoT devices and urban infrastructure systems. This protocol diversity enables the integration of legacy systems alongside modern smart city technologies, providing backward compatibility while supporting future expansion.

Real-time data processing capabilities within the data layer enable continuous monitoring and immediate response to changing urban conditions. The system processes streaming data from thousands of sensors simultaneously, applying data quality checks, normalization procedures, and format standardization to ensure consistent data availability for higher-level processing layers.

Intelligent Data Preprocessing and Quality Management

Advanced data preprocessing functions within the data layer ensure that information feeding into AI agents meets quality standards necessary for accurate decision-making. These preprocessing capabilities include data validation, anomaly detection, missing value imputation, and temporal alignment of data streams from different sources.

The layer implements sophisticated data fusion algorithms that combine information from multiple sensors monitoring the same phenomena to improve accuracy and reliability. For example, traffic flow data from vehicle counting sensors, GPS tracking from public transportation, and mobile phone location data can be fused to create a comprehensive traffic pattern visualization.

Edge computing capabilities within the data layer enable local data processing to reduce bandwidth requirements and latency. Critical decisions can be made locally using edge AI processing, while comprehensive analytics and long-term planning utilize cloud-based processing resources.

Secure Data Management and Privacy Protection

Security and privacy protection are critical aspects of the data layer implementation, particularly given the sensitive nature of urban data and citizen privacy concerns. The system implements end-to-end encryption for data transmission, role-based access controls, and data anonymization procedures to protect citizen privacy while enabling effective urban management.

Blockchain technology integration provides immutable audit trails for data access and modifications, ensuring transparency and accountability in data usage. Smart contracts automatically execute data sharing agreements and compliance protocols, maintaining data governance standards without manual intervention.

The data layer supports federated learning approaches that enable AI model training without centralizing sensitive data. This approach allows multiple urban systems to contribute to AI agent improvement while maintaining data privacy and security requirements.

AI Layer: No-Code Agent Development Platform

The AI layer is the cognitive part of the smart city command center system, providing sophisticated artificial intelligence capabilities through an accessible, no-code development environment. This layer enables urban management teams to create, customize, and deploy AI agents without requiring extensive programming expertise, democratizing AI adoption across city operations.

Advanced Large Language Model Integration

The AI layer incorporates state-of-the-art large language models (LLMs) specifically optimized for urban management applications. These models undergo specialized training on urban planning documents, emergency response protocols, infrastructure management procedures, and city regulations to ensure contextually appropriate responses to urban challenges.

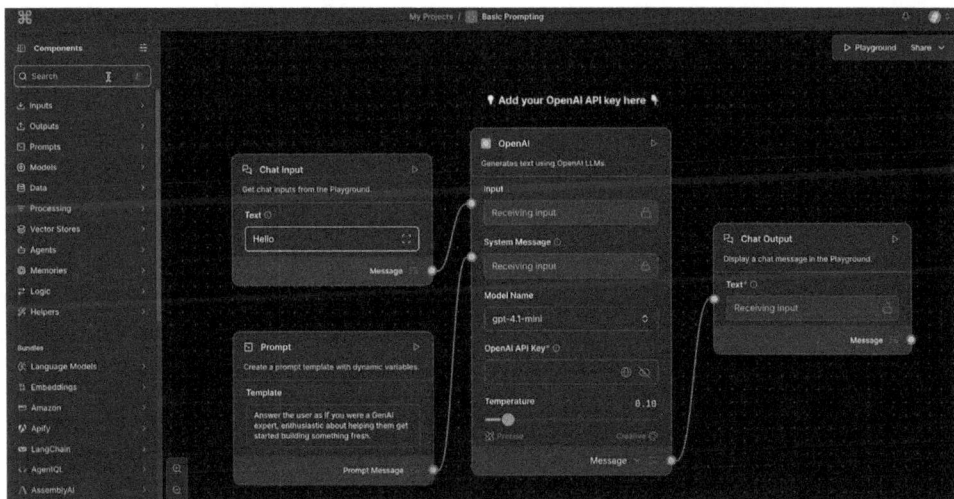

FIGURE 16.3 A no-code AI builder stack.

Multi-modal AI capabilities enable the system to process diverse data types including text, images, video, and sensor data streams. This comprehensive data processing ability allows AI agents to understand complex urban scenarios that require analysis of multiple information sources simultaneously.

The system implements Retrieval-Augmented Generation (RAG) technology that improves response accuracy by integrating real-time urban data with trained knowledge bases. RAG integration improves response accuracy% for strategic development queries and for service accessibility questions, significantly enhancing the practical utility of AI agents in urban management contexts.

Intelligent Agent Orchestration and Coordination

Multi-agent coordination capabilities within the AI Layer enable specialized AI agents to collaborate on complex urban management tasks. Traffic management agents coordinate with emergency response agents to optimize evacuation routes, while energy management agents collaborate with environmental monitoring agents to optimize power distribution based on air quality conditions.

The system implements sophisticated workflow orchestration that enables AI agents to execute complex, multi-step processes autonomously. These workflows can span multiple city departments and systems, coordinating activities such as emergency response, infrastructure maintenance, and public service delivery through automated processes.

Reinforcement learning capabilities enable AI agents to continuously improve their performance based on operational outcomes. The system learns from successful interventions and adjusts strategies to optimize future responses, creating adaptive urban management capabilities that improve over time.

No-Code Agent Development Interface

The AI layer provides intuitive, drag-and-drop interfaces that enable urban planners and city administrators to create custom AI agents without programming knowledge. Visual workflow builders allow users to define agent behaviors, decision trees, and response protocols through graphical interfaces that translate user intentions into executable AI agent code.

Template-based agent creation accelerates deployment by providing pre-configured agents for common urban management scenarios. These templates include traffic optimization agents, emergency response coordinators, energy management systems, and public safety monitors that can be customized for specific city requirements.

Natural language programming capabilities enable users to describe desired agent behaviors in everyday language, which the system automatically converts into functional AI agent implementations. This approach eliminates technical barriers to AI adoption and enables subject matter experts to directly contribute to AI agent development.

Adaptive Learning and Continuous Improvement

Machine learning pipelines within the AI Layer continuously analyze urban data to identify optimization opportunities and update agent behaviors. The system tracks key performance indicators including response times, resource utilization efficiency, citizen satisfaction metrics, and operational costs to guide improvement initiatives.

Automated model updating ensures that AI agents remain current with changing urban conditions and emerging challenges. The system can automatically retrain models based on new data patterns, seasonal variations, or evolving city requirements without manual intervention.

Performance monitoring and analytics capabilities provide detailed insights into AI agent effectiveness, enabling data-driven optimization of urban management processes. Real-time dashboards display agent performance metrics, intervention success rates, and operational efficiency indicators.

This adaptive learning paradigm is best formalized through the SUAL framework (Sense, Understand, Act, and Learn), which is an updated version of traditional SUA models. SUAL emphasizes the ability of AI agents not only to sense their environment, interpret data, and execute actions, but also to learn from outcomes and optimize future behavior autonomously. In the context of smart city command centers, this means agents can analyze intervention results, adjust decision logic, and even reconfigure workflows without human input, enabling a self-improving urban governance system.

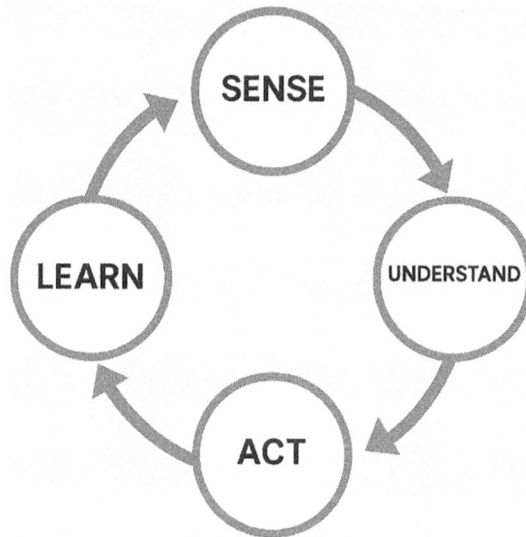

FIGURE 16.4 Sense-Understand-Learn-Act-Learn cycle:Continuous intelligence cycle enabling adaptive decision-making in smart systems.

Interface Layer: Customizable User Experience Platform

The interface layer is the human-machine interaction component of the AI agent architecture, providing customizable, intuitive interfaces that enable city operators, administrators, and stakeholders to interact effectively with AI agents and urban management systems. This layer focuses on delivering actionable insights, enabling informed decision-making, and facilitating seamless collaboration between human operators and AI agents.

Adaptive Dashboard and Visualization Systems

The interface layer implements sophisticated dashboard systems that automatically adapt to user roles, current urban conditions, and operational priorities. These dashboards provide real-time visualizations of city metrics, AI agent activities, and predictive analytics through interactive charts, maps, and alert systems.

Contextual information presentation ensures that operators receive relevant information based on their responsibilities and current situations. Emergency response personnel see prioritized incident information and resource availability, while infrastructure managers focus on maintenance schedules and system performance metrics.

Multi-dimensional visualization capabilities enable comprehensive understanding of complex urban scenarios through 3D city models, augmented reality interfaces, and virtual reality environments. These advanced visualization tools help operators understand spatial relationships, infrastructure dependencies, and the potential impacts of management decisions.

Intelligent Alert and Notification Systems

Adaptive alerting systems within the interface layer prioritize notifications based on severity, relevance, and operator capacity. AI algorithms analyze operator workload, response history, and current priorities to determine optimal timing and channels for alert delivery.

Multi-channel communication capabilities ensure critical information reaches appropriate personnel through various communication methods including mobile applications, desktop alerts, SMS messaging, and integration with existing communication systems. The system automatically escalates alerts if initial notifications are not acknowledged within specified timeframes.

Predictive notification systems provide advance warnings about potential issues before they become critical problems. These proactive alerts enable preventive actions that can avoid service disruptions, reduce emergency response requirements, and optimize resource utilization.

CONCLUSION

The future of smart cities lies not merely in connectivity, but in intelligence that learns and adapts over time. The integration of AI agents into command center architectures enables cities to shift from reactive, siloed management toward unified, autonomous urban orchestration. Through layered architectures (such as those for data, AI, and the interface), these systems utilize heterogeneous data sources, generate predictive insights, and deliver real-time actions across domains ranging from mobility to energy, safety, and disaster management.

As smart cities continue to scale, the true differentiator will be their ability to continuously learn from operational data and evolve system behavior without human reprogramming. This transition demands that AI agents become not just responsive, but reflective: capable of adapting based on experience, context, and feedback. The command center of the future will no longer be a control room, it will be a cognitive, learning entity that governs an urban digital system. In this context, frameworks like SUAL are essential to structure the next phase of AI-driven urban intelligence.

CHAPTER 17

THE FUTURE OF INTELLIGENT IoT ANALYTICS IN SMART CITIES

Throughout this book, we have explored the intricate relationship between IoT technologies, big data analytics, and urban development. As we conclude our journey, it is important to reflect on the concepts we have covered and consider how these technologies will continue to shape the future of our cities. This conclusion synthesizes the major themes discussed and provides a vision for the road ahead.

The integration of IoT devices and big data analytics has fundamentally transformed how we understand and manage urban environments. We began by exploring the core principles of IoT systems, from sensor networks to data processing pipelines. These elements serve as the foundation of smart cities, collecting and transmitting vital information about urban operations. The sophisticated analytics platforms we examined transform this raw data into actionable insights, enabling better decision-making and resource allocation.

Through our exploration of real-time analytics and data lakes, we have seen how organizations can utilize the power of continuous data streams while maintaining historical context for deeper analysis. The implementation of edge computing and cloud integration strategies has shown us how to balance immediate response capabilities with comprehensive data processing needs. This dual approach ensures both rapid reactions to urban events and thoughtful long-term planning based on accumulated insights.

Our discussion of the various smart city applications demonstrated the practical impact of IoT analytics across multiple domains. From public safety systems that protect citizens to intelligent transportation networks that optimize mobility, we have seen how IoT technologies create tangible improvements in urban life. The implementation of smart building management systems and resource optimization platforms showed how technology can enhance both operational efficiency and environmental sustainability.

Case studies throughout the book illustrated successful implementations across different scales and contexts. These real-world examples provided valuable insights into both technical challenges and practical solutions, offering guidance for future implementations. The lessons learned from these implementations emphasize the importance of careful planning, stakeholder engagement, and a systematic approach to technology deployment.

EMERGING TECHNOLOGIES AND TRENDS

The future of smart cities will be shaped by several emerging technologies and trends that promise to further enhance urban intelligence:

1. Artificial intelligence and machine learning will continue to evolve, enabling more sophisticated analysis of urban data patterns. These technologies will move beyond simple prediction to provide complex decision support capabilities, helping city managers anticipate and respond to urban challenges with increasing accuracy and effectiveness. We can expect to see AI systems that not only identify patterns but also suggest innovative solutions to urban problems.

2. Digital twin technology will become increasingly sophisticated, providing detailed virtual representations of city systems and infrastructure. These digital models will enable better planning, testing, and optimization of urban operations through simulation and scenario analysis. The integration of real-time data with digital twins will create powerful tools for urban management and development.

3. 5G and other types of communication technologies will enable faster, more reliable data transmission, supporting new applications and services. This enhanced connectivity will facilitate the deployment of more sophisticated IoT devices and enable real-time processing of complex data streams. The resulting improvements in the communication infrastructure will support more responsive and integrated urban systems.

4. A major leap forward will be the integration of **Agentic AI systems** in urban command centers. Unlike traditional dashboards that rely on human monitoring, Agentic AI can autonomously analyze citywide data, make operational decisions, and coordinate across agencies in real time. For instance, it could simultaneously reroute traffic, dispatch emergency services, and adjust energy loads during a major incident. This form of urban "autopilot" will redefine how cities maintain efficiency and resilience at scale. Example of this is centaurops platform. (centaurops).

5. Autonomous drones will extend IoT's reach into the sky, functioning as mobile sensors and responders. They will patrol infrastructure, monitor environmental conditions, support law enforcement, and provide rapid response in emergencies. Equipped with AI-driven vision systems, these drones will not only collect data but also act as active participants in city management—detecting wildfires, assessing damage, or delivering medical supplies. In doing so, they will create a dynamic aerial layer of the smart city ecosystem.

6. As IoT devices proliferate, relying solely on centralized cloud computing will become unsustainable. Edge computing, processing data near the source will become essential. Micro data centers embedded in city districts will enable real-time decision-making for latency-sensitive tasks such as traffic signal control, accident detection, or energy balancing. This decentralization will reduce bottlenecks, improve resilience, and ensure that critical services continue even during cloud disruption.

7. Securing billions of IoT interactions will demand new trust architectures. Blockchain and decentralized identity frameworks will provide tamper-proof verification of data, devices, and transactions. This will be crucial for applications like peer-to-peer energy trading in

smart grids, secure e-governance services, and trusted healthcare data exchanges. By embedding verifiable trust into IoT ecosystems, cities can minimize fraud, strengthen cybersecurity, and protect citizen privacy.

8. The next generation of IoT will not only serve cities but also the planet. IoT devices will increasingly adopt low-power communication protocols, recyclable materials, and energy-harvesting technologies. Combined with AI optimization, IoT will drive sustainability, from reducing water leaks and energy waste to enabling circular economy practices such as intelligent waste sorting and recycling. In this way, IoT will become a cornerstone of climate-resilient urban development.

CHALLENGES AND OPPORTUNITIES

As we look to the future, several challenges and opportunities will shape the evolution of smart cities:

1. Data privacy and security will remain crucial considerations as cities collect and process more detailed information about urban life. Future implementations must balance the benefits of data-driven decision-making with the need to protect individual privacy and ensure system security. This balance will require ongoing innovation in privacy-preserving technologies and security frameworks.

2. Sustainability and resilience will become increasingly important as cities face environmental challenges. IoT analytics will play a crucial role in optimizing resource usage, reducing environmental impact, and helping cities adapt to changing conditions. Future systems must be designed with sustainability as a core principle rather than an afterthought.

3. Social equity and inclusion must be considered in the development and deployment of smart city technologies. Future implementations should ensure that the benefits of urban intelligence are distributed equitably across all segments of society. This includes considering accessibility, affordability, and cultural sensitivity in technology deployment.

THE PATH FORWARD

For innovators and practitioners in the field of smart city development, several principles will be important for success:

1. Human-centered design should remain at the core of smart city initiatives. While technology provides powerful tools, the ultimate measure of success is the improvement in citizens' quality of life. Future innovations should focus on creating solutions that are not just technically sophisticated but also intuitive and beneficial for users.

2. Collaborative innovation will be essential for addressing complex urban challenges. The most successful solutions will likely emerge from cooperation between different stakeholders, including government agencies, private companies, academic institutions, and community organizations. This collaborative approach enables the sharing of knowledge, resources, and perspectives.

Continuous learning and adaptation will be necessary as technologies and urban needs continue to evolve. Successful innovators will need to maintain flexibility in their approach, continuously updating their knowledge and skills while remaining open to new ideas and methodologies.

As we conclude this exploration of intelligent IoT analytics in smart cities, we encourage innovators to

1. Embrace complexity while seeking working solutions. The challenges of urban development are multifaceted, requiring sophisticated approaches that consider technical, social, and environmental factors. Do not avoid complex problems but strive to find solutions that are both effective and elegant.

2. Think systemically about urban challenges and solutions. Consider how different aspects of urban systems interact and influence each other. Look for opportunities to create solutions that address multiple challenges simultaneously while avoiding unintended negative consequences.

3. Stay curious and maintain a learning mindset. The field of smart city development is constantly evolving, with new technologies and approaches emerging regularly. Successful innovators will need to remain curious, continuously learning and exploring new possibilities.

The future of our cities depends on the creative and thoughtful application of technology to urban challenges. As you move forward in your work, remember that each innovation, no matter how small, contributes to the larger goal of creating more livable, sustainable, and intelligent urban environments. The journey toward smarter cities is ongoing, and your contributions can help shape a better urban future for all.

Through continued innovation, collaboration, and dedication to human-centered design, we can work together to create urban environments that are not just smart, but truly intelligent: serving the needs of current citizens while preparing for the challenges of tomorrow.

ADDITIONAL RESOURCES

For readers interested in implementing the concepts discussed in this book, a collection of related IoT project templates, updates and errata, as well as announcements for future online and live bootcamps, are available at *www.intelligentxhub.com*.

www.ingramcontent.com/pod-product-compliance
Lightning Source LLC
Chambersburg PA
CBHW080904220326
41598CB00034B/5466

* 9 7 8 1 5 0 1 5 2 3 4 1 0 *